Morocco's Africa Policy

Leiden Studies in Islam and Society

Editors

Léon Buskens (*Leiden University*)
Nathal Dessing (*Leiden University*)

Editorial Board

Maurits Berger (*Leiden University*) – R. Michael Feener (*Kyoto University*) – Nico Kaptein (*Leiden University*) Jan Michiel Otto (*Leiden University*) – David S. Powers (*Cornell University*)

VOLUME 20

The titles published in this series are listed at *brill.com/lsis*

Morocco's Africa Policy

Role Identity and Power Projection

By

Yousra Abourabi

BRILL

LEIDEN | BOSTON

Cover illustration: A map of Africa drawn by a Moroccan geographer in the 19th century. Ahmed Chahboune, *Al Jughraphiya Al Maghribiya* (الجغرافية المغربية) 1898. Manuscript of the Royal Library No. 11654, Rabat, Morocco.

The Library of Congress Cataloging-in-Publication Data is available online at https://catalog.loc.gov
LC record available at https://lccn.loc.gov/2024011893

Typeface for the Latin, Greek, and Cyrillic scripts: "Brill". See and download: brill.com/brill-typeface.

ISSN 2210-8920
ISBN 978-90-04-54661-5 (paperback)
ISBN 978-90-04-54662-2 (e-book)
DOI 10.1163/9789004546622

Copyright 2024 by Koninklijke Brill BV, Leiden, The Netherlands.
Koninklijke Brill BV incorporates the imprints Brill, Brill Nijhoff, Brill Schöningh, Brill Fink, Brill mentis, Brill Wageningen Academic, Vandenhoeck & Ruprecht, Böhlau and V&R unipress.
All rights reserved. No part of this publication may be reproduced, translated, stored in a retrieval system, or transmitted in any form or by any means, electronic, mechanical, photocopying, recording or otherwise, without prior written permission from the publisher. Requests for re-use and/or translations must be addressed to Koninklijke Brill BV via brill.com or copyright.com.

This book is printed on acid-free paper and produced in a sustainable manner.

Contents

Foreword   IX
Abbreviations   XII

Introduction   1
1 'Morocco takes the South': Apollonian or Dionysian Impulse?   1
2 The Arab and African Worlds in the Study of International Relations   5
3 A Constructivist Approach to Identity   8
4 The Challenge of Multi-disciplinarity in the Study of Moroccan Foreign Policy   16
5 Book Structure and Objectives   27

1 The Genesis of an Africa Policy in Morocco: The Kingdom in Search of International Recognition   29
1 Introduction   29
2 Measuring Morocco's Emergence in the Light of the New World Order: Africa's Emergence in a 'Multiplex' World   34
3 From the Ambition of Emergence to the Ambition of Power: The Development of the Kingdom's International Relations   41
4 The Discursive Construction of Morocco's International Role Identity around the Concept of the 'Golden Mean'   45
5 Africa as the 'New Frontier'   53

2 The Historical Determinants of Morocco's Diplomatic Interest in Africa   57
1 Introduction   57
2 History as an Objective Determinant of the Geopolitical Order: Allal al-Fassi's 'Greater Morocco' Project   58
3 First Steps towards Building African Multilateralism   64
4 From the Sand War to the Betrayal of the OAU: The Moroccan Western Sahara, an African Problem   68
5 The Search for Leadership in a Regional Union with Libya: A Failed Alternative   73
6 The Cold War Kingdom versus French Power in Africa   77
7 'Renewed Partnership' and a New Policy in Africa at the End of the Cold War   85
8 Ceasefire and Peace Plan in the Aftermath of the Cold War: The Birth of Voice Diplomacy   89

3 The Making of the Africa Policy: Royal Pre-eminence and Diplomatic Mobilisation 100
1. Introduction 100
2. The King's Style in Foreign Policy: A Two-Tiered Role 101
3. Foreign Affairs: A 'Ministry of Sovereignty' 111
4. Modernisation and Professionalisation of the Diplomatic Apparatus at the Service of an African Strategy 116
5. The Specialisation of Diplomacy in the Service of a Golden-Mean Role Identity: Promoting Interculturalism and Trilateralism 126

4 A Framework for Representing Regional Integration 131
1. Introduction 131
2. The Defence of Territorial Integrity: A Political Framework for Defining the Entourage 134
3. Algeria and the Polisario Front: Public Historical *hostis* 137
4. South Africa and Nigeria: Geopolitical Adversaries or Future Continental Allies? 146
5. Shared Perceptions of an Algiers–Abuja–Pretoria anti-Moroccan Axis 151
6. The Representation of a 'Natural Extension' Based On the 'Historical Constants' of the Kingdom 154
7. The French Character of the Kingdom's Africa Policy: The Erroneous Hypothesis of a 'pré carré gigogne' 162
8. The Moroccan Character of the Kingdom's Africa Policy: 'Mohammed VI the African', a Manifestation of the Royal Style in Africa 169

5 A Legitimising Framework for Regional Integration 176
1. Introduction 176
2. The Kingdom Is African: The Inscription of Africanness in the Diplomatic Framework 177
3. The Kingdom's Solidarity: Integrating the Normative Framework of South–South Cooperation and Global Security 180
4. The Kingdom Is Moderate: The Valorisation of a Political-Religious Legacy through the Definition of a Golden-Mean Islam 187

6 Africa as a Field of Expression for an Indirect Strategy 193
1. Introduction 193
2. Fifteen Years of Offensive Bilateralism in the Service of a Sectorisation of Cooperation 196

3 The Acquisition of Material Resources through Trilateral Cooperation 202
4 Circumventing the Absence from the AU through Parallel Multilateral Diplomacy 205
5 Morocco's Return to the AU: The End of the Indirect Strategy? 210

7 **Constructing Diplomatic Levers of Action to Promote a Role Identity** 216
1 The Subordination of the Economic Tool to Political Imperatives 216
2 Sectoral Investment Policies under the Banner of South–South Cooperation 220
3 Promoting State Identity through Nation Branding and Intangible Capital 225
4 Accelerating Trade to Achieve Regional Integration: The Race to Maritime Transport 228
5 Influence Diplomacy: The Role of Cultural and Religious Levers 231
6 The Institutionalisation of Exchanges with trans-Saharan Sufi Confraternity Networks 235
7 The Spreading of a Golden-Mean Islam in Africa through Religious Training 240

8 **The Consequences of Morocco's Africa Policy: Between Relative Gains and Geopolitical Transformations** 244
1 Introduction 244
2 The Effects of Cultural and Religious Diplomacy in the Development of Migration to Morocco 245
3 Towards a Mix of Foreign and Domestic Policies: The Example of Climate and Environmental Policy 249
4 Enshrining the End of a MENA/sub-Saharan Africa Divide: A Socially Constructed Regionalist Project 254

Conclusion—Morocco: A Median Power 258

Appendix 1: State Visits of Mohammed VI Abroad, 2000–2016 273
Appendix 2: The King's Speeches, 1999–2015: Statistics 277
Appendix 3: FDI to Morocco (1) and (2) 278
Appendix 4: Map of 'Greater Morocco' 280
Appendix 5: Countries that Have Withdrawn Their Recognition of the RASD 281

Appendix 6: Map of Diplomatic Postures Regarding the Status of
   Moroccan Western Sahara   283
Appendix 7: Export of French War Material to Morocco
   (2008–2014)   284
Appendix 8: Moroccan FDI in Africa (1)   285
Appendix 9: Legitimisation Framework for the Africa Policy: Example of
   a Document on South–South Cooperation   286
Appendix 10: The Road Linking Morocco to West Africa   288
Appendix 11: Moroccan FDI in Africa (2)   289
Appendix 13: AU Motion of 28 States for the Suspension of the
   RASD   291
Appendix 13: Trade with Africa   293
Appendix 14: Transport Networks in Africa   295
Appendix 15: Shipping Lines, Morocco–Africa   296
Bibliography   297
Index   333

Foreword

Yousra Abourabi's book on Morocco's African diplomacy analyses the Kingdom's policy towards the continent it belongs to. Belonging to a regional group is a geographical fact without necessarily being a fact of identity. At the same time as it is located in Africa, Morocco belongs to another grouping not defined solely by geography: North Africa and the Middle East. There is nothing to unite North Africa with the far west of Asia other than that the states in this area (except Lebanon) recognise themselves as Arabic-speaking and Muslim. For many, these two proclaimed characteristics generate a specific identity that is strongly distinct from the African identity. Morocco claims both, and inscribes them in its 2011 constitution. Its most active diplomacy since the accession to the throne of Mohammed VI has revolved around the African continent. There are several reasons for this (relative) refocusing. The first is geography: Morocco's borders are African, and the Middle East is far away; its problems are not those of the Kingdom. The second is the possibility of exercising regional leadership: this can be done only in Africa. The third, which stems from the first two, is that the continent, starting with West Africa, represents an important economic market for Morocco. The fourth, which is not over-determining, concerns the southern provinces and the defence of the Moroccan position.

Perhaps we could also proceed in the opposite direction and, rather than listing the good reasons why Morocco is primarily interested in the African continent, list the good reasons why Africa, by itself and for itself, arouses interest: it is, unquestionably, the emerging continent, a continent full of promise where positions are not fixed, an intellectually stimulating continent. Of course, there are dramatic counterparts: political instability, conflicts that are difficult to resolve, violence and the pitfalls of development. However, these counterparts are not enough to thwart the promise of emergence. Morocco has good African—not only Moroccan—reasons to turn resolutely towards Africa.

The great merit of this book is that it describes the origin and development of this reorientation. Yousra Abourabi does so with a sure hand, based on a confident mastery of the tools of her discipline (international relations), the use of numerous documentary sources and a thorough investigation, involving the different actors of this policy. It is not, of course, a question of knowing the secret history. This is beyond the reach of researchers. All the events of diplomacy have hidden histories, but what the literature shows is that public data can support the whole explanation. Secrecy is never about specific modalities. It follows that this book allows us to understand, in a clear and substantiated way, why and how Morocco has 'rediscovered' itself as African. It does so by taking a measured stance towards its leading actor, describing the hazards, inadequacies and mistakes of an otherwise winning policy while avoiding over-criticism or over-praise, neither of which ever does justice to a phenomenon.

As is often the case, the description of a state's international policy is an effective tool for analysing its domestic policy and, in particular, the logic of its institutions. Indeed, foreign policy is built on the basis of national interests (an assumption which is often more reasonable than pretending to conduct it based on altruistic motives, which are never fully enacted) and depends on the political functioning of the country. As a result, the monarchy appears to be the main actor in an African diplomacy punctuated by royal trips to the continent, whose relevance is not questioned. Political institutions and actors follow, as do economic actors and civil society. Generally speaking, in Morocco the choice of significant orientations is the responsibility of the monarchy and leads to a broad consensus. This facilitates things and can encourage rapid progress. Morocco's return to the African Union was undoubtedly carried out with great skill, accompanied by the launch of a new migration policy that involved large-scale regularisation of illegal migrants, many of whom were from sub-Saharan Africa. In implementing this, Morocco brought its internal policy into line with its foreign policy: being an African state implied not treating migrants from the continent as Europe does, regularising them where Europe essentially intends to deny them access to its soil. Such a policy could not fail to resonate well in Africa. Joining the ranks of the states of a continent implies establishing symmetrical and supportive relations. Europe does not need this, since it is redeeming (or hoping to redeem) its attitude to and treatment of migrants with development aid. This compensation, however, appears increasingly uncertain, and the obsession with migration increasingly counterproductive both internally and externally. Morocco escapes this constraint because a proportion of its political choices are independent of the outcome of elections, which is not the case on the European continent. There, the fight against immigration is a direct result of the electoral fears of political parties as they compete with extreme right-wingers who are becoming commonplace. Paradoxically, Morocco has an open migration policy supporting its foreign policy rather than one discrediting it, because electoral fears are limited. For a country to have a domestic policy in line with its foreign policy is a rare luxury. As the author shows, Morocco can, moreover, converge several policies to support its African inscription: religious, cultural, environmental and security.

This comparative advantage also has its drawbacks and disadvantages. So far, the ECOWAS accession process has been unsuccessful. Conceived as a follow-up to African Union membership, it quickly became bogged down in procrastination and concern and no longer seems to be supported by the top of the state. It is not certain that Morocco is ready to regionalise its security by accepting the principle of a single identity card for the area (which should normally result from membership of ECOWAS) or to give up the dirham to join a single currency. On the part of the other states, it is evident that the economic power of the Kingdom worries the economic circles of some member countries. If the accession process were to be relaunched, it could only be done by the sovereign. The effort would have to be commensurate with efforts made to join the AU, or even greater, if one considers that the economic and political stakes (especially in light of the instability of parts of the zone) are much higher. Morocco's diplomatic progress on the continent thus seems to be linked to the convergence of several public policies and the sovereign's commitment. Only at this level of commitment can a policy bear fruit.

Professor Abourabi's book is of interest in many ways. It teaches us about the construction of a regional public policy. It provides us with a complete overview of the functioning of public policies in Morocco and their relationship with political institutions. It reminds us, quite rightly, that foreign policy is doubly dependent on the interior and the exterior, even if the dependence on the interior is much less significant than in Europe. Last but not least, it allows us to familiarise ourselves with the continent's teeming diplomatic life. This beautiful book by a specialist in international relations and a talented Africanist provides us with a fascinating account—conducted in the most perfect academic form—of successful diplomatic engagement. Beyond this, it reminds us that policy success is borne out of the convergence of policies and the matching of actors to momentum. It also requires conviction and foresight.

Jean-Noël Ferrié
Director of Research, CNRS, Les Afriques dans le Monde, France

Abbreviations

ADB	African Development Bank
AMU	Arab Maghreb Union
ANC	African National Congress
AQIM	al-Qaeda in the Islamic Maghreb
AU	African Union
BRICS	Brazil, Russia, India, China and South Africa
CEN–SAD	Community of Sahel–Saharan States
CIA	Central Intelligence Agency
CORCAS	Royal Advisory Council for Saharan Affairs
ECCAS	Economic Community of Central African States
ECOMOG	ECOWAS Monitoring Group
ECOWAS	Economic Community of West African States
EU	European Union
FAO	Food and Agriculture Organization of the United Nations
FDI	foreign direct investment
IMF	International Monetary Fund
LOF	Law of Finance
MAECI	Ministry of Foreign Affairs and International Cooperation
MAP	Agence Marocaine de Presse
MENA	Middle East and North Africa
MINURSO	United Nations Mission for the Referendum in Western Sahara
MISMA	International Support Mission for Mali (under African leadership)
NATO	North Atlantic Treaty Organisation
NEPAD-AUDA	New Partnership for Africa's Development
NGO	non-governmental organisation
NHDI	National Human Development Initiative
NPM	New Public Management
OAU	Organisation of African Unity
OECD	Organisation for Economic Co-operation and Development
OIC	Organisation of Islamic Cooperation
OPEC	Organization of the Petroleum Exporting Countries
PKO	Peacekeeping operation
RAF	Royal Armed Forces
RAM	Royal Air Maroc
RASD	Sahrawi Arab Democratic Republic
TICAD	Tokyo International Conference on African Development
UNDP	United Nations Development Programme

UNITA	National Union for the Total Independence of Angola
USSR	Union of Soviet Socialist Republics
WHO	World Health Organization

Introduction

1 'Morocco Takes the South': Apollonian or Dionysian Impulse?

> You had to participate in the 6th Africities Summit, which was held in Dakar from 4 to 8 December 2012, on the theme 'Building Africa from its territories: what challenges for local authorities?', alongside nearly 5,000 people from some fifty countries, half of whom were elected representatives, to measure Morocco's ambition in Africa. The Moroccans, who largely funded the event, had the largest stand of all the countries, thus affirming the receptiveness of Moroccan public authorities and local authorities to set up cooperation in all fields [...] Half a century after the creation of the OAU [Organisation of African Unity] and just under thirty years after its withdrawal, Morocco has never been so present south of the Sahara.[1]

This passage on the Kingdom in a French parliamentary report on coveted Africa aptly illustrates a new phenomenon at work in African international relations: the gradual deployment of an Africa policy by Morocco under the reign of Mohammed VI. As the map on the cover of the book shows, Moroccan geographers, historians and policy-makers have studied and been interested in Africa for centuries. However, Morocco has never been as present on the continental scale as it is today.

A manifestation of the Kingdom's development, this Africa policy is also presented as a natural and historical destiny: 'For Morocco, Africa is much more than a geographical belonging and historical links. It evokes sincere feelings of affection and consideration, deep human and spiritual ties and relations of fruitful cooperation and concrete solidarity. It is, in short, Morocco's natural extension and strategic depth.'[2] While this discursive framework of legitimisation is part of the continuity of Morocco–Africa relations, it reflects an entirely new set of ambitions. The former Cherifian Empire is now a nation-state fully integrated into globalisation, on the road to emergence and searching for a new kind of power. For the past 20 years, the Moroccan presence on the continent has been gradually strengthened. There are more embassies, cooperation

---

1 Jenny Lorgeoux and Jean-Marie BockelL, *L'Afrique est notre avenir* [*Rapport*], Paris, Sénat—Commission des Affaires étrangères, de la Défense et des Forces Armées, 2013, 194–195.
2 "Speech of HM the King to the nation on the occasion of the 63rd anniversary of the Revolution of the King and the People", *Maroc.ma*, August 20, 2016.

agreements are being extended to new areas, Moroccan companies are taking their first steps into the continental market, the armed forces are participating in peacekeeping operations (PKOs) in Africa, and the leaders are getting closer to regional institutional mechanisms.

At the heart of this process, the diplomatic apparatus, consisting of the Ministry of Foreign Affairs, embassies and the Royal Cabinet, is developing, organising and asserting itself. The political dimension of this deployment appears prevalent. A certain number of national interests underpin this new dynamic, while the Palace has set itself up as an institution determined to accomplish the new project that was being planned. Thus, foreign policy is elaborated and constructed in its relationship with its new African terrain of expression.

This diplomatic turning point occurred in the context of internal transformations. The reign of Mohammed VI, which coincides with the political defusing initiated under Hassan II after the Cold War, is also a time of the consecration of a 'political transition', to use the terminology favoured by Abdallah Saaf,[3] Mohammed Tozy,[4] or Jean-Noël Ferrié and Baudouin Dupret.[5] While 'democratic transition' refers to the transition from one regime to another, 'political transition' implies a change of elites within the same regime. In the case of the Moroccan political transition, this change consecrates a neoliberalisation through a set of institutional reforms. The monarchy has made this neoliberalisation its 'reigning project'. This is why one can speak of liberal opening on the economic level without risk of bias, but one cannot say the same of complete political liberalisation. Morocco cannot be considered a liberal democracy in the political sense, but it is not an authoritarian or neo-patrimonial state either. The Kingdom stands in an interstice with subtle and singular contours. On the cultural and technical levels, as Daniel Rivet points out, 'the suffering of maladjustment to the modern world, noted in the middle of the 20th century by Louis Massignon, no longer corresponds to the present time'.[6] In addition to the meteoric growth of urban and rural infrastructures, Morocco is one of the most internet-connected countries in Africa. As a result, civil society has access to alternative self-education systems and information on world changes in realtime. The youth are linking up more with other transnational communities

---

3 Abdallah Saaf, "L'expérience marocaine de transition politique", *IEMed Institut Européen de la Méditérannée*, 2009.
4 Mohamed Tozy, *Monarchie et islam politique au Maroc*, (Paris: Presses de Sciences Po, 1999).
5 Jean-Noël Ferrié and Baudouin Dupret, "La nouvelle architecture constitutionnelle et les trois désamorçages de la vie politique marocaine", *Confluences Méditerranée* 78, no. 3 (2011): 25.
6 Daniel Rivet, *Histoire du Maroc* (Paris: Fayard, 2012), 399.

on issues such as the environment, gender and economic inequality. They are becoming increasingly politicised and mobilised.

The political transition, in many ways, has also accelerated the Kingdom's development, in both its human resources and its material capacities. The time when public policies were promoted without being effective seems to be dissipating as voters gain weight in the political system[7] and citizens mobilise in the public space. The monarchy has also launched many national projects, supported with optimism by this new generation of elites: agricultural reform, consolidation of industries and services, restructuring of the university and professional training, creation of a financial hub, development of the regions, aspiration to defence industry, etc. All of these projects are underway and participate in a 'recognition policy', in the sense given by Axel Honneth,[8] of the Moroccan state. Unlike the recognition of a state in the legal sense (described by the author as 'knowledge' rather than 'recognition'), recognition in international relations refers not to 'the necessary consequence of an established fact, but to the free decision of the governing bodies of a state, wishing to support another state by establishing a positive relationship with it'.[9] The Palace is indeed claiming a place for Morocco within the group of emerging countries and wants to make the Kingdom an African power in its projection space and in its own identity.

On the other hand, it seems relevant to ask how Morocco, which is still in the process of achieving its development, intends to achieve this emergence. The population suffers from significant gaps in education, access to healthcare and civil rights. Its demography is small (36 million inhabitants) compared with African giants such as Nigeria, South Africa or Egypt[10] Its land and sea territory is threatened by an independence movement in the south, coveted by Spain since the discovery of oil off the Atlantic coast in the west,[11] fragmented by the maintenance of Spanish enclaves in the north, and isolated by its rivalry with Algeria to the east. Its army is dedicated to defending the southern provinces as

---

7 Ferrié and Dupret, "La nouvelle architecture constitutionnelle et les trois désamorçages de la vie politique marocaine".
8 Axel Honneth, *La lutte pour la reconnaissance* (Paris: Les Éditions du Cerf, 2000), 232; Axel Honneth, "La reconnaissance entre Etats", *Cultures & Conflits* no. 87 (2012): 27–36.
9 Axel Honneth, *La lutte pour la reconnaissance*.
10 World Bank Population Statistics, 2016: https://data.worldbank.org/indicator/SP.POP.TO TL.
11 Yousra Abourabi, "La découverte de pétrole au large des Iles Canaries: un facteur de conflit entre le Maroc et l'Espagne?", Paris, *Centre Interarmées de Concepts de Doctrines et d'Expérimentations*, 2014.

a legitimate region of Morocco.[12] Does this African vocation, proudly displayed by its leaders, not constitute in this context a chimerical destiny?

The Moroccan impulse on the continent appears to be guided by Dionysian representations of the meaning of its history while being determined by Apollonian considerations in its conduct. Dionysus is the Greek god of excess, wine and madness; he is the only god who can die but is reborn. He symbolises both the enthusiasm of excess and the strength of perseverance. Apollo is the antithesis of Dionysus. As the god of the arts and beauty, he represents order and clarity but also has a proud, vengeful and even belligerent dimension.

On the one hand, despite the material and structural weaknesses that delay and nuance the scope of foreign policy, ambitions prevail over caution, at the risk of widening the gap between the projection of an African presence and the capacity to accomplish it. On the other hand, this royal motivation, visible in the prioritisation of Africa on the Moroccan diplomatic agenda, will push leaders to set the guidelines, come up with a strategy and invent the instruments of this power policy, tailoring it to the ambitions, means and identity values advocated by the Kingdom. We are therefore witnessing the deployment of an actual 'Africa policy', i.e. a policy which determines the design of a set of diplomatic and strategic devices subordinated to the satisfaction of national interests. This differentiates a state that maintains diplomatic relations with a group of countries in a specific geo-cultural area from a country that formulates a policy towards this area perceived as a geopolitical whole. In the case of Morocco, this Africa policy also corresponds more generally to a power policy. It can be said that Morocco is a power constructed in a dialectical relationship with its African environment, affecting both national identity and continental geopolitics. This is the central hypothesis that will guide this book and which will be explained later: that of Morocco's construction of an identity consisting of a 'golden mean' role through its foreign policy.

This does not predispose the Kingdom to claim exception or superiority over its neighbours, as its patriots often do. The Moroccan state is also a state like any other, whose interests, ambitions, constraints and contradictions can be compared with those of its peers and measured against a theoretical and methodological apparatus whose scientific value has been proven in the study of the foreign policy of many states. The interest of the subject matter lies rather in its heuristic dimension to analyse, in an interdisciplinary way, the link between power and role identity in international relations on the theoretical

---

12   Yousra Abourabi, *Maroc*, (Brussels : De Boeck, 2019).

level (notably through a constructivist approach), as well as to illustrate one of the forms that the emergence of Africa can take on the empirical level. The study of Morocco's Africa policy will demonstrate more generally a major transformation at work in the continent: that of a 'top-down' regionalist integration between the Maghreb and West Africa.

2   The Arab and African Worlds in the Study of International Relations

To date, no academic work on Morocco's Africa policy under Mohammed VI has been published. Bakary Sambe's thesis, whose title is the closest to my study,[13] is actually about the history of religious links between Morocco and transnational Sufi brotherhoods, as well as, to a lesser extent, the history of Moroccan–Senegalese diplomatic relations. Irène Fernandez's thesis,[14] revised and published in English,[15] provides a general picture of the relations of Mohammed VI's Morocco with various countries. However, out of the 700 pages of the original thesis, only about 20 pages are devoted to Moroccan–African relations. Abdessamad Belhaj's thesis on the Islamic dimension of Moroccan foreign policy[16] focuses, as its title indicates, on a specific aspect of this policy. The author is also more interested in diplomatic relations with Arab-Muslim countries than in relations with African countries.

On the whole, the scientific contributions that are closely or remotely interested in our subject, although they have been of valuable interest in the elaboration of this study, have left out an analysis of Moroccan–African international relations, in the general sense given by the discipline, namely the study of the political, economic and security interactions between state agents and other recognised actors in the international system, as well as an analysis of the distribution of power and the factors of peace. A range of research perspectives, such as the study of national interest, power relations or diplomatic strategies employed, appear only secondarily in these studies. Moreover, what

---

13   Bakary Sambe, *Islam et Diplomatie: La Politique Africaine du Maroc* (Phoenix Press International, 2011), 286.
14   Irene Fernández-Molina, *La política exterior de Marruecos en el reinado Mohamed VI (1999–2008): actores, discursos y proyecciones internas*, Thesis, (Madrid: Universidad Complutense de Madrid, 2013), 716.
15   Irene Fernandez-Molina, *Moroccan Foreign Policy under Mohammed VI, 1999–2014* (Routledge, 2015), 251.
16   Abedessamad Belhaj, *La dimension islamique dans la politique étrangère du Maroc*, (Louvain : Presses univ. De Louvain, 2009), 302.

Abdallah Saaf remarked on at the end of the 1990s, we still observe today: 'Moroccan perceptions of Africa, unlike Moroccan perceptions of Europe, Latin America, North America, or Asia [...] constitute a relatively untrodden research ground'.[17] All of these limitations inherent to this literature demonstrate the interest in this subject and push us to rethink the instruments of analysis of the 'Arab' and 'African' worlds when, as in this case, they come together and announce a change in diplomatic and geopolitical orientation, but also in identity.

This book is therefore intended to be part of the field of African studies. I make this claim here because in the academic sphere a researcher who works on a Maghreb country is often considered a specialist in the 'Arab world'. Morocco is generally associated with a space composed of North African and Middle Eastern countries and characterised by the sharing of the Arabic language, the Muslim religion and a form of recognition of a collective identity. Similarly, the foreign policies of many countries administratively separate sub-Saharan Africa from the MENA (Middle East and North Africa) region. Conversely, in academic circles, the qualification of Africanists is often applied to researchers who are familiar with one or more regions of sub-Saharan Africa, and not with North Africa or the relationship between these two spaces. However, not only does the existence of a geopolitical system known as the 'Arab world' deserve to be questioned but the existence of an African geopolitical system that covers only part of the continent has been questioned too little. Nevertheless, the inclusion of North Africa in the African geopolitical space is all the more relevant given that the states of this region have expressed their interest in the continent at various points in history by developing an Africa policy. This was the case for Haile Selassie's Ethiopia, Nasser's Egypt and Gaddafi's Libya as it is for Mohammed VI's Morocco. In addition to these power policies, there is a growing interdependence between the North and the South of the continent on issues of development and security, as well as new forms of human and commercial exchanges.[18] The examples of the crisis in the Sahel, the hydropolitics of the Nile, or the challenges raised by migration in Libya or Morocco attest to this dimension, which is becoming increasingly important. On a cultural level, it should also be remembered that the Sahelian states share religious, linguistic

---

17   Abdallah Saaf, *Le Maroc et l'Afrique après l'indépendance*, Actes de colloque organisé par l'Institut des Études Africaines, (Rabat, Morocco: Université Mohammed V, 1996), 15.
18   Laurence Marfaing and Stephen Wippel, *Les relations transsahariennes à l'époque contemporaine: un espace en constante mutation* (Karthala, 2004), 490. Mansouria Mokhefi and Alain Antil, *Le Maghreb et son Sud: vers des liens renouvelés* (Paris: CNRS, 2012).

and commercial links with the states of the North. All of this should reinforce the idea that the countries of the North should be taken into account in African studies.

Moreover, Africa is a neglected object, a poor field of theories of international relations. The inclusion of the study of the Moroccan policy in this prism therefore contributes to ongoing reflections on African international relations. Very often, African states in particular are relegated, as Kevin Dunn so aptly noted, to the position of a 'footnote'[19] to signify their exception to the rules laid down in international relations theory. Not all of the tools and concepts developed by the different theoretical schools are relevant in understanding, explaining or defining African political phenomena. Some Africanists have taken an interest in African international relations from a theoretical perspective, contributing to the emergence of schools of international relations in Yaoundé,[20] Nairobi[21] and Johannesburg[22] striving to orient research towards a change of epistemological perspective..[23] However, the field of international relations in Africa remains largely unexplored. This inherent limitation of the theory of international relations, as recalled by Luc Sindjoun,[24] raises the challenge of formulating an approach that is both nomothetic and ideographic, i.e. an approach that favours both the particularity and the universality of concepts. The concept of power in particular is controversial. Should the stakes of power in Africa be understood in the same terms as in the West, for example? Far from seeking to formulate an exhaustive answer to this question, this study aims rather to add a stone to the edifice by shedding both empirical and theoretical light on the conditions, resources and stakes of Moroccan power.

---

19 Kevin C. Dunn and Timothy M. Shaw (eds.), *Africa's Challenge to International Relations Theory* (Palgrave Macmillan, 2013), 4.
20 See on this subject: Joseph-Vincent Edobé and Frank Ebogo, "Le Cameroun", in *Traité de relations internationals, eds.* Thierry Balzacq and Frédéric Ramel, (Paris: Les Presses de Sciences Po, 2013), 89–112.
21 See in particular the Institute of Diplomacy and International Studies, Nairobi, Kenya.
22 See: Karen Smith, "International Relations in South Africa: A Case of 'Add Africa and Stir'"?
23 For example: Paul Tiyambe Zeleza, *Manufacturing African Studies and Crises* (Dakar: Codesria, 1997), 632.
24 Luc Sindjoun, *Sociologie des relations internationales africaines* (Paris: Karthala, 2002), 250.

3   A Constructivist Approach to Identity

3.1   *Hypothetical-Inductive Reasoning*

In order to justify and solve the equation set by this complex choice (i.e. the balance between a nomothetic and ideographic approach), hypothetical-inductive reasoning seems appropriate: it goes from the particular to the general, while postulating prior hypotheses. These hypotheses are formulated inductively, i.e. they are induced by the empirical observation of a number of relationships; they are then verified methodologically and theologically, with the aim of contributing to the construction of a theory that establishes these relationships. The hypothetical-inductive method is similar to the hypothetical-deductive method in that both postulate prior hypotheses, but while the latter attempts to have them validated by examples without necessarily questioning the hypotheses, the former induces the hypotheses from empirical observation. Deduction seeks to explain facts, and to determine causal relationships, which is why this reasoning has often been used as a means of proof, limiting the weight of observation and experience. In extreme cases, deductive reasoning leads researchers to falsify the empirical result in order to integrate it into the hypothetical framework. Conversely, induction goes from the particular to the general, producing conclusions that are more global than the body of the study. It is based on the interpretation of phenomena. Statements are derived from empirical observation and experience. In extreme cases, induction can lead to inductivism, a form of reasoning that is purely empirical without any preconceived idea of reality, but which ends up becoming a normative epistemic position in itself. This is not my position.

In both cases, hypothetical reasoning is defined by conceptual and theoretical *a priori* argumentation. This is the case here, since I will analyse Morocco's Africa policy through the prism of a constructivist approach (defined below) and a number of concepts from the field of international relations philosophy. The difference between hypothetical-deductive and hypothetical-inductive reasoning lies in the fact that the aim of the latter is to construct knowledge and not to verify existing knowledge in order to eventually produce further knowledge through causality. This constructive process fits in well with the chosen theoretical framework because it makes it possible to take into account the meanings that the phenomena studied have for the actors, while at the same time accompanying it with conceptual analyses that make it possible to identify action strategies not formulated by the actors.

At this point, it is appropriate to further clarify my reasoning by also distinguishing between hypothetical-inductive and empirical-inductive reasoning. Induction seems to go hand in hand with empirical reasoning because this type of approach rejects any predetermined theoretical or conceptual framework. Empirical-inductive reasoning focuses on the actors' representations and analyses phenomena through the prism of their subjectivities. However, observation of facts alone does not lead to good scientific knowledge either. Conversely, in hypothetical-inductive reasoning, the theory is induced throughout the demonstration. It guides the approaches and helps to define the terms and phenomena. This form of thinking therefore lies halfway between hypothetical-deductive and empirical-inductive reasoning. The reader should therefore not be surprised to find that the first part of the book is not entirely devoted to the presentation of a theoretical framework, as is often the case in academic works. This does not mean that it is non-existent, only that it looms in the shadow of the empirical study. I will therefore prefer a presentation of the favoured theoretical approaches in the next section of this introduction. At the same time, the study asserts a definite orientation towards the empirical, insofar as the latter cannot be separated from inductive reasoning. It is therefore a dialogical and interactive process of reasoning, based on a constant back-and-forth between field and theory in several stages. Before starting the work, I proceeded to the empirical observation of the field and the induction of general hypotheses, then I formulated theoretical premises as a starting point for the study (see the next section below). Subsequently, back in the field, I proceeded to the empirical description of the relevant phenomena and their comprehensive analysis in the light of existing theoretical concepts or those developed in an original way according to the observation, in a dialogic logic. This is the core of the work, which consists of all the chapters in this book. Finally, I have modestly attempted to respond to the hypotheses by formulating general conclusions on my subject of study and discussed the theoretical lessons inherited from the analysis.

3.2 *A framework for Theoretical Differentiation*

All of the methods chosen or developed in the direction of hypothetical-inductive reasoning converge towards the constructivist path. Initially born in other disciplines (philosophy, sociology), constructivism became widespread in the field of international relations at the end of the 1980s, notably in the work of Nicholas Onuf. In his book *World of Our Making*,[25] he refers to the philosophy of Foucault, Kant and Wittgenstein to defend the idea that our world is made up of social beings, which may be rational but which are not guided by

---

25   Nicholas Onuf, *World of Our Making*, (Columbia S.C: University of South Carolina Press, 1989).

this law alone. Through, among other things, normative acts of language, we participate in the construction of our international system. Alexander Wendt continues Onuf's work by stating that the anarchy of the international system, described as a natural state of affairs by the realists—for whom the individual is by nature selfish, so that our international system reflects the image of our society at the individual level—is, on the contrary, a social consequence of the behaviour of states.[26] The constructivists re-question, on an epistemological level, the positivist approaches to knowledge.[27] Some clearly take a postpositivist perspective (critical constructivism), while others, primarily Wendt, want to bridge the gap between the two approaches (conventional constructivism).

Thus, for constructivists, our world is formed by 'ideational structures',[28] i.e. the set of rules, norms and representations of the actors that compose it. Far from having a state-centric vision, constructivists will consider all actors that can have an effect on the system in addition to states, such as multinational firms, transnational communities, international and non-governmental organisations, individuals, and epistemic communities. The latter concept was coined by Peter Haas to refer to the normative channels through which expert groups influence international relations. They are 'networks of professionals with recognised expertise and competence in a particular field who can put forth policy-relevant knowledge to the field in question'.[29] All of these actors, therefore, help to shape the system in the same way that the system influences their representations, choices and behaviour. In this sense, the constructivist approach to international relations is neither holistic (or deterministic) nor methodologically individualistic; it is reflexive.[30] The agent (the actor in the international system) and the structure (the system) are seen as co-constituting, in that our environment, while shaping our interests and identities, is not an independent structure. On the contrary, we in turn shape that environment. This is why the main object of study for construc-

---

26   Alexander Wendt, "Anarchy is what States Make of it: The Social Construction of Power Politics", *International Organization* 46, no. 2 (April 1992): 391–425.

27   Stefano Guzzini, "The Concept of Power: a Constructivist Analysis", *Millennium—Journal of International Studies* no. 3 (2005).

28   Alex Macleod and In O'Meara, *Théories des Relations Internationales: Contestations et Résistances* (Athena Éditions, 2010), 243.

29   Peter M. Haas, "Introduction: Epistemic Communities and International Policy Coordination", *International Organization* 461, (Winter 1992): 1–35.

30   Thierry Braspenning, "Constructivisme et réflexivisme en théories des Relations Internationales", in *Annuaire Français des Relations Internationales* (vol. III, 2002), 314–329 (Bruylant).

tivists is to grasp and understand the mechanisms by which our social reality is constructed. Thus constructivism breaks radically with the dominant realist approach, which considers that our international reality is a reflection of humanity's selfish nature (in reference to the pessimistic Hobbesian philosophy).

The constructivist approach is interesting because it bridges the gap between the idealism and materialism[31] that dominates international relations by focusing on the study of actors' representations and how these affect their ideas and interactions, without disregarding the material factors that determine their behaviour. As Wendt reminds us, 'A gun in the hand of a friend is not the same as a gun in the hand of an enemy; enmity is a social, not a material relationship'.[32] This hypothesis will guide the analysis of friendship and enmity relationships in the fourth chapter of this book. Thus, I consider that, contrary to the realist idea, power relations are not the only determinants of social relations on an international scale. Moreover, the constructivist concept of power is not only based on the classical criteria as defined in positivist approaches, such as economy, army, size of territory, demography or sovereignty of power. Other non-material criteria are at work, criteria that have not been pre-established in the constructivist literature but that can be inducted from the empirical analysis if we take this starting assumption into account. This is what I demonstrated with Julien Durand de Sanctis in a study devoted to 'The Emergence of African Security Powers', published a few years ago.[33] In this book, I will therefore try to come up with a renewed examination of the criteria of power induced by the Moroccan experience. On the other hand, if the mutations of the international system can objectively determine the distribution of power, history can also be read and reinterpreted differently according to the actors and participate in shaping new forms of power identities. This hypothesis will be tested in Chapters 2, 4 and 5.

Whether they are critical or conventional, American constructivists come to the same conclusions as Raymond Aron, as well as many French authors, on the need for a sociological approach and the inclusion of historical, geopolitical and security variables. However, it will be a question not of applying the

---

31   In particular, the materialism and determinism that dominate the Marxist approach to international relations.
32   Alexander Wendt, "Constructing International Politics", *International Security* 20, no. 1 (Summer 1995): 71–81.
33   Yousra Abourabi and Julien Durand de Sanctis, *L'émergence de puissances africaines de sécurité: Étude comparative* (Paris: Institut de Recherche Stratégique de l'Ecole Militaire, 2016), 87.

entire constructivist model to the Moroccan case, nor of endorsing all of its normative presuppositions, but rather one of borrowing some of its concepts. Indeed, constructivism should be seen not as a paradigm or theory that fulfils all the requirements to gain this status (ontology, epistemology and methodology) but as a *via media*, bridging rational and reflexive, holistic and individualistic approaches. Such theoretical obedience does not, therefore, exclude occasional reference to other paradigms, as Barry Buzan, in particular, demonstrates, provided that the differentiation necessary for the coherence of the sociological approach employed is made.[34] Therefore, this study is part of this general theoretical framework, because of both the methodological and epistemological choices mentioned above and the importance given to the notion of identity. This concept has been widely studied, defined and developed by constructivists. More precisely, through this study, I will try to define the identity of the Moroccan power, both in its internal characteristics and in the roles it projects. Indeed, one of my starting hypotheses is that understanding the identity of the Moroccan state can help us understand its international behaviour.

3.3 *Plural State Identities*

The advent of the identity approach in the field of human and social sciences is recent. The contemporary meaning of identity in scientific research—no longer the similarity but the fundamental and permanent character of someone or something—originates in the work of the psychologist Erik Erikson in the 1950s on the identity crisis of adolescents.[35] In the 1970s, French researchers began to take an interest in the link between national identity and foreign policy.[36] But it was not until the 1990s that the birth of American reflexivist approaches (constructivism, post-modernism) led to the emergence of the notion in the historical, anthropological or political analysis of societies and states. In international relations, the analysis of identities has become a critical approach to theories of rational choice, making it possible to elucidate the genesis of conflicts, the factors of mobilisation during war, the formation of interests, or the diplomatic and strategic practices of the various actors in the international system. Alexander Wendt's famous postulate is well known:

---

34   Barry Buzan and Mathias Albert, "Differentiation: A Sociological Approach to International Relations Theory," *European Journal of International Relations* 16, no. 3 (2010): 315–337.

35   For a historiography of the concept, see Dario Battistella et al, *Dictionnaire des relations internationales* (Paris: Dalloz, 2012). 277–280.

36   Roger Paret and Jacques Vernant, "Tradition, identité nationale et développement dans la définition et la conduite de la politique étrangère," *Politique étrangère* 40, no. 6 (1975): 663–669.

'Identities are the basis of interests'.[37] As Ted Hopf also states: 'By telling you who you are, identities strongly imply a set of preferences'.[38] Identities are the basis for the unity and power of states. Constructivists advocate reconstructing the 'identity topographies'[39] of states to better understand their behaviour on the international scene. Identity is the result of both global systemic transformations and several internal values (norms, culture, societal values).[40] Identity construction is intersubjective: it is based not only on an actor's idea of themselves but also on the image that other actors reflect onto them and their reaction to this image.

Therefore, identity must be analysed holistically and individually, from top to bottom, exogenously and endogenously. However, while the identity approach is essential in interpreting the behaviour of states, it is not without drawbacks.

The first difficulty with the identity approach is that it does not lend itself to a single, systemic methodology. As a result, many researchers refuse to consider it a comprehensive variable, criticising its elusive and inconstant nature. Indeed, the definition of identity is ultimately based on conjectures, representations or historical facts whose rigour and objectivity of documentation are far from being demonstrated. This approach is, therefore, by no means natural and is the result of a methodological bias. Notwithstanding this fragility, several empirical studies carried out over the last 30 years which have examined the prism of identity have produced convincing results.[41] (It should be noted, however, that they are most often the preserve of the English-speaking scientific literature, whose method is not very sociological in comparison with the French school of international relations, which has only slightly explored

---

37   Alexander Wendt, "Anarchy is what States Make of it: The Social Construction of Power Politics," *International Organization* 46, no. 2 (1992): 398.

38   Ted Hopf, 'The Promise of Constructivism in International Relations Theory', *International Security* 23, no. 1, (1998): 171.

39   To use the term borrowed from Battistella, *Dictionnaire des relations internationals.* 279.

40   On the difference between holistic and individualistic constructivism, see Alex Macleod and Dan O'Meara, Théories des Relations Internationales: Contestations et Résistances (Athena Éditions, 2010), 661.

41   One of the most classic studies is David Campbell, *Writing Security: United States Foreign Policy and the Politics of Identity* (Minneapolis: Univ Of Minnesota Press, 1998), 308. Other contemporary constructivist theorists include Shibley Telhami and Michael Barnett, *Identity and Foreign Policy in the Middle East* (Cornell University Press: 2002). More recently, Adel Altoraifi, *Understanding the Role of State Identity in Foreign Policy Decision-Making. The Rise and Demise of Saudi-Iranian Rapprochement (1997–2009)* (London: The London School of Economics and Political Science, 2012).

the subject to date.[42]) Thus, because many researchers have demonstrated how states' identities can affect their foreign policies, it appears that the notion has scientific value as a framework for Moroccan diplomacy.

A second difficulty also arises. The identity prism implies demonstrating 'the relationship between what actors do and who they are'.[43] Therefore, it can easily lead to causal determinism, or even a 'necessitarianism',[44] visible in the assignment of a unique and unyielding trajectory to a particular identity. To avoid this pitfall, it seems more prudent to distinguish between national and state identities, although they are based on a shared general foundation and are mutually influenced. As MacLeod and his co-authors note about identity, 'The content of the notion is largely a function of the unit of analysis that the researcher intends to favour (the state, the nation, the region, the society, or even the individual)'.[45] But while they make the methodological choice of using national identity and state identity interchangeably, it seems more relevant to distinguish the two expressions. Like the distinction between power and puissance presented by Raymond Aron,[46] national identity belongs to the internal sphere and state identity to the external sphere of the state.[47] In both cases, identity is co-constituted by beliefs and norms that are equally internal and external to the state. While national identity does not necessarily allow for an understanding of what actors do, the superimposed state identity is more appropriate for formulating this relationship because it is also based on projecting a role.

In its context, Alexander Wendt's definition seems to be the most relevant. This definition distinguishes four levels of identity:
1. Body identity: defined as a social entity which allows it to be differentiated from other social structures (be they other states, tribes or groups). This identity must exist as soon as one faces 'an organisational actor linked to

---

42   More generally, some French political scientists deplore researchers' lack of interest in French 'International Relations'—of which Raymond Aron and Marcel Merle are said to be the tutelary figures—as a sub-category of the discipline of 'Political Science'. See in this regard: Dario Battistella, "La France", in *Traité de relations internationales*, ed. Thierry Balzacq and Frédéric Ramel (Paris: Les Presses de Sciences, 2013), 157–180.
43   Wendt, "Anarchy is what States Make of it", 424.
44   A psychological determinism that rejects any idea of contingency or free will.
45   Alex Macleod et al., "Identité nationale, sécurité et la théorie des relations internationales", *Études internationales 35*, no. 7 (2004).
46   Raymond Aron, *Paix et guerre entre les nations* (Paris: Calmann-Lévy, 1962), 804.
47   Paul Kowert, 'The Three Faces of Identity', in *The Origins of National Interests*, eds. Glenn Chafetz, Michael Spirtas and Benjamin Frankel (London, 1999) 4–5.

a society it governs through a political authority structure'.[48] This level of identity is thus also formed by the physical attributes of the state (territory, natural resources, demographic structures). In the case of Morocco, I will look at how the representation of its body identity, marked by the consideration of a territorial amputation (the southern provinces) and a lack of energy resources (in comparison with its Algerian neighbour) marks its geopolitical representations.

2. Type identity: the set of values, rules and political culture around the state regime. History, 'national values', languages, type of law (positive or religious), national beliefs (secular or state religion), and the chosen economic norms (capitalist, socialist, etc.) are all characteristics that define the type identity of a state. In the case of Morocco, I will focus on how the particularities of the monarchical power structure and the choice of redefining a state Islam contribute to the definition of national interests.

3. Role identity: formed by the projection of a role at the international level. To understand this concept, it should be analysed in the light of Kalevi J. Holsti's famous study on the role of states in their foreign policies.[49] In this study, Holsti developed a typology of 17 major roles[50] based on an observation of the foreign policy of a sample of states between 1965 and 1967. The author concludes that a state can play several roles at once (United States) or none (Côte d'Ivoire), estimating an average of 4.6 roles played by each state in the designated period. The interest of Holsti's study is that it shows that the role is defined by endogenous factors (e.g. national values) as well as exogenous factors (e.g. status within the international system). It also shows that some roles are self-assigned by states (e.g. human rights promoters), and others are assigned or reinforced by other actors (e.g. a self-appointed role as 'world policeman' can be supported by soliciting intervention by other states). Wendt goes further than Holsti's conceptualisation of role identity insofar as, if it is co-constructed by the agent and his structure, it seems more stable and perennial. One can easily change one's role, but one will not easily change one's role identity because the latter is interdependent with the other levels of identity

---

48 Wendt, *Social Theory of International Politics*, 201.
49 Kalevi J. Holsti, "National Role Conceptions in the Study of Foreign Policy", *International Studies Quarterly*, no. 3 (1970).
50 Regional leader, regional protector, defender of the faith, defender of liberation, mediator-integrator, bridge, independent, isolated, bastion of revolution, liberation, developer, anti-imperialist agent, internal developer, active independent, regional sub-system, loyal ally and beneficiary.

and takes longer to be constructed. Holsti does not make this distinction, while some of the roles identified by the author (promoter of universal values) seem to be more role identities. In the case of Morocco, the aim will be to define the characteristics and trace the construction process of its role identity. This concept will form the hypothetical core of this work.

4. Collective identity: this refers to regional or international groupings that a state considers itself to share common norms, values and interests with. Unlike alliances (based solely on the dimension of interest), regional (European Union, African Union) or international (NATO) organisations can form the basis of collective identity. In other cases, this collective identity can be postulated without being politically institutionalised; I will help to demonstrate this in this study. Thus, one of the hypotheses that will guide the analysis of Moroccan foreign policy is that its perception of belonging to an Arab or African grouping will influence as well as being influenced by its foreign policy choices in an intersubjective logic. I will then attempt to trace the foundations of these representations and the conditions of their evolution.

4 The Challenge of Multi-disciplinarity in the Study of Moroccan Foreign Policy

This book is intended to be at the crossroads of history, sociology, geopolitics, security studies and international relations, as well as taking into account the economic, anthropological and strategic dimensions of politics. Such multidisciplinary ambition can be rightly accused of masking deficiencies in thinking. Nailed down by some researchers, this approach is nevertheless necessary to understand the evolution of Morocco in its African environment. More importantly, it is the characteristics and implications of Morocco's Africa policy that have prompted my reasoning. However, it is essential to specify how and from what angle each chosen discipline will serve as a framework for the study.

4.1 *The Historical Variable*
A long-standing historical player, Morocco is a territory of Roman, Berber and Arab conquests, ruled by numerous dynasties; extended to the east, south and north, then reduced by its defeats; divided by colonial powers, then successively decolonised; and finally made up of a significant ethnic and cultural mix. It is unclear when the country began as a self-conscious geopolitical unit. For many, the birth of Morocco is associated with the advent of national sentiment and dates back to the protectorate, when the first nationalist movements

INTRODUCTION

appeared. Others show that there was already a sense of national unity in the nineteenth century.[51] Some consider that this entity has existed for a long time, since the advent of the Marinid dynasty in the sixteenth century.[52] Some argue that the Idrisside dynasty, founded in 789, was the first embryo of a politically organised unit with its own identity.[53]

These contradictions in dating, therefore, raised the methodological problem of the place of history in the study of diplomacy: should the deployment of ambassadors to European kingdoms in the eighteenth century be taken into account as an acquired element in the Moroccan diplomatic experience? What is the place *in the collective imaginary* of the conquest of Mali by Sultan Ahmed el Mansour in the sixteenth century? What is the influence of Valéry Giscard d'Estaing's Africa policy on that of the King? Did Morocco's preference for the Western camp during the Cold War count more than the symbolic religious ties forged by the Alawite dynasty in the nineteenth century in its leaders' representations of the former African revolutionary states? As the questions become more and more complex, it becomes clear that the problem was not well posed.

A reflection on the role of history in international relations suggests that it can be a determinant that is sometimes objective (it results in geopolitical data), sometimes subjective (it guides representations) and at other times instrumentalised by politics (it serves legitimisation): dimensions that I will present more precisely in the second chapter of this study. However, a reading of history through these three dimensions shows that we are entitled to speak of Morocco per se, because it is indeed in all this history, ancient or recent, that Morocco's Africa policy draws its identity—to such an extent that the Kingdom's interest in the continent appears in certain regards a predestination of its own history rather than that imposed by the new world order. Therefore, I will mention all the historical facts that objectively, subjectively or in an instrumentalised shape condition this Africa policy, provided that any temptation is avoided to reduce the conducting of foreign policy to these causal factors alone. In contrast to studies on the same topic that have privileged history alone as a guiding thread of analysis,[54] this book also aims to offer a sociological, geopolitical and theoretical analysis of the subject. This is why, in contrast, I will not write a historical and contextual first part, nor will the plan follow a chronolog-

---

51   Germain Ayache, "Le sentiment national dans le Maroc du XIXe siècle", *Revue Historique* 130, (1968): 393–410,.
52   Rivet, *Histoire du Maroc.*
53   This is the version presented in most Moroccan history books.
54   These include the thesis by: Nicodeme Bugwarabi, "La politique sudsaharienne du Maroc de 1956 à 1984" (Thèse de doctorat, Paris, Université Panthéon-Sorbonne, 1997), 467.

ical order. Some historical passages, however detailed, will appear only to serve the argument, even if they are presented anachronistically.

4.2   A Sociological Approach to Foreign Policy

The transformation of the international system has also led Morocco to reconsider its diplomatic posture, reformulate its foreign policy instruments and review its order of priorities. Since the change of era caused by the end of the Cold War, the massive diffusion of the liberal paradigm and the emergence of new transnational security issues, diplomacy has developed. It now encompasses many areas, both strategic (climate diplomacy) and insignificant (culinary diplomacy). The transformation of diplomacy, and by extension of foreign policy, is an institutional consequence of the advent of a new, multipolar, even 'multiplex' world order.[55] Moreover, foreign policy is a public policy exercised in a milieu fundamentally opposed to the domestic milieu, elevated to a noble rank while being trivially determined by the same material, relational and bureaucratic conditions. These new conditions, therefore, pose the challenge of understanding the role of diplomacy as an administrative device in the conducting of the country's Africa policy and determining its orientations and strategy. Does the study of Mohammed VI's personality matter in the interpretation of foreign policy? Is a sociology of decision-makers and diplomats necessary for the study?

Foreign policy is defined by Jacques Vernant as 'the course of events that are currently taking place, in which we are more or less directly involved—and which we assume by rationalist assumption to have a certain structure'.[56] In this sense, foreign policy is, according to the author, more a matter of sociology than of history. It should be remembered that political sociology can be defined as the study of the relationship between the state and its institutions and the power relationships within the various state bodies. It is, therefore, not enough to recount the foreign policy; one must understand its structure and formulate

---

[55] Amitav Acharya, *Rethinking Power, Institutions and Ideas in World Politics: Whose IR?* (London–New York: Routledge, 2014). The author refers to a post-American or even post-Western world, where there are no longer logics of hegemonic poles but rather a multitude of intersecting regional, multilateral and transnational dynamics. More complex than the multipolar world, the multiplex world is not centred around the logic of the balance of state powers. Amitav Acharya's ontological postulates allow the researcher to broaden the study of the international system to include new actors and issues and focus more specifically on regional dynamics.

[56] Jacques Vernant, 'La recherche en politique étrangère', *Politique étrangère 33*, no. 1 (1968): 9–17.

hypotheses on its organisation. Thus, Raymond Aron considered that 'sociology is an indispensable intermediary between theory and event'.[57] While the classical historian is limited by a past time horizon, the sociologist must interpret the present to explain current behaviour in light of new developments in the environment.

Morocco's Africa policy is indeed a policy in constant construction. The sociologist's lenses are therefore necessary for the study. They are compatible with the historical approach, since sociology is interested in the historical depth of phenomena, and with the theoretical approach, since, as Guillaume Devin points out, 'sociohistorical enquiry does not exclude the formulation of general propositions and their discussion with the paradigms of IR theories'.[58] Sociology also offers a reservoir of relevant concepts in the analysis of international relations, but it is more the sociological method of approach that interests me here.

In the analysis of foreign policy, the sociological approach has taken several forms: some will be taken into account and others discarded. First is the perceptual approach, which was brought to international relations by idealist thinkers of the interwar period. Kenneth Boulding,[59] on the one hand, and Robert Jervis,[60] on the other, have both devoted numerous studies to explaining the behaviour of states based on perceptions[61] their decision-makers had of their international environment. In France, the thesis of Julien Freund,[62] an extension of the works of Carl Schmitt, Georg Simmel and Max Weber, has also paved the way for numerous studies on the sociology of conflict. The reconstitution of the world of decision-makers within a perceptual approach is of heuristic interest in understanding decisions. Nevertheless, the contributions of these authors are also limited by the strategic orientation of their approaches, taking away the debate on representation around the issue of war. In order to circumvent this epistemological obstacle, I will therefore consider

---

57 Aron, *Paix et guerre entre les nations*, 26.
58 Guillaume Devin, *Sociologie des relations internationales*, (Paris: La Découverte, 2013), 3.
59 K.E. Boulding, "National Images and International Systems", *The Journal of Conflict Resolution 3*, no. 2 (1959), 120–131.
60 Robert Jervis, *Perception and Misperception in International Politics*, (Princeton, N.J.: Princeton University Press, 1976); Robert Jervis, *The logic of images in international relations*, (Princeton, N.J., USA: Princeton University Press, 1970), 281.
61 For a detailed presentation of the study of images and perceptions in the analysis of foreign policy since then see: Frédéric Ramel, *Recherche ennemi désespérément. Origines, essor et apport des approaches perceptuelles en relations internationales*, (Quebec, 2001), 60.
62 Julien Freund, *L'essence du politique*, (Paris: Dalloz, 2003), 867.

the issue of representation through a sociological and geopolitical approach, as I will explain below.

In addition, I can mention the psychological approach, which is particularly prevalent in anglophone studies.[63] This approach is based on the study of decision-makers' psychology, and therefore carries the risk of biasing the information. As Jean-Noël Ferrié points out, 'if actions are causal, the intentions and intelligibilities that support them are discontinuous. Detailed knowledge of the motivations and interactions within a group does not, therefore, inform us about its interactions with others and so on.'[64] More concretely, the psychology of Mohammed VI, his interests as an individual and his private life are not sufficiently relevant causal factors to be addressed in this study. It is the monarch's social identity, in its discursive, relational and stylistic aspects, that will be the object of particular attention. Thus, emotion will not be understood as an element of understanding an identity[65] but as a means of communicating a representation.[66]

Second, the bureaucratic analysis challenges the state as a unitary or anthropomorphic actor. It breaks it down into a multitude of bureaucratic organisations and competing individuals whose interests are sometimes contradictory. This method was developed by the Foreign Policy Analysis (FPA) school which emerged in the United States in the 1960s, whose main figurehead is Graham Allison.[67] However, it is not really relevant in our empirical case, as the diplomatic apparatus is subordinated to an executive heart constituted exclusively by the monarchy. No conflict of interest within the decision-making unit, no observable bureaucratic competition, can be conceived as a determining phenomenon in the making of the decision. Mohammed Riziki's thesis demonstrates this well.[68] The book carefully and meticulously describes all the sociological characteristics of Moroccan diplomats on the basis of hundreds

---

63   Brian Ripley, "Psychology, Foreign Policy, and International Relations Theory", *Political Psychology 14*, no. 3 (1993), 403–416,.

64   Jean-Noël Ferrié, "Démocratisation de l'Afrique du Nord et du Moyen-Orient: l'impossible accélération de l'histoire", in *Monde arabe, entre transition et implosion: les dynamiques internes et les influences externes*, ed. Hasni Abidi, (Paris, France: E. Bonnier, 2015).

65   Philippe Braud, *L'émotion en politique: problèmes d'analyse* (Presses de la Fondation nationale des sciences politiques, 1996), 276.

66   Todd H. Hall, *Emotional diplomacy: official emotion on the international stage* (Ithaca: Cornell University Press, 2015).

67   Graham Tillett Allison, *Essence of decision: explaining the Cuban missile crisis* (Boston: Little, Brown and Company, 1971), 338.

68   Mohamed Abdelaziz Riziki, *Sociologie de la diplomatie marocaine*, (Paris: L'Harmattan, 2014), 587.

of interviews conducted in a directive or free manner. Still, it does not shed any significant light on the understanding of foreign policy. The encyclopaedic temptation of the study makes it look like a catalogue of different diplomatic profiles and their evolution, disconnected from any political dimension. It provides relevant material to illustrate some of my comments on the development of the diplomatic apparatus while supporting the hypothesis of the weak influence of internal diplomatic interactions in the orientation and development of Morocco's Africa policy. Rachid El Houdaïgui's thesis on the Hasanian period reveals the same trend.[69] Initially focused on a description of the Moroccan decision-making apparatus, this work illustrates once again that political parties, as well as state institutions, constitute marginal 'decision-making units' in the elaboration of foreign policy, to the extent that it is through a historical analysis and not through an analysis of power relations or bureaucratic developments that the author was able to draw the political contours of his subject.

Another methodological approach is based on the idea that all decisions are based on rational, well-calculated, unchangeable interests.[70] Action is presented as the result of this rational choice, while strategic goals are defined according to a predefined list of interests (security, power, economic gains, etc.). This postulate has the advantage of questioning the explanations at the origin of the decision, but it also has its limits in the analysis of our case study. Indeed, although rationality is often sought by the actor, it is not always achieved. The pure rationality of the political actor is a paradoxically anti-realist postulate because of the unpredictable nature of the Other's behaviour, and because of the role of 'passions'—to use Marcel Merle's expression—in decision-making.[71] Moreover, as Franck Petiteville rightly notes, 'there is no "substantial rationality" in foreign policy that does not imply at the same time a normative judgement';[72] any decision is also the result of representations. In the case of Morocco, in addition to the limitations mentioned, the rational approach prevents the exploration of new issues. If it is true that the Kingdom pursues interests defined in terms of power and security, what is the conception of this security? What kind of power identity is being sought? What types

---

69 Rachid El Houdaïgui, *La politique étrangère sous le règne de Hassan II: acteurs, enjeux et processus décisionnels*, (Paris: L'Harmattan, 2003).
70 Graham T. Allison, and Philip D. Zelikowv, "L'essence de la decision. Le modèle de l'acteur rationnel", *Cultures & Conflicts*, no. 36 (2000).see also: Duncan Snidal, "Rational Choice and International Relations", in *Handbook of International Relations*, (Oliver's Yard, 55 City Road, London EC1Y 1SP United Kingdom: SAGE Publications, 2002), 73–94.
71 Marcel Merle, *Sociologie des relations internationales*, (Paris: Dalloz, 1982).
72 Franck Petiteville, "De la politique étrangère comme catégorie d'analyse des relations internationales", *Critique internationale* 20, no. 3, (2003): 59–63.

of resources are mobilised? These are all questions that cannot be answered with any degree of clarity by a rational approach.

Moreover, within this approach, foreign policy is described as the result of the action of decision-makers and not of the constraint of their environment. This methodological individualism also limits the analytical perspectives of Moroccan foreign policy. As a small country, Morocco is subject to a double international influence: normative, on the one hand, since its institutional model is almost entirely inspired by European, and in particular French, norms, determining the bureaucratic organisation of the foreign ministry, the legal structure of cooperation agreements and the choice of concepts in diplomatic discourse; political, on the other hand, since its room for manoeuvre is reduced by the pressures exerted by the great powers in defence of their interests, which determines the list of choices and therefore the conduct of foreign policy. There is no doubt that the influence of the external environment, as well as domestic interests, must be taken into account simultaneously in the interpretation of the decision.

All of these approaches, whether psychological, perceptual, rational or bureaucratic, have their limitations. A reflexivist approach emerged in the 1990s, proposing to interpret perceptions and rational factors in light of the notion of image: for example, it is the image that actors have of the systemic order that leads them to seek power. In contrast to the bureaucratic approach, the state is defined as a unitary actor with anthropomorphic qualities. The reflexivist approach to foreign policy also incorporates cultural and normative factors into the analysis. Reflexivism takes a post-positivist view and is based on an interpretive epistemology, according to which empirical data must be interpreted before results are presented. However, 'reflexivism thus opens the way to a metatheoretical proliferation, which leads some sociologists who claim to be reflexivists to reopen the pluralist path',[73] to the point that it is difficult to identify an objective scientific method.

In order to find a suitable way to observe our object, my method is situated at the intersection of perceptual, rational and reflexive approaches to foreign policy. The state is presented as a coherent decision-making and political unit, not as a set of competing bureaucratic institutions, because, as I have already pointed out, the diplomatic apparatus is subordinate to the orders of the monarchy. It is also conceived as an anthropomorphic structure, so much so that the identity of the King and that of the state merge, and so much so that

---

73   Thierry Braspenning, "Constructivisme et réflexivisme en théorie des relations internationales", *Annuaire français des Relations Internationale III* (2002): 314–329.

a form of state identity seems to emerge. In this respect, at the editorial level, the state will often be referred to as a subject that thinks, that represents itself or that leads, since it refers to the King, his advisors and all the decision-makers who think according to the directives they have been given. This is not an error of language but a methodological bias that suits my observation of the empirical field: I will thus be interested in the decision-making system as a whole. In addition, I will evoke the decision-making style rather than the psychology of the decision-maker in the interpretation of the decision. Interests will be defined in constructed terms, while power and security will be shown to have a strong influence on the conduct of foreign policy. Similarly, the role of perceptions as a determinant influencing the decision will be examined. Finally, the evolution and organisation of the bureaucratic structure will be treated not as a result of the evolution of the external or internal environment, but as a measure of political ambitions. The sociological approach will therefore allow me, more generally, to examine the internal factors of the diplomatic practice. The interest of the sociological approach, in contrast to the purely theoretical approach, is that it makes it possible to minimise the normative influence of international relations theories.

Through these changes of perspective, the main sociological object of this study will then be to demonstrate how the monarchy conducts this foreign policy on the one hand, and the nature of the link between domestic and foreign policy on the other. More generally, the aim will be to understand the superstructures, the institutional and decision-making framework of this foreign policy (the role of the foreign ministry, the Royal Cabinet, the advisors), rather than to focus on the work of Moroccan diplomats in their practice.

4.3 The Role of Geopolitics

On the question of representations, the geopolitical approach is necessary for the analysis. Geopolitics is a discipline in the process of being re-legitimised, as it has become the bearer of a reflection on the heterogeneity of spaces in a globalised society. In this respect, its approach has been assimilated to a spatial ontology,[74] thereby reinforcing the idea of its scientificity. In its classical definition, geopolitics is the study of 'power rivalries or struggles for influence over territories and the populations living in them'.[75] Nowadays, however, most geopolitics textbooks offer a scholastic description of the territorial,

---

74   Gérard Dussouy, "Vers une géopolitique systémique", *Revue internationale et stratégique* 47, no. 3 (2002): 53.
75   Yves Lacoste, *Géopolitique: la longue histoire d'aujourd'hui* (Paris: Larousse, 2009), 8.

demographic, sociological, historical, cultural, strategic and political particularities of a given space. This approach is falsely exhaustive and tends to weaken the relevance of the analysis. Olivier Zajec brings up the limits of this multidisciplinarity, which contributes to making geopolitics 'a method of approach rather than a science',[76] while proposing a new definition that, although state-centric, is both classical and modern.[77] Others focus on non-state actors and non-military strategies. Thus, one can speak of the 'geopolitics of football', the 'geopolitics of the kitchen' or the 'geopolitics of sexual frustration', all of which, according to Yves Lacoste, contribute to making geopolitics an advertising gimmick.[78] This multiplicity of fields of application has for a long time inconvenienced researchers, including Hervé Couteau-Bégarie, who set himself up as the spokesperson through a worrying phrase: in the end, 'we don't really know what geopolitics is'.[79]

However, geopolitics retains some epistemological consistency. Indeed, it is an approach based on representation, a dimension often forgotten by geopoliticians but recalled by the tenants of the school of *critical geopolitics*:[80] '"Critical geopolitics" focuses its attention on the role played by social, cultural and political processes in "giving meaning" and participating in the "construction" of the international political reality'.[81] In other words, in analysing power relations within a space, the study of the discourses that accompany the representation of this space is just as important as the study of geo-economic characteristics. As Gérard Dussouy rightly reminds us, 'it is in intersubjectivity—in other words, thanks to the intersubjective synthesis of paradigms and the models they inspire—that the relevance of geopolitics lies'.[82] This also leads me to emphasise the need to distinguish my approach as a researcher from the point of view of the political actors in the Moroccan space or the structural realities that characterise Moroccan geography in order to maintain some axiological

---

76 Olivier Zajec, *Introduction à l'analyse géopolitique*, (Paris, France: Argos, 2013), 50.
77 'Geopolitics studies the physical and human inertia that affects and guides states' internal and external behaviour. It thus sheds light on the political foundations of peaceful or warlike actions which, by means of military, economic and political strategies with defensive or offensive territorial aims, seek to ensure the continuity of a community in history' Zajec, *Géopolitique: la longue histoire d'aujourd'hui*, 14.
78 Lacoste, *Géopolitique*, 8–9.
79 Hervé Coutau-Bégarie and Martin Motte, *Approches de la géopolitique: de l'Antiquité au XXIe siècle* (Paris: Economica Institut de stratégie comparée, 2013), 31.
80 Anglo-American school of thought born in the late 1980s, under the pen of Gearóid Ó Tuathail, John Agnew and Klaus Dodds.
81 David Criekemans, "Réhabilitation et rénovation en matière de pensée géopolitique", *L'espace politique. Revue en ligne de géographie politique et de géopolitique*, no. 12 (2011).
82 Dussouy, "Vers une géopolitique systémique".

neutrality. Similarly, it seems essential to cross different levels of analysis (spatial, institutional and discursive), since 'there is no geopolitical method per se'.[83]

Taking into account the debates related to the incommensurability of theories in international relations, these methodological precautions aim at supporting the idea of commensurability while admitting the complexity of the theoretical stake that results from it. The need for theories of international relations to take into account the spatial variable, while avoiding an overly normative point of view (characteristic of dominant paradigms), would facilitate this aspect.[84] I will therefore define geopolitics as the study of the representation and organisation of space, of the meanings given by states or transnational actors to a territory, the strategic, political and socioeconomic dynamics that characterise it, and the power relations that result from it. As an approach rather than a science, it completes the analyses privileging the single and dominant prism of the theories of international relations by integrating the spatial variable. The specificities inherent to my empirical field lead me to favour this approach.

4.4   Security Studies

One of the objectives of this study is to demonstrate that security is a vital concern for the Kingdom, thus confirming a classic realist assumption. Security is, however, a polysemous concept defined in Morocco as the defence of territorial integrity, the lives of individuals, the values of the state and national identity, and the defence of a role in external security. A purely realist approach to security is therefore reductive, as it fails to capture the diversity of areas and implications of this policy field. Security has become sectoralised, its actors have diversified, its levels have multiplied and its issues have become more complex.[85] Security studies, particularly the work that is part of or inspired by

---

83   Coutau-Bégarie and Motte, *Approches de la géopolitique*, 24.
84   This point of view is also shared by Gérard Dussouy, according to whom 'the panopticism that legitimises geopolitics must avoid any essentialism, any unique and overhanging point of view, in order to propose alternative configurations, because they are conceived according to different hypotheses of evolution. This approach is undoubtedly indispensable because it is lodged in the hollow of the theory of international relations, which can no longer ignore the spatial variable, in the name of an idealised universalism or because geography is known to have been elevated at the rank of last resort determinant by old geopolitics, while it especially served as support to culturalism.' Dussouy, "Vers une géopolitique systémique".
85   Thierry Balzacq, "La sécurité: définitions, secteurs et niveaux d'analyse", *Fédéralisme Régionalisme* (2006).

the Copenhagen School,[86] consider security in its broadest sense. They therefore constitute a methodological corpus that sheds light on most of the issues relating to Moroccan security.

Two distinctions inherent to security as a national interest will therefore be examined here through the Copenhagen vision. First, threat as a geopolitically observable object will be distinguished from threat as a socially constructed or securitised object.[87] This fundamental nuance will make it possible to measure and separate the different levels of security action linked to this Africa policy, such as the question of the Sahara. Second, it will be a question of showing the nuance while at the same time demonstrating the existing overlaps between a vision of the fields and of security influenced by international norms, taken up as it is by the Moroccan leaders, either by institutional mimicry or intending to legitimise a policy (e.g. global security and human security), and the one constructed by Morocco, which defines new fields of security (illustrated in particular by the appearance of the concept of 'spiritual security'). In the long run, this approach should make it possible to measure the weight, role and levels of security, as interest and instrument of the state, in the conception of the Kingdom's Africa policy.

However, the study of the security dimension will suffer from a notable deficiency of information on issues related to military security and, more generally, defence policy. While the Moroccan defence administration does not publish any activity report or analysis on its activities and does not respond to requests for interviews (unlike many other administrations), few researchers have taken an interest in the subject, certainly for the same reasons that limited my research. Apart from a few rare scientific articles,[88] the academic literature available on this subject is deplorable. To overcome this difficulty, my approach relies on journalistic articles, press releases and diplomatic documents as well as their interpretation given the Kingdom's foreign policy issues. The results of this defence research will be mentioned only to confirm or nuance a previously justified statement, as a precaution to avoid any temptation to over-interpret a phenomenon.

---

86 Barry Buzan et al, *Security : a new framework for analysis* (Boulder, 1998).
87 Mathias Albert and Barry Buzan, "Securitization, sectors and functional differentiation", Security Dialogue 42, no. 4–5 (2011): 413–425; Thierry Balzacq, "The Three Faces of Securitization: political agency, audience and context", European Journal of International Relations 11, no. 2 (2005): 171–201.
88 Brahim Saidy, "La politique de défense Marocaine: articulation de l'interne et de l'externe", *Maghreb–Machrek 202*, no. 4 (2009): 115–131; Brahim Saidy, "Relations civilo-militaires au Maroc: le facteur international revisité", *Politique étrangère Automne*, no. 3 (200):589–603.

5 Book Structure and Objectives

This book is a study of Morocco's Africa policy until its reintegration into the AU in 2017. Through the Moroccan example, it will demonstrate that one of the factors of power and international recognition lies in the diffusion of a strong and syncretic state identity. Abdessamad Belhaj considers, in his study on the Islamic dimension of Moroccan foreign policy, that 'state identities have not yet replaced, In the Arab world, the Islamic supra-state identity'.[89] This book takes the opposite view of the two hypotheses raised by the author. the study of Morocco's Africa policy tends to show that there is indeed a new state identity under construction and in search of recognition, while the idea of the Arab world as a geopolitical entity defined by a form of organic solidarity (through the recognition of a collective religious identity) or mechanical solidarity (through shared institutions and interests) is becoming obsolete in Moroccan representations, to the benefit of the definition of an Islam specific to the Moroccan state, as well as a new interest in the African regional system. In this respect, the Islamic dimension of Moroccan foreign policy, as studied by the author, only partially informs us about the new identity of the Moroccan power in its continental environment, as it is constructed in a triple relationship between the system of internal values and beliefs, political interests and the image reflected by other states, particularly African ones. Here, I will examine Morocco's Africa policy's interests, determinants and consequences. I will also question how the African orientation of this diplomacy contributes to the construction of Moroccan power.

Finally, at the end of this study, it will be necessary to propose a 'hermeneutic definition' of state identity, which can make sense of the relationship between the various constitutive elements of its politics, on the one hand, and the discursive and practical aspects of its diplomatic conduct, on the other. By speaking of a 'hermeneutic definition', although this expression seems contradictory, I insist on the idea that there is no single character in identity, that it must therefore be defined in a representative way and that its causal relationship with diplomacy is not without interpretation.

In order to understand how Morocco is transforming itself in the spirit of integrating its African environment, it will be necessary to identify who is behind this policy and what guides it (Chapters 1, 2 and 3). The evolution of the Moroccan decision-making system in terms of foreign policy, in particular the dominant role and style of the monarch, will be studied in the light of internal

---

89 Belhaj, *La dimension islamique dans la politique étrangère du Maroc*, 77–78.

structural and economic developments to demonstrate how Morocco is gradually asserting a role identity on the international scene, in the sense defined by Alexander Wendt,[90] disseminated by a diplomatic apparatus that is modernising and developing. I will enlighten the reader on Morocco's territorial ambitions in Africa after its independence and the impact of these conditions on the evolution of its relations with African states. In particular, the role of France in constructing Moroccan–African relations during the Cold War will be discussed.

Second, I will question how this role identity is constructed at the normative and discursive level (Chapters 4 and 5), how it is deployed at the strategic and diplomatic level (Chapters 6 and 7) and how it affects the African environment as well as Morocco itself (Chapter 8). I will present the framework of representation and legitimisation that structures this policy, based on the historical conditions analysed above and on Morocco's new ambitions, as well as how these are subject to a discursive legitimisation strategy. I will analyse the strategy of the Africa policy and how it is conducted by studying the different instruments used (political, economic, cultural, etc.) and by reflecting on their use within a diplomacy of influence. More generally, this section aims to define this strategy at the level of foreign policy, drawing on the concept of indirect strategy developed by André Beaufre.[91] Finally, I will look at the consequences of this foreign policy, in terms of both gains (relative or absolute) and its potential to transform Moroccan identity in a reflexive manner.

---

90   Alexander Wendt, *Social Theory of International Politics*, Cambridge (UK; New York: Cambridge University Press, 1999).
91   André Beaufre, *Introduction à la stratégie*, (Paris: Armand Colin, 1963).

CHAPTER 1

The Genesis of an Africa Policy in Morocco: the Kingdom in Search of International Recognition

1   Introduction

Morocco does not have the hydrocarbon deposits of its neighbour Algeria, and it does have a large public debt (nearly 84% of Moroccan GDP). However, the efficiency with which it has undertaken reforms and accelerated its economic development is remarkable. Since the beginning of the 2000s, Morocco has engaged in a policy of internal and external debt reduction, benefiting from a favourable international situation, from the increase in FDI (foreign direct investment) towards Morocco and from the growth of tourism activities. Between 1998 and 2007, the share of the population that was poor, according to the national poverty line, thus fell from 16.3% to 8.9%.[1] Life expectancy is rising, as is gross national income (GNI) per capita, which rose from US$1,310 in 2000 to $8,410 at the end of 2018.[2] More generally, Morocco has had a growth rate of 3.5%[3] on average for almost 20 years, occupying the fifth place in the ranking of the most prosperous African countries[4] and seventh place in the ranking of African economic powers according to GDP.

The emergence model pursued by the government is based on growth, driven by exports and foreign investment in the industrial and service sectors. Initially, under the influence of neoliberal norms and the pressure of the 'Washington Consensus', in the 1980s Morocco adopted, like many other countries in the developing world, a 'structural adjustment' policy.

In a second phase, given the mixed results of this adjustment policy, international organisations, from a neo-institutionalist perspective, then advocated 'economic emergence' based on growth; many countries now subscribe to this paradigm. As Philippe Hugon rightly remarks, 'the Washington Consensus signalled the normalisation, if not the end of development economics […] When the market acquires a status of universality, when spontaneous order prevails

---

1   World Bank data on Morocco: http://donnees.banquemondiale.org/pays/Morocco
2   Ibid.
3   Ibid.
4   "Global Competitiveness Report 2015–2016: African countries ranked", Agence Ecofin, September 3rd 2014.

over decreed order and substantial rationality becomes axiomatic, the economy becomes autonomous and development economics loses its specificity.'[5]

An emerging country, as defined by this consensus, is a country with strong economic growth, political stability and high levels of economic activity.[6] The emergence concept was conceived to recognise developing countries with a favourable business climate.[7] But while many countries appear to fall into this category without being classified as emerging, others are identified as emerging while their economies are still fragile. Although there is no clear consensus on the identification of emerging countries, the notion has become as popular as that of democracy: a holy grail that developing states are striving to acquire. Therefore, because 'the term is fashionable among governments and donors',[8] many countries, such as Côte d'Ivoire, Gabon and even Chad and Togo, have plans to emerge by 2030. Similarly, in Morocco, Mohammed VI estimated that the Moroccan development model 'has reached a level of maturity that enables it to make a definitive and deserved entry into the concert of emerging countries'.[9] It can therefore be seen that the political and economic openness pursued by King Mohammed VI is like a refractive movement, i.e. both the result of the influence of neoliberal norms on an international scale, and the driving force behind emergence on an internal scale in a way that is specific to Morocco. The country's development is linked to the ambition of emergence in its neoliberal sense, as indicated in the King's Throne Speech of 2005,[10] while the monarchical apparatus constitutes the point of impact without which none of the transformations could be effectively initiated. The monarchy recognises, however, that there is no single model for an emerging country and that certain developments can also contribute to creating socioeconomic gaps. In this perspective, the King proposed that the Moroccan emergence model should

---

5   Philippe Hugon, "La crise va-t-elle conduire à un nouveau paradigme du développement?", *Mondes en développement* 15, no. 2 (2010): 53–67.
6   Christophe Jaffrelot et al, *L'enjeu mondial: Les pays émergents* (Paris: Les Presses de Sciences Po, 2008).
7   Dalila Nicet-Chenaf, "Les pays émergents: performance ou développement?", *La Vie des Idées*, March 4, 2014.
8   Marc Innocent, "La quête de l'émergence en Afrique, ou la fin de l'afro-pessimisme", *Abidjan.net*, March 19, 2015.
9   "Speech to the Nation on the occasion of the 61th anniversary of the Revolution of the King and the People", Lavieeco.com, August 20, 2014.
10 'Global development cannot be achieved without upgrading and modernising our economy and without winning the bets on integration into the world economy and free trade. This is a must if we are to accelerate the pace of growth, improve competitiveness, increase productivity and create job-creating wealth', Speech by H.M. King Mohammed VI on the occasion of the 5th anniversary of the Throne Day, *Maroc.ma*, July 30, 2005.

be based on three criteria: 'the level of democratic and institutional evolution, economic and social progress, and regional and international openness'.[11]

It is, therefore, no coincidence that from the beginning of Mohammed VI's reign in 1999, emergence gradually became a national priority, supported by a series of legal and social reforms, industrial and economic programmes, and the construction of numerous infrastructures. The year 2005, in particular, was characterised by the launch of the National Human Development Initiative (NHDI), along with a series of 'emergence plans' whose content and objectives directly aim to affirm Morocco as a power.

The first programme in this direction, 'Plan Emergence', was launched in 2005 and consisted of an industrial policy aimed at consolidating existing sectors and opening new promising sectors (aeronautics, offshoring, automobile, etc.). The 'National Plan for Industrial Emergence' launched in 2009 and the 'National Plan for Industrial Acceleration' launched in 2014 are part of the same objective. According to the Minister of Industry, thanks to these plans, industry share in GDP was projected to increase from 14% to 23% between 2014 and 2020.[12] By 2018, the percentage had already reached 25.9%,[13] exceeding these projected targets. The government has tried to attract as much FDI as possible to its industry while developing foreign trade.[14] This strategy has borne fruit, since many foreign industrial groups (automobile, aeronautics, electronics) have established themselves in Morocco in recent years. However, national industries remain poorly developed and not competitive enough. As an Agence Française de Développement analysis note indicates, this path is strewn with pitfalls: 'the structural transformation of the Moroccan economy, marked by a relatively rapid tertiarisation, reflects the weaknesses of the industrial sector and the lack of competitiveness of the Moroccan manufacturing export sector'.[15] Aware of these shortcomings, the government has therefore oriented its emergence strategy towards other sectors which, although not strictly industrial, still contribute to the industrialisation effort.

In addition to industrial planning, a large number of sectoral projects were launched in a wide variety of fields during this period: the 'Green Morocco

11 "Speech by H.M the King on the occasion of the 61th anniversary of the revolution of the King and the people", *Maroc.ma*, August 20, 2014.
12 Jean-Dominique Merchet, "En 2020, le Maroc entend être une puissance industrielle émergente", *L'Opinion.fr*, April 7, 2014.
13 World Bank data. https://donnees.banquemondiale.org.
14 Ward Vloeberghs, "Quand le royaume rayonne: La géopolitique marocaine au prisme du commerce extérieur", *Confluences Méditerranée 78*, no. 3 (2011):157.
15 Clémence Vergne, "Le modèle de croissance marocaine: opportunités et vulnérabilités", *Agence Francaise de Développement*, no. 14 (2014).

Plan' in 2008 announced significant financial means intended to boost agriculture, the 'Azur Plan' in 2000 provided for the construction of six large tourist complexes in Moroccan seaside resorts, the 'Rawaj Plan' in 2008 for the development of trade, the 'Vision Artisanat 2015' for the development of the jobs of Moroccan craftspeople, the 'Halieutis Project' for the exploitation of fisheries resources, and the 'Digital Morocco' project in 2013 for the development of the information and communication technology sector and digital economy. In order to attract foreign investment to these programmes, the Moroccan Investment Development Agency was created in 2009, supporting the regional investment offices already in existence since 1999. All of this political effervescence, in addition to a government policy of subsidising food and energy products, is once again in line with emergence as conceived from the state's point of view. According to a report published in 2006:

> Skilful integration into the knowledge economy, through alignment with regional and international *benchmarks* in this field, offers an 'exit from the top' for the Moroccan economy. Our country can thus legitimately aspire, over the next two decades, to move from a situation of 'intermediate country' to the status of 'emerging country', with an income exceeding 8,000 constant dollars per capita.[16]

This goal has been achieved, since, as noted earlier, the GNI per capita increased from $1,310 in 2000 to $8,410 by the end of 2018.

The first effects of this national policy are already visible. In terms of infrastructure, for example, connection to the electricity network has reached 90% of rural areas, access to the internet has been extended,[17] road networks and airports have been developed, and many bridges have been built. Residences to accommodate the future families of the emerging middle class, tramways in the major cities, a high-speed train line, and a large commercial port in Tangiers with an export processing zone have all seen the light of day. On the institutional level, several measures aimed at attracting foreign investment have been undertaken and are supervised by the state. All of this shows that the Kingdom is gradually returning to macroeconomic planning after its abandonment

---

16　Mohamed Tawfik Mouline et Anissa Lazrak. *Cinquentenaire de l'Indépendance du Royaume du Maroc—50 ans de développement humain—perspectives 2025*. Document de Synthèse du Rapport Général, January 2006.

17　Morocco is the third most connected African country to the Internet after the Seychelles and Mauritius. Annie Chéneau-Loquay, "L'Afrique au seuil de la révolution des télécommunications", *Afrique contemporaine*, no. 93 (2010): 93–112,.

during the period of structural adjustment, aiming to consolidate its structural resources and be recognised as an emerging country.

At the international level, the quest for emergence has led Morocco to sign several free trade agreements, notably with the Arab and Mediterranean countries (2001), with the United States (2004), and with the European Union ('Association Agreement', 2000). Similarly, the idea of economic interdependence with Africa is emerging. According to an official report, the Moroccan emergence policy corresponds to 'a new approach to South–South cooperation for shared African growth, positioning the country as a privileged partner in the integrated co-emergence of the continent'.[18] In this perspective of 'co-emergence' and 'integrated growth', Morocco has consolidated its trade relations with several countries investing in Africa from the 'global South', such as China, India, Turkey and Brazil.[19] In total, the Kingdom has signed free trade agreements with 54 countries, representing almost one billion inhabitants.[20] However, this type of agreement benefits foreign countries more than it does Morocco and, for the time being, only reinforces a trade balance already in deficit, as well as development gaps.

Thus, despite the speed with which reforms are being carried out, the Moroccan growth model is also likely to run out of steam. First of all, this model seems insufficiently inclusive,[21] insofar as numerous imbalances characterise the labour market, and the subsidy policy—which is insufficient—cannot alone support the low employment rate and the weight of a trade balance deficit. If the financial crisis of 2007 led to a new debate on the responsibility of countries holding international capital in the balance of global development, as well as a new alter-globalist theory of 'post-adjustment', Morocco is still pursuing its quest for emergence on the terms instituted by neoliberal epistemic communities. Moreover, the eco-responsible and social dimension of projects is not always considered, meaning that Morocco's environmental policy remains mainly nested in the energy sector.[22] This is one of the reasons why, despite the many advances made, Morocco was ranked 123rd out of 189

---

18   Economic, Social and Environmental Council of the Kingdom of Morocco, *Annual Report*, 2013.
19   For more details on the various exchanges see: Vloeberghs, "When the kingdom shines".
20   Youssef Aït Akdim, "Interview with Mohammed Bachir Rachdi: 'Morocco must ensure the coherence of its strategies' ", JeuneAfrique.com, June 10, 2014.
21   Vergne, "Le modèle de croissance marocain: opportunités et vulnérabilités".
22   Yousra Abourabi and Jean-Noël Ferrie, "La diplomatie environnementale du Maroc en Afrique: un mix intérieur-extérieur", *Revue Telos*, June 7, 2018, https://www.telos-eu.com/fr/politique-francaise-et-internationale/la-diplomatie-environnementale-du-maroc-en-afrique.html

countries on the Human Development Index by the end of the 2010s. Similarly, income disparities continue to grow. According to the Gini index, one-fifth of the population controls 48% of the national wealth.[23] In a report entitled *Unequal Morocco, Fair Taxation*, the NGO Oxfam noted that 'while the minimum wage is 2,570 dirhams per month [about 237 euros], it would take 154 years for a person at this level of salary to earn the equivalent of the increase in wealth over one year of one of Morocco's billionaires'.[24] Finally, in the area of gender equity, again, the imbalance is alarming. According to the Global Gender Gap Index, Morocco is ranked 137th out of 144 countries.

2   Measuring Morocco's Emergence in the Light of the New World Order: Africa's Emergence in a 'Multiplex' World

Is Morocco really on the road to emergence? As one researcher notes: 'While it is easy to identify rich economies that have finished emerging and others, for example in Africa, that have never emerged, the partition between the two is not so clear: have Korea, Greece or Portugal finished emerging? Have Peru or Morocco entered this enviable club?'[25] Similarly, while it is difficult to establish the degree of Morocco's emergence on a global macroeconomic scale from the figures and national projects mentioned above, to be truly measured its development must be considered in the light of a double global context: on the one hand, that of the structural development of the entire African continent, of which Morocco is one of the reflections; on the other hand, that of the new 'multiplex' world political order,[26] where the weight of the small and medium powers is as recognised as it is effective.

First of all, Morocco's economic and structural development seems to have been amplified by that of the continent as a whole in the aftermath of the Cold War and especially from the 2000s onwards. While post-colonial Africa was preoccupied with the construction of modern and independent states and represented, at the international level, a 'terrain' of ideological confrontation between the two hegemonic poles, post-bipolar Africa, on the contrary, attests to a significant economic and political emergence that stems from several factors:

---

23   Vergne, "Le modèle de croissance marocain: opportunités et vulnérabilités".
24   Oxfam. *Un Maroc inégalitaire, une taxation juste*. Rapport, 2019. https://www.oxfam.org/fr/publications/un-maroc-egalitaire-une-taxation-juste.
25   Jérôme Sgard, "Qu'est-ce qu'un pays émergent?", In *L'enjeu mondial. Les pays émergents*, ed. Jaffrelot, Christophe, (Paris: Presses de Sciences Po, 2008), 41–54.
26   Acharya, *Rethinking power, institutions and ideas in world politic*.

1. First, the end of conflicts related to the definition of borders: as Ali A. Mazrui[27] and more recently Michel Foucher[28] have noted, borders between states, although in most cases they are not natural borders, have been progressively integrated by African countries so that they are now subject to very little dispute. Morocco is one of the few African countries subject to a claim of independence on its borders, as we shall see later.
2. Second, the adoption of liberal constitutions that allow for a multi-party system: as Stephen Ellis[29] notes, the fall of the Berlin Wall in 1989 coincided with the publication of a World Bank report entitled *Sub-Saharan Africa: From Crisis to Sustainable Growth*, which attracted much criticism within the continent. This was the first time the World Bank had introduced the idea of the need for 'good governance' in Africa and called for financial contributions to support the democratisation of different governments. Countries wishing to receive development aid had to agree to 'democratise', even if only superficially. However, the same difficulties inherent in adapting the Westphalian state model to post-colonial Africa were repeated in attempts to adopt a liberal democratic mode of governance in post-bipolar Africa, resulting in a set of reflections on the slowness of democratic transitions[30] or the need to build an 'African-style' democracy.[31]
3. Third, if during the post-colonial bipolar period, ideologies were a significant factor in defining the national interests of African states,[32] it appears that the diplomacy of African countries during the current systemic phase has been modernised, with the development of administrative apparatuses and the enlargement and sectorisation of the field of competence of diplomats (culture, economy, security, religion, etc.). The relative withdrawal of the former colonial powers and the arrival of 'new

---

27 Adekeye Adebajo and Ali A. Mazrui, *The Curse of Berlin: Africa After the Cold War* (Oxford University Press, 2014).
28 Michel Foucher, *Frontières d'Afrique: Pour en finir avec un mythe* (Paris: CNRS, 2014), 61.
29 Stephen Ellis, "Africa after the Cold War: new patterns of government and politics", *Development and change 27*, no. 1 (1996): 1–28.
30 Jean-Noël Ferrié, "Les limites d'une démocratisation par la société civile en Afrique du Nord", *Études et Documents du CEDEJ*, no. 7 (2004).
31 Biléou Sakpane-Gbati, "La démocratie à l'africaine", *Éthique publique. Revue internationale d'éthique sociétale et gouvernementale 13*, no. 2 (2011).
32 Ira William Zartman, *International relations in the new Africa* (Englewood Cliffs, N.J., USA: Prentice-Hall, 1966), 47.

cooperation actors'[33] have also contributed to the gradual autonomisation of state foreign policies.

4. Fourth, the liberalisation of African national economies has partly transformed their ambitions, inspiring for many scholars the idea of 'state privatisation': an observation based on the increasing privatisation of public enterprises and services. Widely interpreted as yet another illustration of African state failure, the privatisation of states can nevertheless be seen as a continuation of their formation.[34] The consequences of privatisation include the production of new spaces of power, the reconfiguration of trade routes, customs rules, etc., so that, as one researcher notes, 'several parts of Atlantic Africa are rediscovering a neo-mercantilist form of trade'.[35] The extraversion of economic activity is one of the factors behind the continent's growth. Since 2000 there has been an average growth of 4.5% per year. While poverty is declining, national income per capita is steadily increasing.[36] Besides these macroeconomic considerations, considering local dynamics (informal economies or clusters) reveals a real development dynamic. Overall, social indicators show progress while the increase in the share of middle classes within African societies is confirmed.[37] This context favours the emergence of new generations of decision-makers, activists and entrepreneurs.

5. Fifth, there is a development of African regionalism, one of the characteristics of which is the growing interest of African regional organisations in security, even though the original purpose of these organisations was economic cooperation. A distinction is made here between regionalism and regionalisation. Regionalism is defined by Daniel Bach as a project that 'postulates the explicit construction of an identity, in opposition to its formation. It refers to the implementation of a programme, or even the definition of a strategy. It can be institutional construction within the framework of an intergovernmental organisation (IGO), but also the conclusion of bilateral political-legal arrangements'.[38] For example, ECOWAS created

---

[33] Philippe Hugon, "Les nouveaux acteurs de la coopération en Afrique", *International Development Policy Review*, no. 1 (2010): 99–118.

[34] Béatrice Hibou, "La 'décharge', nouvel interventionnisme", *Politique africaine 73*, no. 1 (1999): 6–15.

[35] Ellis, "Africa after the Cold War".

[36] World Bank data from 2000–2015. www.banquemondiale.org.

[37] Pierre Jacquemot, "L'émergence de classes moyennes en Afrique", *Afrique contemporaine*, no. 244 (2013): 124–125.

[38] Daniel C. Bach, "Régionalismes, régionalisation et globalisation" in Le politique en

ECOMOG in 1990 and then standby security forces in 1999. The ECOMOG mission in Liberia in 1990 was the first African multilateral intervention on the continent. Since then, several ECOWAS intervention missions have been deployed, including ECOMOG in Sierra Leone (1997) and Guinea-Bissau (1999), MICECI in Côte d'Ivoire (2003), ECOMIB in Guinea-Bissau (2012), and MISMA in Mali (2012). In addition, when the Organisation of the African Union became the African Union in 2002, it established a Peace and Security Council. It created the African Standby Force, recognised as having the right to intervene in serious human rights violations (AU Charter, art. 4) and the capacity to integrate into the PKO mechanism. All of these projects strongly contribute to a progressive regionalisation[39] of the African system.

6. Finally, the paradigm of 'sectoralisation' of security, mainly inspired by the work of the Copenhagen School, has made it possible to account for the different factors and actors in security. This terminology is often used by African states to clarify the objectives of their policies in this area (Kampala Declaration, 1991). This process has enabled them to identify and formulate strategies to respond to new forms of security threat: terrorist activity, the increase in intra-African migration and flows to Europe, maritime piracy, traffic of illegal goods, environmental and health risks, etc. This diversification of states' fields of action in terms of security has favoured the emergence of African security powers characterised by complementary roles in peacebuilding on the continent.[40]

All of these continental developments have made Africa appear as an emerging continent, a land of opportunity for investors, a new 'frontier' of the global capital market and a strategic player in international relations since the beginning of the twenty-first century. While the thesis of Africa's emergence can be criticised for many reasons,[41] the recognition of this status is nonetheless anchored

---

Afrique—État des débats et pistes de recherche, eds. Mamoudou Gazibo and Céline Thirot (Paris, 2009), 346.

39 Still according to Daniel Bach, "Regionalisation refers to processes. These can be the result of the realization of regionalist projects. Regionalisation can also arise from the aggregation of individual strategies, independent of any identified regionalist aspiration or strategy." (Translated from French). Ibid, 347.

40 Yousra Abourabi and Julien Durand de Sanctis, *L'émergence de puissances africaines de sécurité: Étude comparative* (Paris, 2016), 87.

41 Africa is still dependent on external aid, while its natural resources are overexploited by foreign powers and still do not sufficiently benefit local populations. See also: Ndongo Samba Sylla, "From a marginalised to an emerging Africa? A critical analysis", *Review of African Political Economy* 41, no. 1 (2014): S7–S25.

in the discourse. For example, as early as 2002, the OECD, in a report on the emergence of Africa, highlighted the role of growth and its beneficial effects in the fight against poverty.[42] Similarly, the UN organised an 'Emerging Africa' summit to observe the development of the continent's frontier markets. The US, China, Brazil, India, Turkey and the Gulf petro-monarchies are now heavily investing in Africa. At the same time, their leaders declare the strategic importance of Africa in their foreign policy-making. These reports and statements of neoliberal inspiration contribute to the spread of this paradigm as much as they institute the recognition of African emergence and make it an indisputable fact. Thus, French president François Hollande, among others, declared in 2013 that 'Morocco is not a developing country, it is already an emerging country':[43] a diplomatic statement that attests, if not to Morocco's economic emergence, to a much less contested political emergence. All of this consolidates the international recognition of the emergence of Morocco, the second-largest recipient of FDI in Africa, although, as for the rest of the continent, the conditions of this emergence must be nuanced.[44]

Moreover, this recognition comes in a more global context of reconfiguring power poles. The decline of the American hegemony, the rise of China, the emergence of numerous middle powers in different regional areas, the appearance of proactive non-state actors within the institutions of global governance, the diversification of international norms and counter-norms, and the development of South–South cooperation are all manifestations of the formation of a new contemporary, post-hegemonic and multilateral world order. In Amitav Acharya's vision, 'post-hegemonic multilateralism is about formal and informal cooperation among actors, including but not limited to states, based on shared principles and non-coercive leadership at the global and regional levels'.[45] In other words, the current order is no longer based on the balance of one or more hegemonic powers, while many state and non-state actors (civil society, transnational communities, multinational firms, etc.) no longer recognise the absolute dominance of the traditional great powers. The assumption that states' interests are defined solely in terms of power and security, in the realist sense, is no longer so widely accepted, as cooperation takes many forms,

---

42   Jean-Claude Berthélemy et al, *Emerging Africa* (Paris: Organisation for Economic Co-operation and Development, 2002), 232.
43   "Speech by the President of the Republic to the French community at the Lycée Lyautey in Casablanca", www.elysee.fr, April 2013.
44   In this respect, see the chapters on economy and society in: Yousra Abourabi, *Maroc* (Brussels: De Boeck, 2019).
45   Acharya, *Rethinking power, institutions and ideas in world politics*, 141.

both globally and locally. It is therefore easy to see how the norms, ideas, beliefs and identities of states[46] influence the definition of their interests and strategic orientations. Similarly, it is easy to imagine the development of multilateral cooperation without the support and influence of a hegemonic power such as the US.[47] Finally, the development of post-hegemonic multilateralism does not seem incompatible with regionalism, since it can also be observed that many regional structures, of which I mentioned a few examples in Africa above, are evolving in the direction of a better institutionalisation of cooperation, while new interregional dynamics are at work.[48]

In this context, the role of small and medium powers appears more significant. Middle powers are states whose resources are lesser than those of the major hegemonic powers but are sufficiently large to exert influence within their region or multilateral governance structures. Several states can now be classified in this category, such as Canada, Australia and Sweden, which are traditional middle powers, but also Argentina, Brazil and South Africa, which are emerging middle powers.[49] Moreover, small powers today enjoy 'greater international prestige and visibility than ever before in their history'.[50]

This new dynamic is based on a twofold evolution: on the one hand, power is no longer evaluated in terms of traditional resources as defined by the realist and liberal schools,[51] excluding many immaterial, relational and reflexive factors. On the contrary, some traditional power criteria can be a handicap for small and medium powers: this is the case with regard to the DRC's territory or Egypt's demography. On the other hand, the foreign policies of small and medium powers are characterised by their specialisation in one or more domains in which they can effectively act, which makes their actions all the more effective. Based on a comparative examination of the foreign policies of Canada and Australia, Cooper, Higgott and Nossal demonstrate how

---

46 Wendt, *Social Theory of International Politics*.
47 Robert Owen Keohane, *After Hegemony: Cooperation and Discord in the World Political Economy* (Princeton, N.J. Oxford: Princeton University Press, 2005).
48 Haingo Mireille Rakotonirina, "Le dialogue interrégional UE-Afrique depuis Cotonou: le cas de la facilité de soutien à la paix en Afrique", *Politique européenne*, no. 22, (s.d): 125–147; Jean-Raphaël Chaponnière, "Le basculement de l'Afrique vers l'Asie", *Afrique contemporaine*, no. 234 (2010): 25–40.
49 Eduard Jordaan, "The concept of a middle power in international relations: distinguishing between emerging and traditional middle powers", *Politikon 30*, no. 1 (2003): 165–181.
50 Jeanne Hey, "Introducing Small State Foreign Policy", In Small States in World Politics, ed. Jeanne Hey (Boulder, 2003), 1–11.
51 For a review of the concept of power in International Relations theory, see: Abourabi and Durand de Sanctis, *L'émergence de puissances africaines de sécurité: Étude comparative*.

medium powers appropriate new themes on the international agenda and distinguish themselves by their international behaviour. What differentiates a middle power from a state with the same resources that is not a middle power is, therefore, the former's capacity to exercise a recognised activity in one of the areas of global governance. From this perspective, the middle powers have become, as Eduard Jordaan notes,[52] stabilising and legitimising actors in the world order: stabilisers thanks to their ability to bring about profound changes to a regional order; legitimisers due to their absorption of neoliberal institutionalist norms that give them legitimacy, which they, in turn, help to support. In the same way, finally, small powers are distinguished by the concentration of their resources in specific areas of foreign policy, capable of generating benefits. Niche diplomacy,[53] role diplomacy and alliance diplomacy are thus the three main models of action that enable small states to achieve power status.[54]

From these few definitions and given this new context, Morocco can be considered a small power on an international scale and a medium power on a continental scale, despite the weakness of its material resources and the mixed results of its emergence plans. It is indeed a question of perception and projection. The perceptions and projections of Moroccan leaders regarding the evolution of their country and that of the international system also support this representation of emergence. On this point, Morocco's participation in the development of Africa represents, in the eyes of its leaders, a way of being part of the continental emergence dynamic, as confirmed by this royal statement:

> the choice of an African anchorage for our country is part of a logic that is in line with the current reconfigurations of the world economy characterised by the economic catching up of emerging countries and the evolution towards a multipolar world system where our continent is called upon to position itself as a new world growth pole.[55]

---

[52] Jordaan, "The concept of a middle power in international relations".

[53] Andrew F. Cooper (ed.), *Niche Diplomacy: Middle Powers After the Cold War* (Houndmills, Basingstoke, Hampshire: New York: Palgrave Macmillan, 1997), 221.; Jo-Ansie van Wyk, "Nuclear diplomacy as niche diplomacy: South Africa's post-apartheid relations with the International Atomic Energy Agency", *South African Journal of International Affairs* 19, no. 2 (2012): 179–200.

[54] Ziya Öniş and Mustafa Kutlay, "The dynamics of emerging middle-power influence in regional and global governance: the paradoxical case of Turkey", *Australian Journal of International Affairs* 71, (2016): 1–20.

[55] Direction des Études et des Prévisions Financières. Ministère de l'Économie et des Finances. *Relations Maroc-Afrique: l'ambition d'une 'nouvelle frontière'*, Rabat (2014), 29.

3   From the Ambition of Emergence to the Ambition of Power: The Development of the Kingdom's International Relations

Morocco's economic and structural development and the political transition process initiated under Mohammed VI have strengthened the state's confidence in its ability to project its power. New foreign policy orientations have emerged during the last 20 years, aimed at opening up to regions of the distant South such as Latin America and Asia and changing Morocco's relations with its traditional allies. In 2002, the King had already announced these new objectives:

> We seek, above all, to consolidate Morocco's privileged international position as a partner that is listened to by the great powers, as a vigilant defender of the interests of developing countries in the era of globalisation, and as a pole of stability and peace in its regional environment and the international context.[56]

The development of the Kingdom's international relations was therefore initially reflected in a certain number of political choices oriented towards an alliance diplomacy, then, in a second phase, towards a role diplomacy.

The first orientation lies in obtaining 'Advanced Status' with the European Union in 2008: relations between Morocco and the European Union (and its predecessor institutions) have been stable and continuous since 1963—so much so that Morocco is currently the leading regional beneficiary of European financial aid. Therefore, Morocco's economic development has been supported by European and, in particular, French aid and investment.[57] The second phase began with the signing of the Advanced Status, the result of lengthy negotiations based on the Euro-Mediterranean policy and the European neighbourhood policy.[58] Advanced Status includes a fisheries agreement, a security cooperation agreement, an economic free trade agreement, and a framework for cooperation on democracy and human rights. Through this status, Morocco recognises that Europe is not only a strategic ally and a provider of economic aid but also an institutional and normative model.

---

56   "Speech by H.M. King Mohammed VI on the occasion of the 49th anniversary of the Revolution of the King and the People", *Maroc.ma*, 2002.
57   See Appendix 3 and bis3.
58   Larabi Jaïdi and Hassan Abouyoub, *Le Maroc entre le statut avancé et l'Union pour la méditerranée* (2008).

Since 2008, Advanced Status has also served as a framework for strengthening bilateral relations: political consultation, the inclusion of Morocco in European energy and transport networks, the strengthening of links between public and private actors on both sides, and the harmonisation of regulations. Although this status has been criticised because of a lack of legal definition,[59] and primarily because of its low political density, it nevertheless symbolises a diplomatic advance. For Abdallah Saaf, 'Morocco is keen to highlight its lead over the other countries of the South, arguing that it is the only Arab and Muslim country to have engaged in a real dialogue with the EU on governance and democracy issues or respect for human rights'.[60] Indeed, several countries, including Tunisia and Egypt, have expressed a wish to obtain Advanced Status following the Moroccan negotiations, thus far without success.[61]

Second, we can mention the reaffirmation of the strategic alliance with the United States: the interest of the US in the Maghreb has been illustrated, since 2001, by the establishment of a large number of strategic partnerships such as the MEPI (Middle East Partnership Initiative), the Millennium Challenge Account and the TSCTP (Trans-Sahara Counterterrorism Partnership). Morocco took advantage of this situation of securitisation of the Maghreb by the US in the aftermath of 9/11 to engage in an alliance in favour of economic and military cooperation, particularly in the field of counter-terrorism. Let us recall that 'securitisation' refers to the legitimisation of an area as a security issue. It is, according to Buzan, Waever and De Wilde, 'an extreme version of politicisation' and refers to the presentation of a problem 'as an existential threat, requiring extreme measures and justifying actions outside the usual limits of political procedures'.[62] Securitisation is observed by the authors in five sectors: military, political, economic, societal and environmental. A securitised object can be identified by identifying the language and institutional policies that suggest the security importance of a particular issue. Thanks to their particular rhetoric, these speech acts (notably political discourses) 'accomplish a sufficient effect to make an audience tolerate the violation of the rules usually respected'.[63] Indeed, the war in Iraq strongly contributed to the construction of the new post-bipolar enemy, while the Algerian Islamist crisis during the

---

59   Nicolas Delort, "Statut avancé: passer du symbolique au pratique", *Amadeus Institute*, 2010.
60   Abdallah Saaf, "Le partenariat euro-maghrébin", in *Le Maghreb dans les relations internationales*, ed. Khadija Mohsen-Finan (Cnrs Éditions, 2011), 189–211.
61   Khémaies Chammari "Tunisie-UE: confusions autour du statut avancé", *e-Joussour*, June 16, 2010.
62   Barry Buzan et al., *Security: A New Framework for Analysis*. (Boulder (Colo.) London: Lynne Rienner publishers, 1998), 23–25.
63   Ibid.

1992–1996 period reinforced the interest of the United States in the Maghreb space, with the fear that the Algerian Islamist wave would spread in the sub-region.[64] Finally, the attacks of 9/11 definitively reconfigured the objectives of US foreign policy and its re-presentation of the 'Arab-Muslim' space. The initiative for a 'Greater Middle East', from Mauritania to Pakistan,[65] launched by George Bush in 2004, reinforced this new geopolitical representation assimilating the Maghreb into the Middle East. In this context, political Islam has been securitised.

This is why, since 2012, the establishment of the 'Strategic Dialogue', the object of an annual session whose aim is to strengthen the instruments of cooperation between the two countries, has helped to make Morocco a leading regional ally in the fight against terrorism. The signing of an economic free trade agreement (FTA) in 2004 accompanied the signing of an agreement that presents Morocco as a 'major non-NATO ally', which shows, as Larbi Jaïdi also points out, that the FTA is 'essentially a foreign policy issue, rather than an economic issue for the two partners'.[66]

Third, one can note the preference given, within the Arab-Muslim cultural area, to the development of cooperation with Saudi Arabia and the Emirates of the Persian Gulf. As president of the Al Quds Committee and an active member of the OIC (Organisation of Islamic Cooperation), Morocco reaffirms, under the reign of Mohammed VI, its commitment to mediating conflicts within this area and is moving closer to the Gulf countries.

Fourth, the development of cooperation with new countries of the South should be emphasised: Morocco has turned to the Asian and South American continents to consolidate its economic and political openness. The development of its diplomatic relations with Latin America is the result of a series of royal visits in 2004 to the five major countries of the sub-continent,[67] leading to the integration by Morocco into numerous regional organisations as an observ-

---

[64] A stage also observed by Y.H. Zoubir 'During the Algerian crisis, particularly in the period 1992–1996 when Islamist terrorism was ravaging, more than 400,000 Algerian executives (computer scientists, doctors …) fled to Europe and North America. And it was precisely during these years of the Algerian crisis that the Maghreb became important in the eyes of the United States' Yahia H. Zoubir, "Les États-Unis et le Maghreb: primauté de la sécurité et marginalité de la démocratie", *L'Année du Maghreb*, II, (2007): 563–584.

[65] Najib Rfaif denounces the 'Arabness' of American policy in Morocco. According to him: 'Belonging to this nebula is a ball and chain'. Najib Rfaif, "L'arabattitude dans tous ses États", *La Vie Eco*, April 16, 2004.

[66] L. Jaidi, "Trois vérités sur l'accord Maroc-USA", *La Vie Économique*, April 12, 2004.

[67] See Appendix 1 and 1a.

ing member,[68] as well as the granting of humanitarian aid to island states of the Caribbean.[69] At the same time, in Asia, foreign policy was oriented under Mohammed VI towards two main groups of states: what one ambassador calls the 'large countries' (China, Japan, India, Vietnam, Indonesia, South Korea and the Philippines) and the 'small countries, the new oil, gas and mining Emirates' (Kazakhstan, Malaysia, Brunei, Turkmenistan, Mongolia, Azerbaijan).[70] Moroccan policy in Asia has been characterised, as in Latin America, by a constant effort to be represented in multilateral organisations for economic cooperation and interregional forums.[71] In particular, from 2016 onwards, relations between Morocco and China will experience accelerated development through the signing, within the framework of a royal visit to Beijing, of a multitude of public and public–private cooperation agreements.

The African orientation of Moroccan foreign policy is, first and foremost, part of this general framework. Intending to consolidate its relations with all the countries mentioned above, Morocco presents itself as a 'bridge', as an actor in interregional rapprochement. It plans to become a 'regional hub between the Arab-African world and the Ibero-American world', and intends to play a key role in the 'bi-regional rapprochement' between Africa and Latin America.[72] Similarly, with regard to Asia, the Kingdom's ambition is to be recognised as an African platform for investors. However, this ambition equals the need to

---

68 Morocco is an observer member of PARLANTINO, the Latin American Parliament, which groups 22 countries, of the ACS, the Association of Caribbean States, which groups 25 countries, and of the SEGIB, the Ibero-American Conference, which brings together Spanish- and Portuguese-speaking sovereign states of America and Europe. It is the only Arab and African country to enjoy this status.

69 In February 2007, Rabat hosted its first meeting with the member countries of CARICOM (Caribbean Community), for the benefit of the human development of its populations. In February 2013, a Moroccan mission to the Caribbean signed a 'roadmap' for the period 2013–2015, the main objective of which was to strengthen the socioeconomic development of the region.

70 According to the Moroccan ambassador to the People's Republic of China. Jaafar El Hakim, "Le nouveau partenariat Maroc-Asie", in *Annuaire marocain de la stratégie et des relations internationales*, ed. Abdelhak Azzouzi (Rabat: L'Harmattan, 2012).

71 Morocco has joined the FOCAC (Forum for China–Africa Cooperation) launched in 2000, the FSA (Forum for Sino-Arab Cooperation) launched in 2004, the NAASP (New Africa–Asia Strategic Partnership) founded in 2005, the ACD (Asian Cooperation Dialogue) created in 2002 and within which Morocco became a Development Partner in 2008, ASEAN (Association of South-East Asian Nations), of which Morocco has been an observer member since 2008, and AMED (Asia–Middle East Dialogue) established in 2004.

72 According to the Moroccan ambassador to Peru. Oumama Aouad, "Les Relations du Maroc avec l'Amérique latine", in *Annuaire marocain de la stratégie et des relations internationales*, ed. Abdelhak Azzouzi (Rabat: L'Harmattan, 2012).

build and strengthen its foothold in Africa, which now represents a strategic depth necessary for the affirmation of Moroccan power. The projection of the country's economy towards the African continent[73] appears to be linked to the emergence process initiated under Mohammed VI.

Thus, on the one hand, the emergence process appears, in many respects and despite the socioeconomic gaps it may cause, as a catalyst for public optimism. It reveals the strongly regionalist diplomatic orientation desired by society, which aspires to a future power status for Morocco, while projecting it in its specifically relational, interdependent and multilateral dimensions. This vision is also reflected in Mohammed VI's doctoral thesis, according to which Morocco will be inclined in the future to integrate into its region to the detriment of its bilateral relations with Europe.[74] On the other hand, the Kingdom's ambitions reflect its own representation of its place as a geo-cultural and geo-strategic bridge. More generally, these ambitions contribute to the construction of Morocco's role identity, i.e. the role it wishes to play on the international scene based on its perception of its own identity and the image it is given by other states.[75]

4 The Discursive Construction of Morocco's International Role Identity around the Concept of the 'Golden Mean'

A state's role identity is based on a set of norms, values and perceptions shared by the leaders of that state and by the international community. It is co-constructed by the state and those around it in a reflexive manner, and it is a long-term process. A state can change its international role from one decade to another. Still, it could not legitimately claim a role identity on the sole basis of a specialisation of the diplomatic apparatus in a particular area. It is the combination of this specialisation with other dimensions of state identity (type, body

---

73 According to the portal of the Ministry of Economy and Finance: 'The government's ambition is to raise Moroccan industry to higher levels of competitiveness to strengthen Morocco's position as an industrial hub and growth relay for foreign investors. The latter will thus have easy access to sub-Saharan Africa, whose growth could reach 6 to 7% in the years to come. Morocco is also about to conclude preferential agreements with the countries of the West African Economic and Monetary Union (WAEMU).' URL: https://www.finances.gov.ma/fr/pages/strat%C3%A9gies/pacte-national-pour-l%E2%80%99emergence-industrial.aspx.
74 Alaoui, *La coopération entre l'Union européenne et les pays du Maghreb*, 16.
75 Wendt, *Social Theory of International Politics*, 224.

and possibly collective[76]) that can legitimise this posture. On the other hand, a state can find elements in its history that enable it to legitimise a posture that was previously neither officially claimed nor recognised. The valorisation of this reading of history will then take place through discourse.

While the term 'soft power' is now part of the political language, the term 'role identity' is little used, including in academic circles. If a state today easily sells its soft power, it does not do the same with its role identity, but this does not mean that it does not have one or that it does not project it. In the case of Morocco, the stake of this book will be to reveal its existence and describe its consistency through a comparative analysis of African diplomacy and the discursive legitimisation apparatus that accompanies it.

My initial observation is that the notion of the 'golden mean' is a prominent and recurrent feature of political and media discourse. It is possible to identify a 'dialogical network', i.e. a set of speech acts 'made up of successive repetitions of statements oriented towards a single theme [...] linked together by a series of connectors',[77] and carried by different actors around this notion. The golden mean is not officially presented as a character of national identity or a state doctrine in diplomatic and strategic matters. Nevertheless, the collective use of this notion by different actors is such that it gives it an intelligibility of its own that coincides precisely with the Kingdom's foreign policy.

The first official use of the term seems to date back to Hassan II's 1973 'Youth Day Speech', in which he defined Morocco as 'the nation of the golden mean'. Occurrences are, however, revealed before and after this. In 1969, a journalist from *Le Monde Diplomatique* described Morocco's admission to the Conference on Disarmament as 'the consecration of a behaviour which, during the 13 years of independence, has made it a rule to keep a fair measure and a middle ground between rival blocs'.[78] On another note, in 1983, Lhouceine Boubkraoui's thesis presented Morocco as the 'country of the golden mean par excellence',[79] without giving a precise definition. As early as 1989, Driss Basri, in a laudatory campaign for Hassan II, referred to the religious etymology of the term: 'Here, as in other fields, the Sovereign has been inspired by Islam, which has made

---

76 On the definition of these other dimensions of identity, see the introduction.
77 Baudouin Dupre et al. "Derrière le voile. Analyse d'un reseau dialogique égyptien", *Droit et Société*, no. 68 (2008): 4.
78 Louis Gravier, "Le Maroc défend ses intérêts nationaux à l'écart des antagonismes des Grands", *Le Monde diplomatique*, September 1, 1969.
79 Lhouceine Boubkraoui, *Essai de formalisation du fonctionnement de l'économie marocaine*, Reproduction in paper version of the Centre National de Documentation du Royaume du Maroc (Université Paris I Panthéon-Sorbonne, 1983), 15.

its followers a happy and prosperous nation of the just golden mean',[80] In 1992, the researcher Abdelkhaleq Berramdane pointed out 'the implementation of a new political philosophy, that of the golden mean',[81] while Hammad Zouitni noted in 1998 the choice of a golden mean in Moroccan diplomatic behaviour.[82]

The following year, the new King Mohammed VI stated in his very first speech that Moroccan culture was inspired by 'the teachings and precepts of our religion, those that advocate the golden mean, balance, tolerance and openness':[83] a simple statement, which nevertheless has a dialogical resonance. Every year since 1999, the term 'golden mean' has appeared in one of the King's speeches, most often in the annual Throne Speech. If it is not mentioned per se in a Throne Speech, it is replaced in the same context by the terms 'moderation' or 'tolerance' (e.g. in the 2002 Throne Speech). In the wake of the royal speeches, every year since 1999, parliamentary and ministerial reports, journalistic articles, and audio-visual broadcasts have been full of references to the Moroccan culture of the golden mean.

The use of this expression on a large scale, therefore, suggests opposite and diversified representations of the concept. For Abdelkhaleq Berramdane, it is of an economic nature and translates into the Moroccanisation of foreign goods in trade and industry (*dahirs*[84] of March and May 1973).[85] In the writings of Mimoun Hilali, 'golden mean' is used as an adjective that refers to 'the adoption of a so-called measured liberalism, intended to spare the domestic revolutionaries without disappointing the external partners'.[86] On the website of the Moroccan mission to the UN, one can read that: 'This voluntarist approach, adopted since Morocco's independence in 1956, has resulted in the establishment of a multi-party system and freedom of enterprise and has been prolonged in a policy of reforms that place the individual at the centre of the government's concerns'.[87] According to Driss Basri, the golden mean charac-

---

80   Driss Basri, *Le Maroc des potentialités: génie d'un roi et d'un peuple*, Ministry of Information, Kingdom of Morocco (1989), 58.
81   Abdelkhaleq Berramdane, *Le Sahara occidental, enjeu maghrébin* (Paris: Karthala, 1992), 13.
82   Hammad Zouitni, *La diplomatie marocaine à travers les organisations régionales (1958–1984)*, (Casablanca, 1998), 33.
83   "1st Speech from the Throne by His Majesty King Mohammed VI", *Maroc.ma*, July 30, 1999.
84   A *dahir* is a royal decree. More generally, it refers to the King's seal on the texts of laws voted in parliament.
85   Berramdane, *Le Sahara occidental, enjeu maghrébin*, 13.
86   Mimoun Hillali, "Du tourisme et de la géopolitique au Maghreb: le cas du Maroc", *Herodotus 127*, no. 4 (2007): 47–63.
87   At: http://www.mission-maroc.ch/fr/pages/16.html. Accessed June 2016.

terises more generally all areas of politics, including diplomacy: an 'approach to the outside world [...] imbued with liberalism, tolerance, and the middle ground'.[88]

More specifically, Lhouceine Boubkraoui associates the golden mean with a geo-cultural identity which refers to Morocco's African and Mediterranean roots, so that 'it is therefore situated in the golden mean of several civilisations and currents both from the East and the West and from the "North and South"'.[89] Eric Bonnier sees in the Malikite rite practised in Morocco 'a doctrine of the golden mean where the political and the theological correspond'.[90] For Mohsine Elahmadi, the golden mean is also linked to the religious policy reform in 2002, allowing 'the Maliki identity of the Kingdom to be skilfully defended without compromising the irreversible choice of liberalism made by the Kingdom'.[91] In the same perspective, Mounia Bennani-Chraïbi states that the legislative campaigns of 2002 were marked by a series of debates on 'an approach to Moroccanness and Islam, intended to be a vision of the golden mean which would preserve the conservatism of the social and moral order, and which is imbued with the "urban civility" of the "good people"'.[92] More recently, researchers Cedric Baylocq and Aziz Hlaoua published an article demonstrating how Morocco's African religious diplomacy has developed through a symbolic positioning 'which consists in the affirmation of an "Islam of the golden mean" based on three doctrinal and spiritual pillars': the Maliki rite, Acharism and Sufism.[93]

Finally, more generally, many of the Moroccans interviewed (of different ages and backgrounds) recognise the term without being able to define it politically or reconstruct it etymologically with precision. Mostly, they assimilate it from memory to a famous prophetic hadith, erected as an adage: khayru al 'umûr awsatuha (the best way is the middle way). It thus appears that, regardless of the domain or perspective in which it is placed, the golden mean is the right assertion that specifies all public affairs, so much so that the notion possesses a super-leading character. This dialogical network nevertheless reveals

---

[88] Basri, *Le Maroc des potentialités*, 114.
[89] Boubkraoui, *Essai de formalisation du fonctionnement de l'économie marocaine*, 15.
[90] Henry Bonnier, *Une passion marocaine*, (Artège, 2015), Chap. 7.
[91] Mohsine Elhamadi, "Modernisation du champs religieux au Maroc 1999–2009", in *Une décennie de réformes au Maroc (1999–2009)*, (Karthala, 2009), 119.
[92] Mounia Bennani-Chraïbi, *Scènes et coulisses de l'élection au Maroc: les législatives 2002*, (Karthala, 2005), 154.
[93] Cédric Baylocq, Aziz Hlaoua, eDiffuser un 'islam du juste milieu'? Les nouvelles ambitions de la diplomatie religieuse africaine du Maroce, *Afrique contemporaine*, no. 257 (2016/1): 113–128.

three major attributes: first, its religious etymology in the Moroccan reading of the term; second, its ambiguous relationship, at this stage, to liberal philosophy; and third, its political and diplomatic dimension. This constellation of terms or acts linked directly or indirectly to the idea of the golden mean thus forms many stratified and heterogeneous fields of expression that can help us to confer a coherent meaning on this ensemble.

Indeed, the notion of the golden mean, in the Moroccan definition, finds its etymological origins in the Qur'an. The dialogical network studied reveals this connection: Islam is said to be a religion of the golden mean, in reference to Surate Al Baqara,[94] a verse known and quoted several times by the monarch to justify, in the form of a syllogism, that the Moroccan nation, as a Muslim nation, is also a nation of the golden mean. The golden mean refers to the translation of the word 'wasatiya' in theological vocabulary (the middle way) or its political synonym 'i'tidal'. 'Wasatiya' is sometimes translated as 'just', sometimes as 'middle' and sometimes as both, which implies that just and middle are equated. Incidentally, the term 'wasat' and its variations ('al rand', 'awsatuhum', 'awsatna') appear only five times in the Qur'an: in Surate Al Baqara (Verses 143 and 238), Surate Al Ma'ida (Verse 89), Surate Al Qalam (Verse 28) and Surate Al 'Adiate (Verse 5), without systematically signifying a theological principle.

In political terms, the golden mean refers to moderation in the exercise of power. In the Aristotelian definition, the golden mean means the adoption of a constitution that symbolises what is common to citizens, a middle way between idealism and realism in the theory and practice of power and, finally, at the unity point between the space of the city and the space of institutions.[95] The careful consideration of the concept in Aristotle's philosophical literature in Arab countries has influenced the political interpretation of this concept. It could even justify the quasi-natural equivalence that Mohammed VI admits between the golden mean in national identity on the one hand and the golden mean in Islam on the other, since, according to him: 'Moroccans have chosen to adopt Islam because, as a religion of the golden mean, it is based on tolerance'.[96]

However, the epistemological study of this term also demonstrates that it must be situated in a properly ethical sense. The plurivocal character of the

---

94 'We have made you a community of the middle way so that you may be witnesses among men and the Prophet may be witnesses to you' (witnesses among the People of the Book on the Day of Judgement). The Qur'an, Surah of the Cow, Verse 143.
95 Sylvie Vilatte, *Espace et temps: la cité aristotélicienne de la Politique*, (Presses Univ. Franche-Comté, 1995), 241–242.
96 "Royal speech on the occasion of the Throne Day 4th anniversary", *Maroc.ma*, July 30, 2003.

concept is revealed only after interpretation, whether by scholars of the Qur'an or Aristotle. Thus its political dimension cannot be understood as the same value as that brought by Machiavelli to his political ethics, for example— namely, a materialist philosophy of action. On the contrary, the Aristotelian as well as the Qur'anic golden mean appears as a concept linked to a reflexive philosophy of being. The study of the Moroccan dialogical network reveals an understanding of the golden mean that goes beyond the ethical level but also includes levers for political action. To offer a better interpretation of this vision, an analysis of the international context in which the notion has been expressed proves to be more useful for the analysis of the passage from its philosophical to its political version.

Successive kings of Morocco have in turn participated in the extension of this dialogical network and given more precision to the definition of the concept of the golden mean. According to King Mohammed V, the golden mean effectively refers first and foremost to the 'link' between the East and the West. On 18 November 1956, he declared that Morocco was 'firmly resolved to define a policy that would allow it [...] to play a role as a link between the East and the West'.[97] He added, a year later, that this 'historical role played by Morocco, a link between civilisations', was a role that it 'was naturally predisposed to by its geographical position, at the crossroads of four continents'.[98]

King Hassan II also contributed to the consolidation of this definition, in particular with the formula so commonly quoted by Moroccans, taken from the memoirs of the late monarch:

> Morocco resembles a tree whose nourishing roots plunge deep into the soil of Africa and which breathes thanks to its rustling foliage in the winds of Europe [...] Today Morocco is taking back the place that was geographically, historically and politically its own: it has once again become a nation of synthesis, a linking community between East and West.[99]

The use of the metaphor of the tree and the image of the link, in this context, prove to be salutary for the power (and will produce, as we shall see later, other dialogical ramifications concerning the identity of Morocco as a link between civilisations). In the context of the Cold War, of the choice of

---

[97] Throne Speech by Mohammed V, November 18, 1956. Quoted in Charles Saint-Prot, *Mohammed V ou la monarchie populaire*, (Monaco: Éditions du Rocher, 2012), 189.
[98] Declaration of Mohammed V before King Abdel Aziz ibn Saud in 1957, in Ibid.
[99] Hassan II, *Le défi*, (Paris, France: A. Michel, 1976), 189.

a monarchy that proclaims itself to be both social and liberal,[100] and of a diplomacy that claims to be non-aligned without being actively engaged in the developing-world struggle,[101] forces delicacy in the definition of the identity of the state. As former minister Driss Basri formulated it, 'in its quest for the golden mean, Morocco has, since its independence, proclaimed its desire for non-dependence and balance between the great powers'.[102] The concept of 'non-dependence' distinguished the Moroccan position from 'Egyptian positive neutralism', Jordan's 'active neutrality' and Senegal's 'non-suivism',[103] all of which were rhetorical nuances of the non-aligned countries, nascent nation-states, each proclaiming the singularity of its diplomatic posture. In the case of the Kingdom, the alliance with Western Europe seemed as necessary as it was historically desired, while support for the ideologies of formerly colonised peoples made it possible to satisfy the former Moroccan resistance fighters and make France yield to its imperatives. At the same time, maintaining its alliance with the United States seemed as inevitable as maintaining a balance with the socialist regimes.[104] In this context, the rhetoric of the golden mean had the appearance of an attempt at geopolitical equilibrium, not a formalised diplomatic strategy.

In the aftermath of the Cold War the golden mean was no longer debated, but it continued to be a reassuring and defining dimension of state identity in the context of the threat posed by economic and cultural globalisation. Hassan II declared that Morocco

> is an old companion of history. A nation of the golden mean, it is marked by the seal of moderation, imbued with its faith in itself and its intrinsic possibilities, and capable of making the best use of the rule of dialogue and consensus.[105]

This desire to 're-traditionalise' political and social life was prompted by the anti-colonial and nahda (ideology of cultural and intellectual renaissance)

---

100 Ibid., 71.
101 See on this subject: Jean Lacouture, "A chacun son neutralisme : il n'ya pas de non-alignement, il y a des pays non alignés", *Le Monde diplomatique*, October 1, 1961.
102 Basri, *Le Maroc des potentialités*, 121.
103 Thérèse Benjelloun, *Visages de la diplomatie marocaine depuis 1844*, (Casablanca: Éditions EDDIF, 1991), 215; Berramdane Abdelkhaleq, *Le Maroc et l'Occident: 1800–1974*, (Paris, France: Karthala, DL 1987,1987), 164–165.
104 Berramdane, *Le Maroc et l'Occident*, 147–148.
105 "Speech by HM King Hassan II on the occasion of the Youth Day", *Maroc Hebdo*, July 11, 1998.

movements in vogue in the Arabic-speaking region. Re-traditionalisation created an identitarian divide between a fundamentalist and sometimes violent movement idealising a lost golden age, and a modernist movement uncritically absorbing the new international neoliberal norms. In this context, it was difficult for the government to give the nation a cohesive identity. This is why as soon as the new Alawite monarch came to power in 1999, he appropriated the debate on identity, prompting a second 'round of talks'[106] in the dialogical network on the golden mean.

Mohammed VI's very first Throne Speech was entirely focused on the issue of Moroccan identity: an identity now defined as 'plural', composed of 'various civilisations', and whose dialects (Darija Arabic, Amazigh) should be taught in schools. Mohammed VI took on the mission of protecting this identity by promising in this context 'the permanence of a strong power capable of guaranteeing the durability of the state'. This approach confirms Juan Linz's postulate that the stability of democratic states will henceforth depend on their ability to harden the state while at the same time softening the conception of national identity.[107] In this perspective, addressing France in an interview in October 2001, the monarch affirmed that 'Morocco has a different identity' because, as Hassan II had also mentioned, of its geo-cultural particularity, at the crossroads of several regions.[108] Although he did not directly link the golden mean to this geo-cultural identity, the Cherifian monarch made similar use of it to the point that the Moroccan press wondered, 'What is this Moroccan identity that is so envied according to Mohammed VI?'[109]

The Palace remains the primary producer of the meaning of the country's policy due to the frequent use of the expression 'golden mean' in its speeches, its proclaimed role as guarantor of national identity and its political capacity to enact consistent reforms, giving observable meaning to the concept. Since 1999, this rhetorical and institutional work has brought cohesion, as seen in the comments of the most enthusiastic Moroccan observers, such as Centre for International Studies researchers. They are convinced that 'in the space of ten years [...] the image of Morocco as a bridge between the North and the

---

[106] A 'tour de parole' refers to the circulation of an expression or a set of statements around a single theme, forming a dialogical network. Dupret et alii, "Behind the Veil. Analysis of an Egyptian Dialogical Network".

[107] Mohammad-Saïd Darviche, "Exiting the Nation-State: Juan Linz with and beyond Max Weber", *International Journal of Comparative Politics* 13, no. 1 (2006): 115–127.

[108] "Interview given by His Majesty King Mohammed VI to the French daily 'Le Figaro'", *Maroc.ma*, September 4, 2001.

[109] Aïcha Akalay, "Quelle est cette identitié marocaine qu'on nous envie selon Mohammed VI ?", *Telquel.ma*, July 30, 2015.

South, and between the West and the East, has been reinforced'.[110] Similarly, in her comparative study on the contestation of national identities in the Euro-Mediterranean space, Raffaella A. Del Sarto notes that 'Morocco has served as a counter-example to [her] argument. Despite various domestic preferences, the domestic fault lines are much shallower than in Israel and Egypt […] In contrast to Egypt, the historical identity of (modern) Morocco has not undergone major ruptures'.[111]

Thus, the Moroccan experience demonstrates the extent to which the construction of state identity, including role identity, is based on a strategy of discursive legitimisation. The dialogical network, whose main anchor points and discursive connectors I have traced, gives meaning to Morocco's representation of its geopolitical environment. The need for an African depth appears to be linked to this definition of the golden mean as the basis of the country's foreign policy. The study of this dialogical network also shows that the definition of the golden mean as a geo-cultural posture projected on an international scale is as intentional, constructed and instrumentalised as it appears to be inscribed in a collective unconscious.[112]

5 Africa as the 'New Frontier'

Designated as a 'continent of belonging', as a group of 'brotherly countries'[113] or as a 'natural extension' of the Kingdom,[114] Africa thus forms the new privileged

---

110   Centre d'études internationals (dir), *Une. Décennie de réformes au Maroc: 1999–2009*, (Paris, France : Karthala, 2009), 5.
111   Rafffaella A. Del Sarto, *Contested state identities and regional security in the Euro-Mediterranean area*, (Basingstoke New York: Palgrave Macmillan, 2006), 226.
112   On the link between collective unconscious and geopolitical representations, see Sadi Lakhdari, "Nations, representations, inconscient", *Outre-Terre* 2, no. 3 (2003/2): 281–306.
113   'It is in this perspective that the multiple Royal visits made by His Majesty King Mohammed VI, since his enthronement, to many African countries, have created a new dynamic in the relations with these brotherly countries', Press kit—Seminar of the Ambassadors of His Majesty the King accredited in Africa, *Ministry of Foreign Affairs and Cooperation, Directorate of Public Diplomacy and Non-State Actors*, August 2012.
       'With regard to solidarity, Morocco is following a strategic diplomatic approach aiming to consolidate an efficient South-South cooperation, notably with the brother African countries' in "Discours de Sa Majesté le Roi à la Nation à l'occasion de la fête du Trône".
114   'As regards our relations with our African extension, which constitutes a space of promising opportunities, we are keen to follow a constantly renewed approach in this respect', in: "Speech by His Majesty the King to the Nation on the occasion of the Throne Day", July 30, 2011.

field of expression of Morocco's foreign policy, a continent in which it wishes to become a security actor, an economic force and an institutional model. According to the Ministry of Foreign Affairs and Cooperation:

> the Kingdom of Morocco places its home continent at the top of its development priorities and at the heart of its international diplomatic concerns [...] This commitment stems from its belief in an Africa that is strong in its cultural heritage, wealth and potential, but also an Africa that is resolutely turned towards the future.[115]

Since the beginning of the 2000s, Morocco's diplomatic interest in the South has been developing and has been embedded in the construction of an identity for its power. This strategic ambition stems from a royal will, which once again confirms its essential role in the decision-making process of the diplomatic apparatus, in the orientation of the main axes of foreign policy and in control of action. It is nevertheless accepted by all actors of state and public diplomacy. Some of them defy their racial, cultural or security prejudices, now convinced of the advantages that such a diplomatic posture could offer. Indeed, if the strategic importance accorded to Africa is part of this representation of Morocco as a geo-cultural golden mean, how Africa is perceived—or rather, how the proponents of this Africa policy wish to mobilise a wide range of actors, is part of a neoliberal representation shared with other states, that of Africa as a 'new frontier', figuratively speaking.

The concept of the 'new frontier' was first introduced by US president John Kennedy to designate a US policy of openness that was intended to be progressive and anti-isolationist. Gradually, the expression came to be used to accompany interventionist (the US intervention in Vietnam) and imperialist policies (the US flag on the moon), and then neoliberal imperialist policies from the 1970s. In the aftermath of the Cold War, and especially with the acceleration of globalisation in the 2000s, Africa was seen as the new frontier of growth. This vision shared in neoliberal epistemic communities would lead to the publication of several works supporting this representation. Today, the term is synonymous with 'lands of economic opportunity' in common parlance. African actors also use it to refer to their own continent, sometimes with and sometimes without awareness of the normative burden that the term carries. Morocco is not exempt from this trend. In 2014, the Ministry of Economy

---

115   "Press kit—Seminar for Ambassadors of His Majesty the King accredited in Africa", *Ministry of Foreign Affairs and Cooperation, Directorate of Public Diplomacy and Non-State Actors*, August 2012.

published a report on Morocco–Africa relations entitled *The Ambition of a New Frontier*.[116] Many other texts and discourses which I will analyse in more detail later project the same neoliberal representation of the continent.

Thus, while the origins of Morocco's interest in the continent are multiple and diverse, how its leaders project themselves onto it seems to support this powerful normative framework of the 'new frontier'. The Kingdom's ambitions must, however, deal with another framework of a divided geopolitical representation of the continent. On the one hand, for Moroccans, there is the globally friendly Francophone West and Central Africa, a space that corresponds surprisingly to the southern regions of the pre-colonial Cherifian Empire and the departure zones of the Moroccan–African trans-Saharan routes, as well as to the countries that were allied to France and Morocco during the Cold War, and which thus constitutes a privileged area of cooperation. On the other hand, there is also an Africa represented as a historical hostile axis[117] comprising mainly Algeria and its allies, which challenges the projection of Moroccan power. After 2016, the representation of this axis began to change due to the Moroccan–Nigerian rapprochement in 2018[118] and the appointment of an ambassador to South Africa in 2018.

From this framework of representation stems a sectoral and diversified diplomacy, aiming to strengthen the Kingdom's links with, as a priority, the countries most favourable to the establishment of a Moroccan zone of influence. Humanitarian projects, scientific and religious training, economic and security agreements: are all areas in which the diplomatic apparatus now wishes to invest by helping to facilitate the mobilisation and meeting of actors, the legal frameworks of agreements or the media coverage of events that promote the dissemination of a good international image of Morocco. The recent creation of a Directorate of Public Diplomacy and Non-State Actors[119] within the Ministry contributes to the extension of these diplomatic vectors by integrating new actors into this great project. At the top of this edifice, the King,

---

116 Study by the Ministry of Economy and Finance, Directorate of Studies and Financial Forecasts, "Les relations Maroc-Afrique: l'ambition d'une nouvelle frontière", September 2014, 29.

117 As one diplomat put it. Interview with a diplomat, Ministry of Foreign Affairs and Cooperation, April–May 2013.

118 Yousra Abourabi, "Maroc-Nigéria: vers une reconstruction de la géopolitique oust-africaine", *Middle East Eye*, June 23, 2018, https://www.middleeasteye.net/fr/opinion-en/maroc-nigeria-vers-une-reconstruction-de-la-geopolitique-ouest-africaine.

119 "Decree no. 2.11.428" of September 6, 2011 on the powers and organisation chart of the Ministry of Foreign Affairs and Cooperation.

nicknamed 'Mohammed VI the African'[120] by the local and foreign press, is multiplying his 'African tours' in Senegal, Côte d'Ivoire, Gabon and other countries, reviving a legacy from his father, that of high-level bilateral diplomacy. He also 'sets an example' for the most sceptical politicians and entrepreneurs and contributes through his speeches to constructing a shared identity between Morocco and African countries of the Malikite rite. A strong axis of a foreign policy in full expansion, the rapprochement with Africa initially constitutes a policy that is more visible than real: in many areas, the official discourse anticipates with far too much optimism the Moroccan influence on the continent or the benefits it will gain from it. Notwithstanding the structural and human limitations at work in this contingency, the Kingdom's ambition reveals its perception of the role identity it wishes to embody on the external scene and reinforces the recognition of this role by African countries, as much as its African experience plays an essential role in the construction of this identity, in a reflexive way. More generally, Morocco strives to integrate itself into the multilateral continental spheres. These ambitions will lead it to develop a set of diplomatic mechanisms that, when grouped, reveal the practice of an indirect strategy on a diplomatic scale, a strategy defined in Chapter 6. In the long run, this progressive construction of Morocco's diplomatic strategy will help to overcome the state's material weaknesses and offer its leaders new perspectives for diplomatic action.

---

120 "Mohammed VI l'Africain", *Aujourd'hui le Maroc*, September 23, 2013; François Soudan, "Mohammed VI, African King", *Jeune Afrique*, June 15, 2015; "Dossier. Mohammed VI, l'Africain", www.le360.ma, 2015. Mohammed Maradji, *Mohammed VI l'Africain*, (editions la croisée des chemins).

CHAPTER 2

The Historical Determinants of Morocco's Diplomatic Interest in Africa

1   Introduction

History is a perceived time that determines the orientation of foreign policy. On the international scene, state actors constantly try to take into account geopolitical changes and systemic upheavals in order to adapt and be on the right page of the course of history. It is in this perspective that Morocco has pursued a policy of emergence, an aspiration confirmed by a royal speech according to which 'either the Moroccan economy becomes an emerging economy thanks to its potential and the coordination of the energies of all its components, or it will miss its rendezvous with history'.[1] Contemporary history influences the behaviour of state actors, while past history determines their diplomatic orientations. Following this line of thought, it would be futile to try to explain the factors at work in formulating an Africa policy without considering the history of Morocco's relations with its African environment. Far from emerging *ex nihilo*, the notions of strategic depth, greatness, civilisational influence or geocultural crossroads are rooted in a triple understanding of history:
- history as an objective determinant of the geopolitical order;
- history as a subjective determinant of diplomatic orientations;
- history as a framework for legitimising foreign policy.

First, history is an objective determinant insofar as past events are at the origin of a geopolitical, cultural and structural order that cannot be ignored. As Fernand Braudel rightly notes: 'Think of the difficulty of breaking certain geographical frameworks, certain biological realities, certain limits of productivity, or even such and such spiritual constraints: mental frameworks, too, are prisoners of the long term'.[2] These permanences, or historical survivals, constitute frameworks resistant to any attempt at political innovation or breakthrough. Leaders are forced to deal with the facts and outcomes of history, either to overcome them or to be inspired by them. The effects of colonisation, the ide-

---

1   "Speech by HM the King on the occasion of the 61th anniversary of the revolution of the King and the people".
2   Fernand Braudel, "Histoire et Sciences sociales: La longue durée", *Annales. Histoire, Sciences Sociales 13*, no. 4 (1958): 725–753.

ological choices made by independent African states during the Cold War, the socioeconomic and cultural changes on the continent, and the consequences of the diplomatic choices made by the former rulers of Morocco are all decisive historical factors in the formulation of an Africa policy.

Second, the interpretation of historical events by decision-makers influences their reading of any new situation. History thus also appears as a prism, a memory background that determines their representations. In their minds, there is, therefore, a search for cohesion with an interpretation of the meaning of history. This is why the public authorities cannot ignore the past. This dimension poses the epistemological problem of the search for truth, or at least historical objectivity, which can become a political problem or, on the contrary, a driving force of foreign policy. In the case of Morocco, the Sahara problem has often led diplomats to take an interest in history, anxious to understand the nature of this area's cultural and economic relations with the rest of the country or the content of the allegiance of its inhabitants with the central power.

Finally, by using history to aid decision-making, decision-makers move away from the physical dimension and adopt a quantitative approach to time. It is a question no longer of the weight of the past but of the choice of the past. The reconstruction of events or values adopted by the state during its history, and their use in the discourse, make it possible to demonstrate the existence of 'constants' in foreign policy, the persistence of 'ancestral values' of the nation, or the maintenance of 'secular relations' with one or more actors, making history a legitimisation framework of foreign policy.

However, this last dimension (the discursive framework of legitimisation) will be dealt with in Chapter 5.

2   History as an Objective Determinant of the Geopolitical Order: Allal al-Fassi's 'Greater Morocco' Project

'Grandism' is an expression of a desire for state territorial enlargement linked to claims intended to contribute to the nation's greatness and that are considered to be just. Grandism wishes to reunite the territories that have belonged to the state in its history.[3] There are thus two forms of grandism: a realistic or even achievable grandism, and a fantasised grandism, based on a geo-ideological rather than a geopolitical representation of space. In the first case, grandism refers to what is known today as the search for 'territorial integrity'. In the

---

3   Zajec, *Introduction à l'analyse géopolitique*, 132.

second case, grandism is a cartographic maximalism and constitutes an *irrealpolitik*.[4] In both cases, the formulation of a 'grandist' project by a state has often led to a representation of space that has influenced its foreign policy over a long period.

Several countries have, at some point in their history, projected a 'grandist' ideal. This is the case for 'Greater Bulgaria', 'Greater Albania', 'Greater Hungary', 'Greater Greece' and even 'Greater Russia', for example.

In Africa, other manifestations of this type can be mentioned: during the 1960s, Sékou Touré's entourage was said to have retained a nostalgia for a 'Greater Guinea'. At the same time, Modibo Keïta's claims to the Mauritanian Hodh revealed the ambition of a 'Greater Sudan'.[5] In Morocco, the conversion of the Cherifian Empire into a monarchical state, whose territory was almost five times smaller than previous sultanic empires, also gave rise to scenarios of a return to grandeur as independence approached. As a major figure in the Istiqlal independence movement, Allal al-Fassi was also the most fervent negotiator of borders and the herald of a grandist project based on the country's historical and natural borders: a project dubbed the 'Greater Morocco'. This concept appealed to much of the nationalist ruling class in the 1950s and 1960s and significantly shaped the conduct of Morocco's foreign policy in Africa after independence.

According to Allal al-Fassi, the 'Greater Morocco' project aimed to cover all the territories that were historically devolved to it, i.e. the Spanish Sahara, the whole of Mauritania up to the Senegal River, part of north-western Mali along the Niger River, and part of present-day western Algeria (Colomb-Béchar and Figuig).[6] This geopolitical claim was first set out in his book *Al Harakat al Istiqlalia Fil Maghrib* (*Independence Movements in the Maghreb*), published in Cairo in 1946. On his return to Morocco after independence, he reiterated and illustrated his point in the Arabic-language daily *Al-Alam* on 6 January 1956, producing a geopolitical map of this great Morocco as he envisaged it while massively disseminating his message to the foreign press.[7]

Initially, 'Greater Morocco' was of interest only to a small cenacle. Still, al-Fassi's charisma and the campaign led by the Mauritanians for their return

---

4 Interview with the author, Lyon, March 2016.
5 Philippe Decraene, "L'évolution politique: les résolutions adoptées à Casablanca suscitent les inquiétudes de certains Etats", *Le Monde diplomatique*, February 1961.
6 See Appendix 4: Map of 'Greater Morocco'.
7 See in particular the interview given by Allal al Fassi to Jacques Fauvet, "La Mauritanie a toujours fait partie du Maroc", *Le Monde*, April 10, 1956.

to Morocco gradually won the support of the rest of the government.[8] Widely relayed by Moroccan radio and press, once accepted, Morocco's claims on Mauritania were comforted by various arguments. They were supported to varying degrees as much as they monopolised the whole of Moroccan foreign policy vis-à-vis the UN, France and Africa for nearly 15 years. This historical legitimacy claimed in Africa was based on the various territories occupied by the Alawite dynasty at the beginning of the eighteenth century, as well as those that preceded it. For Allal al-Fassi: 'From time immemorial and until the French [military] occupation, the country of Chenguitt, now called Mauritania, as well as the territories that naturally link it to Tarfaya and Sous, were part of the Moroccan provinces as a whole'.[9] Also, Mohammed V was asked by the Mauritanians themselves for this attachment, as a French diplomatic correspondence testifies:

> The Sultan would have received on January 8th a delegation of three Mauritanian leaders: Horm Ould Babana, Ma el Ainin, and Mohammed Ould Jiddou. The latter had read him an address in which the representatives of the Mauritanian National Movement protested against the nationalisation by France of the Saharan zones of Morocco, seeing it as a violation of the agreements concluded between France and the Cherifian Empire and asking the government of Rabat to take all measures with a view to the reattachment to Morocco of the said Saharan zones, which were its own. According to the newspaper El Alam, the Sultan replied that this Moroccan parcel, which is the object of his great concern, cannot be separated from the Moroccan nation.[10]

---

[8] 'When Allal al-Fassi, who had just returned from Cairo, recalled that the Morocco liberated in 1956 represented only one-fifth of historical Morocco, and began to mention the provinces still occupied: Tindouf and Touat, Saoura, Gourara and Tidikelt, Seguia al-Hamra and Chenguit, not to mention Ceuta, Melilla and the Zaffarine Islands, most of the young leaders only listened to these exotic-looking names with distraction. It took a veritable indoctrination campaign with supporting history courses for public opinion to mobilise and take these demands to heart.' Abdallah Laroui, *Les Origines sociales et culturelles du nationalisme marocain* [Book]: *1830–1912 / Abdallah Laroui*, (1977), 11–12.

[9] Allal El-Fassi, "Les revendications marocaines sur les territoires sahariens: le point de vue de M. Allal el-Fassi", *Le Monde diplomatique*, January 1, 1960.

[10] Telegram from M. Maurice Faure, Secretary of State for Foreign Affairs, in charge of Moroccan and Tunisian Affairs, to M. Lalouette, chargé d'Affaires de France à Rabat, Paris, 16 January 1957. T. no. 318 to 323 in *Documents diplomatiques français 1957. Tome I, 1 January–30 June*, Paris, France: Ministry of Foreign Affairs, Commission de publication des documents diplomatiques français, lxix 1990, + p. 1008. In 1957, an offensive campaign was led by Morocco in New York to claim the attachment of Mauritania to Morocco. Telegram

Allal al-Fassi's proposal was convincing for the rest of the Moroccan elite. In this respect, it should be remembered that the Istiqlal, as early as 1956, constituted a 'party-state'[11] for some observers, 'a state within a state'[12] for others. Thus, through the combined pressure of the Mauritanians and the Istiqlal, and as a French newspaper noted, 'the "Greater Morocco" had ceased to be a mystical dream. It had become a political objective.'[13]

It should be noted that, as early as 1956, troops of the National Liberation Army had moved into the Spanish Sahara as well as into the regions of Colomb-Béchar and Figuig.[14] At the same time, the Kingdom was trying to demonstrate that Mauritania was a colonial creation of France and not an emerging nation. Indeed, many tribes had family ties with Moroccans and maintained allegiance to the Cherifian Sultan. Thus, several Mauritanian tribal chiefs, dignitaries or ministers in office, such as the Emir of Trarza (a province close to Senegal) Fall Ould Oumer, or the first deputy of Mauritania Dey Ould Sidi Baba, publicly pledged allegiance to the Cherifian King between 1956 and 1958. At the same time, the Nahda al Watania al Mauritania (Mauritanian Party) movement called for the outright attachment of Mauritania to the Kingdom of Morocco and created a radio programme broadcast in Mauritania, 'La Voix du Sahara Marocain' (Moroccan Sahara's Voice), which was characterised by calls for insurrection and invitations to holy war under the spiritual command of the Cherifian Sultan. The irredentism of a part of the Mauritanians in favour of their attachment to Morocco was also due to the fact that many R'guibat tribes lived and circulated on both territories.

In addition, Moorish traders used to exchange products from the north of Morocco for those from the south of Mauritania, a traffic that would have been tainted by the drawing of borders and the imposition of customs duties.[15] Finally, some Muslim populations in Mauritania preferred the Cherifian power

---

from M. Lalouette, chargé d'Affaires de France à Rabat, to M. Maurice Faure, Secretary of State for Foreign Affairs, in charge of Moroccan and Tunisian Affairs. Rabat, February 23, 1957. n°g to 1385 to 1396, Ibid.

11   Rivet, *Histoire du Maroc*, 357.
12   Bernard Lugan, *Histoire du Maroc: des origines à nos jours*, (Paris: Ellipses, 2011), 312.
13   Jean Lacouture, "Les revendications sahariennes du Maroc s'affirment et s'étendent", *Le Monde diplomatique*, May 1958.
14   Telegram from M. André-Louis Dubois, Ambassador of France in Rabat to the Secretariat of State for Moroccan and Tunisian Affairs, T. no. 5709 to 5714, Rabat, 10 October 1956, in *Documents diplomatiques français: 1956 vol. II*, Paris: Commission de publication des documents diplomatiques français, Ministère des Affaires Étrangères, 1989, 697.
15   Françoise De La Serre, "Les revendications marocaines sur la Mauritanie", *Revue française de science politique* 16, no. 2 (1966): 320–331.

to the Dakar framework law.[16] Beyond these few motivations, as Françoise de la Serre remarks, 'their gesture certainly served the cause of Moroccan claims'.[17]

Thus, on 4 November 1960, the Istiqlal-led government published a white paper in which the historical, geographical, religious and anthropological arguments justifying the attachment of Mauritania to Morocco were presented.[18] In this regard, it should be noted that part of the argument was based on the rules of Muslim law, which differs from international law. According to the former, it was not only the state that founded the territory but the *jus religionis*, illustrated by the fact that a tribe pronounces its Friday prayer in the name of the Sultan of Morocco. In purely legal terms, few treaties were presented to settle the debate.[19] Notwithstanding these challenges, convinced of the legality of this claim, Allal al-Fassi declared that to satisfy it, the government was considering the military option: 'No more than Fez or Rabat does Mauritania have the right to separate from the rest of Morocco. The King and the people would eventually have the duty to force the Mauritanians to safeguard the unity of the fatherland.'[20]

In France, part of the elite recognised this Cherifian suzerainty, following the example of the first French government commissioner in Mauritania, Xavier Coppolani, according to whom Mauritania constituted the 'natural extension' of Morocco.[21] But this was not the opinion of the entire French ruling class,[22] which, as early as 1957, deployed a military contingent in the north of Mauritania to confront possible attempts at Moroccan penetration.

The following year, faced with the Moroccan National Liberation Army on the march towards Mauritania, France deployed 'Operation Swab', causing Morocco's defeat. The French army intervened as often as necessary until Mauritania's independence in 1961. Politically, the French government supported the Mauritanian Progressive Union, while their leader Ould Daddah publicly expressed his attachment to the former colonial power.[23]

16 Lacouture, "Les revendications sahariennes du Maroc s'affirment et s'étendent"*t*.
17 Serre, "Les revendications marocaines sur la Mauritanie".
18 Ministry of Foreign Affairs, *White Paper on Mauritania*, Rabat, 1960.
19 Lacouture, "Les revendications sahariennes du Maroc s'affirment et s'étendent".
20 Allal al-Fassi, *Sahara et Maghreb*, September 17, 1958, Quoted in: Serre, "Les revendications marocaines sur la Mauritanie".
21 Lugan, *Histoire du Maroc*, 316–317.
22 'Mauritania is the natural and political extension of the Cherifian Empire of Morocco. It was France that named these desert areas Mauritania, whereas for the Moroccans they were the 'provinces of Chenguit', a region that has always been part of Morocco'. See Henri Marchat, "Les revendications marocaines sur les territoires sahariens: la réponse de M. Henri Marchat", *Le Monde diplomatique*, January 1, 1960.
23 'At the moment when France, through generous institutions, gives us the right to govern

The King did not pursue bellicose methods and concentrated on his diplomatic offensive. As Mauritania approached independence, he denounced French interference and sought to enlist the support of African countries.[24] In Africa, however, while the role of the colonial powers in drawing borders was evident to everyone, it was not, paradoxically, easy to get it recognised in particular. Many other factors came into play: pressure from France, corruption of the elites and also, a few years later, the ideological alliances of the Cold War.

Morocco's claim to Mauritania thus led the government to the UN, where it requested that the issue be placed on the agenda of the 15th session. Mehdi Ben Abboud, Morocco's ambassador to Washington and the UN, strongly defended the Moroccan position, trying to show how the Mauritanian case was a 'farce', a 'fantasy' of French neo-colonialism.[25] France firmly denied its involvement. This is evidenced by an article in *Le Monde*, which at the time ran the headline 'The Moroccan representative at the UN: We want to turn Mauritania into another Katanga',[26] while the ambassador, quoted in the same article, said: 'We do not want the Katanganisation of Mauritania'. This contradiction speaks volumes about the role of the press in stigmatising and weakening Morocco on the international scene.

Assured, however, of the support of the Arab League (excluding Tunisia), Moroccan diplomacy nevertheless scored a first victory. But it could not obtain the support of other Western and Asian powers, including the USSR.

This was due, in particular, to their disagreement over Mongolia's entry into the UN.[27] In the end, part of the French-speaking Africa, meeting in Brazzaville, adopted a resolution supporting Mauritania's application to join the UN, accentuating the Kingdom's enmity towards this group.

---

ourselves and to determine ourselves freely, I say no to Morocco'. Quoted in: Serre, "Les revendications marocaines sur la Mauritanie".

24   'On 28 November, France is preparing to carry out the plot against our country by granting pseudo-independence to a large part of our territory. After installing a puppet government and putting real Mauritanian representatives in prison, it seeks to perpetuate its domination over Mauritania.' Quoted in Ibid.
25   Intervention by Mr Ben Abboud, official documents, UN PV/aG XVth Session Agenda item 20 'Admission of Mauritania', 988th meeting, April 16, 1961, 342–351.
26   "La question mauritanienne. Le representant du Maroc à l'O.N.U: on veut faire de la Mauritanie un autre Katanga", *Le Monde.fr*, August 27, 1960.
27   Berramdane, *Le Maroc et l'Occident*, 125–127.

3   First Steps towards Building African Multilateralism

From the beginning of the 1960s, the Moroccan government turned to sub-Saharan Africa to reverse the hostile trend, seek diplomatic support for its territorial policy, and, above all, participate in the consolidation of African independence on an international scale. Thus, in 1957, Mohammed V was one of the initiators, along with six other states,[28] of the first conference of heads of state of independent countries, which was held in Accra the following year. The joint declaration from this conference encouraged other states to 'claim an African personality'[29] in the world. This conference is critical in the history of Africa because it raised the interest of the continental elite in the cause of African unity. More importantly, it led to a meeting of the appointed representatives in New York that resulted in the creation of the African Group at the UN.[30]

During this period of bipolar tensions, two groups of elites dominated the African political scene: the 'revolutionaries' or 'progressives' (Kwamé N'krumah, Sékou Touré, Gamal Abdel Nasser, Modibo Keïta) on the one hand, and the 'liberals' or 'moderates' (Leopold Sedar Senghor, Félix Houphouët-Boigny) on the other. These two groups had not only two different diplomatic orientations (Western and Eastern camps) but also different representations of what constituted a decolonisation problem. Given the position adopted by Morocco in the 1970s and 1980s, one could have imagined that the latter would have chosen the 'liberal' camp from the outset. In reality, the Mauritanian question led to a rapprochement of Morocco with progressive countries in the Casablanca Group,[31] without the country claiming any alignment with one specific bloc.

It should be noted that the ideological blocs were not as assertive and divided before the Cuban Crisis. This is evidenced by a 1959 report by James S. Lay, secretary of the US National Security Council, who recognised the powerlessness of the United States to control the aspirations of Africans for non-alignment.[32]

In any case, Morocco constantly reminded others that its territorial claims were an anti-colonial and anti-imperialist[33] act against France and Spain, an

---

28 Ethiopia, Egypt, Liberia, Libya, Sudan and Ghana.
29 Dennis Austin, *Politics in Ghana, 1946–1960*, (London: Oxford University Press, 1970), 396.
30 William Gedney Baker, *The United States and Africa in the United Nations; a Case Study in American Foreign Policy*. (Washington: Offset Composition Services, 1968), 36.
31 Mohammed Bouzidi, "Le Maroc et l'afrique sub-saharienne", *Annuaire de l'Afrique du Nord* 17, (1979): 87–111.
32 Cécile Laronce, *Nkrumah, le panafricanisme et les États-Unis*, (KARTHALA Éditions, 2000), 139.
33 Here are the arguments of Allal al-Fassi in 1960: 'The military, political or economic occu-

argument that found favour with African progressives and, more generally, the Eastern Bloc at first. This was one of the reasons why the Soviet Union briefly opposed Mauritania's independence between 1960 and 1961 as an act of support.

At the same time, Morocco took a more offensive diplomatic approach. For example, it tried to deploy a religious diplomacy, presenting a project on Islam as a unifying link to Sékou Touré.[34] On the economic and security front, Morocco proposed to industrialise its African allies and train their officers and pilots,[35] but this ambition was only feasible in the long term. To illustrate its commitment to continental solidarity, the Kingdom deployed militarily in Africa. At that time, the crisis in Congo was of interest to many African states, which saw it as a threat to their sovereignty.[36] In a leadership spirit, the monarch provided military, logistical and diplomatic assistance to Patrice Lumumba, helping to drive Belgian troops out of Katanga. He first integrated military contingents into the UN forces and then took part in political developments from 1961 onwards. Very soon, General Kettani, commander of the Moroccan troops, was entrusted by the UN to reorganise the Congolese national army. For the observers of the time, the intervention in Congo was ideal grounds for Morocco to affirm its continental role, its 'moderated' ethics and its 'conciliator' role while allowing it to act according to its territorial interests.[37] Kettani had encouraged Mobutu's appointment as the head of the new army.[38]

All of this reinforced the idea of the Kingdom's involvement in Congolese security, the first military expression of Moroccan policy in sub-Saharan Africa.

---

pation of African or Asian territories by European powers, undertaken during the nineteenth or early twentieth century, is today called into question based on unanimously and solemnly proclaimed principles, such as the right of peoples to self-determination and the non-interference of third parties in the affairs of states. It is in this context that the question of the Saharan territories is placed.' El-Fassi, "Les revendications marocaines sur les territoires sahariens".

34   Jean Lefèvre, "À propos de la crise congolaise. Le Maroc confirme la vocation africaine de sa politique étrangère", *Le Monde diplomatique*, September 1, 1960.
35   Ibid.
36   Bouzidi, "Le Maroc et l'afrique sub-saharienne".
37   'The Moroccans have found on the shores of the Congo an ideal terrain to finally rid themselves of the powerlessness complex certain leaders are very close to accusing them of. (...) It is possible that in the face of the outbursts, not to say the demagogic deviations, of Mr Lumumba, the Moroccan leaders will be led to play a moderating role, "of conciliation" as Mohammed V likes to repeat.' Lefèvre, "A propos de la crise congolaise. Le Maroc confirme la vocation africaine de sa politique étrangère".
38   According to Demba Dialo and General Karl Von Horn, see: Bouzidi, "Le Maroc et l'Afrique sub-saharienne".

Similarly, this act illustrated the diplomatic doctrine that was developed in the aftermath of independence and still prevails today. On the one hand, it is manifested in the monarchical centrality of the decision-making process in foreign policy.[39] On the other hand, it expresses Morocco's role identity of the golden mean, considered at the time as a principle that went in the direction of 'the permanent action of Morocco, a link between races and peoples, a bridge between the West and the East, a link between Europe and Africa'.[40] Finally, the Moroccan intervention constituted the starting point of a new multilateral continental diplomacy, confirmed by this communiqué:

> Given the deterioration of the situation in the Congo, and the powerlessness of the United Nations to carry out the mission entrusted to it, and after consultation with the African Heads of State directly concerned by the events in the Congo, His Majesty Mohammed V proposes the holding of a conference at the Casablanca summit from January 3rd to 6th 1961.[41]

The Casablanca Group had set itself the objective of consolidating the African unity project presented in Accra in 1958. For Morocco, it was the crucible of a double hope: to play a decisive role in African multilateral integration and to obtain unconditional support for its historical territorial claims. It was in this dual perspective that Mohammed V welcomed Mali, Guinea, Ghana and the United Arab Republic (Egypt-Syria)[42] to Casablanca, a conference through which was adopted, among other things, the idea of developing a high command of African Major States in order to achieve a common African defence. Mohammed V had a good international image, which is why, for Ahmed Balafrej, 'The observers agreed to give the work of the conference special attention'.[43] Thus, Mohammed V notably obtained approval for 'all the actions carried out by Morocco to recover its legitimate rights in Mauritania'.[44]

---

39   According to this journalist: 'Until now, the king alone, or practically alone, has led Morocco's Africa policy. The country only learned about the sending of troops to the Congo after the decision had been taken'. Lefèvre, "A propos de la crise congolaise. Le Maroc confirme la vocation africaine de sa politique étrangère".
40   Ibid.
41   Quoted in Bouzidi, "Le Maroc et l'afrique sub-saharienne".
42   Algeria and Libya were also represented. Ethiopia, Liberia, Nigeria, Somalia, Sudan, Togo and Tunisia declined the invitation. Other French-speaking African countries were not invited.
43   Ahmed Balafrej, "La charte de Casablanca et l'unité africaine", *Le Monde diplomatique*, June 1, 1962, https://www.monde-diplomatique.fr/1962/06/BALAFREJ/24768, accessed 12 June 2020.
44   Serre, "Les revendications marocaines sur la Mauritanie".

More generally, the Casablanca Conference laid the foundations for continental institutional integration. Together, the various representatives reaffirmed the relevance of the presence of African troops in Congo under the aegis of the UN, and pleaded for an African solution to the conflict. Part of the project of Kwamé N'Krumah (who dreamt of an African supranational institution), notably in terms of continental economic integration through the creation of a common market, and the construction of an African security cooperation mechanism, had found a favourable echo among the members of the Casablanca Group.

However, not everyone viewed this initiative favourably. In many African capitals, the 'expansionist' ambitions of the Casablanca participants were criticised, and their plan to create a high command was seen as a means of military interference in the affairs of other African states.[45] In France, many diplomats considered that this progressive orientation of Morocco would lead, in the long run, to a rejection of Morocco from the group of African powers close to France.[46] In reality, this criticism was more related, for the French, to interests of power and influence, and for the most critical African countries, to an opposition to the foundations of 'African unity' as projected in Casablanca. This was particularly true of the Brazzaville Group, which was enlarged in Monrovia in 1961. Consisting of 'liberal' countries like Nigeria, Senegal, Togo and Liberia, the Monrovia Group opposed the idea of continental integration in favour of a union of sovereign states. There was, therefore, a group of 'integrationists' corresponding to the enlarged Casablanca Group and a group of 'sovereignists' corresponding to the enlarged Monrovia Group. The two groups would eventually unite in favour of the creation of the OAU, as we shall see below. Still, the Monrovia vision would lead to a collective logic of sovereignist capture of multilateralism,[47] a configuration in which it is not the joint obligations or the collective ideal that represent the primary objective of the meeting but the commitments that each one would be ready to make in order to obtain from

---

45 Decraene, "L'évolution politique: les resolutions adoptees à Casablanca suscitent les inquiétudes de certains Etats".
46 Letter from M. Roger Seydoux, Ambassador of France in Rabat, to M. Couve de Murville, Minister of Foreign Affairs, Rabat 28 March 1962. In: *Documents diplomatiques français Tome 1962, I, 1er janvier–30 juin*, Paris, France: Impr. nationale, xlvii 1998, + p. 717.
47 To use an expression used by Zaki Laïdi: 'The sovereignist capture of multilateralism means that, in a non-hegemonic configuration, the strict measure of the cost/benefit ratio of each becomes the exclusive measure of its international commitment' in: Zaki Laïdi, "Négociations internationales: la fin du multilatéralisme", *Esprit novembre*, no. 11, (2013): 108–117.

the group a gain that it would consider relative to its concessions—a manifestation of political realism that dominated the field of ideas in the 1960s.

Finally, this African division weakened the reach of the Casablanca meeting to the point where Western chancelleries were rejoicing.[48] In less than two years, the Casablanca Group was paralysed: several meetings were postponed or cancelled, while the emergence of a revolutionary Algeria worried Hassan II, who preferred to revise his ideological alliances. Thus, while maintaining close relations with progressive Mali and Guinea, Hassan II moved closer to liberal states.

Moroccan leaders thus became involved in creating the OAU alongside the Brazzaville Group.

In 1963, as the birth of the OAU approached, supported by the group of moderates, the Kingdom's position was still fragile: the French press continued to support the French policy of influence and division by spreading the idea that Morocco had 'entered the Addis Ababa circle by the back door, [and] had yet to give proof of its Africanism'.[49] Moreover, Morocco had been absent from the first pan-African meeting in Addis Ababa because of its refusal to recognise Mauritania, and ended up signing the charter with the reservation that it would respect the borders of pre-colonial Morocco. While Morocco witnessed Mauritania's consecration within the pan-African organisation, his chances of obtaining African support for his other claims to territorial integrity had been weakened by the open hostility of many African states.[50]

4   From the Sand War to the Betrayal of the OAU: The Moroccan Western Sahara, an African Problem

After the birth of the OAU, Morocco continued to claim Mauritania's Moroccanness, which the Istiqlal leader called 'the most important national issue'[51]—for almost a decade (until 1969). In 1963, the Istiqlal again published the map of a 'Greater Morocco', while King Hassan II put the Royal Armed Forces to work for the party. The recovery of the Spanish Sahara, in particular, was more than

---

48   Decraene, "L'évolution politique: les resolutions adoptees à Casablanca suscitent les inquiétudes de certains États".
49   Jean Lacouture, "Le Maroc voit se prolonger son isolement diplomatique", *Le Monde diplomatique*, September 1, 1963.
50   Serre, "Les revendications marocaines sur la Mauritanie".
51   Letter from M. Roger Seydoux, Ambassador of France in Rabat, to M. Couve de Murville, Minister of Foreign Affairs, Rabat, 28 March 1962. In: *Documents diplomatiques français Tome 1962, I, 1er janvier–30 juin*.

strategic, as this region constituted one of the foundations of the previously mentioned golden-mean role identity. As Allal al-Fassi declared to France in 1960:

> The proper function, the originality of Morocco, is to be in every respect the link, the place of passage, between Mediterranean Europe and tropical Africa. To ignore either what came to it through the Sahara, or the influence of its action across the desert, is to mutilate it and condemn oneself to not understanding it.[52]

In this respect, to cut it off from its Saharan extension was also to cut it off from its African links.

At first, Morocco chose to negotiate this issue directly with nascent Algeria. When King Hassan II and Ferhat Abbas, head of the Provisional Government of the Republic of Algeria (GPRA), met in Rabat in 1961, Morocco agreed to support the GPRA and to postpone the delimitation of their borders until after Algerian independence. Aware that he would thus lose French support on this issue, he nevertheless preferred to trust the Algerian National Liberation Front based on a convention signed between the two parties.[53] But in 1962, Algeria occupied the Tindouf region, killing and wounding dignitaries who had pledged allegiance to the King of Morocco a few months earlier, while France had, as expected, regained its formal neutrality on the issue.[54] According to Édouard Méric, 'the administrative borders fixed by France had allowed Algeria to launch a real pseudopod towards the Atlantic Ocean. They resulted in Morocco becoming a territory encircled by Algeria.'[55]

---

52 Allal el-Fassi repeats here the words of J. Celerier when he spoke at the eighth congress of the Institut des hautes études marocaines in 1930. See El-Fassi, "Les revendications marocaines sur les territoires sahariens".

53 'The government of H.M. the King of Morocco reaffirms its unconditional support for the Algerian people in their struggle for independence and national unity. (...). The Provisional Government of the Algerian Republic recognises for its part the territorial problem posed by the delimitation arbitrarily imposed by France between the two countries, which will find its solution in negotiations between the Government du Royaume du Maroc et le gouvernement de l'Algérie indépendant' Convention of July 6 1961, signed between Hassan II and Ferhat Abbas, Rabat. Édouard Méric, "Le conflit algéro-marocain", *Revue française de science politique 15*, no. 4 (1965): 743–752.

54 France had recognised in 1957 that it would respect the territorial integrity of Morocco, which, under an agreement with England in 1911, included the whole of North Africa between Algeria, the AOF and the Rio Del Oro.

55 Méric, "Le conflit algéro-marocain".

Thus the Sand War between Morocco and Algeria began in October 1962: it lasted five months and ended in the status quo. While the eastern border was fixed, the southern border was still the subject of heated debate, especially after the discovery of a large phosphate deposit near Laayoune in the same year. Faced with the impossibility of reaching an agreement, the two countries agreed to rely on the mediation of the OAU from 1963 onwards. While waiting for a diplomatic solution, Hassan II tried to repair the state of relations with Algeria, which was working to support the left-wing opposition in Morocco.[56] He first concluded a 'Treaty of Friendship and Fraternity' with President Houari Boumediene in 1969. Then, three years later, he agreed to share the exploitation of the minerals in the Tindouf region and to transport them across the Sahara towards the Atlantic Ocean.

This honeymoon was, however, short-lived. It gave Hassan II time to prepare and launch the Green March on 6 November 1975. Some 350,000 Moroccan civilians marched from the four corners of the country towards the Sahara, unarmed, with flag and Qur'an in hand, at the risk of a war with Franco's Spain, which still occupied the region. The prior organisation of the Green March was a well-thought-out act: a year earlier, Hassan II had sought the opinion of the International Court of Justice (ICJ) on the status of Western Sahara. Was it a territory without sovereignty (*terra nullius*) before colonisation? If not, what links did the inhabitants of this territory have with the Kingdom? The ICJ replied that the people living in Western Sahara had retained allegiance to the Moroccan Sultan. Thus, in May 1975, Franco's Spain announced its intention to withdraw from this region,[57] six months before the peaceful offensive of the Green March. A week after the Moroccan march, the Madrid Accords established the conditions for partitioning the territory between Morocco and Mauritania. On 20 November, the death of the General was announced, and the de-colonisation of the Sahara was officially recognised in the Official Bulletin.[58] Morocco had won, but only for a few months.

On 6 March 1976, the Sahrawi Front, known as Polisario (Frente Popular Para la Liberacion de la Saguia El Hamra et del Rio Del Oro), proclaimed the 'Sahrawi Arab Democratic Republic' (RASD), recognised, hosted and supported by Algeria. It declared war on Morocco after the Royal Armed Forces had just

---

56 Stephen O. Hughes, *Le Maroc de Hassan II*, (Bouregreg, 2003), 299.
57 Abdelhamid Benkhattab, "Le rôle de la politique saharienne franquiste dans l'internationalisation de l'affaire du Sahara occidental", in *Le différend saharien devant l'Organisation des Nations Unies*, ed. Centre d'Études Internationales (Paris, France: Karthala, 2011), 27–45.
58 Law no. 40/1975, *Boletin Oficial*, no. 278, Madrid, November 20, 1975.

militarily confronted—to no avail—Algerian troops in Amgala. The UN invited the OAU to try to settle the dispute. It was then that the issue became genuinely international: the influence of the USSR in newly decolonised Africa was at the origin of the emergence of socialist regimes—whose ideology opposed Western hegemonism—invoking peoples' right to self-determination. As early as 1978, 75 countries recognised the Polisario Front as the legitimate representative of the Sahrawi people.[59] Algeria, Nigeria and Tanzania, emerging regional powers, favoured Sahrawi independence, while several French-speaking countries supported Morocco. For the latter, Algeria coveted the Sahrawi resources (phosphates, minerals, fish) and planned to establish a socialist regime hostile to the monarchy. From the Algerian point of view, the issue was highly strategic, a guarantee of its power. This is why the leaders of the Algerian revolution (including Ferhat Abbas), who had denounced their president's hostility towards Morocco, were immediately placed under house arrest by Algeria.[60] As for the two great powers of the time, the USSR and the United States, they saw the opportunity to pour their weapons into a frozen, low-risk conflict. The arms race between the two neighbours had thus begun.

Initially, the Polisario Front's application to the OAU to have the RASD recognised as a state was rejected.[61]

On the ground, the construction of sand walls and the installation of minefields by the Royal Armed Forces enabled them to gain ground against the Polisario guerrilleros.[62] But a few years later, in 1984, the OAU recognised the RASD as a member state, with a simple majority (26 states out of 50): humiliated, Morocco immediately left the organisation. It was, for more than 30 years and until January 2017, the only African country that was not a member of the African Union. The Sahara War, a specious war, more verbal than martial, had just ended in a diplomatic, not military, defeat on an African scale.[63] Morocco had resisted the temptation of military conflict with Algeria but had lost its place in the continent's most important multilateral organisation.

The Kingdom had also lost the OAU's support because it had not been able to play a decisive role in the organisation's decision-making and action. It did

---

59   Berramdane, *Le Sahara occidental, enjeu maghrébin*, 71.
60   Hughes, *Le Maroc de Hassan II*, 305.
61   Mohamed Lamouri, "L'affaire du Sahara: de l'Organisation de l'Unité Africaine à l'Organisation des Nations Unies", in *Le différend saharien devant l'Organisation des Nations Unies*, ed. Centre d'études internationales (Paris, France: Karthala, 2011), 65–79.
62   Hughes, *Le Maroc de Hassan II*, 327–337.
63   For more details on the military aspects, see Arrigoni, Michael, "La dimension militaire du conflit au sahara occidental: enjeux et stratégies", (Thèse de doctorat, France: Université de Reins, 1997), 408.

attend meetings and advocated for African solidarity, and chaired the organisation from June 1972 to June 1973. Still, it did not carry out large-scale pan-African projects because of a lack of resources, while Algeria dominated the OAU financially. In principle, Morocco was committed to the defence of many African interests: support for national liberation armies in Southern Africa, defence of the right to the sea for landlocked countries, economic and social demands for the development of the continent from foreign powers, defence of the territorial integrity of African states, etc.[64] However, within African regional institutions or offices (WHO, Economic Commission for Africa, African Union of Radio and Television, and other conferences), and in its bilateral relations, Morocco was distinguished by its version of the 'Hallstein doctrine'.

The Hallstein doctrine is named after its inventor Walter Hallstein, Secretary of State in the Federal Republic of Germany between 1955 and 1959. This doctrine aimed at not recognising or breaking diplomatic relations with any country that recognised East Germany. Morocco had pursued a similar policy in Africa in the period before and after its departure from the OAU: it generally broke off diplomatic relations with countries that recognised the Polisario Front as an independent republic. This was the case in Ethiopia, for example, where the Moroccan embassy was closed from 1 October 1979 to 4 April 1996.[65] As one diplomat confirms, 'the period when diplomacy experienced its most important gap was that of M'hamed Boucetta [Minister of Foreign Affairs from 1977 to 1983], who decided to stop diplomatic relations with all countries that recognised the Pseudo-RASD. This policy affected us for almost 25 years.'[66] Furthermore, as explained in the previous section, France's responsibility for the delimitation of the Saharan borders was little considered or ignored by Morocco's rivals.

Finally, the Kingdom's foreign policy was founded on the personal links between the King and African heads of state. Mobutu, Senghor, Bongo and Boigny, presidents for life, had gradually become close friends of Hassan II from the 1970s onwards, as we shall see later. For the Moroccan ruling class, the idea that Africa had betrayed Morocco[67] was to determine the conduct of its foreign policy on the continent for the next 20 years.

---

64   Bouzidi, "Le Maroc et l'afrique sub-saharienne".
65   Information provided by the Moroccan Embassy in Ethiopia, which I contacted by telephone, December 2015.
66   Interview with a diplomat (no. 6), Moroccan Ministry of Foreign Affairs and Cooperation—June 2013.
67   Bouzidi, "Le Maroc et l'afrique sub-saharienne".

5 The Search for Leadership in a Regional Union with Libya: A Failed Alternative

Faced with the difficulties inherent in reconciling its pragmatic interests with an African multilateralism driven mainly by the progressives, Morocco reoriented its action in the regional construction of the Arab Maghreb. At that time, the Libyan Republic was emerging due to coup d'état in 1969 orchestrated by Gaddafi, who had developed a power policy in Africa based on economic and financial cooperation. The victory of Libyan troops in Chad, a stronghold of French influence, confirmed the robustness of this revolutionary power committed to supporting liberation movements on the continent, whose leader soon became president of the OAU. In order to justify its interest in Africa to leaders favouring a more exclusive commitment to Arab solidarity, the Libyan state referred to the 'growing Africanisation of the Arab nation, 70% of whose population and 65% of whose territory is located on the black continent',[68] as a demonstration of the conviction of Gaddafi's commitments. The alliance with Libya was, therefore, essential for constructing a regional union.

While the Moroccan monarchy's relations with the former Libyan monarchy were positive, Gaddafi's new Libya favoured Morocco's isolation by supporting the attachment of the Saharan provinces to Mauritania and openly rejoicing in the attempted military putsch against Hassan II in 1973.[69] From his side, Hassan II was considering restoring the Libyan monarchy by helping King Idris's nephew to get out of prison.[70] At the same time, Morocco drew closer to Mauritania, whose regime was still firmly under French influence. In the context of tensions between Libya and France, Gaddafi openly condemned the new Moroccan–Mauritanian alliance, thus beginning his military support for the Polisario Front. But the historiography of Libya suggests that Gaddafi did not expect the creation of a proto-state group in the Sahara. This analysis error led him to send a personal message to Hassan II on the day of the self-proclamation of the RASD (27 February 1976), indicating that he would finally defend the integration of this region into the Moroccan entity,[71] although he did not initially want this. Hassan II immediately seized this opportunity to dialogue with

---

68 Interview with M. Kikhia, former Foreign Minister of Libya, in *Jeune Afrique*, 1973, see René Otayek, "Libya and Africa: Financial Assistance and Power Strategy", *Politique africaine* 1(2), (1981): 77–98.
69 The Libyan army was put on alert to support the coup elements of the royal army. René Otayek, *La politique africaine de la Libye: 1969–1985*, (Karthala, 1986), 61.
70 Jean-Pierre Bat, *Le syndrome Foccart: La politique française en Afrique, de 1959 à nos jours*, (Paris: Folio, 2012), 331.
71 Otayek, *La politique africaine de la Libye*, 68.

the Libyan leader. This unprecedented rapprochement also allowed a reaction to the signing of an Algerian–Tunisian friendship treaty (Treaty of Fraternity and Concord) in March 1983, which Mauritania joined a few months later.[72] The following year, in 1984 (when Morocco also withdrew from the OAU), Hassan II and Gaddafi signed the 'Morocco–Libyan Treaty', known as the 'Treaty of Oujda', establishing the 'Union of Arab-African States'.[73]

The Treaty of Oujda had set itself the objective of establishing a regional union to defend the interests of Arabs and Muslims in Africa and the Middle East. The Moroccan–Libyan alliance was also intended to support Maghrebian integration at the political and economic levels. The two countries envisaged the creation of four councils (Political, Defence, Economic, and Cultural and Technical Cooperation) that would elaborate propositions in the direction of integration. Beyond this regionalist enthusiasm, the agreement also allowed for an exchange of procedures: Gaddafi saw Morocco as a relay to engage in dialogue with Western bloc supporters, while Hassan II sought support from Eastern Bloc supporters for his policy of territorial integrity.[74] This being the case, while the implementation of the objectives envisaged when the treaty was signed was not pursued, the symbolic value of the alliance for Morocco contributed to the validation of its role as a 'bridge' between two ideological blocs, and of its 'moderate' identity, confirmed by the pragmatism it had shown towards the Libyan power. It also contributed to the reinforcement of Hassan II's legitimacy at the internal level, considered as the precursor to the Arab Maghreb's unity by part of the public opinion.[75]

Seduced by Hassan II's Libyan policy, the Moroccan press and political parties favoured the treaty's ratification, urging the people to vote for the union of Morocco and Libya. In contrast, the Algerian press expressed reluctance to build a future Maghrebian unity, basing its arguments on Morocco's duty to recognise the RASD. According to *Al-Alam*, Algeria had 'done everything in its power to destroy the Morocco–Libyan agreement',[76] and as a result,

---

72 Habib Melyani, *Le Traité de Fraternité et de Concorde de ou 1983, un nouveau droit de la coopération maghrébine* (Annuaire de l'Afrique du Nord, Tome XXiV, Édition du CNrS, 1985), 89–99.

73 Jean Leca, "Le traité instituant l'Union arabo-africaine: Oujda, 13 aout 1984," Monde Arabe 4, n°106, (1984): 101–3.

74 Otayek, *La politique africaine de la Libye*, 71.

75 Mohamed Benkhalloul, "Le traité d'union maroco-libyen d'Oujda (13 August 1984) dans la presse marocaine de langue arabe", *Annuaire de l'Afrique du Nord 23, Centre national de la recherche scientifique; Centre de recherches et d'études sur les sociétés méditerrannes* (CRESM), (1986): 693–704.

76 Ibid., 703. For more on Algeria's behaviour towards the Morocco-Libyan treaty see: Majdi

while 'Morocco had always tried to build bridges between the Maghreb brothers, Algeria had always tried to blow up these bridges',[77] an idea commonly shared within Moroccan public opinion, contributing to the crystallisation of the Algerian–Moroccan conflict. Despite efforts by Morocco and Libya to urge the other Maghreb countries to join the Arab-African Union, their calls went unheeded. Two years later, the reception of Israeli President Shimon Perez in Morocco, criticised by Libya, led Hassan II to break the Treaty of Oujda[78] and move closer to the United States. In an interview given to a journalist a few years later, the Cherifian King enlightened public opinion on the realistic dimension of his policy:

> At the time we are talking about, in 1984, I had two guns against me, one long-range and rather well-fed, the other medium-range. I had to neutralise one of them. The opportunity was given to me while I waited impatiently for the Algerians' response to a federation or confederation project [...] The day I received, in front of several witnesses, the emissary who brought me Gaddafi's letter [...] the idea came to me [...] that there was no reason to exclude a union between Morocco and Libya.[79]

The failure to build an Arab-African Union was partly due to the hostility of Algeria, which had power ambitions in sub-Saharan Africa (and had previously concluded a treaty of brotherhood with Tunisia and Mauritania), but regional alliances also determined it in a Cold War context. The building of a regional union also depended on a rapprochement between the two neighbours. Thus, in 1985, when a new section of the Sahara sand wall was being built, and Hassan II announced his intention to modernise the army, the UN invited Morocco to negotiate directly with the Polisario Front. After several 'proximity talks' in New York, helping to maintain a ceasefire, and as the construction of the wall was nearing completion in 1987, giving a tactical and strategic advantage to Moroccan troops, Algerian President Chadli finally agreed to meet Hassan II in Oujda, in the presence of King Fahd of Saudi Arabia, who mediated the meeting. The two states agreed to an exchange of prisoners and gradually normalised

---

Ali Attya, "Le dialogue algérien libyen à propos de l'union. Hypothèses et conséquences", *Politique internationale*, no. 90, (October 1987): 183–185.
77 Ibid., 698.
78 Abdelgadir Abusitta, "La dimension africaine dans la politique étrangère libyenne 1969–2002" (PhD thesis, Université d'Auvergne–Clermont–Ferrand, 2012), 39.
79 Interview given by Hassan II to Jean Daniel in *Le Nouvel Observateur*, April 4, 1986, quoted in: Claude Nigoul, "De Gaulle et Hassan II", in *De Gaulle et le Maroc, ed.* Sehimi, Mustapha (Paris, 1990), 179–192.

their relations. In Algeria, the exhaustion of the socialist model had indeed pushed the government to stabilise its regional ties in order to focus on internal problems, which led President Chadli to make his first official visit to Morocco in February 1989, initiating a possible rapprochement between the two neighbours. This situation paved the way for the meeting of all the Maghreb heads of state in the same month and the signing of a treaty in Marrakech, creating the Arab Maghreb Union (AMU).

At the time of the birth of the AMU, Morocco was hoping for the organisation's support for its territorial claims. As in previous multilateral union-building projects (the Casablanca Conference and later the OAU, or the Morocco–Libya Treaty), Morocco had defended a clause stipulating that the members of the AMU would agree 'not to tolerate on their territory any movement or activity that could threaten the security or territorial integrity of a member state or its political system'.[80] In other words, Morocco demanded that the Maghreb states refuse to host, meet or support the Polisario Front. This condition had therefore been at the centre of most discussions within the union for many years. At first, intra-Maghreb quarrels faded away, and the Kingdom was able to engage in a policy of regional stabilisation. As one columnist noted, King Hassan II:

> went on board his floating palace in Tripoli to attend the ceremonies marking the 30th anniversary of the overthrow of King Idriss Senoussi by Colonel Gaddafi, an irony that spoke volumes about how things had changed in North Africa. The Polisario was in disarray. Several hundred of its members went to Morocco to obtain a royal pardon.[81]

Second, the Marrakech attack of 1994 led to the closure of the Algerian–Moroccan borders, which had a substantial impact on the AMU, as its heads of state have not met since that date.

Finally, it appears that the 'Greater Morocco' project and its Cherifian variant helped push the Kingdom to engage in an Africa policy that went beyond the Saharan framework. At the same time, Abdallah Saaf considers that from the end of the 1970s, Morocco 'was diverted from its African vocation to orient itself more towards Europe, particularly France'.[82] Illustrating a false contradic-

---

80   Hughes, *Le Maroc de Hassan II*, 363–364.
81   Ibid., 364.
82   Abdelaziz Barre, "La politique marocaine de coopération en Afrique", in *Le Maroc et l'Afrique après l'indépendance*, ed. Abdallah Saaf, (Rabat, Morocco: Université Mohammed V, Publications de l'Institut des Études Africaines, 1996), 17.

tion, French–Moroccan cooperation has, in fact, given the Palace the means to reformulate a singular Africa policy based on bilateral, personal and high-level rapprochements, which have sometimes benefited from, and sometimes suffered from, a French 'invisible hand'.

6   The Cold War Kingdom versus French Power in Africa

Vassal, ally, partner, competitor? Morocco's relationship with France and the consequences of this relationship for its continental relations deserve to be questioned. Several dimensions of the Kingdom's diplomacy, such as its proximity to French-speaking Africa, the close ties maintained by the monarch with many French-speaking African heads of state and the French-speaking dimension of Morocco's Africa policy—characteristics that will be developed later—tend to raise the hypothesis of this influence.

While pursuing the policy of 'non-commitment' formulated by his father (support for liberation movements, rejection of a military alliance with any of the great powers, contestation of foreign bases on national territory, etc.),[83] Hassan II durably consolidated French–Moroccan relations. This balance was possible insofar as, for the Moroccan political parties, 'French–Moroccan normalisation appeared as a necessary counterweight to the extension of American influence in Morocco'.[84] More generally, Hassan II had developed special ties with the French leadership. As early as independence in 1956, when he was still Crown Prince, French diplomats were full of praise for the future King, while he regularly expressed his feelings of friendship towards the French.[85]

Moulay Hassan had seduced France by his personality, his commitment to the Republic, his declared intentions to keep away from the USSR and Nasser's Egypt,[86] and more generally, by his anti-communism. He confided to his French

83   Berramdane, *Le Maroc et l'Occident*, 170–175.
84   Ibid., 390.
85   Moulay Hassan is described in French diplomatic correspondence as a courageous prince endowed with elegance and an art of propriety of terms. The French seem to be convinced of the Francophile spirit of the future king: '*When he speaks of his friendship for France and the French, one can believe him to be sincere insofar as he is convinced, as he said in Cairo, of the need for Morocco to rely on a strong partner whose international authority is unquestionable. His impatience, his impulsiveness, the taste he has for certain material advantages will be blunted and will fade away, one must hope, in front of the feeling that one feels growing in him of his responsibilities towards the crown and his country*'. Telegram from M. Lalouette, Chargé d'Affaires of France in Rabat, to the Secretariat of State for Moroccan and Tunisian Affairs, T. no. 3205 to 3209, Rabat, July 10, 1956, in: *Documents diplomatiques français*.
86   Telegram from Mr André-Louis Dubois, Ambassador of France in Rabat to Mr Savary,

counterparts his fears 'of seeing the emergence of a Ho Chi Minh, champion of a progressive and secular Algerian Republic'.[87] His accession to the throne naturally led him to suddenly and definitively break with the Kingdom's possible revolutionary choice. According to one former French ambassador in Morocco, Hassan II managed to re-establish 'almost overnight better relations with France, and, secondarily, with the United States'.[88] One of the consequences of this rapprochement was the influence of the Gaullist system in the organisation of the monarchical power[89] and how Morocco now viewed its Africa policy. Although the styles of the two leaders were different, De Gaulle and Hassan II conducted their foreign policies according to the same realistic pragmatism.[90]

Despite the accepted influence of the Gaullist Republic on the Hassanian government and the existence of common interests, relations between the two heads of state were strained. It was not until President Pompidou came to power that relations were officially re-established in 1969.[91] The new French–Moroccan cooperation that began with Georges Pompidou and continued with Valéry Giscard d'Estaing proved to be more ambitious while remaining secret in its content. France had adopted a particular policy towards Morocco, primarily due to decisions taken between heads of state rather than ministerial orientations. According to Hubert Durand:

> We observe, on the one hand, that the parliament is never consulted on the possible choices of France's Moroccan policy, and the other hand [...]

Secretary of State for Moroccan and Tunisian Affairs, T. no. 3573, Rabat, July 25, 1956, Ibid.

87 Telegram from Mr. Lalouette, chargé d'Affaire de France à Rabat to Mr. Maurice Faure, Secretary of Foreign Affairs, in charge of Moroccan and Tunisian affairs, Rabat 13 February 1957. T. no. 1039 to 1045. In *Documents diplomatiques français Tome I, January 1-June 30*.

88 Letter from M. Roger Seydoux, Ambassador of France in Rabat, to M. Couve de Murville, Minister of Foreign Affairs, Rabat, March 28, 1962. In: *Documents diplomatiques français Tome, I, 1er janvier–30 juin*.

89 The possibility for the monarchy to proclaim the state of exception and the role of arbiter it embodies was inspired in particular by the Republic of De Gaulle. This role is based '*on the need to defend the general and national interest: it makes the sovereign a superior authority able to represent the will of national life and the legitimacy of the nation*'. Mustapha Sehimi, "L'influence gaullienne sur la constitution marocaine", in *De Gaulle et le Maroc*, (Paris, 1990), 104–122.

90 Nigoul, "De Gaulle and Hassan II".

91 Nicole Grimaud, "L'introuvable équilibre maghrébin", in *La Politique extérieure de Valéry Giscard d'Estaing*, eds. Samy Cohen and Marie-Claude Smouts (Presses de la Fondation Nat. des Sciences Politiques, 1985), 323–347.

that the Ministry of Foreign Affairs plays a secondary role in the elaboration of this policy [...] For thirty years, the Moroccan policy resulted from face-to-face negotiations between the two heads of state.[92]

The constant opacity that characterised French–Moroccan political relations from the 1970s onwards allowed France to maintain formal neutrality vis-à-vis the other Maghreb countries and to avoid the Kingdom facing bitter opposition from the most anti-Western political parties (communists and then Islamists). On the other hand, France needed Morocco's support for its Africa policy and therefore had every interest in protecting the Kingdom's stability. The meeting of Moroccan and French policies in sub-Saharan Africa, thus, began in earnest in the 1970s under Hassan II. As Jean-Pierre Bat notes, he 'took a much more Francophile path than that of his father Mohammed V, becoming for many years a very faithful ally of France in Africa'[93] and, as Raymond Aron notes, Morocco became 'the most pro-Western of the Maghreb countries'.[94] Hassan II confirmed this alliance and officially visited Paris in 1970. He published a laudatory article on French–Moroccan relations in *Le Monde Diplomatique* the same year,[95] while the newspaper prepared public opinion by announcing that 'cooperation with Western Europe, and particularly with France, seems to be postulate inscribed in Morocco's geopolitical data'.[96] The private visit of King Hassan II to France had also confirmed this normalisation, which now took the form of a discreet and loyal alliance.

During the Cold War period, while France was developing its post-colonial strategy in Africa, Hassan II's Morocco established and maintained bilateral and personal relations with many African heads of state to pursue its territorial integrity. Between 1960 and 1987, these bilateral exchanges led to the signing of nearly 120 new cooperation agreements between Morocco and the countries of West Africa (Senegal, Gambia, Côte d'Ivoire, Niger, Cameroon, Zaire, Central African Republic, Chad and Gabon),[97] a rapprochement that did not always benefit France or obtain its support.

The first Moroccan–African cooperation agreements covered various sectors: technical, scientific, cultural, financial, economic, military, etc. However,

---

92 Hubert Durand, "La France a-t-elle une politique marocaine?", *Confluences Méditerranée* 23, (Autumn 1997): 171–177.
93 Bat, *Le syndrome Foccart*, 26.
94 Raymond Aron, *De Giscard à Mitterrand: 1977–1983*, (Fallois, 2005), 416–417.
95 Hassan II, "Assumer son destin", *Le Monde diplomatique*, March 1, 1970.
96 "Dans la voie du développement et du progrès", *Le Monde diplomatique*, March 1, 1970.
97 Barre, "La politique marocaine de coopération en Afrique", 25.

it is worth noting that most of the time, these agreements benefited their African partners *a priori*. Technical assistance to develop the textile sector in Senegal, the offer of scholarships to Guinean students (through the Agence Guinéenne et Marocaine de Coopération created in 1958) and the granting of direct and sometimes interest-free loans (US$ 28 million to Gabon to finance the first section of the Transgabonais in 1975, $10 million to Zaire for the acquisition of military equipment in 1977, $8 million to Chad in 1975, $7 million to Guinea in 1984)[98] are examples of this trend. On the economic level, Morocco hoped to develop trade and increase the export of its products. But this objective was never achieved, mainly because these transactions were conducted through well-established French intermediaries in French-speaking African states. Other reasons, such as a lack of proper Moroccan transport, restrictions linked to the legislation of regional organisations, and the constraints of the GATT (General Agreement on Tariffs and Trade) and the IMF, can be mentioned. On the cultural level, the Kingdom had, very early on, envisaged spreading its model and considered itself, as Hassan II stated, 'invested with the mission of preserving and extending the Muslim religion through universities, mosques, preachers, ulama and professors',[99] which it sent to Senegal, Gabon and Niger. Finally, on the political level, Hassan II had expressly favoured the establishment of a community of interests with the liberal group to fight the communists on the continent, convinced that they represented a threat to territorial integrity because of their support for the Polisario Front. this seemingly ideological posture, guided by much more realistic interests, allowed him to envisage regional leadership and obtain French support, especially when it came to developing the army. As Nicole Grimaud notes, this 'broad convergence of Paris and Rabat in the field of international relations has found concrete application in Africa'.[100]

Initially, the French–Moroccan alliance took the form of an exchange of good will in favour of common interests. Thus, when Paris officially launched the 'Lamantin' operation on behalf of Mauritania, intended to combat the Polisario Front, Rabat was already perfectly aware and very much in favour of the intervention.[101] When Hassan II briefly considered restoring the Libyan monarchy in 1972, the French secret services supported this operation,[102] which

---

98 Ibid., 39.
99 Hassan II, Press conference in Taef (Saudi Arabia), February 9, 1980, quoted in Ibid., 47.
100 Grimaud, "L'introuvable équilibre maghrébin", 340.
101 Walter Bruyère-Ostells, *Dans l'ombre de Bob Denard: les Mercenaires français de 1960 à 1989*, (Nouveau Monde éditions, 2014), Section 10.
102 Bat, *Le syndrome Foccart*, 331.

was in line with France's Libyan policy. The Kingdom had also mobilised fighters from the Kingdom of Jordan to reinforce the French troops, which allowed France to minimise the risk of human losses. All of this suggests *a priori* a critical break with the period of independence, during which France supported Mauritanian independence despite Moroccan claims.

Assured of its position as a loyal ally of the Republic, the Cherifian Kingdom was increasingly solicited by Paris. Many operations remain secret to this day, while others have been made public. In 1977, when the Shaba (formerly Katanga) region of Zaire was reviving its secessionist past, Valéry Giscard d'Estaing wanted to assist the Mobutu regime. He therefore appealed to Hassan II, who immediately sent his Cherifian troops in a multilateral force with logistical support from France, an operation called 'Verveine'. Within this multilateral coalition, Saudi Arabia was in charge of financing the operations, while Egyptian and Sudanese partners served as guarantors.[103] This allowed the Moroccan contingent, made up of 1,500 men[104] under the command of Command Loubaris (facing the 2,000 men of the Front National de Libération du Congo), to deploy rapidly and liberate Shaba. A year later, in 1978, new Katangese separatists, helped by Angola and Cuba, invaded Shaba. Moroccan troops thus intervened twice alongside the French, Belgians and Americans. Both interventions were victorious: in France, the press quickly stated that 'the desired effect was achieved: Paris opposed Soviet penetration of Africa'.[105] For his part, King Hassan II congratulated himself on the success of the operations, which, according to him, marked a real diplomatic breakthrough: Africa now had its coalition to counter the advance of communism, a coalition in which Morocco claimed a leading role.[106] It was then that the monarch tried to rally other African countries under his leadership, stating: 'We want Zaire's friendly neighbours to make an effort, even if it is symbolic, to show that this issue is not just about President Mobutu and myself, but that it is a strategic issue for the whole region'.[107]

From the Kingdom's point of view, the question of neighbourhood was essential. Surrounded by hostile neighbours, the monarchy drew a parallel

---

103   Ibid., 406.
104   "Morocco-France: Ces interventions militaires communes", *L'Économiste, no. 4621*., September 18, 2015.
105   C.J., "Les trois grands mérites de l'intervention française", *Le Monde diplomatique*, May 1, 1977.
106   Berramdane, *Le Sahara occidental, enjeu maghrébin*, 299.
107   "Interview with H.M. Hassan II to the 'Washington Post'", *Speeches and Interviews of H.M. King Hassan II Volume VI*, [1978–1980], (Rabat: Ministry of Information, 1990), 574.

between the Katanga issue and the Sahara issue and certainly hoped that President Mobutu's support could bring it new allies as a matter of reciprocity. Informed that Angola represented a threat to Mobutu's regime,[108] it was with this in mind that the Kingdom hosted training camps for the UNITA (National Union for the Total Independence of Angola) led by Jonas Savimbi in 1979. This training was also done with the support of France, which wanted to place a 'moderate' leader at the head of Angola. To affirm his support for this African Francophile circle, Hassan II participated in the operation.[109] A symbol and standard bearer of the anti-communist struggle in Angola, UNITA was allied with the Western camp (USA, South Africa, France) and fought against the MPLA (Popular Movement for the Liberation of Angola), which was allied with the Eastern camp (USSR, Cuba, GDR). But French support for Savimbi eventually waned as the territory appeared remote and insignificant to France, which did not want diplomatic tensions with Moscow.[110] This did not prevent Morocco from continuing to support the Angolan liberation effort by granting Moroccan passports to the independence fighters, which facilitated their travel.[111]

A few years later, France considered influencing the terms of the Moroccan–Libyan rapprochement of 1984, which was of interest to its policy in Chad, threatened by Gaddafi. In this perspective, Valéry Giscard d'Estaing made two private visits to Morocco shortly before and after the popular referendum on the adoption of the Treaty of Oujda, during which he met with the King, to the point that the media linked these meetings to the situation in Chad.[112] This three-pronged policy benefited Moroccan–Chadian relations: in 1985, Chadian President Hissène Habré visited Morocco. The two states concluded a cooperation agreement, and the first joint cooperation commission was set up.[113]

---

108 'When President Mobutu visited me recently, I asked him, given the friendship that binds us, what had caused his country to be the object of two successive attacks in two years. I was surprised by his answer, which was easy to guess. He reminded me that between 1965 and 1975, peace reigned absolutely. But as soon as Angola achieved independence and adopted a certain ideology, Zaire was attacked twice in two years. It is up to us, Dear People, to draw a lesson from this phenomenon, a lesson concerning the notion of neighbourhood'—Interview with H.M. Hassan II in Ibid.
109 Bat, *Le syndrome Foccart*.
110 Ibid, 400; 392.
111 "Tribute to Morocco for the liberation of Angola", *Tribute to Morocco for the liberation of Angola—The New Tribune*, September 10, 2012.
112 Benkhalloul, "Le traité d'union maroco-libyen d'Oujda (13 August 1984) dans la presse marocaine de langue arabe".
113 Riffi El Mellouki Bouhout, "La politique marocaine de coopération avec l'Afrique Subsaharienne", in *Le Maroc et l'Afrique après l'indépendance*, ed. Saaf, Abdallah (Rabat,

Despite the failure of the Union of Arab-African States, the convergence of French and Moroccan interests in Africa and their asymmetrical balance of power maintained the development of military cooperation between the two countries. Thus, during the Senegal–Mauritania conflict (1989–1991), Morocco participated alongside France, Spain and Algeria in implementing the airlift allowing the repatriation of tens of thousands of refugees after having sent a Maghrebian conciliation mission to Nouakchott. By the end of the 1980s, the balance of diplomatic and strategic cooperation was positive. The French government declared that, in the end, 'France has always considered, through all successive French governments, that French–Moroccan political relations constitute an essential element of our foreign policy, insofar as our historical ties with this country make it a region where the French presence remains important and active, but also insofar as Morocco's political, diplomatic and strategic role in the Maghreb, Africa and the Arab world is important', and its diplomatic positions are 'moderate and balanced'.[114] Here, it is necessary to read between the lines.

Finally, France and Morocco have achieved both relative and absolute gains from their episodic cooperation in Africa.[115] Among the relative gains, one can first mention the effects of French aid to the Moroccan war effort (in the Sahara and sub-Saharan Africa) on the modernisation and development of the Royal Armed Forces on the one hand, and the French economy on the other. Despite competition from the United States, France had become Morocco's leading arms supplier by the end of the 1970s. Given the size of the sums mobilised by the Kingdom (helped by its Arab allies, notably Saudi Arabia), France granted it generous credits and accepted deferred payments.[116] More generally, for Nicole Grimaud: 'Morocco during this period provided perhaps the best illustration of the benefit that the French economy could derive from the financial aid distributed by the State to the Third World'.[117] France was Morocco's largest supplier, delivering 38% of its equipment. More generally, as the Kingdom's largest investor, France had also pleaded with public (Paris Club) and private (London Club) creditors to reschedule the Kingdom's debt in 1983, when the latter was

---

Morocco: Université Mohammed V, Publications de l'Institut des Études Africaines, 1996), 57–86.
114 J. Huntginger, "Les relations économiques entre la France et le Maroc", *Avis et Rapports du Conseil Économique et Social*, no. 10 (1987): 1–25.
115 On the difference between absolute and relative gains, see: Robert Powell, "Absolute and Relative Gains in International Relations Theory", *The American Political Science Review 4*, no. 85 (1991): 1303–1320.
116 Grimaud, "L'introuvable équilibre maghrébin".
117 Ibid.

going through a significant financial crisis and was subjecting its economic policy to a structural adjustment programme.[118]

Reciprocally, the French contributed to the professionalisation and development of the Royal Armed Forces within the framework of bilateral defence agreements. The training of Moroccan officers in France and Morocco and the financial aid provided to the army brought the number of personnel from 60,000 in 1975 to 185,000 in 1981.[119] The strengthening of the Moroccan intelligence service also facilitated the deployment of 'special actions' in Africa, always with the approval of France and sometimes that of the United States. The development of the Moroccan army allowed it, from the 2000s onwards, to develop a training programme for African officers on the one hand, and to deploy an effective anti-terrorist cell within the intelligence service on the other—two axes to which we will return later.

Throughout the Cold War, Morocco generally reinforced its role as a mediator in Africa, outside the French fold. For example, the day after the successful military operation in Shaba in 1977, Hassan II was asked by General Mobutu to help him normalise his relations with Belgium. At that time, Morocco had excellent relations with the Kingdom of Leopold III: Crown Prince Mohammed was staying there for an internship at the European Commission, the country was home to a large Moroccan community of 120,000 people, and Morocco had just allowed for the F-16 of the Belgian aerial forces to train in the Saharan south.

The Belgian Minister of Foreign Affairs, Henri Simonet, therefore readily accepted the King's invitation to visit Rabat to discuss Belgian–Zairian relations with him.[120] Following the success of this first mediation, Hassan II reiterated his diplomatic role between Zaire and Belgium in 1989, during the debt crisis, and asked the Moroccan government to enlighten the Belgian side on Zaire's needs.[121] On 25 July 1989, after numerous negotiations, the Belgian and Zairean

---

118   Édouard Moha, *Histoire des relations franco-marocaines ou Les aléas d'une amitié*, (Paris, France: Picollec, DL 1995), 288–289.
119   Grimaud, "L'introuvable équilibre maghrébin".
120   'The Moroccan Sovereign will telephone the Zairian president in his presence to inform him of what has just been said, in substance: that Belgium is not seeking in any way to promote a change at the head of the Zairian state. The royal mediation (thus) puts an end to the political ostracism that Mr Simonet had suffered. In early August, he travels to Zaire' in : Gauthier de Villers, *De Mobutu à Mobutu: trente ans de relations Belgique-Zaïre*, (De Boeck Supérieur, 1995), 96.
121   It was the Minister of Foreign Affairs, M. Filali, who explained that 'once Belgium has formulated consistent proposals on debt, agreeing to go beyond what the Paris Club en-

parties signed a protocol of agreement in the Royal Palace in Rabat, putting an end to their dispute.[122] This was a diplomatic victory for the Kingdom, which thereby affirmed its mediation role within the continent. It should be noted, however, that this effort was deployed only towards a small group of friendly countries since Morocco had, it should be recalled, gradually broken off its relations with the states that recognised the RASD from the 1980s.

The 'Hallstein doctrine' had been a tangible limit to its diplomatic influence in Africa in the 25 following years.

7 'Renewed Partnership' and a New Policy in Africa at the End of the Cold War

At the end of the 1980s, Hassan II was, in the eyes of the French public opinion, 'the most popular Arab head of state ahead of Chadli, Arafat and Gaddafi'.[123] According to a *Figaro Magazine* Sofres poll conducted in May 1989, 32% of respondents felt sympathy for Hassan II.[124]

According to another survey of French left-wing supporters, 63% of respondents said they had a good opinion of the Cherifian King,[125] despite the existence of an 'anti-Moroccan lobby' within the French left since the Ben Barka affair. According to the journalist Jean Daniel, Hassan II appeared to the French as an 'atypical' man: 'he surprised them with his way of being so concerned about being and appearing French while remaining himself',[126] which made him fascinating and attractive. However, this relationship deteriorated very quickly after the fall of the Berlin Wall, leading to a reformulation of the terms of the French–Moroccan alliance in Africa. First of all, in June 1990, François Mitterrand, in his famous speech at La Baule, initiated a strategic turn in French diplomacy in Africa. France would henceforth prioritise multilateralism and economic cooperation, and would no longer distinguish between its traditional allies, its 'pré carré' and other African states. As a sign of good faith, Mitterrand

---

visages, Zaire will have no difficulty in putting the problem of the global "dispute" between the two countries back on the agenda', Ibid., 203.

122 Colette Braeckmann, "Belgians and Zairians sign reconciliation agreement in Rabat", *Lesoir.be*, July 25 1989.
123 Marie-Hélène Jouve, "Effet et usage de l'opinion publique dans les relations franco-marocaines: la crise des années 1990–1991", (Paris, France: Mémoire de D.E.A., Université de Paris Panthéon-Sorbonne, 1991), 18.
124 Ibid.
125 Ibid, 19.
126 Ibid.

acknowledged French politico-military interference in Africa during the Cold War and officially announced the end of this practice.[127] The La Baule speech had revealed France's ambition to work towards the democratisation of African regimes, thereby subscribing to the principle of 'democratic conditionality', which was in vogue in the international *doxa*. However, Hassan II immediately took the opposite view of this discourse, which he considered excessive. He became the spokesperson for an African Group (notably including Togo and Chad)[128] which was opposed to implementing democratic reforms in a hurry. He immediately declared that Western countries should 'help the young democracies to develop without putting the knife to their throats, without moving brutally to a multiparty system',[129] and accused France of causing 'cancer in Africa by using horse doses, while democracy was to be introduced in homoeopathic doses'.[130]

Hassan II's reaction to Mitterrand's call was the cause of diplomatic troubles between France and Morocco. In September of the same year, this was accentuated by the publication of Gilles Perrault's book, *Notre Ami le Roi* (*Our Friend the King*), in which the author made an indictment of the regime. To re-enhance the country's image, the Palace launched an initiative which consisted in organising a cultural and folkloric event from October 1990 to March 1991 in Paris called 'Le Temps du Maroc'. However, the event was cancelled due to the active opposition of French associations. At the same time, President Mitterrand had become closer to Algeria, while the First Lady, Danielle Mitterrand, had established direct links with the Polisario Front. The increase in tensions between the two states, fuelled partly by the activism of humanitarian organisations (Amnesty International in particular) and media publications, finally led to the infamous French–Moroccan crisis of 1990.

This crisis symbolised the beginning of a reorientation and a redefinition of the French–Moroccan policy. First, it officially marked the end of French covert operations aimed at overthrowing African regimes. It committed the two

---

127 'In the same way, I will always prohibit a practice that sometimes existed in the past and consisted of France trying to organise internal political changes through plotting or conspiracy. As you well know, this has not happened for the past nine years, and it will not happen.' Speech by François Mitterrand at La Baule, June 1990.
128 "Mitterrand and Africa: a relationship marked by the La Baule speech", RFI *Afrique*, January 8, 2016.
129 Quoted in: Jouve, *Effet et usage de l'opinion publique dans les relations franco-marocaines*, 38.
130 "Speeches and Interviews of H.M. King Hassan II", March 1991–1992, p. 101, quoted in El Houdaïgui, *La politique étrangère sous le règne de Hassan II*, 275.

countries to a new, more institutionalised form of military cooperation. Thus, the Royal Armed Forces intervened alongside France in Somalia in 1992 as part of a humanitarian operation under the aegis of the UN. On 11 October 1994, Morocco and France signed their first official intergovernmental agreement on technical military cooperation, covering the training of military personnel and the management of weapons. The agreement repealed and replaced the previous military agreement, which consisted of a series of letters exchanged between the government of the French Republic and the government of the Kingdom of Morocco since 1973.[131] As a result of this new agreement, between 1997 and 2007, 31 Moroccan officers received training at the French Defence College; between 2001 and 2006, 38 short-term missions were organised on-site by 88 trainers and experts.[132] The entire bilateral cooperation is to this day based on this intergovernmental agreement, which goes in the direction of formalising military cooperation.

On the other hand, Morocco became closer to the United States. Many US officials, including Secretary of State James Baker, prepared Hassan II's visit to Washington in 1991. This meeting allowed the US to exert discreet pressure for the economic and political liberalisation of Morocco. As one researcher noted: 'The idea of the Americans consisted in using secret diplomacy directly involving the high officials of the two States [...] to dialogue far from all media hype. This approach, which particularly pleased Hassan II, was the antithesis of the French approach, which was particularly media-friendly'.[133]

However, Morocco did not turn away from its Francophile inclination. This is why many French leaders and journalists continued to defend the development of bilateral cooperation with Hassan II. Among them were those who, like Charles Pasqua, considered the French debate on the universality of democratic and liberal values a new form of colonialism, and those who, like Claude Imbert, recalled Hassan II's stabilising role in the Arab world or his contributions to the appeasement of the French suburbs.[134] The arrival of Jacques Chirac in power finally restored the French–Moroccan relationship of trust, particularly through his recognition of Morocco's claim to a golden-mean role. He thus declared: 'There is a constant in the moderation and balance of Moroccan diplomacy that makes its strength. We do not forget that Morocco has never

---

131 Jean Roatta, "Rapport sur le projet de loi (no. 3276) autorisant l'approbation de l'accord entre le Gouvernement de la République française et le Gouvernement du Royaume du Maroc relatif au statut de leurs forces", Assemblée Nationale, February 6, 2007.
132 Ibid.
133 El Houdaïgui, *La politique étrangère sous le règne de Hassan II*, 277.
134 Jouve, *Effet et usage de l'opinion publique dans les relations franco-marocaines*, 61–65.

been tempted by extremism. Morocco's path has always been specific. This is one of the reasons why our two countries are natural partners.'[135]

On the Moroccan side, the leaders envisaged, at the time of Jacques Chirac's election, revisiting the terms, both literally and figuratively, i.e. in the discourse as well as in the content, of French–Moroccan cooperation. Mohammed Berrada (former Minister of Finance, and former Moroccan ambassador) defended, for example, the establishment of a 'renewed partnership', where Morocco would 'accompany' France on the international scene. According to him:

> Morocco, with its privileged geographical position, its political stability, the solidity of its institutions, and the moderation of its diplomacy, is well placed to bring points of view closer together and to serve as a companion to an imaginative and bold French policy on the international scene. The example of military cooperation in Bosnia and the presence of a Moroccan battalion in the SFOR [Stabilisation Force in Bosnia and Herzegovina] are very useful in this respect.[136]

In the eyes of this former leader, this accompaniment would be highly desirable insofar as it would allow Morocco to develop tripartite agreements with France on the one hand and with African countries on the other in order to place itself at the centre of negotiations and cooperation.[137]

The instruments of French–Moroccan cooperation in Africa have therefore been extended to cultural and technical fields, while the decision-making mechanism has been extended to various government and civil society actors. According to Laurent Fabius:

> Morocco wants to work more and more with Africa, both economically and in other areas. France works a lot with Africa. Our idea is that our cooperation should not be simply bilateral—France/Morocco, Morocco/France—but that it should be directed towards third countries, particularly in Africa. We are working in this direction on an economic and

---

[135] "Speech by the President of the Republic Jacques Chirac on the occasion of the State dinner offered in honour of His Majesty Hassan II, King of Morocco", May 7, 1996.

[136] Mohammed Berrada (former Minister of Finance, former Ambassador of Morocco), "Les relations maroco-françaises pour un partenariat rénové", *Défense Nationale*, no. 10, (October 1999), 10.

[137] 'Morocco's proposal to establish triangular cooperation with France and African countries is worth considering in more than one respect, as its effect would be so beneficial, particularly in the areas of management training and agricultural development', Ibid.

cultural level. This is one of the elements of the renewal of our cooperation that I mentioned.[138]

More generally, the end of the Cold War allowed Morocco to renew its continental diplomacy. This progressive reconfiguration marks a change in strategic and military paradigm vis-à-vis France, on the one hand, from which it has gradually become autonomous. As an illustration of this first trend, Morocco's military interventions in Africa have taken on a more multilateral form since 1990, integrating the RAF into several UN blue helmet missions.[139] On the other hand, Morocco has repositioned itself concerning the Sahara issue by putting an end to the application of its 'Hallstein doctrine'. As an example of this second trend, Rabat gradually re-established its relations with countries that had recognised the Polisario Front as an independent state, such as Benin (1990) and Ethiopia (1996). Finally, new efforts were made to participate in the African integration process despite Morocco's exclusion from the OAU. With France, the renewed partnership has thus evolved into a 'South–South Win-Win' partnership, as we will see later in the section on the contemporary period. In the immediate future, however, with the end of the myth of 'françafrique' and the gradual emergence of new autonomous African powers, the resolution of the Saharan case was also, more than ever, dependent on continental support.

8 Ceasefire and Peace Plan in the Aftermath of the Cold War: The Birth of Voice Diplomacy

The Saharan southern provinces—to use the national terminology—constitute, in the geopolitical representation of the Kingdom, a 'link between Morocco and its African extension'.[140] To better understand the meaning of this discourse, it must be interpreted in two ways. On the one hand, the Sahara constitutes a geographical link between Morocco and sub-Saharan Africa, without which it would not be able to legitimise its power and strategic depth to external powers; on the other hand, it is also a political link with Africa, since the recognition of the Moroccanness of Western Sahara has largely conditioned its

---

138   French Ministry of Foreign Affairs and Development, 'Morocco—Politique africaine—Entretien de M. Laurent Fabius, Ministre des affaires étrangères et du développement international, avec la radio marocaine 'Medi1'', *diplomatie.gouv.fr*, March 10, 2015.
139   See in this regard: Saidy, "La politique de défense Marocaine".
140   "Royal speech on the occasion of the 40th anniversary of the Green March", *Maroc.ma*, November 6, 2015.

diplomatic relations with many African countries. The reconfiguration of the world order at the end of the Cold War and its consequences in Morocco will further determine this last condition.

In 1991, a new chapter in Morocco's history began with the ceasefire and the peace plan proposed by the UN for the Sahara: the conflict has been seen since then as a legal dispute to be resolved by defining a legal status. The UN planned a referendum consultation with the Sahrawi tribes—taking up a solution that had already been discussed during Franco's time—by setting up MINURSO (United Nations International Mission for the Referendum in Western Sahara). The challenge was twofold: on the one hand, it was necessary to define the electorate that would participate in this referendum (and to make the parties accept the outcome of the referendum), and on the other hand, it was necessary to monitor the ceasefire between the two parties. However, from the outset the Kingdom had employed a policy of 'fait accompli': at the beginning of the 1990s, it *de facto* controlled nearly three-quarters of the territory, and from the inside, the 'pseudo-RASD' (to use the official terminology) represented only 'a puppet government supported by the enemies of the Monarchy'.[141]

No citizen could question this principle, on pain of being considered a traitor. For the rest, Hassan II's policy in the 1990s was based on his famous formula that 'everything is negotiable except the stamp and the flag'. Thus, as the Polisario Front began to lose weight due to the weakening of developing-world organisations in the aftermath of the Cold War, Hassan II set out to demonstrate that the demographic statistics in the Sahara converged towards the idea that they were indeed Moroccan citizens. In 1992, Morocco was able to organise a referendum on constitutional reform, including the vote of the Sahrawi people, without any significant protests.

For several years, Morocco managed to limit the implementation of UN plans while convincing the organisation to register new voters. For many observers, it is clear that Morocco's support from France and the United States in the UN Security Council contributed to the delay of the referendum. For others, these two countries did not do enough for Morocco, in a spirit of regional division for power purposes, while the UN was doing an impartial job due to pressure from Spain in particular. As a result, after announcing the provisional suspension of the voter identification process in 1996, due to a disagreement over the criteria, the UN proposed a provisional list of 86,383 voters in 2000.[142]

---

141 Interview with a diplomat (no. 7)—Moroccan Ministry of Foreign Affairs and Cooperation—June 2015.
142 Catherine Lalumière, "L'évolution de la situation au Sahara Occidental", European Parliament—Ad Hoc Delegation to Western Sahara, 2002.

This result had been cleared by both parties (another 170,000 voters were eligible for Morocco to include in the list but were not taken into account, under pressure from the Polisario Front). In the event that either side contested the referendum, a second solution based on autonomy was envisaged. The problem was pressing. As the 2001 UN report stated: 'Twenty-six long years have passed since the conflict began [...] During this time, a whole new generation of Sahrawi refugees has been born and raised in the Tindouf camps, while many of the first generation have died without being able to return to their homes.'[143]

The Security Council, therefore, proposed a framework agreement (only one page long) in 2000, known as the 'first Baker plan',[144] which proposed partial autonomy for the Sahara under Moroccan sovereignty.

Morocco accepted it, and the Polisario Front rejected it. In its official communiqué, the Kingdom declared its agreement in principle to 'a transfer of competencies to the local populations, taking into account the specificities of the Sahara, within the framework of the sovereignty and territorial integrity of the Kingdom',[145] while recalling its refusal to raise the idea of future independence. It wished to propose its own Autonomy Plan in the hope that it would be more acceptable to all. The UN then submitted a second Baker plan in 2004, but while the Polisario Front eventually accepted it, Morocco considered that the option envisaged did not sufficiently guarantee the sovereignty and territorial integrity of the Kingdom. The main reason given was that the plan proposed to establish a transitional period of autonomy under the authority of the monarchy, pending the Sahrawi peoples' decision to determine their status; Morocco saw this as a source of instability.[146] In the end, despite the numerous proposals for legal and institutional arrangements suggested by the UN Security Council, the conflict seemed insoluble. While Morocco did concede the idea of partial autonomy, the Polisario Front entrenched its position on self-determination.

After several setbacks, James Baker resigned. For its part, throughout this period Algeria officially denied taking part in the conflict while being actively involved. Indeed, Algeria hosted the Sahrawi refugee camps near Tindouf and their batch of political prisoners, as well as Polisario dignitaries in the capital. But above all, it helped to support the recognition of the Polisario Front as

---

143   Report of the Secretary-General on the situation in Western Sahara, Official Records, United Nations, 2001.
144   Named after the UN's special envoy to Western Sahara: James Baker.
145   "Peace Plan for Sahara", Official Portal of the Embassy of the Kingdom of Morocco, https://themoroccanembassy.com/moroccan_embassy_sahara_peace_plan.aspx.
146   "Western Sahara: Kofi Annan's Personal Envoy James Baker resigns", June 11, 2004 https://news.un.org/en/story/2004/06/10661

an independent state by its African allies and among several South American (socialist) and North European (sensitive to human rights rhetoric) countries. As a result, in the same year as Baker's resignation, 2004, South Africa officially recognised the RASD as an independent state. Nigeria reaffirmed its support for the Polisario Front in the same stride, and Kenya recognised the independent Sahrawi state the following year. Overconfident in European support, the Moroccan policy lost many battles.[147] The involvement of the major African powers thus paved the way for a third period of intensified diplomatic mobilisation to win back regimes hostile or indifferent to its position—a policy called '1 State = 1 Voice in the UN'.[148]

Therefore, the strategy pursued since the early 2000s is more specifically oriented towards the search for diplomatic recognition. The outcome of the conflict now depends on Morocco or the Polisario Front's ability to have the Sahrawi region's status recognised as either Moroccan or independent by the other states represented at the UN, and more specifically by the major powers and African states. It appears that it is no longer the referendum resulting from the legal process initiated by MINURSO that has the value of recognition but the proclaimed position of the various UN member states regarding the political status of this territory. One diplomat recognises that the settlement dynamic has moved from a 'diplomacy of resolutions to a diplomacy of votes'.[149]

Thus, Morocco engaged in a vast operation of media-covered openness: in 2004, as mentioned in the previous section, Mohammed VI created the Equity and Reconciliation Commission (following the model of the Truth and Reconciliation Commissions), which is responsible for giving a voice to the victims of the abuses committed under the Hassan II regime, including many families of Sahrawi opponents.[150] This commission aims to promote a democratic image of the country vis-à-vis its international environment as well as part of the Sahrawi population. At the same time, the state has developed and fervently defended its own Sahara Autonomy Plan,[151] which it submitted to the UN Security Council on 11 April 2007: a strategic gamble. Unlike the second Baker plan, this proposal excludes the option of future independence. To reinforce the legiti-

---

147 Carlos Fernández-Arias, "Sahara Occidental: Un ano después de Baker", *Política Exterior* 19, no. 107 (2005): 73–82.
148 Interview with a diplomat (no. 7)—Moroccan Ministry of Foreign Affairs and Cooperation—June 2015.
149 Ibid.
150 See on this subject: Susan Slyomovics, "Témoignages, écrits et silences: l'Instance Équité et Réconciliation (IER) marocaine et la réparation", trans. Hammadi Safi, *L'Année du Maghreb*, IV, (2008): 123–148.
151 A state website is dedicated to the presentation of this plan: http://plan-autonomie.com/.

macy of this plan, the monarchy created CORCAS (the Royal Advisory Council for Saharan Affairs) in Laayoune in 2006, with the aim of, as formulated in its founding speech by the monarch, 'allowing our fellow citizens to make their contribution, through concrete and practical proposals, on all issues relating to our territorial integrity and the economic, social and cultural development of the southern provinces'.[152]

More concretely, CORCAS was intended to allow the Saharawis to participate in the elaboration of the Autonomy Plan in order to respond to regional socioeconomic and cultural expectations. The conduct of parallel diplomacy was also thought out with the aim of sending emissaries to the most influential European capitals, in order to promote a good reception of the Moroccan project.[153] At the same time, the government proposed to the Polisario leader, Mohamed Abdelaziz, that he occupy the position of governor of the future autonomous region of the Sahara: a hand-holding policy that divided the Polisario Front for a short while.[154] To avoid any social and political contestation in the other regions of the Kingdom, some of which have historical pro-independence tendencies, the government simultaneously launched a vast 'advanced regionalisation' project in 2010, granting greater administrative and financial autonomy to the elected councils in the various territorial collectivities, including the Saharan provinces.[155]

From the UN perspective, this was a period of 'renewed dialogue',[156] especially since representatives of both parties, in addition to Algeria and Mauritania, agreed to meet for UN-supervised negotiations in Manhasset (a suburb of New York) in 2007. The designers of the Autonomy Plan were inspired by the configuration of the Catalan and Northern Irish autonomous regions. Thus, the text proposes that

> the people of the Sahara manage their own affairs democratically through legislative, executive and judicial bodies with exclusive competencies. They will have the financial resources necessary for the region's devel-

---

152 Full speech on the Royal Advisory Council for Saharan Affairs website: www.corcas.com.
153 Aomar Baghzouz, "Le Maghreb, le Sahara occidental et les novueaux défis de sécurité", *L'Année du Maghreb*, III, (2007): 523–546.
154 Ibid.
155 On the link between autonomy and advanced regionalisation, see Raquel Ojeda García, and Ángela Suarez Collado, "El Sáhara Occidental en el marco del nuevo proyecto de regionalización avanzada marroquí", RIPS: *Revista de Investigaciones Políticas y Sociológicas 12*, no. 2 (2013), 89–108.
156 Note on the history of MINURSO on the UN website. https://minurso.unmissions.org/background

opment in all fields and participate actively in the Kingdom's economic, social and cultural life. Finally, the State will retain its competences in the regalian domains, in particular defence, foreign relations and the constitutional and religious attributions of the King.[157]

France, the UK and the US supported the proposal in principle as a basis for negotiations. The US considered the Moroccan proposal 'serious' and 'credible'.[158] Russia has acknowledged Morocco's 'willingness to explore mutually acceptable ways out of the conflict situation',[159] while China has maintained positive neutrality towards the Kingdom. While these different powers have stated in principle that they want to support the Moroccan proposal, they have not become more involved, thus participating in the perpetuation of a status quo. On the other hand, maintaining this tension constitutes an effective lever of pressure vis-à-vis Morocco in the framework of economic negotiations (fishing agreements or agricultural agreements with Europe in particular), as we will see later in this study.

Even today, while European countries do not have a clear-cut common foreign policy on the issue, the United States, despite its 'pro-Moroccan' position,[160] does not take a clear side either: on the one hand, because US oil and gas companies have invested in Algeria, and on the other hand, because Democrats defend human rights movements in the Sahara. The 'MINURSO crisis' of 2012, triggered by the US proposal to expand the UN mission in the Sahara to include human rights, is a prime example. Although Morocco succeeded, through numerous negotiations and diplomatic offensives, in having the proposal dropped, it was warned that the human rights situation in the region would receive separate attention, which would undermine the Autonomy Plan.[161]

On the other hand, the strength of the Polisario Front lies in its ability to motivate public opinion by using the register of human rights and the right of peoples to self-determination, even though the situation of the refugees

---

157   Official presentation on the Autonomy Plan website: http://plan-autonomie.com/.
158   "Congress reiterates US support for Moroccan autonomy plan for the Sahara", http://plan-autonomie.com/5265-le-congres-reitere-lappui-des-usa-au-Moroccan-autonomy-plan-for-the-Sahara.html, accessed on August 182016.
159   "Russia welcomes Morocco's efforts to settle the Sahara conflict", CORCAS, March 2, 2007.
160   For more details on US policy towards the Western Sahara conflict, see: Yahia H. Zoubir, "Stalemate in Western Sahara: Ending International Legality", *Middle East Policy 14*, no. 4 (2007): 158–177.
161   Amnesty International, "L'Ombre de l'impunité. La torture au Maroc et au Sahara occidental", Report, 2015.

sequestered in the Algerian camps of Tindouf constitutes a humanitarian disaster. And it should be emphasised here that the Kingdom has several times offered residents of the Tindouf camps a safe return to the Moroccan regions. The Polisario Front has nevertheless managed to build up a considerable network of associations and activists, as well as being an observer member of the Socialist International. Part of its funding comes from humanitarian aid granted by European actors and NGOs, as well as aid from the former Gaddafi regime (arms in particular).[162] The movement also benefits from the support of several northern European NGOs, part of Spanish civil society,[163] and African and South American countries sensitive to the revolutionary ideology. In the United States, where the Polisario Front is less popular, Algerians defend the independence project by projecting the existence of a terrorist movement in the region.[164]

This is why the Manhasset negotiations failed after four rounds between 2007 and 2008: the Polisario Front did not envisage a solution without a referendum, while Morocco considered that it had already shown much good will and that it could not offer more than autonomy. The partition of the Sahrawi territory was not an option either. In the end, the situation remained hopeless, as the UN note states: 'Despite the persistence of divergent positions, the renewed dialogue represented the first direct negotiations between the parties to the conflict in more than seven years [...] However, none of these meetings achieved progress on substantive issues'.[165]

The Sahara issue undoubtedly constitutes a vital and 'sacred'[166] national interest for Morocco. It is a question of territorial integrity, at the same time as it constitutes a lever for citizen mobilisation. Finally, it dynamises diplomacy while being the Achilles heel of Moroccan foreign policy.

---

162   Maâti Monjib, "Kadhafi et Hassan II, des ennemis de trente ans", *Zamane.ma*, March 24, 2014.
163   See the actors present at the annual European Conference of Support and Solidarity with the Sahrawi People, http://www.eucocomadrid.org/. Accessed July 2016.
164   'The imposition of an unjust solution on the Sahrawis may well lead to the implosion of this movement and although the Polisario has never been involved in terrorist acts, a fraction of it could be tempted, out of desperation, to join one of these subversive movements and thus lead to the destabilisation of the whole region', According to a series of interviews conducted with Algerian and American officials by Yahia H. Zoubir, "Les États-Unis et L'Algérie: antagonisme, pragmatisme et coopération", *Maghreb–Machrek* 200, no. 2 (2009): 71–90.
165   Presentation of MINURSO on the UN website: http://www.un.org/fr/peacekeeping/missions/minurso/background.shtml.
166   "Royal speech on the occasion of the 4th Throne Day anniversary".

The third chronological phase of the Sahara's history, that of voice diplomacy, coincides with the modernisation of the diplomatic apparatus, several aspects of which will be discussed in the next chapter. The message conveyed by the King at the first Ambassadors' Conference also supports this connection. For the monarch, efforts to modernise diplomacy must be supported with the aim of 'being more present in this new space where our absence has long been taken advantage of by the adversaries of our territorial integrity'.[167] The preparation of new diplomatic staff also contributes to this objective. For example, during their compulsory training at the diplomatic academy, recruits are asked to draw up 'country files' in which they must pay particular attention to the relations of the studied country with Algeria, such as its position vis-à-vis the Polisario Front, but also vis-à-vis Kosovo and Taiwan, which are considered to represent similar issues.[168] More generally, new and old diplomats are obliged to defend the Moroccanness of the Sahara, whatever their field of diplomatic action or speciality. Any means are admissible as long as the goal is achieved. Ambassadors, in particular, are unanimous: the first subject on which diplomacy is or should be focused on is the Sahara issue.[169]

Thus, within the Legal Affairs and Treaties Directorate, the search for an argument justifying the Moroccan nationality of this territory takes precedence over issues concerning the delimitation of maritime waters with the Canary Islands, illegal immigration or the status of Spanish enclaves.[170] Within the European Affairs Directorate, the emphasis is placed on defending the Moroccan nationality of the Sahara in the European Parliament, as well as on gathering information on the networks of alliances and diplomatic manoeuvres of Algeria and the Polisario Front. As one diplomat confirms: 'In our directorate, we analyse the trends in the Parliament. Algeria and the Polisario have developed an influential lobby, the "Intergroup for Western Sahara". We actively monitor it.'[171] Within the Multilateral Affairs Directorate, the instruction is also to observe and try to prevent any active presence of Polisario Front members in international bodies, mainly using legal arguments.[172]

---

167   "Message of the Sovereign to HM the King's Ambassadors' Conference", *Maroc.ma—Le portail officiel du Maroc*, September 1, 2013.
168   Consultation of some 20 'Country Fact Sheets' drawn up by young diplomats. Moroccan Ministry of Foreign Affairs and Cooperation—May–June 2013.
169   According to a series of interviews with various ambassadors between and 20132015.
170   Interview with an ambassador (no. 5), Rabat, Moroccan Ministry of Foreign Affairs and Cooperation, May 2013.
171   Interview with a diplomat (no. 8), Rabat, Moroccan Ministry of Foreign Affairs and Cooperation—June 2013.
172   Interview with a diplomat (no. 11), Rabat, Moroccan Ministry of Foreign Affairs and Cooperation—June 2013.

In parallel to this laborious watch, the Kingdom has approached countries that recognise the Polisario Front as the legitimate representative of the Sahrawi population: royal visits, special envoys, the opening of embassies, signing of cooperation agreements, humanitarian projects; the approaches are diversified and interested, even with small countries. As one diplomat notes, 'Morocco has established diplomatic ties with the Pacific islands for the first time, as these countries represent a voice in the UN'.[173] Alongside opening new diplomatic representations in South American and Asian countries, one of the strategies of decision-makers is an intense lobbying policy in the United States. According to Moroccan and American press reports, $20 million was spent in this area between 2007 and 2014[174] by the Cherifian state, employing nearly nine lobbying companies.[175] Over the same period and in the same sector, by comparison, Algeria spent $2.4 million and the Polisario Front some $42,400.[176] Morocco was thus the first country on the African continent and the sixth in the world in terms of investment in lobbying in the United States during this period.[177] While it mainly uses specialised companies (such as the Moroccan American Center for Policy, MACP), certain personalities also appear as special envoys, such as Mostafa Terrab, CEO of the Office Chérifien des Phosphates (OCP), or Edward M. Gabriel, former US ambassador to Morocco. The objective is clear: to undermine the credibility of the Polisario Front. The arguments are mainly security-related: the terrorist threat in the Sahel is a source of fragility in the Sahara, which only a stable state like the Kingdom of Morocco can control. This threat has already reached the Tindouf camps, where candidates for jihad were recruited by al-Qaeda in the Islamic

---

173 Interview with a diplomat (no. 11), Rabat, Moroccan Ministry of Foreign Affairs and Cooperation—June 2013.
174 Matt Johnson, "The $20 Million Case for Morocco", *Foreign Policy*, February 26, 2014.
175 Lobbying groups approached: HL Group Partners LLC, Moroccan National Tourist Office, Moffett Group, LLC, CRAFT I Media Digita, Gerson Global Strategic Advisors LLC, LeClairRyan, A Professional Corporation, BLJ Worldwide LtD (Brown Lloyd James), The Gabriel Company, LLC, Moroccan-American Center for Policy, Inc, Western Hemisphere Strategies, LLC, The Amani Group, Dutko Worldwide, LLC, Avalanche Strategic Communications, Vision Americas L.L. v., Nurnberger & Associates, Inc. See Elena Blum and Nadia Lamlili, "Lobbying: What African countries spend in the United States", JeuneAfrique.com, May 16, 2014.
176 Yassine Majdi, "Les secrets du lobbying marocain aux Etats Unis dévoilés", *Telquel.ma*, February 27, 2014.
177 Figures for 2013. See the Foreign Influence Explorer tool created by the Sunlight Foundation, for more details on Morocco's spending in the United States, as well as other countries, at https://www.influenceexplorer.com/foreign_subdomain/index/

Maghreb (AQIM). The Polisario Front is an entity without a political project or defence capacity against Islamic terrorism. The poverty in the refugee camps, the porous borders, the structural weakness of the states in the region and the multitude of terrorist hotbeds operating in the Sahara contribute to these arguments.

The current period thus contrasts with the 1970s–1990s, when Morocco systematically broke off dialogue with countries that supported the Polisario Front. Although the Sahara issue is an obvious dividing line, many diplomats now believe that the recent turn of events on the issue has paradoxically contributed dramatically to the dynamism of foreign policy. The quest for recognition has significantly developed the Moroccan diplomatic apparatus and strengthened its relations with many states. Between 1999 and 2016, 34 countries that recognised the Polisario Front as a state officially withdrew this recognition.[178] Half of these withdrawals were declared from 2004 onwards, which tends to show that the Moroccan Autonomy Plan had a certain weight in the negotiations. However, the countries that have withdrawn this recognition are mostly small states (St Vincent and the Grenadines, Seychelles Islands, etc.) that carry little weight in international negotiations. Moreover, the idea of diplomatic recognition appears uncertain and fluctuating in this context. The examples of Mauritius, which withdrew its recognition in 2014 then retracted it in 2015, or Haiti, which declared its recognition in 2006 before rejecting its declaration in 2013, illustrate this dimension. More generally, the fact that a state does not recognise the Polisario Front as an independent republic—since it is not *de jure* or *de facto* anyway—does not mean that the state supports the Moroccan position on this territory. The recognition of the Western Sahara region as a province of southern Morocco should be declared in itself and supported through bilateral cooperation with Morocco that integrates it as part of the Kingdom.

Therefore, whether de *facto* or de *jure*, diplomatic recognition could not be considered a definitive achievement. Morocco is desperately seeking a resolution rather than prolonging the status quo, which will become infirm in the long run. Among the states that still support the statehood of the Polisario Front, there are many African countries, notably Nigeria, South Africa, Angola, Mozambique and Kenya, which are sufficiently influential to overturn the balance within the AU in favour of the exclusion of this actor if they so wish. More than voice diplomacy in the UN, it is an Africa policy that seems to be the actual outcome of the conflict. Yet it is precisely this conflict that prevents

---

178   See Appendix 5 and 5bis.

Morocco from gaining geographical and political access to Africa. The Sahara is therefore, in every respect, an essential historical and diplomatic determinant in the African orientation of Morocco's foreign policy under the reign of Mohammed VI.

CHAPTER 3

The Making of the Africa Policy: Royal Pre-eminence and Diplomatic Mobilisation

1   Introduction

To fabricate a political phenomenon means to politicise it through a number of speech acts, according to the constructivist definition. Thus, everything, or almost everything, can be politicised or depoliticised according to the electoral context and the definition of national interests: sports, health, identity, sexual relations or the incarceration of an individual. Therefore, the 'political fabrication process' is characterised by the enunciation of representations and strategies, their translation into commitments, their legitimisation, and their implementation in a decision-making system. If the making of domestic policies depends to a large extent on the type of regime in place, the making of foreign and defence policies, the rebel sisters of public policies, depends to a large extent on the type of world regime in force. Thus, they partially or entirely escape the constraints that may characterise the implementation of public policies and are most often under the direct supervision of the executive. The more politicised an object is, the less it can be kept secret.[1] This is why defence policies, in particular, are rarely the subject of a public debate like other public policies. As far as foreign policy is concerned, it can be considered that the more politicised it is, the more it will have to undergo the process of political fabrication described above, which becomes synonymous with a process of publicisation (making decisions public and legitimising them) and governmentality (through the administered involvement of a set of actors in the implementation of this policy).

In the case of Morocco, the construction of foreign policy reflects this double posture. On the one hand, it constitutes a reserved domain of the monarch, just like defence policy. It therefore reflects the King's style and the role he projects on the international scene. On the other hand, the Africa policy under the reign of Mohammed VI has been highly politicised, to the point where it has become partly subject to the process of fabrication that tends to make actions public and mobilise a set of actors via the diplomatic lever.

---

[1] Juan J. Linz, *Totalitarian and Authoritarian Regimes*, (Boulder, Colourado, Lynne Rienner Publishers, 2000).

Therefore, understanding the process of making Morocco's Africa policy comes down to identifying the monarch's style in power and analysing how the diplomatic apparatus is used for the publicisation and the governmentality of foreign policy.

2   The King's Style in Foreign Policy: A Two-Tiered Role

Morocco's new Africa policy stems from royal orientations. It can only be so, as the monarchy, since the Cherifian Sultan, has historically been at the centre of decision-making in foreign policy. The Sultan was deprived of his diplomatic prerogatives throughout the protectorate period and regained his powers in this area when he became King of Morocco on 2 March 1956. At first, the attitude of King Mohammed V favoured consultation with the Independence Party and its leaders, in terms of both domestic and foreign policy, while contributing to the popularity of the image and role of the monarchy. In a second phase, the arrival in power of Hassan II led to the institutionalisation of the monarch's leading role in foreign policy, enshrined in the first constitution drafted in 1962. Until today, this constitution has made the King the warrantor of 'the independence of the nation and the territorial integrity of the kingdom' and the 'supreme leader of the royal armed forces'. In this capacity, Hassan II appointed the prime minister and ministers, presided over the Council of Ministers, promulgated the law, and accredited ambassadors.[2] Although some rules have changed since then—the prime minister is now a member of the ruling majority party—the governmental system designed by Hassan II remains prevalent today.

The question is not 'Did the King initiate this Africa policy?' but 'How does the King view this Africa policy?' The current monarchical system, while based on the new powers acquired since independence, is very different from that of Hassan II. Is it necessary to try to understand the personality of Mohammed VI in order to understand the new political orientations that have marked his reign? The many books devoted to the rule of Mohammed VI caress the contours of his identity without piercing its mysteries, which causes frustration among readers. For example, Ignace Dalle wrote about the book by Pierre Vermeren[3] that, beyond a historical approach to the policy conducted by the King, sprinkled with some questionable judgements, 'a portrait of Mohammed VI [...]

---

2   Constitution of the Kingdom of Morocco of December 7, 1962.
3   Pierre Vermeren, *Le Maroc de Mohammed VI: la transition inachevée*, (Paris, France: la Découverte, 2011), 331.

would also have been welcome [...] Who is Mohammed VI, really? What does he want? The reader is left wanting.'[4] Does this voyeuristic appetence bring with it scientifically treatable elements? Some intentions are causal, but the psychological approach can bias the information and lack relevance. It would seem that it is first and foremost the public actions and image that Mohammed VI wishes to project, as well as his political and religious status, that form tangible elements of understanding as to the nature of royal interests that may influence the conduct of foreign policy. This book will focus on his public rather than his private persona.

The study of the new public identity of the monarchy prefigured, as early as 1999, the legal, political and social changes that followed. Indeed, the King allowed the reform of the family code (*Moudawana*) in 2004, the creation of the IER (the Equity and Reconciliation Commission, charged with examining the exactions demanded by the state under the Hassan II regime and giving a voice to the victims) the same year, the creation of the IRCAM (the Royal Institute of Amazigh Culture) in 2001 and the creation of a commission to fight against corruption in 2006. All of these reforms (this list being far from exhaustive) were invested with the royal seal. The possibility to publicise and criticise crimes committed by the government before the 1990s,[5] and to denounce political corruption or police violence, are new freedoms that indirectly contribute to legitimising the usefulness of monarchic action.

From the beginning of his reign, the King thus asserted himself by his style, expressed by a highly publicised personal involvement in social development. In addition to creating a philanthropic foundation (the Mohammed V Foundation for Solidarity), Mohammed VI initiated or inaugurated numerous social works and visited several neglected regions of the Kingdom. To implement and monitor these projects, many para-public organisations have been set up, acting in a concerted or parallel manner alongside conventional public policy. The monarch's popularity with society is truly notable. The example of the 75,000 women who had benefited from a literacy programme in mosques offering the King a transcription of the Qur'an written by all of them (at the rate of one word per person) illustrates this particular form of recognition.[6] Even critics of the regime observe the myth carried by the Cherifian style. Thus, the dissident journalist Ahmed Benchemsi, referring to the sympathetic reactions of internet

---

4   Ignace Dalle, "Pierre Vermeren. Le Maroc de Mohammed VI. La transition inachevée", *Afrique contemporaine 239*, no. 3 (2012): 154–156.
5   See on this subject: Hughes, *Le Maroc de Hassan II*; Abdallah Laroui, *Le Maroc et Hassan II: Un témoignage*, (Casablanca: Centre culturel arabe—Presses inter-universitaires, 2005), 248.
6   "75.000 Women offer an unexpected gift to King Mohammed VI", *H24info*, June 19, 2015.

users following a media appearance of the King leaning on a crutch during one of his daily political activities, acknowledges that 'Mohammed VI is, on a personal basis, extremely popular'.[7] As a result, the demands of the 'February 20th Movement' during the 'Arab Spring' were more about the governmental system than the monarchical institution.

For Jean-Noël Ferrié and Baudouin Dupret, the particularity of the Moroccan monarchy lies in its stability, the legitimacy of royal power and its capacity to reform: 'Morocco is the only country in North Africa and the Middle East to have succeeded in initiating reforms in such a profound manner that one can no longer—except in a polemical manner—simply say that it is an authoritarian country'.[8] It is for this reason that the country was soon described as the 'exception' of the Arab Spring in the press and then in official discourse. Of course, the claim of Moroccan exception is both true and false. True, because Morocco's political opening coincided with the end of the Cold War, although several more domestic events encouraged Hassan II to accept political alternation. False, because, unlike Hassan II, it was Mohammed VI's notoriety preceding the Arab revolts that consolidated this assurance. Mohammed VI was widely publicised and presented as the king of the poor, king of development, king of women, Commander of the Faithful, king of Moroccans living abroad, protector of territorial integrity, warrantor of stability and security, and defender of national interests abroad. In this context, do the monarchy's interests lie primarily in preserving its power? It appears that this dimension is almost non-existent, as power is already consolidated.

The power-seeking hypothesis is based on the assumption that the strategy of rational actors is to maximise their gains or minimise their losses (realist and liberal assumptions). In this perspective, ideology is seen as having no function other than to conceal actors' rationality. But is the principle of rationality rationally based? Does it not stem from an overly simplistic view of things? Challenging the prejudice of rationality requires distinguishing between interest and passion. The former is the result of a cold and objective calculation. The latter is the result of 'the "perception" or "representation" that decision-makers (and even more so the less informed and more emotional public opinion) have of the identity of their partners, if not the nature of the problems to be resolved'.[9] Thus, beliefs, preconceived ideas, value systems and norms shared within a society help to determine the interests of the decision-maker.

---

7 Ahmed Benchemsi, "Mohammed VI, despote malgré lui", *Pouvoirs 145*, no. 2 (2013): 19–29.
8 Baudouin Dupret and Jean-Noël Ferrié, "L 'exception' marocaine: stabilité et dialectique de la réforme", *Moyen-Orient*, no. 14 (2012).
9 Merle, *Sociologie des relations internationales*, 258.

Although the monarchy does not seem to need an ideology to exist, it is nonetheless shaped by the image that society sends back to it and which it must reflect. Its interests are not immutable but evolving.

Indeed, the monarchy is not without enemies, but the threat they represent is derisory. For example, the radical Islamist party Justice et Bienfaisance (Al 'adl Wal Ihsan), led by Sheikh Yassin until his death in 2012, refuses to recognise the legitimacy of the monarch's status as Commander of the Faithful and is clearly republican. Still, it has never been authorised to form a political party, as was the moderate Islamist party Justice et Développement, winner of the 2011 early elections.[10] This differentiation has beneficially divided the Islamists in Morocco.

Similarly, the socialist opposition is fiercely critical of the royal sanctity, privileges and wealth. Consisting mainly of non-governmental parties such as the Democratic Voice (Marxist-Leninist), the Democratic Avant-Garde Party and the United Socialist Party, the opposition makes its voice heard through trade unions or associations and, to a lesser extent, the parliament.[11] However, the Socialist Union of Popular Forces (USFP), the main governmental socialist party, has stayed away from these movements. Thus, from 2001, the USFP lost the support of the CDT (Democratic Confederation of Workers) union, and the governmental left was reduced to a mere 'opposition to the Islamist opposition'.[12] As Jean-Noël Ferrié and Baudouin Dupret note concerning the protests in 2011:

> it is not the same thing to say 'nothing is moving' as to say 'it is not yet enough'; nor is it the same thing to say 'Mubarak out!' as to say 'We want a parliamentary monarchy'. From the outset, the protesters' demands were in the realm of the socially acceptable: we don't criticise the King, and we don't criticise Islam.[13]

Other opponents, consisting of a few scattered personalities, tried to take their demands abroad. For example, the 'Red Prince' Hicham Ben Abdallah Alaoui, the King's cousin and third in the order of succession to the throne, has pub-

---

10 Khadija Mohsen-Finan and Malika Zeghal, "Opposition islamiste et pouvoir monarchique au Maroc", *Revue française de science politique 56*, no. 1 (2006): 79–119.
11 Myriam Catusse, "Au-delà de 'l'opposition à sa Majesté': mobilisations, contestations et conflits politiques au Maroc", *Pouvoirs 145*, no. 2 (2013): 31–46.
12 Abderrahim El Maslouhi, "La gauche marocaine, défenseure du trône. Sur les métamorphoses d'une opposition institutionnelle", *L'Année du Maghreb*, v, (2009): 37–58.
13 Dupret and Ferrié, "Maroc: le 'printemps arabe' de la monarchie".

lished numerous critical writings for Grasset,[14] in the magazine *Pouvoirs*[15] and in *Le Monde Diplomatique*[16] from Stanford University, where he is an associate researcher. However, he remains attached to his lineage: for the Prince, the election of a constituent assembly to revise the constitution is 'unrealistic and would mean the end of the regime'. He thus believed that the monarchy should be maintained as 'an institution of arbitration and the symbol of the unity of the nation'.[17]

The last opponents, finally, crystallised around a few self-proclaimed imams and their fatwas, or journalists from Casablanca and Paris, but they did not constitute an organised and sufficiently influential or threatening force. This situation is, therefore, in no way comparable to that of Hassan II, who was targeted by two military coups (1971, 1972) and an attempted coup by the revolutionary left (1973). While the act of opposition under Hassan II was synonymous with liquidation,[18] the act of opposition under Mohammed VI is synonymous with demands. Moreover, during the Hassanian period, opposition to the King's foreign policy was more an expression of global opposition to the monarchy than an expression of opposition to a particular decision or policy direction.[19]

At the same time, Mohammed VI cultivates an empathetic approach to the people in his speeches. Thus, he declares: 'Everything you experience concerns me: what affects you also affects me, and what brings you happiness also brings me joy. What worries you is always at the top of my list of concerns.'[20] By claiming the role of arbiter of public and private disputes, the monarch thus replaces the state while simultaneously distancing himself from it. In particular, the act of pardon plays a fundamental role in this process. The amnesty of political prisoners (Islamists, journalists, activists) after their conviction by the state constitutes a lever through which the monarch affirms his moderation vis-à-vis legal practices aimed at protecting his sovereignty. The end of the exile of former political opponents such as Abraham Serfaty also illustrates this

---

14   Moulay Hicham el Alaoui, *Journal d'un prince banni : Demain, le Maroc*, (Paris: Grasset, 2014), 368.
15   Hicham Ben Abdallah El Alaoui, "L'autre Maroc", *Pouvoirs 145*, no. 2 (2013)–: 59–69.
16   Hicham Ben Abdallah El Alaoui, "Le 'printemps arabe' n'a pas dit son dernier mot", *Le Monde diplomatique 719*, no. 2 (2014): 19–19.
17   See the interview by Jean-Michel Demetz and Dominique Lagarde, "Moulay Hicham: 'La solution au Maroc: une monarchie réformée'", *L'Express*, May 15, 2011.
18   Maslouhi, "La gauche marocaine, défenseure du trône. Sur les métamorphoses d'une opposition institutionnelle".
19   Benjelloun, *Visages de la diplomatie marocaine depuis 1844*, 193.
20   "Royal speech on the occasion of the 16th Throne Day anniversary", *Maroc.ma*, July 30, 2015.

trend. Similarly, communication plays an important role. The King's speeches are increasingly critical of leaders and officials for their lack of professionalism in implementing the reforms he has initiated.

It can be observed that as the development of the media has made domestic differences more visible, the construction of the symbolic power[21] of the monarchy—and consequently of its interests—is part of a process of absorption and fusion of cultural and political heterogeneity, to strengthen its role as arbiter. This is a process the monarchical apparatus is becoming more aware of, as illustrated by this statement: 'Our doctrine for the exercise of power consists essentially in serving the citizen, sanctifying his identity, preserving his dignity and being constructively receptive to his legitimate aspirations.'[22] The sanctification of identity is a crucial issue at a time when the definition of national identity, as we will see later, constitutes a strategic bet in the preservation of sovereignty and the survival of the Moroccan state within the international system.

This attitude broadens the potential of the sovereign's symbolic power beyond his traditional fields, stemming from his Cherifian descent (the prophet's family) and his religious status as Commander of the Faithful (Amîr Al Mu'minîne), to whom the people, as well as some transnational religious brotherhoods, pledge allegiance (through the Bey'a ceremony[23]). The symbolic power of the King will also have to reside in his capacity to take on roles that are sometimes difficult to reconcile: king of the poor and defender of economic liberation, Commander of the Faithful and defender of religious tolerance, supporter of women's rights and warrantor of traditions, 'proximity monarchy' and parliamentary monarchy.

This is a dimension which the government also prides itself on when it claims the identity of a citizen's monarchy.[24] In short, its symbolic power lies

---

21   The expression is understood here in the Bourdieusian sense: 'Symbolic power is a power that can make itself recognised, to obtain recognition; that is to say, a power (economic, political, cultural or other) that has the power to make itself known in its truth of power, of violence and arbitrariness. The proper effectiveness of this power is exercised not in the order of physical force, but in the order of the sense of knowledge. For example, the nobleman, as the Latin says, is a *nobilis*, a "known" man, "Recognised"'. Pierre Bourdieu, *Interventions, 1961–2001: science sociale & action politique*, (Marseille, Agone, Contre-feux, 2002), 173–174. See also: Pierre Bourdien, "Sur le pouvoir symbolique", *Annales. Histoire, Sciences Sociales 32*, no. 3 (1977): 405–411.
22   Royal speech on the occasion of the 16th anniversary of the Throne Day.
23   Ceremony of allegiance to the King.
24   'While remaining attached to the specificity that distinguishes the Moroccan Monarchy in its essential features, namely its religious and constitutional legitimacy, its popular fibre and its historical patriotism, We have raised it to the rank of citizen Monarchy, through

in its ability to represent a heterogeneous nation. This is initially a function of the King's inclusive religious status: as a spiritual leader, he symbolically stands above the conflicts that divide the nation while embodying it in its own identity and when confronted with an external threat.[25]

Therefore, because the style of King Mohammed VI is different from that of his father, diplomacy has been transformed. Consequently, it appears that to elucidate the nature of Mohammed VI's foreign policy orientations, other factors must be taken into account, going beyond the principle of a simple quest for power, as this has already been consolidated. However, style is a difficult concept to define, as everyone has their vision of it. Thus, determining a 'good style' or a 'bad style' is as tricky as judging taste. For Kant,[26] taste is the faculty of judging the beautiful, but carries with it the apparent contradiction of being both universal and subjective. One recognises someone who has taste while admitting that everyone has their own taste. We can draw a parallel here with style: we can know someone has style while admitting that everyone has their own style.

Nevertheless, it is possible to determine what constitutes style, although several distinctions must be made here. In the artistic field, as in the political field, style can be spontaneous or worked out, it can be personal or that of a group, and it can reside in a coherent and recognisable repetition (one will then recognise the belonging of a touch or a modus operandi) or, conversely, in unpredictability or in the fact of claiming an incoherent 'non-style' (which in this case becomes a style in itself). Among political scientists, style is often used to define the style of a state as a group in order to understand foreign policy orientations. Stanley Hoffmann, for example, in 1968, talks about the 'national style'[27] of the United States, determined by a set of historical, geopolitical and ideological representations.

In the same vein, the French political scientist Marie-Christine Kessler defines style as 'the use of standardised ways of doing things that characterise the processes of forming and implementing public policies in different political systems'.[28] It would be difficult to apply such definitions in the Moroccan

---

the democratic progress achieved, the action carried out in the field of development and the work of mobilisation and proximity carried out on the ground'. "Royal speech on the occasion of the Throne Day's 16th anniversary of the Throne Day".

25   Abdessamad Belhaj, "L'usage politique de l'islam: l'universel au service d'un État. Le cas du Maroc", *Recherches sociologiques et anthropologiques 37*, no. 2 (2007): 121–139.
26   Immanuel Kant, *Critique de la faculté de juger*, (Paris, Flammarion, 2015 (1790)).
27   Stanley Hoffmann, *Gulliver empêtré: essai sur la politique étrangère des États-Unis*, (Paris, Éditions du Seuil, 1971).
28   Marie-Christine Kessler, "La politique étrangère comme politique publique", in *Politique*

case, as they approach style as that of a historical group and not that of an individual in a given period. However, it is clear that Morocco's foreign policy style corresponds to the style of the ruling monarch: first, because of the centralised nature of the decision-making system, and second, because the current Moroccan monarchy has made style an identity of action. Hassan II said in one of his interviews about the education of his son Mohammed VI:

> I hope he will have a good career. I spend my time telling him one thing, because it is not easy to succeed to Mohammed V. I spend my time repeating Pascal's phrase: 'style is man'. I tell him: I wouldn't have deviated from what my father would have done—may God rest his soul—but I would have done it my way. By trying to mimic my father—because I would have mimicked him, I wouldn't have imitated him because he had his own style—I would undoubtedly have missed everything—I apologise for the term. What is important is the goal and the educational and virtuous way, but the style is the man.[29]

Mohammed VI thus has his own style, which finds its coherence in reproducing this inclusive function mentioned above within several areas. This attitude facilitates the embodiment of these different roles projected by society while simultaneously allowing him to contribute to their formulation and orientation. It can thus be said that the King defends roles rather than interests. One of the consequences of this practice is that it consolidates the interdependence between domestic and foreign policy: there is a close concordance between the internal role of the monarch and his diplomatic choices, the most important of which are summarised in Table 3.1.

First, the function of the 'king of the poor', as attributed by the press, is illustrated by the mediation of the monarch's presence on all development fronts. The King's distribution of foodstuffs to poor people during the month of Ramadan, his visits to hospitals and prisons, as well as his direct contact with the sick and prisoners, and, more generally, the media coverage of the inauguration of all the development projects implemented under his leadership, are convincing examples of this dynamic. Abroad, the 'king of the poor' behaves in the same way: the cancellation of the debts of the Least Developed Countries to Morocco, the construction and inauguration of a rural hospital in Niger, devel-

---

 étrangère: nouveaux regards, ed. Frédéric Charillon, (Paris: Presses de Sciences Po, 2002), 174.
29 See the video of the interview on the following link: https://www.youtube.com/watch?v=DyYN4-yJMO0

TABLE 3.1   Internal and external roles of the King

Mohammed VI—internal role	Mohammed VI—external role
King of the poor	Development of South–South cooperation; humanitarian initiatives in the Least Developed Countries
Commander of the Faithful	Defending a Moroccan Islam on the international stage; chairing the Al Quds Committee; financing transnational religious brotherhoods; training foreign imams
Entrepreneurial king	Promoting economic diplomacy
Warrantor of the nation's traditions	Leading the Moroccan community abroad (MRE) through institutions specially dedicated to culture
Defender of territorial integrity	Supervision of all high-level international negotiations related to the Sahara issue

opment cooperation with Hawaii,[30] development aid in the Caribbean and the visibility of the monarch on construction sites in West Africa are all marks of the personal involvement of the sovereign in this field, as well as revealing the astonishing continuity of the Cherifian style in the conception and mediatisation of his political actions on a domestic as well as on an external scale.

The function of Commander of the Faithful is also characteristic of this extension of roles. Internally, the status of the monarch allows him to control the body of ulemas, interpret religious texts and instigate legal reforms linked to Muslim law, and allows a real ritualisation of his symbolic power. The Bey'a ceremony (allegiance to the Commander of the Faithful), which takes place yearly at the Royal Palace, is the most representative illustration of this ritual aspect. This ceremony gathers every year the ulemas, the government, the parliament and the dignitaries around the court, dressed in traditional clothes, singing the Sultan's praises and kissing the King's hand—all symbolic relics of

---

30   To the point that the State of Hawaii, after instituting a national day dedicated to Morocco, "Morocco Appreciation Day", signed in 2013 the stablishment of an annual week exclusively dedicated to Mohammed VI, named *'His Majesty King Mohammed VI Week in Hawaii'* and held each year from 28 November to 2 December. Driss Guerraoui, "'His Majesty King Mohammed VI Week in Hawaii' in book form', *Quid.ma*, July 28, 2015. See also official documents at: http://www.morocco-in-hawaii.com/governors_proclamation_2005.htm.

the Cherifian Empire. This religious function also appears in the conduct of foreign policy, in its both institutional and ritual aspects. The institutionalisation of the secular links between the King and the transnational Sufi brotherhoods, which are very active in the Sahel region, as well as the inauguration of a policy of training foreign imams in Moroccan Islam since 2012, are convincing examples of this trend. On the ritual level, the prayers performed by Mohammed VI in the mosques of foreign countries, such as Mali, mirror the regular prayers performed in Morocco. The same is true of the gifting of Qur'ans and other donations to African religious communities.

Moreover, the economic liberalisation of the country, whose consequences for the emergence of Morocco will be discussed later, is the work of the monarchy. Thanks to the systemic transformations and the evolution of international norms since the end of the Cold War, Mohammed VI embodies the economic liberalisation initiated by his father. As such, the King is also the head of a royal holding composed of various banking, financial, mining and agricultural firms.

This entrepreneurial fibre of the monarch is also expressed in his domestic policy management. The King governs as much as he reigns, to the extent that the Kingdom is referred to as an 'executive monarchy',[31] an 'entrepreneurial monarchy' or a 'governing monarchy',[32] all of which illustrate the maintenance of the royal prerogatives inherited from Hassan II as well as his strong involvement in the management of the country's affairs. This managerial style influences government officials and is reflected in the management of public policies, as we shall see with the diplomatic apparatus. On the external level, the entrepreneurial style of the monarch is characterised by the development of an economic diplomacy combining the action of the Ministry of Foreign Affairs and that of private companies. The presence of royal companies abroad forms, in this process, a 'guide' to the countries towards which diplomacy should be directed.

Finally, according to the old constitution and the new constitution of 2011, the King represents the state and is the symbol of the unity of the nation. He is, more broadly, the warrantor of the nation's traditions. This means that he represents the state politically and diplomatically, but he also represents, in the words of Mohammed VI, 'the Moroccan identity'—an aspect I develop in more detail below.

---

[31] Thierry Desrues and Said Kirhlani, "Dix ans de monarchie exécutive et citoyenne: élections, partis politiques et défiance démocratique", *L'Année du Maghreb VI*, (2010): 319–354.

[32] Omar Bendourou, "La consécration de la monarchie gouvernante", *L'Année du Maghreb VIII*, (2012): 391–404.

3   Foreign Affairs: A 'Ministry of Sovereignty'

In order to ensure the defence of these roles, the monarchy is at the heart of the foreign policy decision-making process. If the King is to embody the nation, the image he reflects in the international environment must enhance the country's image. The Ministry of Foreign Affairs has therefore been retained as a 'ministry of sovereignty'. This status is illustrated by the appointment of an independent minister who is not part of the opposition. The expression 'ministry of sovereignty', echoing that of the 'reserved domain' in France, appeared in Morocco immediately after independence, in the very nature of the 1962 constitution[33] drafted under Hassan II, and was reinforced in practice at the time of the changeover.

The Royal Cabinet had then opened several ministries to opposition parties, except for the Prime Minister's Office, the Interior (which has included the Secretariat of Defence and Security since the abolition of the Ministry of Defence by the King in 1972), Foreign Affairs and Justice, which implicitly became ministries of sovereignty.[34] Even when, in 1998, Aberrahmane Youssoufi became the prime minister from an opposition party, this appointment was part of a royal strategy to include the opposition, which reciprocally agreed to keep the principle of sovereignty ministries. Youssoufi said: 'When I was appointed by H.M. the King, he told me to suggest the list of ministers while confiding in me that he did not want to change the holders of three ministries that were in charge of certain important issues. I was in complete agreement. This is what happened in February 1998.'[35] Thus, alongside the Interior (including defence), Justice and Islamic Affairs, Foreign Affairs has become, since 1962, a ministry of sovereignty.

While the new constitution resulting from the Arab Spring opened, for the first time and for a short time, the possibility for the winning party to lead this ministry, the diplomatic apparatus has not been invested in by the new ruling party. Since 2012, three ministers of Foreign Affairs have succeeded each other at the head of this institution: Saad Eddine Al Othmani (from a left-wing Islamist party with a majority in the elections, the Justice and Development Party/PJD) until 2013, then Salaheddine Mezouar (from the liberal centre party, the National Rally of Independents/RNI) and finally Nasser Bourita (a

---

33   See in this regard: Sehimi, "L'influence gaullienne sur la constitution marocaine".
34   Mohamed Benkhalloul, "La fin des ministères de souveraineté?", *La vie eco*, November 28, 2011.
35   Interview with Abderrahmane Youssoufi, in "Les ministres de souveraineté", *Aujourdhui le Maroc*, August 20, 2002.

career diplomat with no party affiliation) since 2017. These ministerial reshuffles (partly due to the withdrawal of the Istiqlal Party, in power since independence, from the government coalition) raise the nuance of this unprecedented experience. In this respect, the decision-making process of Moroccan foreign policy has shown the same continuity since the nineteenth century: the Sultan or King traditionally defines the Kingdom's interests, assisted by his advisors, and appoints the ambassadors in charge of negotiations.[36] What Thérèse Benjelloun observed in 1990, we still observe today: 'diplomacy remains the work of the head of state, according to the spirit of the old Makhzenian structure, brought back into the democratic fashion of the 20th century'.[37] The scope of the King's control over foreign policy must, however, be contrasted with the fact that only specific important issues are concerned. As this former advisor to Hassan II reminds us: 'Foreign Affairs and the Sahara are indeed the reserved domain of the Monarch. But the King only determines the main orientations of our policy. Implementation is the responsibility of the state apparatus, and in particular of our diplomacy.'[38]

Therefore, to limit the effects of mismanagement by the diplomatic apparatus and to circumvent the new democratic representation resulting from the Arab Spring, the Palace has strengthened its group of foreign affairs experts within the Royal Cabinet: Taieb Fassi Fihri, former Minister of Foreign Affairs (from 2002 until the Arab Spring in 2012) became the King's advisor in this area. Youssef Amrani, former Minister Delegate to the Minister of Foreign Affairs, was appointed 'Royal Cabinet Officer' for several years. Since 1955 when it was created, the Royal Cabinet has generally grown a lot. During the reign of Hassan II, the Royal Cabinet was used to supervise the activities of the government, but it consisted only of a few advisors with an extremely limited role.[39] Under the reign of Mohammed VI, the Cabinet has become resolutely professional. If its functioning remains discreet, the list of its members, recruited by *dahir* (royal decree), is public: in addition to a dozen special advisors to the King, there are about 20 officers and a hundred senior collaborators. Each member is in charge of one or more files considered strategic: Mohamed Rochdi Chraibi, former Private Secretary to the King, has been the director since 2000; Fouad Ali El Himma, former Minister of the Interior and close friend of the King, became

---

36 Benjelloun, "*Visages de la diplomatie marocaine depuis 1844*", 195.
37 Ibid.
38 A.R. Guédira, Interview in Jeune Afrique, no. 994, January 23, 1980, Quoted in: Sehimi, "L'influence gaullienne sur la constitution marocaine".
39 John Waterbury, *Le commandeur des croyants: la monarchie marocaine et son élite*, (Presses Universitaires de France, 1975).

an advisor in charge of domestic policy in 2011; Zoulikha Nasri (the only female advisor, who died in December 2015) was entrusted with the promotion of the Mohammed VI Foundation for Solidarity as well as the development of the solar energy park and the high-speed train; and Yassir Zenagui was responsible for the development of tourism, Omar Azziman, former Minister of Justice, the file of the regionalisation of the Moroccan territory, and Karim Bouzida public relations and communication of the Palace since the retirement of Chakib Laaroussi in 2014.

In the case of Foreign Affairs, the recruitment of advisor Taieb Fassi Fihri was intended, among other things, to pursue the monarchical policy on the Sahara issue. The former minister played an essential role in the negotiations for the withdrawal of the US proposal to extend the mandate of MINURSO to human rights in May 2013. This proposal was at the origin of a crisis between Morocco and the United States, the solutions of which were discussed behind closed doors at the Royal Palace in Fez, effectively sidelining the Minister of Foreign Affairs (who tried in vain to set up his crisis unit within the Ministry[40]). Thus, when Hillary Clinton visited Morocco, she was first received by Taieb Fassi Fihri before being received by Foreign Minister Saad Eddine al Othmani.[41] The collaboration of this special envoy of the King working within a 'diplomatic cell' exclusively dependent on the head of state, and which is superimposed on the authority of the Minister of Foreign Affairs, perfectly illustrates this tendency to centralise action in the hands of the monarchy.

More generally, the circle of foreign policy advisors is made up of former ambassadors or ministers, such as El Mostapha Sahel[42] (former Moroccan ambassador to France and the United Nations, former Minister of the Interior, who died in 2012), or Omar Kabbaj (former member of the board of directors of the World Bank and the IMF and then director of the African Development Bank). The latter is more notable for having become the 'Africa advisor' of the Palace.[43]

From the Cabinet's point of view, the government is not sufficiently well equipped to manage the country's strategic affairs on its own.[44] From the point

---

40 Observations during my observation fieldwork at the Ministry of Foreign Affairs during the same period.
41 Driss Bennani, "Enquête. Voyage au cœur de la diplomatie marocaine", *Telquel*, March 28, 2012.
42 Réda Mouhsine, "El Mostafa Sahel. Adieu conciglieri!", *Telquel.ma*, October 17, 2012.
43 Fahd Iraqi, "Omar Kabbaj: le conseiller Afrique de Mohammed VI", *Jeune Afrique*, June 21, 2016.
44 "Morocco: Fassi Fihri, the return", JeuneAfrique.com, May 3, 2013.

of view of the members of the government, the support of the Cabinet is indispensable. Mohammed VI's style is truly entrepreneurial: he guides, inspects and encourages if necessary. He defines the significant diplomacy orientations in his speeches and during official meetings with diplomats. The Royal Cabinet agrees on strategies directly with the King, sometimes including ministries that also have to interpret the content of royal speeches to formulate their own roadmaps. The monarch's speeches, letters and official messages are numerous and thus constitute the primary source of guidance: a body of strategic foreign policy texts.[45]

Furthermore, if the monarchy is not satisfied with the effectiveness of the Ministry, it can sanction those responsible in a speech, following which the Ministry will have to take the necessary measures. The analysis of these discursive interactions between the King and the Ministry and the resulting policies consistently reveal this dynamic. This was the case, for example, with the King's admonition to the consular body in the Throne Speech, in 2015, in which he stated:

> We, therefore, draw the attention of the Minister of Foreign Affairs to the need to work with all the necessary firmness to put an end to the dysfunctions and other problems experienced by certain consulates. On the one hand, anyone who has been found guilty of negligence, disregard for the interests of community members, or ill-treatment of them must be removed from office. On the other hand, care must be taken to select Consuls from among those who meet the requisite conditions of competence, responsibility and dedication to the service of our children abroad.[46]

To this, the minister replied a few days later at a press conference:

> In application of the high royal instructions, the Ministry of Foreign Affairs and Cooperation has taken immediate and urgent measures and others programmed in the short term: these measures concern human resources, interaction with the members of the Moroccan community residing abroad and the improvement of the quality of consular services [...] The Ministry foresees heavy and immediate administrative sanctions.[47]

---

45   See Appendix 2—The King's speeches: statistics.
46   "Royal speech on the occasion of the 16th Throne Day anniversary".
47   "Mezouar announces a large movement in the consular corps concerning about 70% of the consulates", Video, *Medi1TV*, August 6, 2015.

These measures included the dismissal of nearly 30 consuls. This example shows how the royal discourse is a 'high instruction' in contrast to traditional political discourse. The Ministry had to subordinate the conduct of its policy to the consideration of royal orders.

In addition to guidance and inspection, the executive style of the monarchy is also expressed through the diplomatic action of the head of state during official visits abroad. The King's official trips have an essential function in Moroccan diplomacy: on each trip, the King is accompanied by his Cabinet, a ministerial delegation, generals, and businesspeople. The visit usually ends with the signing of many cooperation agreements in fields as diverse as the economy, finance, telecommunications, transport, education, scientific research, health, buildings, mines, etc. In 20 years of reign, Mohammed VI and his Cabinet have made more than a hundred such visits abroad, leading to the signing of countless cooperation agreements.[48] This policy has aroused the interest of Moroccan businesspeople in foreign countries, contributed to bringing together the diplomatic body of representatives of other sectors (health, economy, education, etc.) and reassured the most reluctant diplomats to transfer to countries of the South.

The monarchy, thus, has a decisive influence on the conduct of foreign policy. Partisan wills are at odds with a politically organised Royal Cabinet. The royal discourse is the unquestionable frame of reference for diplomatic policy and must not be refuted. There are, however, objectives that are described as the 'higher interests of the nation'.[49] As defined by the monarchy, these interests are 'sovereignty', 'territorial integrity' and the 'society project'. The sovereignty of the King and the state are merged into a single prism and are therefore linked to the centrality of monarchical power, as presented above. Territorial integrity refers to the claim to the Spanish enclaves in Morocco, the definition of territorial waters on the Atlantic coast and, above all, the international recognition of the Moroccan identity of the Sahara. Finally, as I shall examine later, the social project crystallises around the Kingdom's emergence policy.

The pursuit of these higher interests, defined in a context of political transition, has led to the opening up of Morocco's foreign policy, illustrated by the consolidation of diplomatic ties with the European Union and the United States, the development of South–South cooperation (Latin America, Africa,

---

48 See Appendix 1 and Appendix 1bis—Official visits of Mohammed VI abroad.
49 'If our country's domestic policy is essentially intended to serve the citizen, its foreign policy is intended to serve the higher interests of the nation'. "Royal speech on the occasion of the 16th anniversary of the Throne Day".

Asia), the growing representation within international and regional organisations, the search for new non-Western allies, and the extension of diplomatic action into new areas (cultural, economic etc.).

The evolution of Morocco's foreign policy also reflects the course of systemic transformations in post-bipolar Africa. On the one hand, like the rest of the continent, its path seems to be conditioned by the influence of international norms and the pressure of foreign powers. On the other hand, its structural and economic development continuously supports the stability of its institutions and the consolidation of its diplomacy: emergence seems to be within reach, an objective for which the monarchy has launched an ambitious programme.

4 Modernisation and Professionalisation of the Diplomatic Apparatus at the Service of an African Strategy

Since Morocco's accession to international sovereignty in 1956, the progressive opening of Moroccan embassies abroad has accompanied the building of the modern state. However, they were not the first manifestations of Makhzenian diplomacy. Over the course of the successive sultanic empires that reigned in Morocco since AD 789, several emissaries of the state were sent abroad on non-permanent missions.[50] Although few in number, they were mostly close to the Sultan and enjoyed prestigious status. They represented the figure of the classical ambassador, whom Marie-Christine Kessler describes as a figure of the 'international society of sovereign states',[51] as opposed to a modern world without sovereignty.[52] The birth of a modern state in Morocco thus reinforced the institutionalisation of the ambassador's function and its contribution to the decision-making system. The quantitative study conducted by Augustin Kontchou on the African diplomatic network from 1960 to 1970 reveals, through a calculation of the number of diplomatic representations received and sent, that Morocco was already among the top five diplomatic powers on the continent at that time.[53] However, no sooner had the diplomat's status been rede-

[50] See in particular: Benjelloun, *Visages de la diplomatie marocaine depuis 1844*; Mohammed Nabil Mouline, *Le califat imaginaire d'Ahmad al-Mansûr légitimité, pouvoir et diplomatie au Maroc*, (Paris: Presses Universitaires de France, 2008) 1 vol. (500 p.).; Germain Ayache, *Études d'histoire marocaine*, (Rabat, Morocco: SMER, 1979).

[51] Marie-Christine Kessler, *Les ambassadeurs*, (Paris: Les Presses de Sciences Po, 2012), 11.

[52] Bertrand Badie, *Un monde sans souveraineté, les états entre ruse et responsabilité*, (Fayard, 1999).

[53] Augustin Kontchou Kouomegni, *Le Système diplomatique africain: bilan et tendances de la première décennie*, (Paris, France: A. Pedone, 1977).

fined than their function was called into question. As Marie-Christine Kessler puts it, 'globalisation has created a theatre so vast that ambassadors often appear as sidekicks. This raises questions about the purpose of the ambassador's "profession": has it not withered away with the state? All that remains is a title of honour, the residual symbol of a profession in the process of disappearing.'[54] Thus, post-bipolar Morocco was faced with a double challenge: the need to project itself beyond its regional environment to ensure its recognition as an independent power was matched by the need to rethink the instruments of its diplomacy.

The King's speech at the 1st Ambassadors' Conference in 2013 reveals his awareness of this new configuration. While admitting the thesis of a 'new world order' marked by 'the entry on the scene of new actors such as international NGOs and multinational firms, as well as the diversification of global decision-making centres', the monarch emphasised the need to diversify the ambassador's fields of action and called for more 'professionalism' within the diplomatic body. He assigned ambassadors the role of 'soldiers'[55] at the service of the nation's interests, thus expressing the Aronian principle of a symbolic concordance between the soldier and the diplomat.[56] This discourse reflects the new role assigned to the diplomatic apparatus and the ambition of its modernisation. However, the specific nature of the Ministry of Foreign Affairs as a ministry of sovereignty meant that this approach was fraught with contradictions. The modernisation of the Moroccan diplomatic apparatus occurs in a context where all public institutions are subject to reforms. Examples include the definition of a 'new concept of authority', the territorialisation of public policies, and the integration and promotion of information and communication technologies within ministries.[57] These reforms began following the political opening allowed by the 'Alternance' in 1998 before being definitively introduced under the reign of Mohammed VI. As Jean-Noël Ferrié notes: 'The reforming action is taken over by the Monarchy, from the reign of Mohammed VI. This action certainly has legitimising effects, but these effects are based on

---

54   Kessler, *Les ambassadeurs*, 13.
55   "Message of the Sovereign to the 1st Ambassadors Conference of HM the King".
56   According to Raymond Aron: 'Inter-state relations are expressed in and through specific conducts, those of the characters I will call symbolic, the diplomat and the soldier. Two men, and only two, act fully not as any members, but as representatives of the communities to which they belong: the ambassador in the exercise of his functions is the political unit in whose name he speaks; the soldier on the battlefield is the political unit in whose name he gives death to his fellow man'. Aron, *Paix et guerre entre les nations*, 17.
57   For a more specific approach to the internal reforms undertaken by Morocco, see Centre for International Studies (ed.), *A decade of reforms in Morocco*.

effective policies. Firstly, it is a question of perfecting the political defusing launched by the changeover.'[58]

This political defusing has contributed significantly to the autonomisation of public institutions in relation to the monarchy. The Ministry of Foreign Affairs recognises 'the active role played by civil societies as a form of effective and fundamental influence in the decision-making process'.[59] The King promotes 'the intervention of new actors in diplomatic action' and underlines the importance of preventive diplomacy within this new mechanism.[60] These actors include local collectivities, the parliament, economic actors, non-governmental organisations and private personalities (artists, sportspeople, etc.). The resulting sectorisation of the Ministry's budget has led to the emergence of parallel diplomacies (economic,[61] parliamentary,[62] religious[63] and public[64]) whose role is to contribute to the promotion of national interests abroad. In addition to a broadening of the actors who represent Moroccan diplomacy, a political opening is taking place within the Ministry. The modernisation of the administrative apparatus started in 1995, with the definition of the different directorates and services of the Ministry, as well as their attributions.[65] The interest of the opposition parties—now in power thanks to the changeover—as well as that of part of civil society in the transparency and efficiency of foreign policy, led to media inquiries about the state of corruption in embassies. In 1999, for example, *Le Journal* published the results of a controversial investigation into corruption in the Moroccan embassy in Washington. The case led to the conviction of the two journalists, Ali Amar and Aboubaker

---

[58] Jean-Noël Ferrié, "Dispositifs autoritaires et changements politiques. Les cas de l'Égypte et du Maroc", *International Journal of Comparative Politics* 19, no. 4 (2013): 93–110.

[59] Ministry of Foreign Affairs and Cooperation, *Presentation on the draft sectoral budget of the Ministry of Foreign Affairs and Cooperation*, November 5, 2015.

[60] "Royal message to the participants of the symposium organised in Rabat on the occasion of the celebration of the National Day of Moroccan Diplomacy", *Maroc.ma—Le portail officiel du Maroc*, April 28, 2000.

[61] See in this regard: Amine Dafir, "La diplomatie économique marocaine en Afrique subsaharienne: réalités et enjeux", *Géoéconomie 63*, no. 4 (2013): 73–83.

[62] The objectives of parliamentary diplomacy, the agenda and the diplomatic activities of the House of Representatives are presented on the official website: http://www.chambredesrepresentants.ma/.

[63] Belhaj, *La dimension islamique dans la politique étrangère du Maroc*.

[64] Ismaïl Regragui, *La diplomatie publique marocaine une stratégie de marque religieuse?* (Paris: l'Harmattan, 2013), Vol. 1.

[65] Ministry of Public Service and Modernisation of the Administration, *Decree on the attributions of the Minister of Foreign Affairs and Cooperation and the organisation of the Ministry of Foreign Affairs and Cooperation*, Decree no. 2-13-253 of 11 Shaaban 1434, June 20, 2013.

Jamaï. However, it introduced new terms to the debate on the democratisation of institutions. This debate has also spread within the diplomatic body. Thus, a white paper on foreign policy (which criticised, among other things, the new appointment of ambassador to Washington Mohamed Benaïssa as Minister of Foreign Affairs) was reportedly circulated to a dozen high-ranking ambassadors in 2002.[66]

The issue of democratisation of foreign policy as a basis for its professionalisation is now a matter of public debate. The royal speech of 2002, evoking the idea of a reform of the diplomatic apparatus, constituted the first response to this general discontent:

> We have given Our High Directives so that our diplomacy endeavours take advantage, judiciously and optimally, of the democratic evolution that our country is undergoing [...] We have, in this respect, given Our High Instructions to ensure the upgrading, the modernisation and the redeployment of our diplomatic tool. The approach envisaged to carry out this reform must concern both the structures of the Ministry of Foreign Affairs and Cooperation, its mission of incitement, coordination and monitoring, as well as the activities and working methods of our diplomatic representations and consular offices.[67]

This discourse is part of an almost neo-institutional vision of public management. It places foreign policy in the perspective of 'new governance' as formulated by the UN within the framework of Agenda 21,[68] which promotes users' participation in public decision-making. In Morocco, Agenda 21 was mainly applied to land use policies, but the influence of this process can be found in other sectors.

More generally, the reform of the diplomatic apparatus is part of the New Public Management (NPM) perspective. Promoted by the European Union, this concept refers to the practice by the public sector of management techniques borrowed from the private sector. For Georges A. Larbi,[69] there are several reasons for this trend, including the influence of neoliberal ideas in the 1970s,

---

[66] Fernández-Molina, *La política exterior de Marruecos en el reinado Mohamed VI (1999–2008)*.

[67] "Speech by HM King Mohammed VI on the occasion of the 49th anniversary of the Revolution of the King and the People", *Maroc.ma—Le portail officiel du Maroc*, August 2002.

[68] For more information on the Agenda's programme in Morocco, see the UN website at: https://staging.unhabitat.org/content.asp?cid=650&catid=219&typeid=13

[69] George A. Larbi, "The New Public Management and Crisis States", *Geneva: United Nation Research Institute for Social Development*, September 1, 1999, 65.

the development of international management consultants and the pressure exerted by loans (contracts with performance obligations). According to the author, while this phenomenon is more common in developed countries, some developing countries have applied variants of NPM since the 1990s. We have notably witnessed the apparition of autonomous institutions in the public sector, as well as a will to modernise the public function. This trend is illustrated by the fact that the Moroccan Ministry of Administrative Affairs was renamed the Ministry of Public Service and Administrative Reform in 1998 and the Ministry of Modernisation of the Public Sectors in 2002.[70]

In this perspective, Morocco participates in several international programmes for the modernisation of public policies. Since 2003, it has benefited from a World Bank loan programme for Public Administration Reform (PARAP), whose objectives are to improve budget management and transparency by introducing performance measures, simplify procedures through e-government, improve the efficiency of human resources management and improve the working conditions of employees.[71] In 2007, it ratified the United Nations Convention against Corruption (UNCAC), which led to the creation of a Central Corruption Prevention Commission (ICPC) in the same year. Its mission is to observe and monitor corruption in several public bodies, including the Ministry of Foreign Affairs and International Cooperation (MAECI).[72] In addition, the OECD is accompanying Morocco in the area of open government, intending to integrate it into the Open Government Partnership (OGP).[73] All of these institutional policies (among which I have cited only a few significant examples) constitute the third actor and factor in the modernisation of the diplomatic administration, alongside the demands of civil society and the interests of the monarchic apparatus. Within this framework, three areas of reform will be the focus of our attention: (1) the training and profile of the diplomat, (2) the distribution and monitoring of expenses, and (3) the systematisation of working methods.

---

70 See the Ministry's website at: http://www.mmsp.gov.ma/.
71 See details of the PARAP Project on the World Bank website at https://www.worldbank.org/
    en/news/loans-credits/2010/04/29/morocco-fourth-public-administration-reform-development-policy-loan
72 See ICPC website: https://inpplc.ma/fr
73 The 2008 financial crisis made the concept of 'open government' prominent. The OGP, launched in 2011, brings together more than 60 countries committed to transparency and citizen participation in public policy. Morocco has officially applied for membership but is 1/12 points short of being eligible. See OECD, *OECD Public Governance Reviews Open Government in Morocco*, (OECD Publishing, 2015). See also the OGP website http://www.opengovpartnership.org/.

The opening of an entrance exam that allows the diversification of the socio-academic profiles of recruits and the reorganisation of the steps and possibilities of career diplomats' evolution has transformed the Ministry.

Since 2004, internal promotions have benefited 1,449 staff members, including 817 managers, out of the 3,000 civil servants at MAECI.[74] The professionalisation of civil servants is now subject to a programme of continuous training and internships abroad. The training of recruits has also been promoted since the creation of the Royal Moroccan Academy of Diplomacy at the English-speaking Al-Akhawayne University (in the city of Ifrane) in 2008. This institution was replaced in 2011 by the Academy of Diplomatic Studies, located within the Ministry, where the diplomatic history of Morocco, international law and negotiation techniques are taught. At the same time, the Ministry trains its senior staff in other institutions. This includes, for example, with Sciences Po Rabat, which offers executive training on diplomatic practices and European and African expertise. The training courses help to broaden the diplomat's knowledge while mitigating potential academic weaknesses: mastery of languages, research and communication methods, etc. While appointing ambassadors and certain other diplomats to strategic positions is still a political decision, intermediate positions are now obtained following a public or internal competition.

Furthermore, marked efforts can be observed in the adaptation of the choice of academic profiles, age and gender according to foreign policy orientations. Traditionally, a large proportion of Moroccan graduates are from the National School of Administration in Rabat (ENA) or the various faculties of legal sciences (Rabat, Casablanca, Fez). According to a study conducted by Mohamed A. Riziki, based on the biographies of 245 diplomats, about 44% studied in Morocco, 31% in France, 8% in the United States, 6% in Egypt, 3.5% in Switzerland, 3% in Spain, 2% in the Netherlands and 2% in other countries;[75] 62% of the diplomats who studied in Morocco graduated in Rabat, half of them at the National School of Administration.[76] Traditionally, ambassadorial positions were reserved for political elites from the same socio-cultural background (large Moroccan families or career diplomats),[77] in a logic of reward.[78] The creation of a master's degree in governance and international intelligence at the International University of Rabat and other such master's degrees will progres-

---

74 Mustapha Sehimi, "La réforme silencieuse", *Maroc Hebdo*, September 3, 2004.
75 Riziki, *Sociologie de la diplomatie marocaine*, 285.
76 Ibid., 390–391.
77 Riziki, *Sociologie de la diplomatie marocaine*.
78 Ali Anouzia, "Ambassadorial appointments, what has changed?", *Lakome*, March 12, 2013.

sively contribute to the diversification of profiles. A more significant renewal of senior diplomatic staff, however, occurred during the waves of ambassadorial replacements ordered by the King between 2008 and 2013.

In 2008, Mohammed VI appointed 25 new ambassadors, including five women (Morocco had three women ambassadors in 2008, two in 2002), with an average age of 53 (compared with 61 for outgoing diplomats), 19 of whom were taking up the position for the first time.[79] In 2009, he appointed 15 more ambassadors, including two women in important countries (the UK and Canada).[80] In 2011, 28 ambassadors were appointed, including four women (14%), in 2013, 17, including three women (17%).[81] In 2016, almost 70 ambassadors were appointed, including 14 women (20%).[82] Within the Ministry, the feminisation rate in 2014 was 33.1%, while the share of women in departmental management positions was 22.7%.[83] Overall, the proportion of women in positions of responsibility is increasing. Finally, the rights of women diplomats have been significantly improved. For example, they are no longer required to provide a court order granting them legal custody of their children to benefit from their rights and family allowances.[84]

On the one hand, the feminisation of the diplomatic body testifies to the desire to better inscribe the institutionalisation of gender equality in public reforms.[85] These transformations echo the reform of the Moudawana (Family Code) instituted in 2004 and respond to the implementation of the provisions of the Committee on the Elimination of Discrimination Against Women (CEDAW)[86] while at the same time constituting a media operation aimed at enhancing the image of Moroccan diplomacy.[87] Mbarka Bouaida, former Min-

---

79 Soufiane Belhaj, "Rajeunissement du corps diplomatique", *Aujourd'hui le Maroc*, November 10, 2008.
80 "HM King Mohammed VI appoints new Ambassadors", *Aujourd'hui le Maroc*, January 23, 2009.
81 Aziza El Affas, "Mouvement dans le réseau diplomatique", https://www.leconomiste.com/article/904385-mouvement-dans-le-r-seau-diplomatique, March 2013.
82 Benjamin Bousquet, "Mohammed VI appoints new ambassadors, here is the complete list", *Jeune Afrique*, October 13, 2016.
83 Ministère de l'Économie et des Finances, Projet de Loi des Finances pour l'année budgétaire 2015, *Rapport sur le budget genre*, (Rabat, 2014).
84 Sehimi, "La réforme silencieuse".
85 Sophie Brière and Andrea Martinez, "Changements et résistances en matière d'institutionnalisation de l'égalité entre les sexes: le cas du Maroc", *Recherches féministes 24*, no. 2 (2011), 153.
86 *Committee on the Elimination of Discrimination against Women—UN Convention ratified by Morocco in 1993*.
87 Ministry of Foreign Affairs and Cooperation, *International Women's Day: La femme diplomate à l'honneur*, March 8, 2012.

ister Delegate to the Minister of Foreign Affairs appointed in 2013, represents this effort. She was young at the time of her nomination (42 years old), of Sahrawi origin, she studied in Morocco and France but also in England, and was consecrated 'Young Global Leader' by the World Economic Forum in 2012.[88] She therefore represents the diversity of gender, age and socio-academic profile, modernist and consensual, desired by the reform movement. Despite these advances, the number of women diplomats who reach positions of responsibility remains very low. Several factors are at work: first, the domestic factor, linked to family constraints—in a society where inequality in the division of domestic work and time spent on childcare and education is persistent—limiting the time devoted to building a career; second, the domestic-professional factor linked to the spouse's resistance to leaving his job and following his wife to a country where he would not have the right to work (this factor also concerns the wives of diplomats, but the concession is more difficult to accept for the husbands). Finally, a third factor, strictly professional, lies in Moroccan political culture, which, like domestic culture, struggles to normalise and standardise gender equality in gestures, words, practices, promotions and networks. These three factors are observable in all states of the world,[89] but they are more exacerbated in highly patriarchal countries such as Morocco,[90] where many women have also integrated these practices as normal and also contribute to their diffusion.

On the other hand, these large waves of appointments have sought to mitigate the reproduction of elites through clientelistic co-optation. This trend is changing slowly,[91] but the new appointments should be able to ensure a better match between the strategic objectives of the foreign policy and the profiles chosen to fill the positions. For example, the appointment in 2010 of Ahmed Ould Souilem (a former founding member of the Polisario who joined Morocco's cause in 2009)[92] as ambassador to Spain appears to be a

---

88 "Mbarka Bouaida, Minister Delegate to the Minister of Foreign Affairs and Cooperation", *Jeune Afrique*, April 5, 2015.
89 See in particular Jennifer Cassidy, *Gender and Diplomacy*, (London: Routledge, 2019). Glenda Sluga, Carolyn James, *Women, Diplomacy and International Politics since 1500*, (London: Routledge, 2015).
90 Houria Alami M'Chichi "Les feminismes marocains contemporains", *Nouvelles Questions Féministes 33*, no. 2 (2014): 65–79. Rabéa Naciri, "Le movement des femmes au Maroc", *Nouvelles Questions Féministes 33*, no. 2 (2014): 43–64.
91 Anouzia, "Nominations d'ambassadeurs, qu'est ce qui a changé?".
92 Given the empathy of Spanish society for the Sahrawi activist Aminatou Haidar during her 2009 hunger strike, this nomination was intended to influence public opinion. See Leïla Silmani, "Un Ambassadeur pas comme les autres", *Jeune Afrique*, May 3, 2010.

well-calculated diplomatic manoeuvre to disenchant a Spanish public opinion imbued with independence propaganda.

In parallel with the professionalisation of the diplomatic body, the distribution and monitoring of expenditure has been inexorably subjected to the combined pressure of the three main actors of the reform (international organisations, the Royal Cabinet and civil society). The digital publication of reports on draft finance laws since 2001 illustrates and contributes primarily to the transparency of this major undertaking. Between 2001 and 2014, the Ministry of Foreign Affairs' budget grew by an average of 3.4% per year.[93] Between 2014 and 2015 alone, the Ministry's budget increased by 13% to reach 2.5 billion dirhams.

A significant part of the MAECI budget is used for staff remuneration and new staff recruitment. Still, the majority was devoted to acquiring material goods at that time. Two-thirds of the MAECI budget was used to construct diplomatic infrastructures, rehabilitate real estate assets or modernise IT management tools.[94] The Ministry's headquarters has not been exempt from these renovations: it has acquired new buildings that are better located, larger and better adapted to the image that the diplomatic apparatus wishes to project. In addition, the number of diplomatic representations has increased tenfold: by the time Morocco joined the AU in 2016, it had over 90 embassies and 50 more general consulates general[95] in the world.

The objective of increasing and controlling the MAECI budget is also part of the project to professionalise diplomats. The objective of the Organic Law relative to the Law of Finance (LOF) is to establish a performance culture,[96] to ensure the transition from a 'normative approach to expenditure to a presentation by programme and project/action',[97] and to introduce the principle of 'budgetary sincerity': all discursive and institutional practices widely used in NPM. A report by the French Senate, which adopted a similar law in 2001, clearly states the purpose of these reforms: 'modernise public management to reform the State'.[98] The objective of the Moroccan administration, in this same perspective, is to consolidate the democratic gains obtained in recent years and to

---

93   "Rapport sur le budget genre".
94   Ibid.
95   Official website of the Ministry of Foreign Affairs and Cooperation.
96   Ministry of the Economy and Finance, Directorate of Financial Studies and Forecasts, *Loi des Finances 2015* [Report], (2014), 87.
97   Ibid.
98   Alain Lambert, "Rapport du Sénat sur la proposition de loi organique relative aux lois de finances", Sénat, 2001–2000, 19 See also: Alain Lambert and Didier Migaud, "La loi organique relative aux lois de finances (LOLF): levier de la réforme de l'État", *Revue française d'administration publique* 117, no. 1 (2006): 11–14.

strengthen the efficiency of the diplomatic apparatus by introducing modern management tools, as well as the control of expenditures by the parliament. This initiative was supported by the World Bank, the Expertise France group and the Moroccan Ministry of Finance, which awarded a trophy to the Ministry of Foreign Affairs and Cooperation as the institution that prefigured the implementation of the LOF.[99] The adoption of the LOF also demonstrates that Morocco is following in the footsteps of its foreign partners by copying their actions.

Finally, the rationalisation of working methods is the third prominent area of reform: electronic mail is standardised, the diplomatic protocol is clarified and royal roadmaps are refined. An entrepreneurial spirit is spreading in favour of modern management. To make diplomats aware of their new functions, a significant brainstorming operation (to use the ministerial term) was organised within MAECI in 2009. This meeting led to the production of the 'Charter of Values of the Moroccan Diplomat'[100] and the 'Guide to the Moroccan Diplomat'[101] indicating the functions and missions of the various diplomatic agents. A meticulous description specifies elements of protocol, such as the type of traditional dress the ambassador must wear during a reception, the table plan to adopt, the kind of meal to be preferred and the speaking time to be respected during a speech. This protocol already existed within the Makhzen but was not as formalised publicly within the government administration.

The monitoring of diplomats' performance is also assiduous: the cancellation of diplomatic staff's annual leave in August 2015, following complaints from Moroccans living abroad (of ill treatment, abuse of power or gender violence), is one example which reminds us of the monarchy's executive role in controlling the exercise of diplomatic functions. Thus, a special commission was charged with studying officials' performance and compliance with prescribed working methods in Morocco's embassies and consulates. The seditious report sent to the Royal Cabinet in September 2015 led to the immediate and unprecedented recall of some 30 consuls. Of the new consuls appointed to replace them, 80% were first-time consuls, and 25% were women.[102] In addition, some 40 executives under the age of 30 were appointed to follow a

---

99   Ministry of Foreign Affairs and Cooperation, *The Ministry of Foreign Affairs and Cooperation's endorsement of the new LOF's ownership seminar*, October 21, 2015.
100 Ministry of Foreign Affairs and Cooperation, *Charte des valeurs du diplomate marocain*, Rabat, 2011.
101 Ministère des Affaires étrangères et de la Coopération, *Guide du diplomate marocain*, Rabat, May 2009.
102 "Morocco: Appointment of 31 new consuls", *Bladi.net*, October 19, 2015.

three-month training course to join the various consulates in support of this professionalisation policy.[103]

The reforms of the diplomatic apparatus are little known. The media discretion with which these transformations were carried out earned them the title of 'silent reform' by the press.[104] An analysis of the media's treatment of the changes in the Ministry of Foreign Affairs since the beginning of the 2000s nevertheless reveals a semantic consensus around the notion of 'new diplomacy'.[105] Confined by journalists to the idea of a readjustment of diplomatic orientations to the new international stakes, the 'new diplomacy' expresses two tendencies: on the one hand, a strict framing of diplomacy by public policy, providing it with its structural and normative base, and on the other hand, a manifest reaffirmation of the centrality of the monarch, who is revealed as the prior designer and inspector of this diplomacy. Gradually, this two-tier arrangement led the Palace and the government to specify foreign policy guidelines based on the definition of national interests and the identity of the state's role on the international scene.

5   The Specialisation of Diplomacy in the Service of a Golden-Mean Role Identity: Promoting Interculturalism and Trilateralism

On the website of the Permanent Mission of Morocco to the United Nations in Geneva, one can read the following statement:

> Due to its privileged geographical position, at the meeting point of Europe, Africa and the Arab-Muslim world, Morocco has always advocated openness and respect for others, and favoured the dialogue of nations and civilisations. As a result, the policy of the golden mean and moderation has been a constant in the conduct of the Kingdom's domestic and foreign policy.[106]

---

103   "Moroccans of the world: Mohammed VI wants 'exemplary consulates'", *Bladi.net*, August 16, 2015.
104   Sehimi, "La réforme silencieuse".
105   Omar Dahbi, "La nouvelle diplomatie en œuvre", *Aujourd'hui le Maroc*, November 24, 2004; "Retraits de la reconnaissance de la pseudo-RASD: la nouvelle diplomatie marocaine porte ses fruits", *MAP Express*, January 15, 2014; Aourid, "Penser notre diplomatie", *Zamane*, January 12, 2015; Pascal Airault, "La nouvelle diplomatie de M6", *Jeune Afrique*, January 26, 2009.
106   At: http://www.mission-maroc.ch/fr/pages/16.html. Accessed July 2016.

Confirming a previously demonstrated geo-cultural representation, this statement forms the prelude to the gradual formation of a bridging role by the diplomatic apparatus. This posture translates into what a Moroccan diplomat has called 'bridge-building diplomacy.'[107]

This term can be defined as a niche diplomacy that allows a small state to compensate for its low weight in international relations by playing an inescapable role—if successful—in bringing two countries or communities together. Building a diplomatic bridge requires few material resources but excellent relational skills, including the ability to mobilise non-state actors. Thus, bridge diplomacy both reinforces and relies on the construction of a mediating or moderating identity and the recognition of this identity by peers. Although the expression is not used in the academic literature, it nevertheless has a significant meaning in the case of Morocco.

Indeed, there are several areas of expression of this bridge diplomacy, which makes it so relevant. First, we can mention the interest of diplomacy in the politics of mediation and 'inter' roles (interfaith, intercultural, interregional), legitimised by a 'moderate', 'open' and 'tolerant' state identity. In his capacity as Commander of the Faithful, let us recall that in 1985 Hassan II received Pope John Paul II, who gave a speech in front of nearly 80,000 young Moroccans who cheered him on in front of the cameras of the national television channel. The Kingdom marked its singularity as the first Muslim state to officially invite a Pontiff to speak to its citizens.

Although the event was achieved thanks to the force of particular circumstances (a few years earlier, Hassan II had been mandated by the Islamic countries, in his capacity as president of the Al Quds Committee, to go to the Vatican to discuss the status of Jerusalem, a trip at the end of which he confided that he had felt a particular admiration for John Paul II[108]), it marked the begin-

---

107   Interview no. 6 with a diplomat, Ministry of Foreign Affairs and Cooperation, Rabat, May 2013.
108   Hassan II wrote of Pope John Paul II: 'He is a man with a striking personality, in the literal sense of the word, because it really marks you. He gives me the impression of being both down to earth and, at the same time, between heaven and earth. It is a mixture of the spiritual and the concrete. (…). I think it must be said that John Paul II is not a pope like the others. He was once a trade unionist, a theatre actor and even engaged. That changes everything. He is sui generis. When he tackles a problem, you cannot say that it is the approach of the Vatican or the approach of the Church. It is, first and foremost, the analysis of John Paul II. I don't think other popes like him will come along soon. (…) At one of our meetings, I asked him: Holy Father, whenever you have the opportunity, pray for me.' Hassan II and Éric Laurent, *La mémoire d'un roi: entretiens avec Eric Laurent*, (Paris, France: Plon, 1993), 304.

ning of a form of institutionalisation of interreligious dialogue at the scale of the Moroccan diplomacy. A few years later, Mohammed VI affirmed that 'dialogue between religions is the other side of the dialogue between civilisations and cultures'.[109] In this respect, Morocco's ability to validate its expertise in interreligious mediation would consolidate its bridge-building diplomacy on a geo-cultural scale. Morocco's efforts in resolving the Israeli–Palestinian conflict are a clear manifestation of this trend.[110] On other issues, the diplomacy of intercultural dialogue is embodied mainly by the figure of André Azoulay.[111] To a lesser extent, other personalities such as Serge Berdugo, president of the Rassemblement mondial du Judaïsme marocain, Assia Bensalah Alaoui, president of the Association d'Amitié maroco-japonaise, and Hassan Abouyoub, former Moroccan ambassador to Djibouti, Somalia and Saudi Arabia, who were nominated as the Kingdom's itinerant ambassadors in 2006, have participated in this vigorous enterprise. The first ecumenical institute of theology in Morocco (the Al-Mowafaqa Institute), created in 2012, was also built based on this trend.

Confirming this preference of the state for 'inter' diplomacy, the former Minister Delegate of Foreign Affairs, Youssef Amrani, affirms that 'Morocco has played a key role as a mediator in Africa, the Middle East and the Balkans' and advocates at the UN for the establishment of a security agenda focused more on 'mediation and conflict prevention' than on 'peacekeeping and peacebuilding'.[112] While Morocco's commitment is not yet evident, it seems to be evolving towards a proactive attitude at the diplomatic level. At the governmental and public levels, initiatives to institutionalise mediation practices have multiplied. For example, since 2012, the Moroccan–Spanish Initiative for the Promotion of Mediation in the Mediterranean has been helping to enable researchers, asso-

---

109 "Message of HM the King, Amir Al Mouminine, to the participants of the interconfessional meeting in Brussels on 'God's peace in the world'", *Maroc.ma*, December 18, 2001.
110 Morocco's role in mediating the conflict was revealed during the official visit of Shimon Peres to Rabat in 1985. However, many observers of the conflict assume that several unofficial meetings between the monarchy and the Israeli and Palestinian authorities took place before and after this date.
111 A Jewish Moroccan, Azoulay has been a special advisor to the monarchy since 1991. He was also president of the Anna Lindh Foundation for the Dialogue between Cultures from 2008 to 2015 (Cairo), president delegate to the Foundation of the Three Cultures (whose headquarters are in a medieval building in Seville ceded by Morocco for the use of the Foundation), a founding member of the 'Aladdin' project for interreligious dialogue (Paris) and finally, a member of the Committee of Wise Men for the Alliance of Civilizations at the UN since 2005.
112 "Youssef Amrani at the UN: Morocco, adept at preventive diplomacy", *La Nouvelle Tribune*, May 24, 2012.

ciations and private consultancy firms to establish a network and think about mediation tools in the region.[113] Finally, at the state level, the search for African depth will push the monarchy, as we will see later, to confront conflict theatres and to test its political aptitude in direct negotiation in times of crisis (such as mediation attempts during the Malian crisis and the conflict around the Mano River basin).

The second notable area of this bridge diplomacy is in the choice of tripartite, triangular or trilateral interregional cooperation.[114] This refers to a form of North–South–South cooperation that includes three actors: a donor, a recipient and a pivotal actor. Morocco has negotiated numerous agreements of this type with institutional donors (FAO, ADB) or states (France, Japan).[115] In some cases, the funding obtained allows Morocco to think about and carry out actions in Southern Africa; in other cases, it is a matter of making experts available within the framework of projects already planned by the donors.[116] For diplomacy, it is a question of 'having additional means at its disposal thanks to the participation of international donors' to 'make Africans benefit from Moroccan expertise'.[117] This report, supported by a series of official speeches calling for this form of arrangement,[118] states that 'Morocco could play an important role in generating a triangular cooperation strategy, which consists of channelling international aid funds to finance infrastructure projects in Africa and entrusting the management of these projects to Moroccan service providers, including consultancy offices, civil engineering companies and oth-

---

113 "Opening in Madrid of the 1st seminar on the Moroccan-Spanish Initiative for the mediation in the Mediterranean", *Atlasinfo.fr: News France, Maghreb, Morocco, Algeria, Tunisia, Libya, Mauritania*, February 11, 2013.
114 I refer here to the concepts of triangular, tripartite and trilateral cooperation in an undifferentiated way, as is customary in Moroccan discourse. In the academic field, a distinction is often made between these concepts, which are subject to delicate nuances. Rhee, for example, notes that triangular cooperation refers to multilateral support from the North for South–South cooperation, while he defines trilateral cooperation as formalised North–South–South cooperation. H. Rhee, "South-South Cooperation", KOICA—*Working paper*, (2010).
115 Ministry of Foreign Affairs and Cooperation, *Morocco and Tripartite Cooperation*, 2015.
116 This is the case, for example, with the tripartite cooperation between Germany, Morocco and Costa Rica. "Tripartite Cooperation", *Deutsche Gesellschaft für Internationale Zusammenarbeit (GIZ) GmbH*, December 2013.
117 "Le Maroc et la Coopération Tripartite". See also: Ministère de l'Economie et des Finances, Direction des Études et des Prévisions Financières, *Point sur les relations du Maroc avec les pays de l'Afrique Subsaharienne*, Rabat, October 2008, 15.
118 'Morocco is an essential link in tripartite and multilateral cooperation, particularly in ensuring security, stability and development in Africa'. "Speech by HM the King on the occasion of the 61st anniversary of the Revolution of the King and the People".

ers'.[119] Through this form of cooperation, Morocco, as a pivotal state, would be able to enhance its experience in the South while benefiting from financial support and learning in the North. On the diplomatic level, this configuration makes it possible to reinforce the legitimacy of its identity as a golden mean in interregional exchanges.

The Kingdom's efforts to deploy a bridge or mediation diplomacy are part of an ambition consistent with its golden-mean role identity as described in the previous chapter and in line with other states' perception of Morocco's place in the concert of nations. Promoting the golden-mean role identity is, therefore, a lever of intangible power. In any case, this is what the royal speech suggests: 'if Morocco has neither oil nor gas, while the other party has a "greenback" which it believes opens the doors to it, in defiance of the law and legality, we have, on the other hand, our principles and the justness of our cause.'[120] In this perspective, the diplomatic apparatus is duly called upon to ensure the dissemination of this identity:

> We have developed an integrated and coherent diplomatic vision that affirms and consecrates the secular civilisational identity of Morocco [...] It is also the duty of Moroccan diplomacy to work, with the same ardour, to highlight the fundamental assets of the Kingdom and to make the most judicious use of them, through a coherent and effective positioning, in phase with the values and the best interests of Morocco, and with the fundamental evolutions of international relations.[121]

Without being enshrined as an official doctrine, the golden mean appears in this context as a hypothesis likely to bring meaning and coherence to the whole of Moroccan foreign policy. The coincidence of the dialogical network around this notion with the conduct of Moroccan diplomacy is such that it can be interpreted as the principle justifying Morocco's stated preference for 'inter' diplomacy and triangular cooperation in the field of action, the role of bridge in the field of representation, and moderator in the field of ethics. This specialisation will be put at the service of a *conditioned* Africa policy, as we will see in the next chapter.

---

119   *Point sur les relations du Maroc avec les pays de l'Afrique Subsaharienne.*
120   "Speech by HM the King to the nation on the occasion of the 39th anniversary of the Green March", *Maroc.ma*, November 5, 2014.
121   "Message of the Sovereign to the 1st Ambassadors Conference of HM the King".

CHAPTER 4

A Framework for Representing Regional Integration

1   Introduction

Representations determine foreign policy decisions. Yet even though the different representations of actors reveal more complex distinctions than the Schmittian typology of friend and foe,[1] they are regarded as epiphenomena of international politics. However, a branch of political science research turned very early on to studying the role of perceptions[2] and images in forming and resolving conflicts,[3] demonstrating the heuristic interest of such an approach and opening the way to several theories. Some of these studies are limited by their divisive approaches, hijacking the debate on representation around the issue of war;[4] others more finely examine the origins and different degrees of friendship in politics[5] and highlight the pursuit of a common idea of world order as a factor influencing the perceptions of actors, demonstrating, in fine, that 'under certain circumstances and by means of skilful diplomacy, enemies can become friends'.[6] The issue of building a common future brings us directly back to the importance of the criterion of multilateralism. For many states, it appears that their commitment to the construction of the future world order within regional or thematic multilateral spheres (disarmament, environment, finance, etc.) is a criterion as crucial as the search for security or power, or the quest for recognition and the diffusion of their own identity, and it also actively participates in constructing their representations.

---

1   Carl Schmitt, *La notion de politique*, (Paris, France: Flammarion, 1992), 64.
2   James F. Voss and Donald A. Sylvan, *Problem representation in foreign policy decision making*, (Cambridge, UK: Cambridge University Press, 1998), viii+ 347.
3   For a detailed history of the study of images and perceptions since then, see the introductory chapter of Ramel's study, *Recherche ennemi désespérément. Origines, essor et apport des approches perceptuelles en relations internationales*.
4   I refer in particular to the work of Robert Jervis, Kenneth Boulding and Julien Freund.
5   Simon Koschut and Andrea Oelsner, *Friendship and international relations*, (Basingstoke, UK, United Kingdom of Great Britain and Northern Ireland: Palgrave Macmillan, 2014).
6   Charles A. Kupchan, *How Enemies Become Friends: The Sources of Stable Peace*, (Princeton, N.J.; Woodstock: Princeton University Press, 2012), 13.

The different theories that deal with the role of perceptions are not epistemologically commensurable. Still, they all demonstrate that the representation of the Other is a decisive factor in foreign policy-making, so that the criterion of representation completely ignores the divisions in the discipline of international relations.[7] Indeed, in the same way that action theory forms a metatheory in analytical philosophy, the representational approach constitutes a transversal and indispensable component in the analysis of foreign policy. This approach nevertheless requires many methodological precautions, as the fragmentation of the theoretical base could easily alter the purpose. Thus, on the theoretical level, while the representational approach to decision-making is at the antipodes of the so-called rational approach, one being comprehensive and the other explanatory, it can be observed that the two forms of reasoning are often engaged simultaneously, on the empirical level, by the political actor. Therefore, two obstacles inherent to the analysis of Morocco's representation of Africa must be raised. The first is the definition of 'representation' as a political concept, and the second is the link between representation, legitimisation and demonstration of friendship or enmity relations.

Representation is not legitimation: while the former is based on a series of arbitrary or unconscious assumptions, the latter is the conscious legitimation of this representation through language. Other authors also make this distinction. According to Julien Durand de Sanctis, the representational framework refers to the 'perceptual, phenomenological and epistemological foundation of any strategic consciousness that thinks and decides in a conflictual environment [...] Without a representational framework, it is the power to say "I" in strategy that disappears, meaning its very essence which consists in theorising action individually and consciously to decide how to act.'[8] Conversely, according to the same author, a legitimation framework is 'a regime of discourse that develops knowledge in the service of power'.[9] This distinction appears all the more relevant as the ideas at the origin of the representations and those formulated in the framework of a justification do not always coincide. On the contrary, as Michel Foucault rightly put it, 'the limit of knowledge would be the perfect transparency of representations to the signs that order them'.[10] Confus-

---

7 Frédéric Ramel, "Représentations, images et politique étrangère: anciens débats, nouveaux outils", *Revue française de science politique 50*, no. 3 (2000): 531–538.
8 Julien Durand De Sanctis, *Philosophie de la stratégie française. La stratégie continentale.* (Paris, Nuvis, 2018), 28.
9 Ibid., 33.
10 Michel Foucault, *Les mots et les choses: une archéologie des sciences humaines*, (Paris: Gallimard, 1990), 91.

ing representation and the legitimisation of this representation is part of the same arrangement of ideas.

We therefore call representation a cognitive system formed by a set of associations of ideas, beliefs and images constructed by representatives of a state or non-state agent about their international environment, based on a teaching they have received. These private representations, fed by the interactions of decision-makers with the Other and by a part of the imaginary,[11] are transformed into a political phenomenon from the moment they are aggregated. Finally, the memory of the state forms the substratum within which the representation is preserved and developed.[12]

On the other hand, let us call legitimation the speech acts and other forms of symbolic communication by which the representatives of a state or non-state agent explain and justify their representations to public or international opinion, or to the actors they wish to rally to their causes.

Finally, let us call demonstration the political behaviour and rituals related to representation and justification. According to hypothetical-inductive reasoning, these behaviours and rituals are illustrated through a set of mechanisms which are reconstituted in Table 4.1. Thus, the different criteria put forward form not an exhaustive list, but one adapted to the observations related to our case study.

The criteria at work in the representation of friendship and enmity are as follows:

- Sameness: this criterion applies to countries, often border or regional neighbours, which share a common culture, history, beliefs or language, and perceive each other as part of a common collective identity, in the sense given by Wendt.[13]
- Security: this applies to countries that perceive each other through the prism of national interests conceived in terms of security, broadly defined.[14] The

---

11 Imagination plays a fundamental role in the association of ideas or phenomena. As Foucault reminds us, 'without imagination, there would be no resemblance between things [...] There must be, in the things represented, the insistent whisper of resemblance; there must be, in the representation, the always possible withdrawal of imagination' Ibid., 83.
12 The State's history thus constitutes the link between the individual who fought against the enemy to protect their region and the individual who finds themselves detached from this vision 20 or 50 years later. It should be noted at this point that the role of the historian appears to be just as essential as that of the political actor in constructing this representation through language.
13 Wendt, *Social Theory of International Politics*, 201.
14 Buzan *et alii*, *Security*.

evolution of their relations depends mainly on threat perceptions and the geopolitical context of their time.
- Influence: this applies to countries that perceive each other through the prism of national interests defined in terms of influence, diplomatic power relations and historical relations. Power here is based on a non-coercive, more cultural, economic and normative will to influence. The exercise of power is based on consent or soft domination.
- Multilateralism: this applies to countries strongly engaged in multilateral or supranational projects with a significant degree of ownership or production of multilateral standards.

The behaviours related to representation are summarised in Table 4.1.

The frameworks mobilised in the legitimisation of representation are:
- the accountability of the Other in triggering action;
- the emphasis on peace, development and collective security issues in the geopolitical context;
- the use of state historical memory in discourse;
- the inclusion of the civilian population in the relationship and the reference to national pride.

Using the methodological framework developed above, this chapter aims to highlight the nature and weight of the Kingdom's representations of its African geopolitical environment and those of certain African states vis-à-vis Morocco. To what extent do these representations, once shared, condition Moroccan–African diplomatic relations?

2 The Defence of Territorial Integrity: A Political Framework for Defining the Entourage

During the Cold War, Nicholas Spykman, one of the first US geopolitical scientists, warned his country's leaders of the danger of a Manichean reading of the world. He wrote: 'I do not believe that the world can be divided into good and bad, and I do not believe that the bad would want war and live east of the Atlantic, while the good would want peace and live west of the same ocean'.[15] Indeed, this type of representation can accentuate and extend the enmity relationship to the whole of society and all domains, whereas it may initially con-

---

15 Nicholas Spykman, "Neutrality laws and exceptions to commercial treaties", Lecture, American Society of International Law, April 24, 1936, in *Proceedings of the American Society of International Law at Its Annual Meeting* (1921–1969), Vol. 30 (April 23–25, 1936), 138–162.

A FRAMEWORK FOR REPRESENTING REGIONAL INTEGRATION   135

TABLE 4.1   Behaviour of agents in the international system and likely examples

Representations	Sameness	Security	Influence	Multilateralism
Friendship	Regionalist behaviour or multisectoral cooperation (Morocco–Senegal)	Searching for an alliance or a security community (Morocco–France)	Influence diplomacy or balance of powers (Morocco–Côte d'Ivoire)	Affirmation of mechanical solidarity (Morocco–Rwanda)
Enmity	Conflict behaviour or economically and ideologically competitive (Morocco–Algeria)	Security dilemma or armed conflict, expression of enmity in discourses (Morocco–Algeria)	Coercive diplomacy or economic and normative conflict (Morocco–Nigeria)	Exclusion and political stigmatisation (Morocco–South Africa)

cern only one aspect of the behaviour of the actor in question. The United States, like many other countries, formulates its representations of the world according to its perceptions of friends and foes, which are based on another perception, that of threat. Pierre Conesa notes that a country always seeks to clearly define or designate enemies.[16] Although Conesa's study focuses exclusively on Western democracies, Morocco is not exempt from this analytical framework. Its geopolitical representation of Africa is linked to its perception of the threat (attack on its territorial integrity) and the definition of friends and enemies in relation to it, with the interests and limits that such an approach entails.

According to one diplomat: 'one must see the state as a human being and be ever vigilant, especially towards Algeria, Nigeria and South Africa'.[17] From the Moroccan point of view, these three countries have long formed a 'hostile axis'[18] that the Kingdom wanted to break. These representations are entirely linked to the Sahara issue. Vital interest, cement of national unity, geo-strategic depth and land of natural resources, the Sahara, as I demonstrated earlier, constitutes the indispensable compass for the Moroccan diplomat, the pilot of the Kingdom's foreign policy. Although Morocco abandoned its Hallstein doctrine in the aftermath of the Cold War, the recognition of its friends and enemies still

---

16   Pierre Conesa, *La fabrication de l'ennemi*, (Paris, Robert Laffon, 2011).
17   Interview with a diplomat in Rabat no. 11, Ministry of Foreign Affairs and Cooperation, May–June 2013.
18   Anthony Drugeon, "En Afrique, la diplomatie marocaine a listé ses pays hostiles", *Telquel.ma*, January 7, 2015.

depends closely on the latter's relations with the Polisario Front. This posture is the measure that allows the Moroccan diplomat to separate the wheat from the chaff.

For a long time, the 'enemies of Morocco' have been, as simple as it sounds, the 'enemies of the territorial integrity of the Kingdom': corollary and redundant formulations in official discourse. By comparison, non-state actors such as African terrorist groups appear as global threats, not as enemies in the political sense.

The betrayal syndrome, inscribed in the historical memory of the Moroccan state and the imaginary of its representatives, plays a fundamental role in this representation. Morocco considered itself betrayed by Algeria when, at the time of its independence in 1962, the latter did not fulfil the terms of their political contract (Moroccan support for Algerian independence in exchange for the delimitation of common borders outside the French sphere), as mentioned in the second chapter. The Kingdom then considered the recognition of the RASD by the AU in 1984 a defeat and a betrayal, given its commitment to the construction of African unity. Today, this representation still dominates the field of discourse, including that aimed at Moroccan citizens. For the monarchy: 'either the citizen is Moroccan, or he is not [...] There is no middle ground between patriotism and treason. One cannot enjoy the rights of citizenship and at the same time deny them by plotting with the enemies of the homeland'.[19] In this way, as Moroccan citizens, the politician and the diplomat have an institutional obligation coupled with a moral duty to be as partial and proactive as the dialectic of patriotism and treason demands. This condition reinforces the diplomatic representation of Morocco's 'enemies', as much as it allows the identification of the space in which Morocco can exercise its policy.

By placing the Sahara issue at the top of its interests, Morocco does not exhaust itself by pursuing too many enemies, which confers a singular clarity and simplicity on its diplomatic conduct. However, while the authentication of a hostile actor in a publicly defined political framework helps to determine a strategy to be adopted, it does not inform on the differentiations made within this same hostile category. In the case of Morocco, it can be seen that some of the actors on the hostile axis do not constitute (South Africa) or no longer truly constitute (Nigeria) enemies in the sense of *hostis*. Only the Polisario Front and Algeria do.

---

19   "Speech of HM the King to the Nation on the occasion of the 34th anniversary of the Green March", MAP, November 6, 2009.

3 Algeria and the Polisario Front: Public Historical *hostis*

The Algerian state in the first place, as the main promoter of Polisario's claim and as an African power, constitutes the real political *hostis* for Morocco. This representation is based on the fact that since 1975, Algeria's Africa policy has been polarised around the Sahara issue: it has supported the Polisario Front militarily, financially and diplomatically, at both the African and the international level.

More than a regional *hostis*, Algeria represents a continental *hostis* insofar as it is in Africa that Algiers has found the most consistent support for its anti-Moroccan theses.[20] The defence of the independence of the Sahara has thus gradually become a leitmotif of its diplomacy.[21] Already, during the Cold War, in the year 1978/1979 alone, the number of Algerian diplomatic representations in Africa had practically doubled, going from 15 to 25. In parallel with its commitment to African revolutionary movements,[22] Algiers had also quickly developed a programme of cultural cooperation and financial support for students, and granting aid through the ADB. It was within the OAU that its action was particularly offensive. After submitting a 'Memorandum on the Sahara Affair' in 1977, Algeria actively campaigned for the recognition of the Polisario Front as a liberation movement by the OAU.[23] In this respect, the recognition of the RASD by the OAU in 1984 and the withdrawal of Morocco from the organisation are considered by Algerian leaders one of their most important diplomatic victories. Moreover, despite the collapse of the Algerian economy in 1985, the rise of Islamism and the end of the ideological divide inherited from the Cold War in the early 1990s, Algeria continued to include the Western Saharan independence project among its diplomatic priorities. Between the riots of 1988 and the bloody years from 1991 to 1999, Algerian diplomacy had to withdraw from the African and international scene while maintaining its support for the Polisario

---

20　Slimane Chikh, "La politique africaine de l'Algérie", *Annuaire de l'Afrique du Nord 17*, (1979): 9.
21　Ibid., 50.
22　Algeria has been particularly committed to the internationalisation of decolonisation issues in Africa within multilateral organisations, accusing Zionism. Delloul Malaïka supported liberation movements (the Polisario Front, but also the South African ANC, the Mozambican FRELIMO, the Guinean PAICG, the Namibian SWAPO, etc.) and hosted their leaders at the famous 'Villa Boumaraf' in Algiers. The Rhodesian Affair also mobilised the Algerian government, which went as far as to break off relations with the British alongside eight other African countries. Algeria was then described as a veritable 'Mecca for revolutionaries'.
23　Berramdane, *Le Sahara occidental, enjeu maghrébin*, 65–75.

Front. From this point, it is noteworthy that, beyond the material aid granted to the Sahrawi independence fighters, almost all of the speeches made by the Algerian president to a foreign president mentioned Western Sahara at least once.[24] Clearly, the Polisario Front could not have existed militarily or developed diplomatically without Algeria's involvement.

The Sahara border dispute appears today an outdated conflict insofar as, on the African level, almost all of the borders inherited from colonisation are now accepted,[25] the continent has not undergone the balkanisation that was predicted, and the 24 secession attempts that broke out between 1948 and 1998 practically all failed. One wonders, then, why Algeria continued to support the Polisario Front and to frame its Africa policy within the framework of a 'cold peace' with Morocco after the 2000s. Three hypotheses can be put forward. The first relates to the historical unconscious of the Algerian state, or what Ted Hopf identifies as 'a logic of habit in international relations',[26] meaning an irrational foreign policy practice linked to ideological routines in the definition of friends and enemies. In this sense, Algeria continues to do what it has always done until a significant change abruptly alters this orientation. The second hypothesis is linked to the principle of national pride ('nif' in the Algerian dialect) and the desire for revenge[27] inherent to a feeling of betrayal (particularly concerning the Sand War mentioned in the second chapter). To paraphrase Raymond Aron,[28] it can be said that not admitting defeat is the primary condition for Algeria's final success. Finally, the third hypothesis is more rational and linked to the diplomatic interest that the adversity with Morocco represents and the strategic interest that the control of the Sahara represents. These three reasons, both rational and irrational, are subtly intertwined.

President Bouteflika represented the last actor of a fossilised diplomatic golden age,[29] which Algeria wanted to recover. Moreover, the main objective of Algerian foreign policy from 1990 onwards was to avoid diplomatic isola-

---

24   See the President's full speeches on the official website of the Presidency of the Algerian Republic, http://www.el-mouradia.dz.
25   Foucher, *Frontiers of Africa*.
26   Ted Hopf, "The logic of habit in International Relations", *European Journal of International Relations 16*, no. 4 (2010): 539–561.
27   On the issue of revenge in state foreign policy, see the analysis by Oded Löwenheim and Gadi Heimann, "Revenge in International Politics", *Security Studies 17*, no. 4 (December 2008): 685–724.
28   Aron, *Paix et guerre entre les nations*, 36–37.
29   This corresponds to the period before 1985. See: Ardavan Amir-aslani, *L'age d'or de la diplomatie algérienne*, (Éditions du Moment, 2015).; Akram Belkaïd, "La diplomatie algérienne à la recherche de son âge d'or", *Politique étrangère Été*, no. 2 (2009): 337–344.

tion. However, it was precisely from this period on that, taking advantage of Algeria's withdrawal, Morocco was able to gradually regain its place on the continent. The withdrawal of many African countries from their recognition of the RASD was therefore defined as a betrayal by the Algerian leaders.[30] In this respect, Bouteflika intended, as early as the 2000s, to restore Algeria's position as a diplomatic power, which implied a victory for the Polisario Front, weakening Morocco, cutting it off from its African depths, and giving Algeria the possibility of gaining access to the Atlantic Ocean. The recognition of the RASD is, therefore, a fundamental strategic dogma for Algerian leaders,[31] who go as far as to demand the Sahara to be shared with Morocco[32] and refuse the offer to freely operate a port on the Moroccan Atlantic coast.[33] Thus, the Algerian representations are dual, both emotional and rational.

This is why, at the end of the 1980s, to compensate for its diplomatic weaknesses, Algeria's strategy consisted of buying its political positions on the continent, using the money from its oil revenues. Algeria was also the fourth-largest African shareholder in the ADB in 2008 and obtained a seat on its board of directors.[34] Many Algerian officials also occupy senior positions in the AU, contributing to disseminating Algerian perceptions and defending its interests.[35] As an example of this activism, the Pan-African Parliament called for the closure of Moroccan embassies in African states to pressure Morocco,[36] following an Algerian request.

More generally, the perceptions of Morocco and Algeria are characterised by a deficit of shared identity going beyond the Sahara. Marked by a revolutionary and republican socialist heritage, Algeria has a negative perception of the Moroccan regime as a constitutional monarchy of divine right and fears the power that a 'conspiracy' of Arab monarchies would represent.[37] In this respect, it can be observed that on the scale of the Arab-Muslim space, a cleavage inher-

---

30 Belkaïd, "La diplomatie algérienne à la recherche de son âge d'or".
31 Jean-François Daguzan, "La politique étrangère de l'Algérie: le temps de l'aventure?" *Politique Étrangère Automne*, no. 3 (2015): 31–42.
32 United Nations Security Council, "Report of the Secretary-General on the situation concerning Western Sahara, February 19, 2002". https://digitallibrary.un.org/record/458559?ln=en&v=pdf
33 Lugan, *Histoire du Maroc*.
34 "AfDB and Algeria redefine the basis for a strengthened partnership", *African Development Bank Group*, April 21, 2016.
35 Salim Chena, "Le Maghreb après les indépendences: (re)definition, (re)composition, (re)-construction", *L'Espace Politique. Online journal of political geography and geopolitics*, no. 18, (2012).
36 "Diplomacy: African Parliament wages war against Morocco", *le360.ma*, October 19, 2015.
37 Halim Benattallah, "Par-delà la participation du Maroc au Sommet des pays du CCG, quels messages en direction de l'Algérie?", *Le Quotidien d'Oran*, April 25, 2016.

ited from the ideologies of the Cold War and the influence of the United States and Russia in the region is illustrated in the different foreign policy positions of the Arab monarchies, Tunisia and Egypt on the one hand, and Algeria, Syria, Iran and Yemen on the other. Negatively labelled as a republic of atheists, Algeria was also accused by Saudi Arabia and other Arab monarchies of facilitating the financing of terrorism in the Middle East.[38] The Arab League, in particular, is a clear arena for these diplomatic confrontations and differences. The debate that pitted Algeria against the Arab monarchies on the designation of Hezbollah as a terrorist organisation is a convincing example. While Algeria officially refuses 'to speak for the Lebanese in a matter that concerns them',[39] the monarchies consider that Hezbollah's involvement in the Syrian and Iraqi theatres should be the subject of a univocal condemnation by all states in the region.

On the other hand, while Algeria made anti-Zionism one of the major principles of its foreign policy during the Cold War[40] and continues today to defend the idea of a Zionist conspiracy, Morocco distinguished itself by welcoming Shimon Peres in 1986 as part of its policy of mediation for peace in the Middle East, and by its punctual and discreet cooperation with Moroccans in Israel. Many Algerian leaders voluntarily associate the Kingdom with a hostile Israeli–American alliance.

In addition, Moroccan leaders negatively perceive the military's dominance in the Algerian Republic. Indeed, as early as 1991, to escape a potential Islamist regime, many democrats supported stopping the legislative elections in favour of the military institution, considering that it would prevent Algeria from sinking into radical Islam,[41] which facilitated the military coup of 1992. Today, the Republic is constituted by a 'special army' that controls both the regular army and civil society.[42] Conversely, the monarchy had been targeted by two attempted military coups, which led to the abolition of the Ministry of Defence and its replacement with an administration under the supervision of the head of government. At the operational command level, the Moroccan army is under the direct command of the King as Supreme Chief and Chief

---

38 Daguzan, "La politique étrangère de l'Algérie".
39 "Hezbollah case: towards a tussle between Algeria and the Gulf monarchies at the Arab League", *Al Huffington Post*, July 4, 2016.
40 Chikh, "La politique africaine de l'Algérie".
41 Louisa Dris-Aït Hamadouche, "L'Algérie face au 'printemps arabe': l'équilibre par la neutralisation des contestations", *Confluences Méditerranée*, no. 81 (2012): 55–67.
42 See on this subject: François Gèze, "Armée et nation en Algérie: l'irrémédiable divorce?" *Herodote 116*, no. 1 (2005): 175–203.

of Staff of the Armed Forces. Moreover, while the history of modern Morocco was characterised by a depoliticisation of the military apparatus (due to the abolition of the Ministry of Defence), that of Algeria was marked by a militarisation of the political apparatus (due to political representation by the military). These different trajectories reinforce the differentiated perceptions of the two actors.

This is why the feeling of enmity towards Algeria in Moroccan public opinion goes beyond the Sahara. A part of the press and civil society considers Algeria responsible for all of Morocco's problems, while the Algerian media, relaying the perceptions of their leaders, regularly accuses Rabat of plotting against Algeria's security. For many years, Moroccan leaders have suspected Algeria of preventing oil companies from exploring the Kingdom's subsoil, which is why Morocco has reportedly not found any oil.[43] More recently, Algeria has been blamed in the official Moroccan press for trafficking psychotropic drugs to 'destroy Moroccan society'.[44] Conversely, the Algerian media accused the Moroccan government of being at the origin of hashish trafficking in Algeria and financing terrorist operations in Tunisia.[45] The Algerian and Moroccan populist press regularly convey feelings of enmity through their constant accusations.

At the leadership level, Moroccan diplomats also point to Algeria's responsibility for the failure of their bilateral relations, denouncing Algeria's 'provocative and hostile acts towards the Kingdom, particularly concerning the regional dispute over the Moroccan Sahara'.[46] While elaborating a rhetoric of reaching out to Algeria in favour of Maghrebian regional integration, Moroccan press releases describe its leaders as 'prisoners of a bygone era' suffering from a 'total geopolitical amnesia', a 'serious strategic myopia', and assert that its discourse 'belongs to another era, another time'.[47] The Algerian leaders also contribute to this climate of mistrust. This was the case when the head of Algerian diplomacy publicly accused Royal Air Maroc (RAM) of transporting Hashish and Moroccan

---

43 Akram Belkaïd, "L'obsession des complots dans le monde arabe", *Le Monde diploma tique*, June 1, 2015.
44 "Algeria uses the weapon of psychotropic drugs to harm Morocco", MAP, *LeMatin.ma*, August 2014.
45 Olivier Ribouis, "Terrorisme en Tunisie: Alger accuse le Maroc", *La Nouvelle Tribune*, December 16, 2013.
46 "Morocco decides the recall in consultation of the ambassador of His Majesty the King in Algiers", MAP *Maroc.ma*, October 30, 2013.
47 "Bouteflika's provocative speech triggers tension in Moroccan-Algerian relations", MAP *Maroc.ma*, October 31, 2013.

banks of laundering money in Africa.[48] Many diplomats reported the extreme animosity that characterises direct exchanges between Moroccan and Algerian diplomats within multilateral organisations or foreign embassies, sometimes hijacking the debate of the day on the Sahara issue.

Morocco is actively seeking recognition from the international community of Algeria's direct role in the birth and development of the Polisario Front. From the Moroccan point of view: 'Without making Algeria assume its responsibility as the main party in this conflict, there will be no solution. And without a responsible perception of the tense security situation in the region, there will be no stability.'[49] Therefore, the Kingdom's strategy is to minimise the role of the Polisario Front as an actor and to demonstrate the non-existence of the RASD as a government in order to emphasise the role of Algeria. In this way, the Moroccans hope to be able to negotiate directly with their neighbour, which, it should be remembered, also supplies them with half of their national imports on a continental scale.[50] However, Algeria officially denies any responsibility in this conflict. For the president, 'There is no problem between Morocco and Algeria; there is a problem between the Kingdom of Morocco and the Polisario'.[51] This Algerian posture prevents any possibility of directly arranging an agreement or setting rules and political limits that should not be exceeded.

These shared perceptions also reveal the existence of a security dilemma,[52] which, over the past decade, has led to an arms race. Initially conceptualised by Herbert Butterfield, John Hertz and Robert Jervis, a security dilemma is a situation in which the many means deployed by one state to ensure its security are perceived as a threat by another, sometimes resulting in an arms race.

Algeria, on the one hand, became in 2011 the first arms buyer in Africa, and the first defence budget, representing 4.8% of its GDP, thus overtaking South Africa. With a budget of US$10.4 billion in 2013, Algeria is the first country in African history to have spent more than $10 billion on military matters and the

---

48 "Indignation in Morocco after the remarks of an Algerian minister on 'hashish money'", *Le Monde.fr*, October 23, 2017.
49 "Speech by HM the King to the nation on the occasion of the 39th anniversary of the Green March".
50 In 2013, 53% of Moroccan imports from Africa came from Algeria and consisted mainly of energy resources. "Morocco-Africa relations: the ambition of a new frontier".
51 "Intervention by President Bouteflika at the NEPAD-AUDA Stakeholders' Dinner-Debate'", *El Mouradia—Presidency of the Republic*, October 22, 2004.
52 For a more recent study on the different behaviours related to the security dilemma, see: Ken Booth and Nicholas J. Wheeler, *The Security Dilemma: Fear, Cooperation and Trust in World Politics*, (Basingstoke New York, N.Y: Palgrave Macmillan, 2008).

sixth-largest importer of arms in the world.[53] In parallel with the increase in the defence budget, all sectors of the Algerian army have been renovated. Its relations with its traditional supplier, Russia (which provides 90% of its imports), have also been strengthened. In exchange for the important purchases made by Algeria between 2006 and 2010[54] (120 tanks to the company Rosoboronexport, Su-30MkA fighters to the same company for an amount of 5.5 billion euros, etc.), Russia erased the 3.6 billion euro debt contracted by Algiers during the Soviet era.[55]

The objectives of the Algerian arms policy are equivocal. On the one hand, it is clear that 'Algerian threat analysis and the strategic models taught to its staff are always centred on an attacker from the West'.[56] On the other hand, for the former secretary-general of the Algerian Ministry of Foreign Affairs, Ramtane Lamamra, 'Algeria's large arms purchase from Russia should not be interpreted as an aggressive measure or as targeting Morocco. We are coming out of almost 15 years of internal struggle against the Islamist maquis.'[57] Since 2009, Algeria has concentrated its forces against AQIM by equipping itself with mine and explosive-resistant vehicles.[58] Since 2012, the army has reinforced its means to protect its eastern and Sahelian borders following the collapse of the Libyan state and the war in Mali. The fight against terrorism has gradually become the official *leitmotif* of Algerian foreign policy, to the point that today's supporters of jihadist terrorism are now equated with 'those of yesterday's colonialism'.[59] This does not, however, exclude the threat posed towards its neighbour by Algeria's military force. Indeed, Algeria regularly organises troop landing exercises. This type of activity is no longer a demonstration of force but a form of force projection.

As Brahim Saidy rightly reminds us, 'Morocco's defence policy has always been defined in terms of its fight for the country's territorial integrity and the

---

53 SIPRI Yearbook 2013, SIPRI 2013.
54 Sukhoi Mk fighter aircraft, Mig 29 SMB fighter aircraft, Yak-130 trainer aircraft.
55 Mathieu O. "Course aux armes et leadership algérien", JeuneAfrique.com, May 5, 2012.
56 Interview with Peter Cross, analyst at Middle East Tactical Studies (METS), Paris, 27 April 2007, in "Western Sahara: the cost of conflict", Middle East/North Africa Report, International Crisis Group, June 11, 2007.
57 Interview with Ramtane Lamamra in Ibid.
58 Gelfand L. "Spend to Thrive, Country Briefing: Algeria", *IHS Janes Defense Weekly*, January 28, 2009.
59 Ahmed Gaïd Salah (Lieutenant General, Deputy Minister of National Defence, Chief of Staff of the National People's Army), in "L'Armée de Libération Nationale, arme de l'information et de la diplomatie", Colloquium organised by the *Directorate of Communication, Information and Orientation of the National People's Army Staff*, Algiers, October 22, 2014, http://www.mdn.dz/site_principal/index.php?L=en#undefined.

threats posed by its neighbours'.[60] Thus, it can be observed that in reaction (in part) to Algeria's arms policy, Morocco increased its imports of major conventional weapons, or heavy weapons, by 443% between 2002 and 2011,[61] while the share of military expenditure in GDP increased (3.4% in 2004, 3.9% in 2014) over the period 2004–2014, at the same time as GDP rose from US$56 to $105 billion dollars, i.e. doubled in ten years. This brought the Moroccan defence budget to nearly $3.8 billion in 2014, the highest in its history. In ten years, Morocco has gone from being the 69th- to the 12th-largest arms importer in the world.[62] The RAF (Royal Armed Forces) is since 2014 the fourth-largest army in Africa in terms of manpower (195,800 men) and the fourth-largest spender on armaments on the continent,[63] making the Kingdom the 7th largest military power in Africa since 2014.[64]

The reasons for this armament policy are just as multiple as for Algeria. Officially, Morocco is modernising its military apparatus at a time when it is constantly growing. Moreover, it is consolidating its weight as a regional power at a time when foreign policy priorities are oriented towards economic diplomacy and security in Africa. Through the modernisation of its naval arsenal, it wishes to protect its maritime borders, threatened by territorial disputes with Spain (in the Mediterranean Sea and the Atlantic Ocean), as well as its economic interests (due to the discovery of potential oil deposits on the Atlantic coast and the construction of the new international port of Tanger-Med). Through the modernisation of its land and air warfare arsenal, the army can actively participate in the anti-terrorist fight within its territory and beyond through the multilateral mechanism of NATO's Mediterranean Dialogue, and within a bilateral framework (training soldiers in the fight against terrorism). These forces also participate in the control of migratory flows and of trafficking (arms, drugs), as well as in PKOs (peacekeeping operations).

On the other hand, the modernisation of the Moroccan army also stems from the desire to counter the Algerian threat in the Sahara.[65] According to

---

60 Saidy, "La politique de défense Marocaine".
61 "Growth in international arms transfers driven by Asian demand", *Press release, SIPRI*, March 19, 2012.
62 Paul Holtom, Mark Bromley, Pieter D. Wezeman and Siemon T. Wezeman, "Trends in International Arms Transfers", *SIPRI Fact Sheet, SIPRI*, (March 2013), 4.
63 The World Factbook, CIA, 2014.: https://www.cia.gov/library/publications/the-world-factbook/rankorder/2034rank.html?countryname=Morocco&countrycode=mo&regionCode=afr&rank=14#mo.
64 Global Fire Power, Rank, 2014.: http://www.globalfirepower.com/countries-listing-africa.asp.
65 Anthony H. Cordesman, and Aram Nerguizian, *The North African Military Balance. Force*

a study by Anthony H. Cordesman and Aram Nerguizian, the Moroccan army makes considerable efforts to protect the territory against invasion or targeted attacks by the Polisario Front.[66] Morocco's acquisition of armoured personnel carriers in recent years is, therefore, also linked to the protection of its southern provinces. The Kingdom has indeed acquired nearly 320 M-113 armoured personnel carriers from the United States (2005–2007), 13 other M-113s from Belgium (2009)[67] and 250 US Abrams tanks (2015–2018).[68] Its vehicles also include 0 EBR-75s, 80 AMX-10RCS, 190 AML-90s, 38 AML-60-7s and 20M-1114s,[69] all usable devices in desert zones like the Sahara.

Finally, the army uses some of its aircraft for transporting troops and equipment and for logistical support during its operations in the Sahara region, but it has also acquired fighter aircraft, such as the F-16.

While Morocco's acquisition of land and air equipment was a reaction to its neighbour's armament policy, the priority given to the modernisation of the Algerian navy's equipment seems to be a response to the development of the Kingdom's fleet. For many observers, Algeria undertook the modernisation of its fleet in response to the development plan of the Moroccan navy.[70] Comparing the dates of orders or purchases of naval equipment makes it possible to partly verify and illustrate this hypothesis. It can be noted that to follow up on Morocco's purchase of a Frégate from France in January 2014 (500 million euros),[71] Algeria ordered two German MekoA200 frigates in April of the same year (2.2 billion euros).[72] Following Morocco's order of three SIGMA frigates from the Netherlands in 2011,[73] Algeria ordered three Chinese C28A corvettes

---

Developments & Regional Challenges, (Center For Strategic and International Studies—Burke Chair in Strategy, 2010), 124.

66   Ibid., 98.

67   *Arms Transfers Database*, SIPRI, in Simon Pierre Boulanger Martel, "Transfert d'armes vers l'Afrique du Nord. Entre intérêts économiques et impératifs sécuritaires", *Note d'Analyse*, GRIP, (March 24, 2014): 7.

68   "Morocco receives American Abrams tanks", *Bladi.net*, https://www.bladi.net/maroc-chars-abrams-etats-unis,48485.html, accessed on June 14, 2020.

69   Cordesman and Nerguizian, *The North African Military Balance. Force Developments & Regional Challenges*, 58.

70   Fanny Lutz, "Une décennie de frénésie militaire Dépenses militaires au Moyen-Orient et en Afrique du Nord", *Analysis Note*, GRIP, (February 26, 2013): 14–15.

71   M. Cabirol, "Défense: la France a exporté pour 6,3 milliards d'euros d'armes en 2013", *La Tribune*, January 29, 2014.

72   "The first images of Chinese corvettes destined for Algeria", https://medias24.com/2014/08/25/les-premieres-images-des-corvettes-chinoises-destinees-a-lalgerie/, August 25, 2014.

73   "Damen delivers a second Moroccan SIGMA frigate", MerEtMarine.com, February 13, 2012.

in 2012.[74] Nevertheless, contrary to appearances, this arms race does not constitute a risk of escalation of violence. It reinforces each of the two states in their capacities but is not part of a logic of imminent armed conflict: it is instead part of a logic of deterrence and balance of power.

Finally, it is clear that Algeria (and, by extension, the Polisario Front) is a public historical *hostis*. Historical, because the conflict between the two neighbours began in the run-up to Algeria's independence. Public, because Morocco has publicly and officially accused Algeria of being responsible for the conflict.

However, the definition of the enemy must be nuanced in this context: while in many historical cases, the designation of the enemy was accompanied by a strategy of annihilation or extermination resulting in the declaration of a military offensive—a similar example in Africa today is the threat of all-out war made by Ethiopia against Eritrea–Morocco, in fact, rules out the option of war. Contrary to the Ethiopian–Eritrean example, Algeria's denial of its role in the conflict and the existence of a third actor, the Polisario Front, diminish the interest in declaring war. Moreover, the strategic cultures of the two countries show that the outbreak of a direct war is unlikely. While Algerian military doctrine forbids the army to intervene in combat missions outside the borders, eliminating any risk of a direct attack on Morocco, Morocco is characterised by a defensive strategic culture. As such, the participation of the RAF in external operations is limited to PKOs, and to a lesser extent to specific multilateral coalitions (Iraq, Yemen). All of this supports the idea that the confrontation is more on the diplomatic, economic and informational fronts than the military front, especially in Africa.

4   South Africa and Nigeria: Geopolitical Adversaries or Future Continental Allies?

In the wake of Algeria's Moroccan policy, South Africa and Nigeria have adopted the same positions and have long been represented, in the aforementioned official phrase, as 'enemies of the territorial integrity' of the Kingdom. However, unlike Algeria, they are not enemies in the Schmittian sense but political adversaries. The adversary, unlike the enemy, is not strategic but only geopolitical. Indeed, Moroccans have little knowledge of and share few ties with Nigeria and South Africa: they do not historically project negative stereotypes on the identity and culture of these two countries. Similarly, the

---

74   "The first images of Chinese corvettes destined for Algeria".

Moroccan state does not reveal any contemptuous or depreciatory perceptions in its discourse. The adversarial relationship is framed within a limited political framework and is expressed through opposing representations of the Nigerian and South African problems.

First of all, South Africa has historically supported the self-determination of the Sahrawi independence fighters. As one researcher recalls, 'Algeria was and still is the ANC's best friend in North Africa and perhaps even on the continent'.[75] Thus, South Africa established ties with the Polisario Front in the late 1970s, and the ANC president-in-exile, Oliver Tambo, visited Polisario-controlled territories in late 1988. At the end of apartheid, Nelson Mandela acknowledged the assistance Mohammed V had provided to the ANC and thus maintained moderate positions on the dispute.[76] Therefore, while continuing to support the Polisario Front within the OAU, the ANC government refrained from commenting strongly on the Moroccan position while Nelson Mandela was in power. For some, Mandela was dissuaded by the diplomatic interventions of France, the United States and Boutros Boutros-Ghali, the then UN secretary-general, from supporting Saharan independence.[77] For others, the relationship with the Polisario Front was not as good as it could have been. For still others, Hassan II's relationship with Nelson Mandela, who had visited Morocco several times, was the reason for the South African leader's political moderation.[78] In any case, Morocco and South Africa decided to open a diplomatic mission in 1994 and signed the first cooperation agreements, while maintaining a certain formal restraint. South African positions towards Morocco became more radical in 2000 after the election of President Thabo Mbeki. The government officially declared its support for the Polisario Front, which, according to a former Moroccan ambassador to South Africa, reflected the rise of the radicals at the expense of the pragmatists within the ANC.[79]

---

75 Alain Vircoulon, "L'Afrique du Sud et le Maghreb", in *Le Maghreb et son Sud: vers des liens renouvelés*, eds. Mokhefi, Mansouria and Antil, Alain (Paris: CNRS, 2012), 59–72.
76 Samir Lakmahri, "Maroc-Afrique du Sud: les dessous d'un gâchis", *Zamane*, December 6, 2013.
77 Vircoulon, "L'Afrique du Sud et le Maghreb".
78 "Nelson Mandela and Morocco: a long history of friendship and loyalty", *Medias24*, December 6, 2013.
79 'The Sahara issue had become a recurrent issue in the ANC's internal debate (along with Zimbabwe and major economic choices), around which moderates and radicals within the ruling alliance (ANC, Pc and central COSATU) were divided. So much so that it represented a cumbersome weight that Mr Mbeki chose to shed in order to guarantee the chances of success of his neo-liberal economic programme, which was a priority for his second term (2004–2009) and which met with strong opposition from the radicals within

Against a backdrop of crisis, Mohammed VI visited South Africa in 2002 for the first and only time, for the World Summit on Sustainable Development. On the margins of this conference, a meeting between Mohammed VI and Thabo Mbeki led to short-lived appeasement of South African positions, with the result that the government now affirmed its support for UN efforts to resolve the dispute. Two years later, in 2004, Pretoria hosted a permanent diplomatic representation of the Polisario Front, while the South African ambassador in Algiers was accredited to the latter. Since then, South Africa has increased its contacts and aid to the Sahrawi independence movement. Together, Algeria and South Africa reaffirmed their common position against the Moroccan policy on their fifth bi-national commission in 2010; the ANC also directly condemned Morocco on the occasion of its national conference in 2012. While the Kingdom did not break its relations with the first African power, it chose to symbolically reduce its diplomatic representation to the rank of chargé d'affaires.

The perception of adversity was thus shared between the two countries. While South Africa may have seen Morocco as an ideological adversary in North Africa, Morocco perceives South Africa as an illegitimate adversary in the sense that it cannot rationally explain Pretoria's interest in the matter. According to one ambassador, 'unlike other African countries that have recognised the so-called "RASD" (e.g. Ghana, Mozambique or Ethiopia), South Africa has positioned itself in the front line of this conflict in international forums (UN, NAM, etc.), in place of our adversaries'.[80] It thus forms a substitute for the real *hostis* that Algeria constitutes in the Moroccan representation.

The reasons for South Africa's re-engagement with the Polisario Front, while not fully explainable, can be contextualised. First, 2004 was marked by the legislative elections in which the ANC won a majority and the parliament re-elected Thabo Mbeki. Among the party personalities who supported the president's re-election was Nkosazana Dlamini-Zuma, former wife of President Jacob Zuma, several times minister under Mandela, Mbeki and Zuma, who became head of the AU Commission and candidate for the position of South Africa's presidency in 2019, and who was supported by Algeria in her candidacy for the chairship of the Commission. Her pro-Sahrawi positions and her political activism with UN secretary-general Ban Ki-moon in favour of self-determination reveal Algeria's involvement, according to Moroccan leaders. The positions of the South African government were indeed clearly influenced by the future candidate. According to one ambassador:

the ruling Alliance.' Talal Rhoufrani, "Les relations Maroc-Afrique du Sud: réalité et perspectives", *Royal Institute for Strategic Studies*, (2012).
80   Ibid.

Ms Nkosazana D. Zuma, leader of the pro-Polisario camp, has taken advantage of the 'collateral damage' caused by the fierce competition around the World Cup of 2010[81] and the untimely resignation of Mr James Baker, Special Envoy of the UN Secretary-General for the Sahara in June, to make President Mbeki and some of his close associates give in to the need for restraint and realism on this issue.[82]

On the other hand, it seems that Morocco has not been able to make any efforts to develop its relations with this power. On the contrary, Moroccan diplomats have been absent from ANC meetings on several occasions and have cancelled mixed commissions planned by the countries.[83] In this regard, former ambassador Talal Rhoufrani acknowledges that on the Moroccan side,

> We have to admit that we did not do all that was necessary to encourage President Mbeki to persevere in his balanced attitude and to strengthen his position within the leading bodies of the party and the Government, in the face of constant pressure from the declared opponents of our thesis.[84]

This attitude is indicative of a defeatist representation of the Moroccan–South African relationship, in the sense that it was difficult for Moroccan diplomats to commit to an order of things that seemed impossible to reverse, which tended to prolong the state of enmity for an indefinable period. This representation continued until Morocco's re-adherence to the AU and the organisation of the AU–EU summit, during which the heads of state of the two countries shook hands and announced the resumption of more sustained cooperation through the appointment of an experienced ambassador, Youssef Amrani. The choice of this former Minister Delegate for Foreign Affairs and head officer to the Royal Cabinet was a way of ensuring high-level diplomacy and a symbolic act to mark the importance of this renewal.

Unlike South Africa, Nigeria, the third major 'adversary' of the Moroccan cause, in the words of one former ambassador,[85] is a particular case in Moroc-

---

81 In 2003, Morocco and South Africa simultaneously submitted their bids to host the World Cup 2010.
82 Rhoufrani, "Les relations Maroc-Afrique du Sud : réalité et perspectives".
83 Lakmahri, "Maroc-Afrique du Sud".
84 Rhoufrani, "Les relations Maroc-Afrique du Sud : réalité et perspectives".
85 Cherkaoui Mustapha former Moroccan ambassador to Nigeria, "Le Maroc et la lutte contre l'extrémisme religieux: le cas de Boko Haram au Nigéria", in *Journée d'étude sur*

can representations. Nigeria recognised the Polisario Front as an independent state in 1984 when the latter was admitted to the OAU, without Morocco deciding to break off diplomatic relations with it, contrary to the policy it had adopted at that time towards the countries that supported the Polisario Front. Indeed, the Kingdom considers Nigeria a long-standing ally with which it shares age-old ties. For one former ambassador:

> Nigerians, especially the Muslim community in the North, hold Morocco and Amir Al Mou'minine in high esteem, in memory of the Khalifate of Sokoto founded in 1803 by Sheikh Outhmane Danfodio, with the support of the Sultan and the ulemas of Morocco. It should be recalled that at the time of the advent of the Cherifian Empire on the one hand, and the Khalifates of Sokoto and Borno on the other, the two countries at one time shared common borders.[86]

Moreover, as we shall see in the next chapter, Nigeria is geographically located in Morocco's privileged area of cooperation, namely West, Central and Sahelian Africa.

More confident about the possibility of a future turnaround and aware of the need to cooperate with this regional power to develop the Moroccan presence in this region of the continent, the Moroccans wish to maintain flexible positions towards Nigeria. The hosting of a diplomatic mission of the Polisario Front by the Nigerian government in 2000 thus did not lead to a rupture in diplomatic relations. The election in 2015 of Muslim president Muhammadu Buhari, who succeeded Goodluck Jonathan, was even expected to allow a rapprochement between Morocco and Nigeria. Although Buhari reiterated Nigeria's support for the Polisario Front and commended Algeria's commitment to the issue,[87] Morocco has not undertaken any hostile diplomatic action. Even though the Kingdom sees Nigeria as a political adversary, it has chosen to develop its economic and cultural relations with the latter, as we will see in more detail in the following section.

---

    les relations maroco-africaines, Rabat, Centre Jacques Berque, Centre d'Études Sahariennes, Conseil National des Droits de l'Homme, Fondation kAS, October 3, 2014, Rabat. Coordination: Yousra Abourabi. URL of the video: https://www.youtube.com/watch?v=MsSEGV2NRAc.

86 Mustapha Cherkaoui, "Quel potentiel de développement des relations de coopération Maroc-Nigeria", *Royal Institute for Strategic Studies*, May 10, 2012.

87 "Morocco/Nigeria: La normalisation des relations pas prête d'avoir lieu", Yabiladi.com, June 1, 2015.

Finally, contrary to its representation of the South African problem, Moroccan diplomacy reveals a much more optimistic representation of the evolution of Moroccan–Nigerian relations based on geo-cultural and tactical considerations. On the one hand, Nigeria's belonging to the West African grouping reinforces Morocco's view of the possibility of future regional integration; on the other hand, the balance of power with Nigeria is not the same as with South Africa. Nigeria has shown itself to be open to dialogue. Also, it faces security problems (terrorism, maritime piracy) which Morocco believes it can help to address,[88] as we will see in more detail below.

5 Shared Perceptions of an Algiers–Abuja–Pretoria anti-Moroccan Axis

Is the perception of a hostile axis between Algeria, Nigeria and South Africa, the main actors of 'relentless entryism of Morocco's adversaries',[89] justified? The three countries indeed joined forces in the early 2000s, along with Egypt and Senegal, to support the launch of NEPAD-AUDA, a manifestation of historical cooperation. At the same time, presidents Bouteflika and Mbeki, who shared excellent personal relations, established in 2000 a bilateral commission that met at a high level on a regular basis to help each other on strategic issues relating mainly to African affairs.

Algeria thus supported Mbeki's efforts to promote NEPAD-AUDA, to transform the OAU into the AU at the Durban Summit in 2002 and to support Nkosazana Dlamini-Zuma's candidacy for the chair of the AU Commission, a strategic and highly diplomatic position. Algiers also maintains close military cooperation with South Africa: it is one of the few capitals to host an office of the South African arms company Denel, and in 2007 it appointed a military attaché to its embassy in Pretoria. Generally, the two states stand together in the AU, illustrating the Bouteflika–Mbeki strategic alliance that persists under the current presidency.

Similarly, Algeria and Nigeria launched an Algerian–Nigerian gas pipeline project called the Trans-Saharan Gas Pipeline and a highway project linking the Maghreb to the Sahel called the Trans-Saharan Road in the following years.

---

88   Mustapha Cherkaoui (former Moroccan ambassador to Nigeria), "Le Maroc et la lutte contre l'extrémisme religieux: le cas de Boko Haram au Nigéria", *Journée d'étude sur les relations maroco-africaines*.
89   "Adoption of the Tannock report: The relentless entrism of opponents defeated", MAP Maroc.ma, October 23, 2013.

For one Moroccan ambassador, the first of these projects was in reality 'politically motivated, as Algeria wanted to counter the construction of a gas pipeline to Europe through Morocco at all costs', while the second was 'to compete with the now almost completed Tangier–Lagos route'.[90] Although the first Algerian–Nigerian project is still frozen and the second not very profitable, and while the NEPAD-AUDA has been criticised by many African leaders, fearing South African industrial influence,[91] the entire African and foreign press has nonetheless confirmed the constitution of a geopolitical axis committed to the development of the continent, formed by the triumvirate of Bouteflika, Mbeki (then Zuma) and Obasanjo (then Buhari).

On the other hand, these three states appear more like rival powers in the political arena: the dissension between South Africa and Nigeria over the Ivorian crisis[92] is an example of this. It was also in the spirit of rivalry that Algeria, Nigeria and South Africa fought for a permanent seat on the UN Security Council via the Ezulwini Consensus in 2005. The three countries have also failed to define common policy positions on the future of African cooperation. Within the AU, while South Africa and Nigeria are among the 'unionist-gradualists', a group that opposes the creation of an African government *ex tempore*, but in favour of political harmonisation within the framework of the Regional Economic Communities, Algeria falls into the category of 'undecided-sceptics' that appeared in 2007, to which is added a party of 'minimalists', a group of states which have not genuinely formulated their positions and which contribute to the status quo.[93]

The three countries do not form a political axis per se but historically share ideological ties that have fostered consultation and joint interest arrangements in the post-Cold War era.

The Nigerian and South African positions vis-à-vis the Moroccan problem can also be interpreted in light of the criterion of multilateralism suggested at the beginning of this chapter. The persistence of Nigerian and South African positions vis-à-vis Morocco originates in Morocco's departure from the OAU. Together with Algeria, these two countries are among the largest African financial contributors to the UN, the best-represented and most active in pan-

---

90 Cherkaoui, "Quel potential de développement des relations de cooperation Maroc-Nigéria".
91 Ian Taylor and Roland Marchal, "La politique sud-africaine et le NEPAD-AUDA, *Politique africaine*", no. 91 (2012): 120–138.
92 Vincent Darracq, "Jeux de puissance en Afrique: le Nigéria et l'Afrique du Sud face à la crise ivoirienne", *Politique étrangère Été*, no. 2 (2011): 361–374,.
93 Delphine Lecoutre, "Vers un gouvernement de l'Union africaine?", *Politique étrangère Automne*, no. 3 (2008): 629–639.

African organisations,[94] and the most influential in the AU. Until Morocco's return to the AU, South Africa alone contributed almost 25% of the institution's operating budget. What Nigeria and South Africa have in common is the projection, at one or more points in their history, of a multilateral pan-African ideal. Nigeria's 'Manifest Destiny'[95] and Thabo Mbeki's 'African Renaissance'[96] are clear examples of this multilateralist trend towards building conditions for cooperation, development and security in Africa. These two countries, along with Algeria, Senegal, Mozambique and Mali, have strongly contributed to the development of pan-Africanism in the twenty-first century, illustrated by the creation of new organs within the AU: the African Parliament, the Peace and Security Council, and the African Standby Forces. Thabo Mbeki, in particular, although no longer in power, is the architect of South Africa's continental development and, to some extent, of the AU's diplomatic development on the international scene. His cooperation with Algeria and Nigeria has thus strengthened the association between these two countries in the 2000s.

In this respect, the participation, integration and reappropriation of Nigerian and South African ideals projected within the AU, in particular, appear to be determining criteria in the representation of the friends and enemies of these two states. By practising an empty chair policy at the AU, although it seemed rational in its context, Morocco reinforced its 'hostilisation' by Nigeria and especially by South Africa. As a result, the latter helped to reinforce Morocco's exclusion from multilateral negotiations.

The shared representations of Nigeria and South Africa, on the one hand, and Morocco, on the other, are thus expressed in the exclusion of Morocco from their multilateral projects. As one diplomat notes: 'Along with Algeria, South Africa (as well as its neighbours in English-speaking Southern Africa such as Zimbabwe) and Nigeria (and its allies in Central Africa) are the countries that most often pose problems for us within multilateral organisations'.[97] The phenomenon of exclusion is illustrated by Morocco's absence for many years from African multilateral meetings organised by the various AU organs and offices, political opposition in UN debates and projects, and the lack of participation of these three countries in multilateral projects initiated by Morocco. It there-

---

94 André Lewin, "Les Africains à l'ONU", *Relations internationales*, no. 128 (2006): 55–78.
95 Daniel C. Bach, "Nigeria's 'Manifest Destiny' in West Africa: Dominance without Power", *Africa Spectrum 42*, no. 2 (2007): 301–321.
96 Ivan Crouzel, "La 'renaissance africaine': un discours sud-africain?", *Politique africaine*, no. 77 (2012): 171–182.
97 Interview with a diplomat no. 3, May–June 2013. This analysis was confirmed by other diplomats with whom I had informal discussions in subsequent years.

fore appears that Morocco has more to gain by reintegrating into the AU and working to exclude the Polisario Front from within by truly playing the game of African multilateralism. The option of reintegration was not, however, envisaged without conditions, because it would have constituted a form of symbolic recognition of the existence of the RASD in the Moroccan representation. This vision has since changed, leading to Morocco's application for membership in 2016.

However, it appears that Moroccan–African relations are sometimes irreconcilable with the principles governing internal life. The current adversarial relationship with South Africa could evolve into continental economic cooperation. Indeed, while Morocco is currently deploying economic diplomacy in South Africa, Pretoria's North Africa policy was enriched with an economic dimension after Jacob Zuma came to power in 2009.[98] Morocco is not a threatening economic competitor on a continental scale—compared with external powers—but the degree of liberalisation of its economy, the amount of FDI it receives and reinvests on the continent,[99] and finally its geo-strategic position have made it a continental economic power and the second-largest African investor on the continent, after South Africa.

It would seem, moreover, that it is by this means that the Kingdom envisages, in the long term, and in parallel with the completion of its Saharan Autonomy Project, to make its rivals yield to its imperatives. Therefore, the need to think of new forms of economic and security cooperation in Africa equals the need to integrate Morocco into these initiatives as it establishes itself as a continental power. Ultimately, the perceived hostility of the South African and Nigerian positions and the development of Algerian military power have helped to animate Morocco's African diplomacy both economically and politically. This new dynamic could eventually contribute to transforming the situation from one of political rivalry to one of building economic alliances.

6   The Representation of a 'natural extension' Based On the 'Historical Constants' of the Kingdom

In Moroccan geopolitical representations of the African continent, West, Sahelian and Central Africa form a privileged area of South–South cooperation: Senegal, Côte d'Ivoire and Gabon are the main axis, but there are also Guinea-

---

98   Vircoulon, "L'Afrique du Sud et le Maghreb".
99   See Appendix 7.

Conakry, Niger, Burkina Faso, Benin, Mali, the Democratic Republic of Congo (DRC), Congo, Guinea-Bissau, Equatorial Guinea and Togo. This preference is illustrated in particular by the density and quality of diplomatic exchanges: Mohammed VI's visits and signing of numerous 'win–win' cooperation agreements with countries in these regions attest to this preference. In this respect, the King has repeatedly declared 'the importance of political and economic ties between the Kingdom and the countries of Central and West Africa'.[100]

This preference can be explained in the first place by what Pierre Grosser calls 'faith in history', i.e. the belief in a historical destiny. According to the author, 'to refer to history, to analyse events in terms of historical evolution, is not only to have faith in the supposed explanatory power of history, but also to have faith in a history that would have a meaning and, by the same token, would give one to the scum of events'.[101] In this case, the meaning conferred on events by this faith in history is that of the 'civilisational influence' of Morocco based on 'national constants', two expressions often used in speeches and official communiqués. In this respect, the monarch states that he has oriented Moroccan diplomacy towards the objective of 'highlighting the assets of its spiritual influence, its historical heritage and geo-strategic situation [...] and shaping a better cultural influence'.[102] This effort is all the more directed towards West Africa 'because of the geography and history [...] between Morocco and the kingdoms that have developed in the region south of the Sahara, from Ghana to Chad, via Nigeria, and this from the Idrissid dynasty to that of the Alaouite *Chorfas*'.[103] More generally, what one French ambassador observed in the 1960s we still observe today: 'there is, in various official circles, the conviction that this country has a mission of liaison between the Arab world and the Black world'.[104]

Morocco thus recognises the weight of history in its relations with West Africa as a determining element of its foreign policy. However, as Pierre Grosser

---

100 "Speech by HM the King at the Moroccan-Ivorian Economic Forum in Abidjan", *Maroc.ma*, February 24, 2014.
101 Pierre Grosser, "De l'usage de l'Histoire dans les politiques étrangères", in *Politique étrangère: nouveaux regards*, ed. Charillon, Frédéric (Paris: Presses de Sciences Po, 2002), 376.
102 "Speech by HM King Mohammed VI on the occasion of the 49th anniversary of the Revolution of the King and the People".
103 Ministry of Habous and Islamic Affairs, *Press release on the occasion of the announcement of the constitutive act of the Mohammed VI Foundation of African Ulemas*, July 13, 2015.
104 Letter from M. Roger Seydoux, ambassador of France in Rabat, to M. Couve de Murville, Minister of Foreign Affairs, Rabat, 28 March 1962. In: *Documents diplomatiques français 192 Tome I, 1er janvier–30 juin*.

also notes, 'invoking the weight of history [...] provides less information on the history of the qualified region than on the weight of representations and the static and selective vision of those who convey these expressions'.[105] However, the origin of these representations cannot be understood without looking at the history of Morocco through the prism of its Saharan ambitions since the first Arab conquests. This is why I will attempt to summarise, in a few paragraphs, the main historical events that have structured this representation: what are the age-old links that Morocco shares with sub-Saharan Africa, to which official statements sometimes refer?

It should be recalled that since the first Arab conquests in the seventh and eighth centuries, the *as-Saby* policy, i.e. the acquisition of enslaved people from conquered populations, and the trade in raw materials led the Moroccan empires to establish caravan routes crossing the Sahara.[106] Under the rule of the Umayyads (661–750) and then the Abbasids (750–1258), all families in Morocco and throughout the Muslim West owned slaves, and even poor families could acquire at least one slave.[107] Thus, when the Almoravid Empire (1040–1147), once in power, expanded into West Africa, new caravan routes were established with the mighty kingdom of Ghana. The Marrakech–Sijilmassa–Ghana axis was the most frequented.[108] Taking advantage of these profitable commercial exchanges (salt and gold in one direction; dates, copper and wool in the other), the Almoravid Empire played a decisive role in the Islamisation of the black Saharan and West African populations through the propagation of the maraboutic networks still active today.

Successors of the Almoravids, the Almohads (1147–1269) strengthened the Cherifian power in relation to brotherhood networks in Africa by instituting the bonds of allegiance. Leader of the Almohads at the beginning of their rebellion against the Almoravids, Ibn Toumart was at the origin of a set of texts constituting a doctrine that combined Sunni and Sufi ideas (1121–1124). This federating messianic doctrine earned him the title of Mâhdi (person guided by God). On his death, the Almohads conferred on Ibn Toumart's successor the title of Amir al Mou'minine (Commander of the Believers, a title still held by the King today) and led a decisive battle against the Almoravids, resulting in the

---

105 Grosser, "De l'usage de l'Histoire dans les politiques étrangères", 363.
106 Chouki El Hamel, *Black Morocco a history of slavery, race, and Islam*, (Cambridge New York: Cambridge University Press, 2013), 116.
107 Ibid., 117.
108 Olivier Pétré-Grenouilleau, *La Traite des noirs*, (Paris: Presses Universitaires de France–PUf, 1998), 127.

death of nearly 3000 Gnaoua soldiers (black people from the Gulf of Guinea at the service of the Sultan).[109]

Following the fall of the Almohads, under Marinid rule (1269–1465), the control of the trans-Saharan caravan routes continued to be seen as a strategic lever of the empire's power. The Moroccans approached the great Malian kingdom of the Songhai to create a framework for sustained cooperation in this mercantilist enterprise. It must be said that at that time, the alliance of the Makhzen with the Songhai kingdom was facilitated by the presence in this region of numerous peoples mixed with Berbers fleeing the Arab conquest, as well as Arab traders married to natives. The two peoples already knew each other. Moreover, if the empire of Ghana was not truly Islamic, that of Mali was based on the legitimacy of the chiefs of the Malinke tribes, claiming descent from Bilal, the black companion of the prophet. This did not prevent the slave trade from existing, demonstrating that slavery followed mercantile and religious differentiation rules but that it was not fundamentally racialised. According to Ibn Battuta's travel accounts, for example, the number of enslaved people per caravan and per year for each Maghreb merchant was estimated at several hundred people on the route from Takadda to Timbuktu.[110] Throughout this period, the Islamisation of West African societies was spreading, with traders and local elites being the first to convert.[111] In the other direction, the mixing of Moroccan society was increasing.

The arrival of the Portuguese in Morocco (1415–1769) and the establishment of trading posts along the Atlantic coast had, for a short time, a severe impact on trans-Saharan trade. Coming to terms with this presence after a short period of withdrawal, Morocco's trade with Africa expanded again. It reached its peak during the reign of Sultan al-Mansur of the Saadian dynasty (1549–1660). The latter is renowned for his conquest of Bilâd al-Sûdan, one of the most important periods in the history of Morocco. Motivated by the extension of his empire and uninterested in the alliances sealed by his predecessors with the West African kingdoms, al-Mansur led a military offensive against the Songhai kingdom in 1591. His strategy was first to send his black slaves to obtain intelligence on the internal politics of the Songhai and then to set up a diplomatic mission composed of Bedouin marabouts for future negotiations.[112] Historio-

---

109   El Hamel, *Black Morocco a history of slavery, race, and Islam*, 123.
110   Ibid., 125.
111   Ibid., 132.
112   In 1583, according to Al Sa'di's account of the diplomatic mission to Songhai: 'the Prince gave the most brilliant welcome to the Moroccan envoy and gave him, as he returned to his country, a quantity of presents double that which he had received. These presents con-

graphic accounts also assume that the Sultan's chronicler was Prince Ali, son of Askia Daoud, Songhai emperor from 1549 to 1592,[113] who had informed the Sultan precisely about the strengths and weaknesses of his clan (note in this regard that the Daoud family still exists in Morocco). In the time of the Saadian Sultan, beyond the economic interests offered by the control of gold or salt mines or the messianic interests of al-Mansur, the conquest of Bilâd al-Sûdan was considered a way of extending and concretising the Islamic Umma under his command and acquiring a strategic depth that would allow him to escape from the Spanish-Ottoman pincers to the east and north.[114] The correspondence between the Sultan and Queen Elizabeth of England in 1589[115] thus demonstrated that no matter how cooperative the Songhai were, the Sultan planned to expand south.

Al-Mansur the Saadian's victorious military expedition took the city of Gao. As a sign of recognition of his suzerainty, several convoys of captive black people were sent to al-Mansur, amounting to nearly 1,200 men, women and children.[116] Gao, Timbuktu and Djenné became the main markets for enslaved black people bound for the Saadian Empire, a trade managed by the 'Pachaliks of the Sudan', pashas of the Cherifian Bilâd al-Sûdan, often from the ethnic group of the Armas, Arab-Andalusian-Songhai mixes in the service of the successive Saadian sultans[117] (it should be noted that the Armas bear the family name Touré in Mali and Guinea today). Finally, the conquest of Songhai, if it had lasted, would have given the Moroccan empire the means to be Sudanese as well as Arab-Berber; but the Cherifian occupation had rapidly diminished.[118]

With the advent of the Alawite dynasty (1631 to the present day), the later Alawite sultans could renew the allegiance of many of the ulemas-marabouts of the West African and Sahelian regions who had sworn allegiance to the earlier Saadian sultans through the ceremony of the Cherifian Bey'a.[119] Around 1690, even though the Moroccan territory had been amputated from its Saha-

---

sisted of slaves, musk, etc. and they also included eighty eunuchs'; quoted by Mouline, *Le califat imaginaire d'Ahmad al-Mansûr légitimité, pouvoir et diplomatie au Maroc*, 336.

113 El Hamel, *Black Morocco a history of slavery, race, and Islam*, 147–152.
114 Mouline, *Le califat imaginaire d'Ahmad al-Mansûr légitimité, pouvoir et diplomatie au Maroc*, 334.
115 Ibid., 338.
116 Maurice Delafosse, "Les débuts des troupes noires du Maroc", *Hespéris—Institut des Hautes Études Marocaines*, (1923): 1–12.
117 Michel Abitol, *Histoire du Maroc*, (Paris, 2009), 235–245.
118 Mouline, *Le califat imaginaire d'Ahmad al-Mansûr légitimité, pouvoir et diplomatie au Maroc*, 350.
119 Ibid., 352–353.

ran depth, the Alawite Sultan Moulay Ismaïl obtained the allegiance of the Pachalik of Timbuktu.[120] In parallel to the northern Malian allegiance, the Sultan established his authority on the borders of present-day Mauritania.[121] Admiring the exploits of Louis XIV, with whom he exchanged regular correspondence, Moulay Ismaïl set up an army of 80,000 men and 40,000 cavalry, intending to reunify the empire according to the borders established at the time of the Marinids[122] and to regain control of the Moroccan pashaliks of the Sudan, who had long since turned their deference to the sultans of the empire in favour of the Bambara king of Segou.[123] Composed of many tribes, including the indomitable Rifans, the Sultan's army also included a body of black 'janissaries',[124] nicknamed 'Abid al-Bukhari (slaves of Bukhari or Bukharas), in reference to the sacred book of Imam al-Bukhari on which the slaves had pledged allegiance to the Sultan. To organise this black army, the Sultan created a bureaucracy to establish and manage its constitution[125] based on a register containing the numbers of the former black troops formed by al-Mansur the Saadian.[126] The Black Army of the Bukharas thus played a major role in the defence of the Alawite throne against foreign attempts, but not only that. Some chroniclers report that it had conquered 'several provinces of Sudan and that its positions in the Black country went beyond the banks of the "Nile" (Niger or Senegal), extending beyond the limits reached by the conquest of Ahmed El Mansour in the previous century'.[127]

After the death of Moulay Ismaïl (1727), the 30 years of 'Moroccan anarchy' benefited from the arrival of the first European settlers. The joint pressure of the European colonial powers led to the weakening of the Sudanese tribes' allegiance to the Alawite Sultan, as well as to the abolition of slavery in the majority of the countries of the Maghreb and the Sahel, except in Morocco, the last country in the region to yield apart from Mauritania. After half a century of infighting between the Alawite power and its military garrisons, resulting in sporadic salaries, the black soldiers gradually became mercenaries who plun-

---

120 Quoted in: Abitol, *Histoire du Maroc*, 244–245.
121 Ibid., 246.
122 Ibid., 234–239.
123 Delafosse, "Les débuts des troupes noires du Maroc".
124 The Janissaries were Ottoman special troops created in the fifteenth century and abolished in 1826.
125 El Hamel, *Black Morocco a history of slavery, race, and Islam*, 156–184.
126 Ibrahima Baba Kaké, "L'aventure des Bukhara (prétoriens noirs) au Maroc au XVIIIe siècle", *Présence Africaine*, no. 70 (1969): 67–74.
127 El-Oufrâni, *Nozhat el-hâdi*, in Delafosse, "Les débuts des troupes noires du Maroc".

dered the Berbers and were soon decimated by them.[128] At the state level, the Sultan's Black Guard was maintained throughout the protectorate period before being renamed the Royal Guard in 1956. Lyautey, himself inspired by this Sultanian guard, created for himself a close guard composed of Senegalese riflemen.[129]

Finally, the expansion of the Sultanian empires, the establishment of trans-Saharan trade routes, the slave trade, the Islamisation of black Africa and the establishment of allegiance ties to the Sultan, Commander of the Faithful, always took place towards the West, starting from the Souss region in Morocco. The Almoravid (eleventh century) influence south of the Sahara, breaking the Ghanaian empire and Islamising the region, appears to be a golden age in Moroccan history. The military expedition of the Saadians to Songhai (sixteenth century) also marked the historical memory of the state to the point of being a determining exploit, among others, for the 'Greater Morocco' project of Allal al-Fassi in the aftermath of independence.[130] At the time of modern Moroccan independence, the claim to Mauritania and the maintenance of links with tribal chiefs in the Sahara and with African religious brotherhoods that once recognised the spiritual authority of the Commander of the Faithful also attest to a historicist representation of Morocco's identity. Numerous official documents, such as the Ministry of Economy study on Moroccan–African relations entitled 'The Ambitions of a New Frontier',[131] also convey this representation constructed in the 'historical consciousness' (defined in the Aronian sense[132]) of the Makhzenian state.

This history reinforces the feeling among Moroccans of a historical role for their country in this region. This is the case at the level of civil society. As Mostafa Hassani-Idrissi notes in a study on school textbooks, the 'medieval period is visited in order to deliver (to students) the prestige of a past likely to reassure the children of a people whose complexes vis-à-vis the West are sought to be reduced and to comfort their heritage'.[133] This is also the case at the level of diplomats. For example, one diplomat proudly stated that 'there are Moroccans whose families are in Mali like the Touatis; Morocco has also

---

128 Ibid.
129 Daniel Rivet, *Lyautey et l'institution du protectorat français au Maroc: 1912–1925 Tome II*, (Paris, France: L'Harmattan, 1996), 17.
130 See Title 2.
131 "Les relations Maroc-Afrique: l'ambition d'une nouvelle frontière".
132 Raymon Aron, *Dimensions de la conscience historique*, (Paris, Les belles lettres, (1961), 2011).
133 Mostafa Hassani-Idrissi, "Manuels d'histoire et identité nationale au Maroc", *Revue internationale d'éducation de Sèvres*, no. 69 (2015): 53–64.

contributed to the spread of Islam in West Africa'.[134] Helping to demonstrate this postulate, many outside observers will also see, in the development of the different aspects of Morocco's Africa policy that I will study throughout this section, the idea of historical continuity. Thus, for the historian Bernard Lugan, 'Morocco is in phase with its historical realities [...] Moroccan influence was manifested by the circulation of a single currency from Tangier to the Senegal River valley and by the same system of weights and measures'.[135]

For all of these reasons, Moroccan leaders refer to this part of Africa as a 'natural extension'.[136] According to Mohammed VI, 'the West African and Sahel region is particularly important in our strategic vision, insofar as it constitutes the natural extension of Morocco's neighbourhood'.[137] Similarly, one diplomat considers that 'Morocco's presence in West African countries is natural'.[138] Within this representation, the question of the Moroccanness of the Sahara appears to be all the more strategic as, in the Moroccan vision, this region historically constitutes the link between Morocco and its Southern African neighbours. After independence, Allal al-Fassi declared that the Sahara played for Morocco 'the political stalk role linking Maghrebian Islam, [and] the Muslims of the entire south-western Sahara'.[139] Even today, the monarch reaffirms that the 'southern provinces have constituted, throughout history, the African extension of Morocco, embodying the age-old geographical, human and commercial links that unite our country with the states of sub-Saharan Africa'.[140]

The recognition of a collective identity uniting Morocco and the countries of West Africa, based on a common history, commercial and religious links, and geographical proximity of which the Sahara is the epicentre, is developing all the more as African countries discursively participate in the recogni-

---

134   Interview with a diplomat from the Ministry of Foreign Affairs and Cooperation no. 9, April–May 2013.
135   Adam Sfali, "Bernard Lugan: L'Africanité du Maroc, d'historique à agissante", *Lemag. ma*, March 03, 2014.
136   According to a statement by the deputy minister of foreign affairs: 'Mr. Amrani stressed that the last visit of HM King Mohammed VI to Côte d'Ivoire has opened new prospects for Morocco-Ivorian relations and injected them with a strong and renewed dynamic. He added that it is also a strong signal of Morocco's attachment to its natural extension and the importance it attaches to its home continent': "Amrani talks to the Ivorian Minister of Industry", *Maroc.ma*, May 22, 2013.
137   "Speech of HM the King on the occasion of the Throne Day", *Maroc.ma*, 2004.
138   Interview with a diplomat no. 15, Ministry of Foreign Affairs and Cooperation, May–June 2013.
139   El-Fassi, "Les revendications marocaines sur les territoires sahariens".
140   "Speech by HM the King on the occasion of the 38th anniversary of the Green March", *Maroc.ma*, November 6, 2013.

tion of this history. For example, at a conference organised at the Ministry of Foreign Affairs in Rabat, a Senegalese diplomat stated that 'every family in northern Senegal has found a way to find a Moroccan ancestor' and adhered to the Moroccan reading of Africa's post-colonial history, stating that 'Africanists did not do much for Casablanca in 1961: they forgot that the Congo was attacked'.[141] Another example is Senegalese president Macky Sall's reference to the existence of a 'Senegalese–Moroccan exception, a relationship strongly rooted in the fertile ground of our shared values of faith, kinship, trust and mutual esteem'.[142]

Pre-colonial historical exchanges and the religious and political links that stem from them are not the only factors in this historical representation of the West African region. This discursive construction of the shared memory between the Kingdom and these states was also reinforced by the political links maintained with the latter in the context of France's Africa policy during the Cold War.

7 The French Character of the Kingdom's Africa Policy: The Erroneous Hypothesis of a 'pré carré gigogne'

The development of French–Moroccan cooperation in Africa during the Cold War, by pushing Hassan II to establish links with many heads of state in French-speaking Africa, renewed the historicist ambition of Morocco, discussed earlier. The cooperation with France also allowed him to get closer to presidents of more distant countries, such as Zaire or Gabon. The young Crown Prince and future King Mohammed VI befriended many children of African presidents, such as Ali Bongo, son of Omar Bongo. After becoming president, Omar Bongo often received foreign dignitaries in his Gabonese residence, which was inspired by Moroccan architecture and decoration, dressed in a traditional jellaba that was extremely similar in cut and decoration to the one worn by the Cherifian monarch in the same period. From the beach of Libreville, one cannot miss the island on which Mohammed VI has a sumptuous palace. Similarly, the Moroccan and Senegalese press regularly report on the many expressions of friendship between Karim Wade, son of former Senegalese president Abdoulaye Wade, and Mohammed VI.[143] Such a close relationship can be

---

141   Ministry of Foreign Affairs and Cooperation, *Conference on the occasion of World Africa Day*, Rabat, May 25, 2013.
142   "Official visit of the Senegalese President to Morocco", *MAP–Maroc.ma*, July 24, 2013.
143   "Affaire Karim Wade: Mohamed VI, négociateur de l'ombre?", *DAKARACTU.COM*, March

observed with several other African political figures. Thus, at the same time as it adheres to the postulate of a 'Francophone family',[144] Morocco sees West and Central Africa as countries linked to Morocco by a club diplomacy.[145] For several hostile observers, Morocco gives the impression of having built a form of 'pré carré gigogne' from its relations during the Cold War. Moreover, part of African civil society now sees Moroccan continental integration as a form of reproduction of French hegemonism. This is why it is necessary to try to reveal and understand the elements that give rise to such a representation. This section will show, in particular, how Morocco, while using the levers inherited from France to its advantage, is part of a non-hegemonic trajectory that is well differentiated, in both its objectives and its foreign policy practice.

It is true that the countries to which Mohammed VI has made the most regular visits over the past 15 years[146] coincide precisely with the most representative actors of the former French 'pré carré' (a term which can be translated into English as 'preserve'), namely Gabon, Côte d'Ivoire and Senegal, and more generally the countries of the AOF (French West Africa) and AEF (French Equatorial Africa). However, the expression 'pré carré' carries a conceptual burden that is inapplicable to Morocco. It should be recalled that the term was coined by Vauban, considered one of the first French geopoliticians.[147] According to the author, it refers to a defensive system made up of fortifications to secure the borders of the Kingdom of France during the Ancien Régime. The 'pré carré' also refers to the organisation of a space of economic influence: 'With Vauban, the territory organised according to the principles of an absolute space becomes—in the form of the pré carré—emblematic of a form of struggle waged according to the very precepts that the mercantilists had been developing for a century: war with the means of the economy'.[148] More generally, Vauban's pré carré refers to a space conceived as a resource of power and a

---

15, 2013., Abdoulaye El Hadji, "Mohammed Chraibi, Honorary Consul of Senegal in Morocco: 'Le Sénégal a la chance d'avoir un homme de dossiers'", April 2, 2012.

[144] "Morocco welcomes Mali back into the Francophone family", *Maroc.ma*, November 8, 2013.

[145] For the definition of club diplomacy, see: "Penser les relations internationales africaines à travers l'étude des régionalismes", *Revue Française de Science Politique* 67, no. 5 (2017): 931–945. This is a critical review of Daniel Bach, *Regionalism in Africa, Genealogies, Institutions and Trans-State Networks*, (Abingdon, Routledge, 2016).

[146] See Appendix 1 and Appendix 1bis: Mohammed VI's official visits abroad.

[147] The expression appears in a letter from Vauban to the minister Louvois dated 3 January 1673. Olivier Kempf, "Le Maréchal de Vauban, premier géopoliticien français?", *Stratégique*, no. 99 (2010): 35–50.

[148] David Bitterling, *L'invention du pré carré: construction de l'espace français sous l'Ancien Régime*, (Paris, France: A. Michel, 2009), 138.

potential ground for rivalries. While the expression was never used by French leaders per se, in either their correspondence or their statements, to describe France's Africa policy, it has nevertheless resonated with observers of French strategy in Africa in the post-colonial era.[149]

At that time, the pré carré strategy meant, first, the geometric definition of a territory and its control by a surveillance and intelligence apparatus; second, the repression of the use of military threat; third, the establishment of a network of commercial exchanges; and fourth, the placing of this apparatus, at the decision-making level, under the direct control of the president. On the defensive level, the pré carré strategy in Africa aimed, on the one hand, 'to prevent the extension of communist subversion and penetration, in particular in the countries of French black Africa bordering Guinea: Mali, Senegal and Côte d'Ivoire, and on the other hand, to ensure that the Americans did not encroach on our zone of influence, particularly at the economic level'.[150] For the historian Jean-Pierre Bat, Jacques Foccart's strategy in Africa ultimately followed the same rules established by Vauban through his concept of the pré carré: 'almost three centuries later, the application of this strategy is the keystone of the decolonisation of sub-Saharan Africa'.[151] The difference is that while Vauban's pré carré was essentially defensive, Foccart's was also intended to ensure France's prestige and international influence.

It can thus be observed that the Moroccan strategy in Africa aims, in this same vein, to secure the Kingdom's Saharan borders and to repel its adversaries by establishing a privileged cooperation zone in Africa. The organisation of this cooperation is based, first, on maintaining close links with the political and religious leaders of a geographically defined area; second, on a doctrine of the use of the army subject to the international legal framework applicable to the neighbouring states; third, on the development of economic and cultural cooperation serving both mercantile and security interests; and finally, on the supervision of this strategy, at the decision-making level, directly by the King.

Nevertheless, while the geographical limits of the space favoured by Morocco, namely West and Central Africa, are clearly defined in the discourse, the constitution of an intelligence network is carried out by employing a global representation of security threats. Terrorism, drug and arms trafficking, migra-

---

149 Bat, *Le syndrome Foccart*.
150 Maurice Robert and André Renault, *Maurice Robert 'Minister' of Africa. Entretiens avec André Renault*, (Paris: Seuil, 2004), 112.
151 Jean-Pierre Bat, *Le Syndrome Foccart. La Politique française en Afrique, de 1959 à nos jours*, (Paris: Gallimard, 2012), 81.

tion regulation, and natural disasters are seen as common problems.[152] In this respect, it appears that the Kingdom has also modernised its intelligence apparatus since the appointment of Mohamed Yassine Mansouri in 2005. Thus, these information networks seem to serve not a logic of domination comparable to France's but primarily regional security interests.

Moreover, the Moroccan military presence in Africa has increased, not only through participation in PKOs but also through the training of African troops within the framework of multilateral cooperation agreements. Thus, Morocco does not conduct military offensives in Africa and no longer supports liberation movements, as was the case in the 1970s. Its strategic activity is limited to UN peace operations on the multilateral level, to humanitarian action on the bilateral level (the construction of a field hospital in Niger by the army, or the triggering of artificial rain in Burkina Faso by the air force, for example).

Moreover, though Morocco's Africa policy does indeed favour increased use of diplomatic tools and economic and cultural levers to build a community of interests and shared values within this zone, the diplomatic lever serves first and foremost an international recognition logic rather than a hegemonic logic, insofar as most of the agreements are oriented towards South–South cooperation and forms of partnership that are committed to promoting a win–win dimension.

Finally, the King, surrounded by his Royal Cabinet, is effectively at the heart of this enterprise to the extent that Morocco's foreign policy in this specific space is associated, as much as the Sahara defence policy and more than any other area of the Kingdom's foreign policy, with the style of Mohammed VI. Nevertheless, the centrality of the decision-making apparatus relating to the Africa policy is not an exclusive phenomenon: it is already possible to observe the increasing involvement of ministries, economic operators and many multilateral institutions in shaping this policy in a logic of publicisation and governmentality, as described above.

To sum up, Morocco does seem to project a space of privileged cooperation that corresponds geographically to the historical French space of influence (even if the limits of this space are more restricted). However, the hegemonic meaning given to the expression 'pré carré' is not relevant to Morocco's Africa policy objectives. Moreover, Morocco is not a colonial power and does not have

---

152 'In addition to the traditional threats arising from inter- or intra-state armed conflicts, new dangerous phenomena of a transnational and complex nature have been added, such as trafficking of all kinds, organised crime, piracy and terrorism. The global nature of these threats requires the search for collective, coordinated and concerted responses': "Message of HM King Mohammed VI to the 25th Africa-France Summit", *Maroc.ma*, May 31, 2010.

the material means France had during the post-colonial period. In this sense, its ambitions are more modest. The Kingdom still has to rely on French aid to exercise its policy while maintaining its autonomy and its own specificity, and without putting itself in a situation of competition, rivalry or antagonism in relation to French interests. Finally, Morocco's desire to differentiate itself from the French approach to the pré carré and not to be seen by African states as a vassal or a sub-power reproducing French hegemony has led the latter to review the terms of French–Moroccan cooperation in Africa.

Indeed, the arrival of Mohammed VI to power in 1999 and the gradual confirmation of a new Africa policy has comforted the implementation of the French–Moroccan 'renewed partnership' on the continent, mentioned in the second chapter of this study (Section 7). This consists of positioning itself as an actor country, wishing to strengthen its close ties with France and assert itself more as an independent partner, notably through triangular cooperation agreements (North–South–South). From the outset, Mohammed VI strengthened Morocco's representation at the annual Africa–France summits, where the government now supports the importance of France's role in African security and its historical responsibility for the continent's development. He has also developed a rhetoric that aims to present Morocco's Africa policy as an opportunity for France while highlighting the Kingdom's specific assets. Morocco's objective is to reaffirm its political autonomy in terms of foreign policy vis-à-vis France while continuing to benefit from its diplomatic support (on the Sahara issue in particular), strategic support (in terms of modernising the Moroccan military apparatus) and financial support (loans, direct investments and development aid, but also financial support for Moroccan–African programmes).

On the economic front, Morocco emphasises the:

> need to establish a genuine co-development partnership between the two parties, going beyond the traditional principal/subcontractor pattern, relying on the Kingdom's position as an economic hub for Africa [...] noting that the complementarity between French and Moroccan operators constitutes an asset for co-development in Africa that is beneficial to both parties.[153]

In terms of security, the Kingdom invited the Republic to define close cooperation regarding intelligence and military training. More generally, it is the theme of tripartite or triangular cooperation that spearheads the Moroccan

---

153 "Morocco-France Partnership Forum in Paris", *MAP–Maroc.ma*, May 20, 2015.

political campaign in favour of a renewed partnership which makes it possible to reinforce the golden-mean posture. This theme has been addressed since the first year of Mohammed VI's reign, was emphasised on the occasion of Jacques Chirac's visit to Morocco[154] and then was reiterated during the 25th Africa–France summit,[155] as well as on the occasion of numerous multilateral events. In the military field, for example, as a 2007 French report emphasises, this cooperation has since evolved into a 'genuine partnership', which is illustrated in four areas, including the development of higher military education, the modernisation of the Moroccan army, the pooling of defence resources in a joint framework and, above all, 'support for the reinforcement of Morocco's African and international vocation, in particular by helping it to receive a greater number of foreign interns, especially Africans, in its schools or by promoting the emergence of Moroccan centres of excellence in the field of military training'.[156]

However, although French–Moroccan cooperation in Africa appears to be more formalised and institutionalised in the aftermath of the Cold War, it is not more transparent. Several agreements have been discussed behind closed doors at the level of heads of state, their cabinets or their staffs without being made public. For example, the intergovernmental agreement on military cooperation signed in 1994 and still in force today concerns only French military personnel managed by the Ministry of Foreign Affairs.

As the 2007 report underlines: 'At present, it is, therefore, ad hoc arrangements at the ministerial level that provide a framework for exchanges of French and Moroccan personnel in a wide range of areas of cooperation, including joint actions in operational theatres, joint training and exercises, and training or exchanges in the field of military history'.[157] It therefore appears that this 'renewed partnership' between France and Morocco should be established at two levels.

---

154 'We salute your pioneering and sustained efforts in favour of Africa, its development and stability. (…) Morocco's African vocation naturally associates us with any tripartite cooperation approach aimed at improving the living conditions of the African peoples': "The speech of H.M. King Mohammed VI during the official dinner offered in honour of President Jacques Chirac", *Maroc.ma*, March 20, 2000.
155 'I would like to say here how much Morocco is attached to the additional opportunities that would be offered by a deepening of our triangular cooperation, where the contribution of one is usefully combined with the know-how of the other for the realisation of concrete projects for the benefit of third party African populations', Ibid.
156 Roatta, "Report on the draft law (no. 3276) authorising the approval of the agreement between the Government of the French Republic and the Government of the Kingdom of Morocco on the status of their forces".
157 Ibid.

The first level now includes the Moroccan government and contributes to the validity of a bridging role between Africa and Europe through tripartite cooperation. For example, Philippe Faure, former French ambassador to Morocco, is convinced that 'Morocco, like France, has a good knowledge of sub-Saharan Africa and very dense relations with most African countries. One of the future avenues of our bilateral cooperation is precisely to open up to Africa and conduct what is called trilateral cooperation.'.[158] These projects include an AIDS and infectious diseases research centre with an African focus and several joint training institutes.

The second level of cooperation involves diversified actors and contributes to the strengthening of this special French–Moroccan relationship, i.e. a relationship that is based not on a formalised politico-military constraint but instead on economic dependence and an interest in the French,[159] and more broadly, European, normative and structural model. It can therefore be observed that Mohammed VI has largely contributed to the revaluation of the French language in Morocco after a long period of 're-traditionalisation' of political and cultural life. Thus, his inclusion in French Africa policy is reflected more in a preference for the French-speaking world than in the deployment of a Francophile diplomacy.[160]

For Thérèse Benjelloun, beyond the links with France, 'the weight of the past was bound to lead Morocco to mimic the Western liberal multi-party model'.[161] Institutional mimicry is often a pragmatic and rational strategy: small powers evolve in an uncertain environment, pushing them to look for solutions to their problems in solutions tried by other actors which they consider to be successful.[162] In other cases, mimicry results from pressure from an external power which intends to impose its norms and facilitate exchange by establishing

---

158 Philippe Faure, "Le partenariat franco-marocain: une relation exceptionnelle", *L'ENA hors les murs*, no. Hors Série, *'Le Maroc pays en mouvement'*, (February 2006): 6.
159 This preference for the French model has been observable since independence in 1956. As the author of this French diplomatic note remarks on Moroccan-Spanish cooperation: 'judicial, cultural and economic issues are more difficult to address, given that in these areas Morocco seems willing to treat us much more favourably than Spain'. Note from the Directorate General of Political Affairs, "Franco-Spanish Conversations on Morocco", Paris, July 6, 1956 in *Documents diplomatiques français*.
160 Yousra Abourabi, "Le Maroc francophone: identité et diplomatie africaine", *Revue Internationale des Francophonies* [On line], La Francophonie dans les politiques published on December 12, 2019, URL: https://rifrancophonies.com/index.php?id=966
161 Benjelloun, *Visages de la diplomatie marocaine depuis 1844*, 196.
162 Martha Finnemore, *National Interests in International Society*, (Cornell University Press, 1996), 11.

common rules. In this context, both the problem and the solution are brought to the state by external actors.[163] Both of these cases apply to Morocco, which makes it doubly attentive to France's Africa policy: a tendency illustrated in Morocco's numerous diplomatic actions in Africa.

Consequently, Morocco effectively but paradoxically follows in France's footsteps: first, by reproducing a certain number of French institutional, diplomatic and defensive mechanisms, and second, in its desire and need to cooperate with France in the framework of common interests. The geographical definition of a privileged space for the exercise of this Africa policy, which corresponds to the traditional French space of influence, allows Morocco to mobilise a set of institutional mechanisms and already established cultural or political links, such as Francophone cooperation.[164] However, beyond its reproductive or inclusive aspects of French mechanisms or the French language, Moroccan policy, due to its intrinsic specificities, projects itself according to its own strategy, which cannot be qualified as pré carré or assimilated to an expansionist power logic. According to a constructivist approach, its objectives lie in the search for international recognition of a role identity qualified as a golden mean.

8 The Moroccan Character of the Kingdom's Africa Policy: 'Mohammed VI the African', a Manifestation of the Royal Style in Africa

In France, each of the presidents of the last half-century, from de Gaulle to Hollande, including Pompidou, Giscard d'Estaing, Mitterrand, Chirac and Sarkozy, has defended a singular Africa policy, to the point that each of them has been called 'African' by the media and researchers. Each of them also wanted to mark a break with his predecessor while recovering the French political-normative heritage that the previous one had helped to implement. The famous formula according to which 'everything must change so that nothing changes', an expression of the constant renewal of the conditions of French power to maintain, or even strengthen, its historical role in Africa, also applies to Morocco, in a certain sense. While Cold War Morocco suffered from a neo-patrimonial

---

163   Ibid., 12. Seealso on the issue of mimicry in International Relations: Benjamin Goldsmith, "Imitation in International Relations: Analogies, Vicarious Learning, and Foreign Policy", *International Interactions* 29, no. 3 (2003): 237–267.
164   Yousra Abourabi, "Le Maroc francophone: identité et diplomatie africaine".

and sometimes subservient image in Africa,[165] the Royal Cabinet is working assiduously to positively enhance the image of Mohammed VI among African countries, through communication strategies aimed at strengthening his recognition as an African king, at the head of a democracy, while reinforcing the prerogatives of the monarch at the institutional, religious and political levels. Thus, everything must change regarding the orientation, conditions and levers of Morocco's foreign policy so that its role identities are preserved.

Thus, while Hassan II had never been decorated with this expression, the current King was very quickly referred to as 'Mohammed VI the African' by the French, Moroccan and, more generally, African press. For example, *Aujourd'hui le Maroc* headlined an article 'Mohammed VI l'Africain' to highlight the idea that 'with King Mohammed VI, the Kingdom is bringing back to the agenda a diplomatic tradition that has always been lacking in our neighbours, despite the petrodollars generously poured into the capitals of the black continent'.[166] Similarly, in France, *Jeune Afrique* titled its article 'Mohammed VI, *African king*' to show that 'Rabat has managed to carve out the status of autonomous regional power and relay power between Europe and the southern Sahara. A strategy directly steered from the Royal Palace by a personally invested sovereign, to the point that the African tours of this 51-year-old head of state do not resemble any others.'[167] Many Senegalese,[168] Malian[169] and Ivorian[170] newspapers have reported on the monarchy's diplomatic offensive in Africa. More generally, the electronic press has devoted numerous articles to describing the unprecedented nature of this royal enterprise and relaying the expression 'Mohammed VI the African'.

Whether the result of editorial inspiration or a suggestion from the Palace, the origin of this qualification is of little importance, since it reveals a genuine involvement of the monarch in this Africa policy at several levels. First of all, Mohammed VI is 'African' in this context because he first decided on the African orientation of diplomacy, placing his 'home continent at the top of his development priorities and the heart of his international diplomatic con-

---

165 Alain Antil, "Le Royaume du Maroc et sa politique envers l'Afrique sub-saharienne", *Étude, Institut français des relations internationales*, (2003): 27–28.
166 "Mohammed VI l'Africain".
167 Soudan, "Mohammed VI, African King".
168 Amadou L. Mbaye, "Le Roi du Maroc en Afrique Subsaharienne: Mohammed VI, l'Africain", SeneNews.com, May 24, 2015.
169 Adam Thiam, "Mohammed VI's African Tour: Majesty, the people are waiting for you", *maliweb*, May 22, 2015.
170 "Le roi Mohammed VI attendu dimanche en Côte d'Ivoire", *Connection ivoirienne*, February 22, 2014.

cerns'.[171] As the head of the foreign policy decision-making process, he also instituted specific monitoring of issues related to Africa and considered strategic. For example, the dual position of Inspector General of the Armed Forces and Commander of the Southern Zone, the second highest position of responsibility in the army after that of the King, was granted in 2014 to a general close to the monarch: Bouchaïb Arroub. With this new appointment, the general was entrusted with two specific files that are not usually directly dealt with at this level: coordinating the installation and deployment of field hospitals in Africa and supervising African officers undergoing training in Morocco.[172] Another example is the appointment by the King in 2013 of Moulay Hafid El Alamy (a Moroccan entrepreneur and Africa's 40th-richest man) as the new Minister of Industry, Trade, Investment and the Digital Economy in a government supposedly composed of a majority of representatives of the Islamist party elected in the aftermath of the Arab Spring. This new appointment was also intended to direct the Moroccan economic policy towards the African market.[173]

Second, Mohammed VI is politically African in addition to his African identity, as he regularly visits the countries of the continent accompanied by a procession of ministers and advisors: visits that help to promote his charitable and modernist policy. Mohammed VI's visits to Africa are an opportunity to seal ties with heads of state, to sign cooperation agreements in various fields and above all, to make the monarchy known and to spread a positive image of the Kingdom. This diplomatic scenography takes place on two levels: the first relates to the development of emotional diplomacy exchanged during meetings and speeches. The second relates to the public behaviour of Mohammed VI, his roles and his style in the digital age.

During his African tours, Mohammed VI, dressed in traditional clothes, accompanied by his ministers, civil servants and servants, bringing numerous gifts, inaugurating humanitarian projects and drawing up cooperation agreements ready for signing, offers a diplomatic spectacle that attracts many journalists. These are forms of political rituals, defined by Bourdieu as 'social magic' that allow, through appropriate words and deeds, to claim a difference.[174] The

---

171 Ministère des affaires étrangères et de la coopértaion, *Seminar of Moroccan Ambassadors in Africa. Diplomatie marocaine en Afrique: une approche renouvelée au service d'une priorité stratégique*, Dossier de Presse, (Rabat: August 2012).
172 "What the wave of ambassadorial appointments means for Moroccan diplomacy", *Al Huffington Post*, February 7, 2016.
173 Ibid.
174 Pierre Bourdieu, "Les rites comme actes d'institution", in *Actes de la recherche en sciences sociales*. vol. 43, June 1982. Rites and fetishes. 58–63.

agitation that characterises the reception of the monarch in the countries he visits illustrates the strength of these rituals. Through this protocol, based on a staging of power in the Bourdieusian sense, the King asserts his sovereign function while showing his availability and interest in African integration. These royal visits have progressively become real institutional rites, still in the Bourdieusian sense,[175] serving to validate Moroccan action in Africa (in particular the multiple South–South cooperation agreements discussed in the following two chapters) and to institute cooperation. As Pierre Bourdieu notes: 'To institute is to consecrate, that is to say, to sanction and sacrifice a state of affairs, an established order, as does a constitution in the legal-political sense of the term'.[176]

This form of ritual is illustrated in particular by the welcome these countries reserve for each visit, a manifestation of their enthusiasm for emerging cooperation prospects. In Gabon, Senegal, Mali, Côte d'Ivoire and Guinea, one can see images of hundreds of enthusiastic citizens, sometimes wearing T-shirts bearing the effigy of the monarch, cheering the arrival of the Moroccan representatives around the airport and along the main roads where the royal procession passes by, waving to the crowds. In Guinea-Bissau, the government even decreed a paid day off on the day of the royal visit.[177] In Gabon, one journalist observes, on the eve of Mohammed VI's arrival, 'the main avenues were given a special cleaning. Workers put a coat of white paint on the avenues' outskirts.'[178] In Côte d'Ivoire, another journalist reported that 'Abidjan was dressed in its finest and the Ivorian population, as well as all the members of the Moroccan community living in this country, did not hesitate to take to the pavements along the route of the official motorcade to cheer the distinguished guest of the Republic, to wish him Akwaba' (welcome in the Baule language) and reiterate their total attachment to their sovereign by brandishing flags of the two countries and portraits of the two heads of state, all to the sound of you-you, tam-tam, bendirs and songs.[179] On the occasion of another visit, members of the Ivorian delegation rushed to kiss the hand of the Cherifian monarch as Moroccan citizens would do in an official setting, to the extent that the

---

175   Ibid.
176   Pierre Bourdieu, *Ce que parler veut dire: l'économie des échanges linguistiques*, (Paris, Fayard, 1982), 124.
177   "En Guinée-Bissau, un jour chômé pour la visite de Mohammed VI", *Telquel.ma*, May 28, 2015.
178   Stevie Mounombou, "Mohammed VI in Libreville", *Gabonreview*, June 2015.
179   "Popular reception for King Mohammed VI in Abidjan", *Connectionivoirienne*, May 31, 2015.

King's refusal to be kissed by these former friends of his father was paradoxically misinterpreted and treated as a minor diplomatic scandal by the Ivorian press.[180]

This formal and sometimes spontaneous effervescence reveals a clear interest on the part of the leaders of these states in the Kingdom's Africa policy. In Senegal, for example, Alassane Ouattara expressed his sensitivity to the 'tokens of affection' transmitted by the royal family, as well as his 'great admiration for the modernisation and development effort [...] which makes the Kingdom of Morocco a respected country and a top-tier partner'.[181]

In Guinea-Conakry, President Alpha Condé also announced that 'Our ambition is for Guinea to become Morocco's first partner south of the Sahara, and we will do everything to achieve this'.[182] On the whole, the press in this region conveys an equally optimistic and favourable perception of the Moroccan presence.[183]

This is true emotional diplomacy. As Todd Hall puts it, 'emotional diplomacy is coordinated state behaviour that explicitly and officially projects the image of a particular emotion as a response to other states'.[184] This emotional diplomacy, consisting of deliberate speech acts and political staging, is a measure of the interest of African states. It also significantly impacts the development of relations between the two parties, as it reinforces the Moroccan side's perception of West Africa as a group of benevolent and interested states. Thus, the King of Morocco, referring to his relations with Gabon, welcomes their shared 'identity of view',[185] an expression also used by Moroccan leaders to characterise Moroccan–Senegalese[186] or Moroccan–Malian[187] relations. Together, the

---

180 "Affaire Georges Ouégnin humilié: Mohamed VI a plutôt honoré l'ancien Chef du Protocole d'État", *Abidjan.net*, March 22, 2013.
181 RTI CHAINE, *Statement by President Alassane Ouattara on his return from Morocco*, January 25, 2015.
182 "Interview with Alpha Condé, President of the Republic of Guinea", *Le Matin.ma*, May 3, 2014.
183 See, for example: Thiam, "maliweb.net—Tournée africaine de Mohammed VI".
184 Hall, *Emotional diplomacy*.
185 "HM the King sends a message of thanks to President Ali Bongo at the end of His official visit to Gabon", *Maroc.ma*, April 13, 2013.
186 "Morocco/Senegal: A perfect identity of views and a common will to promote a bilateral cooperation as fruitful as diversified", *MAP Express*, July 31, 2013.
187 'I would like to tell You how pleased I am with the positive and promising results achieved during this visit, as well as with our shared views on issues of common interest, at the bilateral, regional and international levels',: "HM the King addresses a message of thanks to the Malian president at the end of His official visit to Mali", *MAP Maroc.ma*, February 23, 2014.

West African countries closest to Morocco and the Moroccan state representatives perceive and refer to each other as brothers or friends. This mutual appreciation, charged with affective discourse, confirms the existence of both a historical and a political friendship.

To support this emerging representation, the royal visits to Africa are organised in the same way as the King's movements within the Kingdom. The monarch inaugurates each project, greets all the representatives and travels to all the places, however insignificant, in the same way he has done in Morocco since the beginning of his reign. The two-tiered game mentioned in the first chapter of this study, i.e. the continuity of the Cherifian style in domestic and foreign policy, is particularly evident in this Africa policy. Indeed, I demonstrated in the third chapter how the monarch is perceived through his public roles. It should be recalled that he has inaugurated several projects since he acceded to the throne, escorted by his officials and representative delegations of the associative or private sector to the point that many observers have described the regime as an 'executive monarchy'. It should also be remembered that the King travelled to villages ignored by Hassan II, immersed himself in spontaneous crowd baths, and came into physical contact with hospitalised people, prisoners, orphans, the unemployed and other marginalised groups, to the extent that Mohammed VI was soon described as the 'King of the poor'. The same political style is now being replicated at the African scale.

One of the other particularities of Mohammed VI's style in this communication device is that he has lent himself to the game of selfies, in the image of showbusiness celebrities and English-speaking leaders such as Barack Obama, David Cameron and Justin Trudeau. In the many photos of the monarch posted on the internet, he can be seen dressed in jeans, a flowery shirt, a T-shirt or a patterned hoodie, and trainers or platform shoes, holding the arm of the stranger who asked for the photo. This behaviour breaks entirely with the rigour of the royal protocol, which, let us remember, institutes, among other things, the ritual of the royal hand kiss. The selfie, which does not always present the monarch at his best, gives the King a more accessible and human character, which makes him more popular. Selfies completely break down the divide between conservatism and liberalism, between elites and the general public, and between noble and popular culture. Their intrusive nature and the impression of proximity they create between the monarch and the people have made the King's selfies a sought-after object for a new generation of citizens marked by the development of digital technologies. In Morocco, the terrain is favourable: traditionally, Moroccans like to display official photos of the King in public and private spaces. The selfies will help to perpetuate this tradition among young people, except that this display will take place on social networks.

It can be seen, therefore, that in the projection of his two-tiered roles described in the third chapter of this book, the king reproduces these same political rituals in Africa. On the one hand, he inaugurates several humanitarian, real estate, financial and agricultural projects, which he also monitors by regularly returning to the sites.[188] He takes care to receive each political, religious and social representative involved in the cooperation agreements, during an interview held in the presence of one or two ministers. On the other hand, on the margins of official events, he willingly accepts requests to take selfies with African residents, including Moroccans living in these countries.

The Moroccan representation of this part of the continent and the confirmation of this representation in royal speeches have allowed the signing of a series of South–South cooperation agreements in fields as diverse as the economy, finance, public works, education, health, the army and culture. The marks of friendship shared between Morocco and the states that make up the West African space effectively contribute to the validity of a regional system of beliefs and collective norms between sub-Saharan West Africa and north-Saharan West Africa. Similarly, they promote the emergence of a geopolitical community, i.e. a group of countries allied by a political will to recognise a common geo-cultural space. This representation goes in the direction of regionalism, in the sense of Daniel Bach, defined by the author as a project that 'postulates the explicit construction of an identity, as opposed to its formation'.[189] This regionalism, as a promise of future regionalisation,[190] has therefore led Moroccan leaders to develop a discursive framework for legitimising their Africa policy that is conducive to the realisation of these projects.

---

188   See the detailed reports on royal visits to Africa on the MFAc website. For example: Ministry of Foreign Affairs and Cooperation, *Visit of King Mohammed VI to Côte d'Ivoire*, (2014), 21; "Official visit of HM the King to Guinea-Conakry", *MAP Maroc Arab Press*, March 2, 2014, 49.

189   Bach, "Régionalismes, régionalisation et globalisation", 346.

190   According to Daniel Bach, 'Regionalisation refers to processes. These can be the result of the realisation of regionalist projects. Regionalisation can also result from the aggregation of individual strategies, independent of any identified regionalist aspiration or strategy.' Ibid., 347.

CHAPTER 5

A Legitimising Framework for Regional Integration

1 Introduction

From a regionalist[1] perspective, Morocco resorts to a discursive strategy of legitimation: a process that mobilises symbolic references for the construction of an official framework of interpretation and justification of Morocco's diplomatic actions. It should be remembered that a legitimation framework refers to 'a regime of discourse that develops knowledge in the service of power'.[2] The legitimisation of a role in Africa constitutes, in this respect, a fundamental lever in the acceptance or even the support of political practice (foreign or domestic) by civil society and the leaders of foreign states, just as the legitimisation of power does. One cannot engage in a cooperation policy without legitimising it to its actors, recipients or even observers. The current world order is marked by the multiplication of international power regimes; multilateral decision-making centres, sources of funding for public policies and legal bodies for global control and condemnation;[3] and the development of digital technologies favouring the emergence of a new space of democratic control.[4] All of these configurations demonstrate the need to define a legitimisation strategy capable of supporting the autonomy of the foreign policy of sovereign states. Morocco must necessarily develop a framework for legitimising its diplomacy.

Thus, the inclusion of the African character of the national identity in the 2011 constitution enhances Morocco's historical geopolitical and cultural anchorage in West Africa. Similarly, the inclusion of Morocco's Africa policy in the framework of South–South cooperation and the highlighting of shared security interests on the continent constitute both a framework of legitimisation and a framework for action. Third, the assertion of a golden-mean role identity, particularly through religious diplomacy, is both a legitimisation framework and an action framework for asserting the particularity of the Moroccan system in Africa.

---

1 Ibid.
2 Julien Durand De Sanctis, *Philosophie de la stratégie française. La stratégie continentale*, 33.
3 A. Hurrelmann *et alii*, *Legitimacy In An Age Of Global Politics*, (Basingstoke: Palgrave Macmillan, 2007), 273.
4 Dominique Cardon, *La démocratie Internet: Promesses et limites*, (Paris: Seuil, 2010).

2 The Kingdom Is African: The Inscription of Africanness in the Diplomatic Framework

From the perspective of defending his two-level roles, the Alawite monarch has been involved in the identity debate since the beginning of his reign. Addressing the nation, he drew up a first Throne Speech entirely devoted to the issue of Moroccan identity: an identity now recognised as 'plural', enriched by 'varied civilisations' and whose different dialects, in addition to Arabic, should henceforth be taught in schools. As King, he set himself up as the custodian of the mission to protect this identity. He promised 'the permanence of a strong power capable of guaranteeing the continuity of the State'. Addressing France, he criticised the existence of a 'security reflex because there is an amalgam between Morocco and other countries south of the Mediterranean'; he stressed that 'Morocco has a different identity' for a reason already mentioned by Hassan II, namely its geo-cultural particularity, at the crossroads of several regions,[5] The Kingdom's foreign policy had been based on two normative bases since the beginning of the 2000s: 'its identity and its irreversible commitment to its home continent. This identity comprises history and geography, human intermingling, common cultural values and ancestral spiritual links',[6] including the age-old link with the African continent.

Thus, taking advantage of the Arab Spring, which led to the writing of a new constitution in 2011, the Kingdom attested through this text, for the first time in its history, to the African character of its national identity.[7] More than a strategy for integrating ethnic plurality in the service of a unifying symbolic power, the recognition of Morocco's African identity contributes to validating the Kingdom's geo-cultural anchorage within the continent. The claim to this African identity is based also on the cultural dynamics of the black-Maghrebi populations, symbolically represented by the Hausa, Gnawa and Derderba brotherhoods, which recount the memory of their journeys in music sung in particular

---

[5] "Interview given by His Majesty King Mohammed VI to the French daily newspaper 'Le Figaro'".
[6] "Press kit—Seminar of the Ambassadors of His Majesty the King accredited in Africa".
[7] The preamble of the Kingdom's fundamental law states that: 'As a sovereign Muslim State, attached to its national unity and territorial integrity, the Kingdom of Morocco intends to preserve, in its fullness and diversity, its single and indivisible national identity. Its unity, forged by the convergence of its Arab-Islamic, Amazigh and Saharan-Hassan components, has been nourished and enriched by its African, Andalusian, Hebrew and Mediterranean tributaries.' Kingdom of Morocco, General Secretariat of the Government, Directorate of the Official Printing Office, *Constitution du Royaume du Maroc*, Documentation Juridique Marocaine, Série, (2011).

dialects. Morocco is, therefore, right to claim its African identity, both because of the African character of the ethnic groups that make it up and because of the density of economic and religious exchanges that link it to Sahelo-Saharan, West and Central Africa. These exchanges result in shared communities or families, cultural similarities and secular confraternal networks.[8] However, as the nation's Africanness has been little institutionalised, as illustrated by the small place given to the continent's history in school textbooks, Moroccans have acquired little knowledge of African history compared with their knowledge of the Arabic-speaking world and the Euro-American West. This trend is also visible in the sporadic treatment of the continent's news by the Moroccan press for many years. The claim of Morocco's Africanness is therefore an *a posteriori* official recognition of the centuries-old ethnic mix. This is why this inscription constitutes, first and foremost a framework of historical and identity legitimisation at the service of a diplomacy justifying the Kingdom's Africa policy.

Let us remember that Morocco presents itself as the centre of all exchanges, as a 'civilisational crossroads' within which African or Western cultures form 'tributaries' from which it feeds. This diplomatic discourse perfectly aligns with its identity as one of a golden-mean role. The claim of Morocco's historical Africanness allows it to consolidate its Africa policy by offering historical depth to its union with the continent. The Palace presents Morocco as 'a land of meetings and dialogue [...] faithful to the age-old ties that unite it with its African environment'.[9] This is why part of the state budget is devoted to supporting cultural events that promote black Moroccan and, more broadly, African culture (the Gnaoua Festival in Essaouira, the African Film Festival in Khouribga, the African Cultural Centre in Rabat), while parallel diplomacy participates in this dynamic. In France, for example, the Institut du Monde Arabe (Arabic World Institute) devoted two days in January 2015 to the historical presentation of 'Plural Morocco', a meeting of multidisciplinary researchers discussing, among other things, the historical aspects of the African identity of Morocco,[10] as part of a major exhibition on the 'Contemporary Morocco' supported by the Moroccan government. At the same time, at the Louvre Museum, the National Foundation of Moroccan Museums organised an exhibition on 'Medieval Morocco: an empire from Africa to Spain', bringing to the attention of the general pub-

---

8   See on this subject: Steffen Marfaing and Laurence Wippel, *Les relations transsahariennes à l'époque contemporaine*, (Paris: Karthala, 2003), 490.
9   "HM King Mohammed VI addresses a message to the participants of the first African conference on human development", *Maroc.ma*, April 6, 2007.
10 See the programme at the Institut du Monde Arabe: http://www.imarabe.org/colloquium/maroc-plural-history-and-identity.

lic the conquests of Moroccan dynasties south of the Sahara. More generally, Moroccan newspapers help to support the premise of the country's African anchorage as a 'historical reality' and a 'natural' identity,[11] which the African media is helping to promote.[12]

Although civil society is mobilised to support the assumption of an African national identity, the primary addressees of the discursive strategy for legitimising the Kingdom's Africa policy are the African states in question, the major foreign powers and international donors, and Moroccan civil society, with the aim of mobilising the latter in the aforementioned effort of publicisation and governmentality.

The Palace formulates Afro-optimist ideas similar to those of the pan-Africanists in the aftermath of independence: 'Africa must trust Africa';[13] 'a dynamic and developed Africa is not just a dream for tomorrow, it can be a reality';[14] 'Africa needs less assistance than partnerships';[15] 'it is time for Africa to regain its rights to History and Geography';[16] all of these formulas are sufficiently similar to be associated with this movement while being completely new. At the governmental level, following on from the royal declarations, the 'Marrakech Declaration', drawn up in the context of the launch of the Media Forum on the African Continent, is equally illustrative of this discursive strategy, which is both identity-based and political. The declaration speaks of the 'right of the African people' and the 'renaissance of Africa' and calls for 'a consecration of a multipolar world through the launch of initiatives aimed at making Africa's voice heard in the free world'.[17] Thus, more than a political recognition of the African character of the national identity, more than a strategy institutionalising the promotion of African culture in Morocco or of the Kingdom's African roots abroad, this theme constitutes, by embedding, a framework of legitimisation within another framework of legitimisation, that of the King-

---

11 For example: Abdeljalil Didi, "L'ancrage africain enrichit l'identité locale et nationale du Maroc", Almaouja.com, November 19, 2014.
12 Mamadou Dabo, "Au Mali de l'hospitalité et de l'africanité: Adieu les visées Azawadiennes, le Roi marocain s'installe", *Mali Actu*, February 21, 2014. "L'africanité du Maroc ne s'est jamais démentie", *Afrique 7*, September 19, 2013.
13 "Full text of HM the King's speech at the Morocco-Ivorian Economic Forum in Abidjan", Maroc.ma, February 24, 2014.
14 "Speech by HM the King at the Moroccan-Ivorian Economic Forum in Abidjan".
15 "Full text of the speech delivered by HM the King to the 3rd India-Africa Forum Summit", Maroc.ma, October 29, 2015.
16 "Message of HM the King to the participants of the Crans Montana Forum in Dakhla", Maroc.ma, March 18, 2016.
17 "Marrakech Declaration on the occasion of the African Media Forum", *Maroc.ma*, December 17, 2015.

dom's commitment to the development of the continent and its association with African issues. Morocco cannot claim to speak on behalf of Africa if it has not demonstrated its identity and cultural attachment to the continent. All of these discursive policies are nevertheless relevant and can be decisive. During the reign of Hassan II, national identity was defined in terms of Arabness and Islam, while expressions of political solidarity were directed mainly towards the Arab-Muslim world. During the reign of Mohammed VI, Africa was gradually presented as a 'continent of belonging', a space of historical exchange, but also a continent towards which the Kingdom has a duty of solidarity.

3 The Kingdom's Solidarity: Integrating the Normative Framework of South–South Cooperation and Global Security

On the basis of the African character of its identity, Morocco also places its Africa policy within the framework of South–South cooperation and the defence of collective security. The King has clearly stated this framework of legitimisation and action: 'Africa must rely first on its many assets, its rich potential and its own resources. This is the meaning that I have wanted to give, since my accession to the Throne, to the Kingdom's African strategy. This strategy is based on the virtues of South–South cooperation and the imperative of human development'.[18] Thus, all documents relating to cooperation with West Africa, and more generally to Morocco's foreign policy, emphasise the priority given to South–South cooperation. In this perspective, the Kingdom organised, with the support of the UNDP, the first African Conference on Human Development in Rabat in 2007—an opportunity for the Palace to reaffirm this framework of legitimisation and action of its Africa policy: 'We have therefore placed the development of South–South cooperation at the top of our foreign policy priorities, particularly in Africa, and have given it concrete content in the economic and social fields'.[19]

More than development aid, South–South cooperation refers to a system of economic, cultural and technical exchanges that emphasise solidarity rather than profit.[20] South–South cooperation, advocated in the 1960s and 1970s by

---

18 "Speech of HM the King to the participants of the 4th Africa-EU Summit in Brussels", *Maroc.ma*, April 3, 2014.
19 "HM King Mohammed VI addresses a message to the participants of the first African conference on human development", *Maroc.ma*, April 6, 2007.
20 Francisco Simplicio, "South-South Development Cooperation: A Contemporary Perspective", in *South-South Cooperation*, ed. Modi, Renu (Palgrave Macmillan UK, 2011): 19–41.

the Non-Aligned Movement,[21] was initially a way for these countries to protest against the economic and political supremacy of the former colonisers and, more generally, of the great powers of the North. The first manifestation of this demand was the formation of the Group of 77 (G77) in 1964, followed by the creation of a Special Unit for South–South Cooperation within the UN in 1978 (the High-Level Committee (HLC) on South–South Cooperation (SSC)).[22] However, the countries of the South were too dependent on financial aid from the rich countries to instigate real upheaval in international relations. Therefore, only in the 2000s did a new form of South–South cooperation, defined as a complement to rather than a substitute for North–South cooperation, develop on a global scale. More consensual, this new paradigm has gradually become one of the main frameworks for UN action—advocated in the context of the Millennium Development Goals (MDGs)—as well as a privileged funding niche for emerging powers and oil states in the South.

In 2000 the G77, therefore, held its first South Summit in Havana, followed by two action plans to institute the development of South–South cooperation by states: the Marrakech Framework, adopted by the Ministerial Conference on South–South Cooperation held in Marrakech in 2003,[23] and the Doha Plan of Action, adopted by the second South Summit of the Group of 77 in 2005.[24] As an act symbolising its support for these plans, the UN instituted a UN Day for South–South Cooperation in 2004.[25] Gradually, the UN has emerged as the most important vehicle and promoter of South–South cooperation through the development of standardised methodological approaches and implementation tools, the facilitation of South–South exchange networks, and the support of the agencies involved in this new networking.[26]

The Kingdom is actively participating in the consolidation of this new development paradigm and is showing a certain optimism in this respect. To assert

---

21 Renu Modi, *South-South Cooperation: Africa on the Centre Stage*, (Springer, 2011): 1–13.
22 See the institution's website at: http://southsouthconference.org/.
23 "Marrakesh Declaration on South-South Cooperation", United Nations Group77, General Assembly, January 19, 2004.
24 On the various conferences that followed the first South Summit see: "Report of the High-level Committee on South-South Cooperation", United Nations General Assembly, June 2007.
25 United Nations General Assembly, "Resolution adopted by the General Assembly 58/220: Economic and technical cooperation among developing countries", February 19, 2004.
26 For a recent summary of the actions undertaken by the UN in favour of the development of South-South cooperation, the actors mobilised, and the funding allocated, see United Nations High-level Committee on South-South Cooperation, "Review of the Reports of the Administrator of the United Nations Development Programme", New York, May 22, 2012.

its new role in South–South cooperation, its first symbolic act was the cancellation of the debt of the Least Developed Countries in 2000.[27] Moroccan leaders also participated in elaborating the Paris Declaration on Aid Effectiveness (2005) and the Accra Agenda for Action (2008), initiatives that aim to strengthen, monitor and evaluate international development cooperation and encourage support for South–South cooperation from the North.[28] The Moroccan government's involvement in this area has also increased as it has taken part in NEPAD-AUDA, the Monterrey Conference and TICAD.[29] These accessions also contribute to consolidating the rhetorical framework of action and legitimisation of the Moroccan presence on the continent. The South–South cooperation presentation document published on the MAECI website is notably illustrative of this discursive correspondence. The paper largely addresses Moroccan–African relations, in particular Morocco's duty of 'active' solidarity towards the continent as the main responsibility of its leaders in Africa.[30] Thus, from 2005, the RAF took charge of constructing a field hospital staffed by 28 Moroccan doctors and delivering foodstuffs to Niger. In 2010, the government sent three new aircraft loaded with humanitarian aid.

In 2012, two other aircraft were sent to Niger on the King's orders. The King's visit to Niger in 2005 in the context of a humanitarian crisis and the aid provided to African countries since then are examples of commitment that the Kingdom's representatives do not fail to highlight in their speeches.

In addition to emergency aid, US$ 300 million, equivalent to 10% of Moroccan trade with the continent, is allocated to Africa each year as part of public development assistance. The private sector also participates in this solidarity effort. For example, in the name of the Kingdom's solidarity with Africa, RAM was the only airline to fly regularly to Sierra Leone, Liberia and Guinea-Conakry during the Ebola crisis, thus following the recommendations of the WHO, which deemed it inappropriate to cut these countries off from the rest of the world. The spokesperson for RAM, Hakim Challot, argued that the company's initiative was part of 'a solidarity-based and non-mercantile approach, which echoes the Kingdom's constant commitment to Africa'.[31]

---

27 Note that 30 out of 42 LDCs are African.
28 "Paris Declaration on Aid Effectiveness and the Accra Agenda for Action", *OcDE*, 2008.
29 Ministère des Affaires Étrangères et de la Coopération, *Le Maroc et la Coopération Sud-Sud / Pays les moins avancés (PMA)*, Synthèse, Rabat, 2.
30 Ministry of Foreign Affairs and Cooperation. *Morocco, a country of solidarity: South-South cooperation*, See also the full document in Appendix 8.
31 Guillaume Klein, "Au nom de la politique africaine du Royaume: Le Maroc solidaire des pays touchés par Ebola", *L'opinion.ma*, September 1, 2014.

The rhetoric of South–South cooperation and the institutionalisation of development aid help to shape the role of a supportive Kingdom. This type of initiative puts Morocco on the right side of the fence, referred to by its partners as a country that 'shows the way to proper development in Africa'.[32] The African media also relay this idea. For example, one Cameroonian newspaper considers that 'relations between H.M. Mohammed VI's country and Paul Biya's country know a singular success story of south–south cooperation'.[33]

Moreover, South–South cooperation is closely associated with triangular cooperation, which, as mentioned at the beginning of this study, constitutes a fundamental diplomatic lever for Morocco in the affirmation of its identity as one of a golden-mean role. The government does not have sufficient financial means to provide substantial aid to the South, unlike the aid provided by South Africa, India, Kuwait or Argentina;[34] North–South–South triangular cooperation, therefore, appears to be a good compromise solution.

On a financial level, this discursive theme is equally fruitful. According to various sources, South–South and triangular cooperation have become major development funding sources. In 2006, they accounted for 10% of global aid,[35] or US$12 billion.[36] By 2008, this figure had already reached $16.2 billion.[37] There are no global statistics on the current scale of such aid, but it would appear that it is still growing. Southern providers now include oil states such as Saudi Arabia and Venezuela, industrial powers such as Korea, India and China, and Southern multilateral organisations such as the Arab Bank for Economic Development in Africa (BADEA), the Islamic Development Bank and the OPEC Fund for International Development. More generally, South–South and triangular cooperation programming conditions will tend to be more standardised

---

32   Statement by the President of the Crans Montana Forum, a Swiss NGO, an economic forum aimed at encouraging global growth, but highly political for Morocco as it was organised in Dakhla for two consecutive years, postulating an unofficial recognition of the Moroccanity of the Sahara by the participants present. "Dakhla 2016: Africa and South-South Cooperation at the heart of the debate", *Guinea Matin–Les Nouvelles de la Guinée profonde*, February 17, 2016.
33   "Maroc-Cameroun: Main dans la main", *Journal Du Cameroun*, August 8, 2013.
34   United Nations Economic and Social Council (ECOSOC), *Background Study for the development cooperation forum. Trends in South-South and triangular development cooperation*, (New York: United Nations, 2008).
35   "South-South Cooperation", *Development Finance International Group*, 2006.
36   Cheryl McEwan and Emma Mawdsley, "Trilateral Development Cooperation: Power and Politics in Emerging Aid Relationships", *Development and Change 43*, no. 6 (2012): 1185–1209.
37   United Nations Economic and Social Council (ECOSOC), *Background Study for the development cooperation forum. Trends in South-South and triangular development cooperation*.

and generalised at national, regional and global levels, as affirmed by a recent UN Framework Plan on this subject.[38] Several UN agencies have established units to support such cooperation. New banks (e.g. the BRICS Development Bank) and new trust funds specific to South–South cooperation are continually emerging, to the extent that, as one OECD study points out, 'South–South cooperation is reshaping the development finance landscape'.[39]

Among the thematic priorities targeted by the various donors of South–South cooperation, human security,[40] as a concept that embraces various sectors of security (economic, food, health, political, environmental, etc.), geared as much to conflict prevention as to conflict resolution, occupies a central place in this system. Security thinking has broadened from an exclusive concern with state security to one of individual security, in which the negative approach to peace (peace as the absence of war) has to be replaced by a positive approach.[41] In this context, human security aims to enable the development of the individual and postulates a double strategy: protection and empowerment. The UNDP first advocated this approach in a 1994 report, but it has been an objective that has been debated in the UN General Assembly since 2008.[42]

In Africa, the continent most affected by forms of insecurity as defined by the Commission on Human Security, this notion is included as a primary objective by the African Union, NEPAD-AUDA (now AUDA, the AU Development

38   United Nations–High–level Committee on South-South Cooperation, *Framework for operational guidelines on United Nations support for South-South and triangular cooperation*, (New York: May 22, 2012).
39   Sachin Chaturvedi, "Le dynamisme croissant de la cooperation Sud-Sud", in *Coopération pour le développement 2014: Mobiliser les ressources au service du développement durable*, (Paris, 2015).
40   The notion of human security refers to a definition of threat that is not limited to the violence of armed conflict but includes other forms of deprivation: poverty, pollution, disease, illiteracy, and lack of freedom are also forms of insecurity. In this sense, human security complements the areas defined by state security and places the human being at the centre of the state's concerns. More Rather than protecting, human security is about empowering people. Finally, the method advocated in this objective is to include non-state actors and foreign actors in a framework of shared sovereignty to solve human security challenges. See in particular: Commission on Human Security (ed.), *Human Security Now: Report of the Commission on Human Security*, (Paris: Presses de Sciences Po, 2003).
41   Charles-Philippe David and Jean-François Rioux, "Le concept de sécurité humaine", in *La sécurité humaine: une nouvelle conception des relations internationales*, ed. Jean-François Rioux, (Paris: l'Harmattan, 2002).
42   UN Office for the Coordination of Humanitarian Affairs, *Human Security in Theory and Practice. Application of the Human Security Concept and the United Nations Trust Fund for Human Security*, (2009), 86.

Agency) and regional organisations in West Africa.[43] While some countries, such as Sudan and Algeria, have expressed scepticism about the concept, which is considered vague and opens the way to interference in the internal affairs of states and the imposition of 'civilisational norms', many countries are fully committed to it. Gabon, for example, has stated that 'human security is at the centre of the government's priorities',[44] while Guinea has declared that 'it is essential to develop the practice of human security'.[45] In Europe, many parties, organisations and institutions now frame their African actions within this new normative rhetoric.

For example, the Swiss Centre for the Democratic Control of Armed Forces (DCAf) organised a conference in Rabat to promote the integration of human security into national security policies in North-West Africa, which representatives of many West African states attended.[46]

In Morocco, the King referred to human security in his message to the UN Millennium Summit,[47] the 11th Francophonie Summit[48] and the 21st Africa–France Summit[49] without giving this theme a legitimising role in Moroccan external action. The Kingdom has a nuanced position on this point. Like Mexico and Egypt, it neither rejects nor adheres entirely to the notion of human security but declares itself in favour of a more restrictive approach that distinguishes the responsibility to protect from human security: in other words, an approach that distinguishes national security from that of the individual.[50] Although the Palace and the government do not always refer to the concept of human security *talis qualis* concerning Morocco's Africa policy, the con-

---

43 Sahel and West Africa Club/OECD, *Human Security in West Africa: Challenges, Synergies and Actions for a Regional Agenda*, (Lomé, Togo: October 2006).
44 "The definition of human security continues to divide Member States in the General Assembly", *UN General Assembly*, May 21, 2010.
45 Ibid.
46 Geneva Centre for the Democratic Control of Armed Forces (DCAF), *Intégrer la sécurité humaine dans les politiques de sécurité nationale dans le nord-ouest de l'Afrique*, Synthesis Report, (November 2010), 64.
47 "Message from His Majesty King Mohammed VI to the UN Millennium Summit", *Maroc.ma*, July 2, 2006.
48 "Message of HM the King to the XIth Summit of Heads of State and Government of the Francophonie", *Maroc.ma*, August 2006.
49 "Speech by H.M. King Mohammed VI at the 21st Summit of Heads of State and Government of Africa and France", *Maroc.ma*, January 17, 2001.
50 Rahim Kherad, *Sécurité humaine: théorie et pratique(s) en l'honneur du doyen Dominique Breillat colloque international*, [5 et 6 février 2009, Faculté de droit et des sciences sociales de Poitiers], (Paris: A. Pedone, 2010).

cept of 'global security',[51] a postmodernist corollary of the liberal concept of human security, is prevalent in the discourse. Also defined as a broad approach to security, global security emphasises the interdependence between internal and external security and the value of a systematic response to global threats. Unlike human security, which questions the dominance of states and downplays the military's role, global security emphasises the role of sovereign states. It fully reaffirms the value of the defence mechanism. It is therefore a concept that better suits the Moroccan vision—all the more so as all of the areas of security referred to as human security, as defined by the Commission,[52] are also considered in the context of global security: transnational crime, ethnic and religious conflicts, pandemics, biotechnological attacks, mass migration, and environmental and climate crises.

The use of the concept of 'global security' by Moroccan leaders is also a way of referring to the different dimensions of security as defined by international organisations while preserving the idea of the supremacy of the state over these issues.[53] In many speeches, the monarch has emphasised his support for consolidating global security while recalling the need to develop mutual aid for the African continent.[54] The Moroccan government has also used the concept of 'global security' in its policies. The issues of terrorism in the Sahel, drug and arms trafficking in West Africa, food problems in Chad or Niger, the development of the role of women in African societies, and environmental challenges are all reasons raised to justify and legitimise cooperation between Morocco and its African environment. In this context, Morocco resorts to the principle of subsidiarity, which makes it possible to reconcile the principles of the need to act and those of state sovereignty. It makes its diplomacy appear more human-

---

51 For a full analysis of the concept, see: Alain Bravo et alii, *La sécurité globale: Réalité, enjeux et perspectives*, Roujansky, Jacques (éd.), (Paris, France: CNRS éditions, 2009). Mark Bevir et alii, *Interpreting Global Security*, (London New York: Routledge, 2014).
52 Commission sur la sécurité humaine (ed.), *La sécurité humaine maintenant*.
53 The Monarchy proposes its own expanded definition of global security: 'We also reaffirm Our commitment to global security, in its strategic, political, economic, cultural and human dimensions, security that guarantees the sovereignty, national unity and territorial integrity of each people. We further call for the adoption of an operational strategy to usher in a new era in our internal relations and our relations with our international environment': "Speech by HM King Mohammed VI at the Arab Summit in Tunis", *Maroc.ma*, March 29, 2004.
54 "Speech by HM the King to the participants of the UN General Assembly meeting", *Maroc.ma*, September 14, 2005. "HM King Mohammed VI addresses a message to the participants of the first African conference on human development", "Royal speech on the occasion of the 4th anniversary of the Throne Day".

ist than realistic. As a result, many non-African actors diplomatically support Moroccan action in this region.

Discourses related to South–South cooperation and global security are echoing in Africa, especially since the current context is marked by the development of peace diplomacy on the continent. Since the beginning of the 2000s, Africa has strongly reaffirmed the need to give itself the means to take charge of the security and development issues of the continent.[55] This context is conducive to recognising Morocco's role in development and security among African leaders. For example, the First Lady of Guinea has stated that the Kingdom has become 'a model for African countries in just a few years'.[56] Some extra-African actors also adhere to the Moroccan legitimisation framework, most notably France, which has reiterated its support for Morocco's diplomacy in Africa.[57] The United States also supports Morocco's security policy in the Sahel, a topic I will discuss later. The countries of the South, and more specifically the Gulf monarchies, facilitate meetings and Moroccan integration in West Africa when necessary.[58]

4   The Kingdom Is Moderate: The Valorisation of a Political-Religious Legacy through the Definition of a Golden-Mean Islam

Another discursive theme in the legitimisation of this Africa policy is the promotion of the Kingdom's 'moderate' character, particularly in the religious sphere, which has been consolidated by the threat posed by Islamic terrorism. More generally, the resurgence of the religious issue in international relations[59]

---

55   Jean-Luc Stalon, "L'africanisation de la diplomatie de la paix", *Revue internationale et stratégique 66*, no. 2 (2007): 47–58.
56   "HM King Mohammed VI has made the Kingdom 'a model' for African countries (First Lady of Guinea)", *MAP*, March 8, 2014.
57   According to President François Hollande: 'Couldn't we federate our forces, Morocco and France, to serve the development of the African continent, to carry out projects in Africa, to invest together in Africa? Our two countries share the desire to help a certain number of countries in Africa and to work in the same direction with our specific assets, with our respective strengths', Presidency of the Republic, "Speech by the President of the Republic to the French community at the Lyautey School in Casablanca", www.elysee.fr, April 5, 2013.
58   Saudi Arabia contributes, for example, to the normalisation of Moroccan-Mauritanian relations. "Saudi Arabia facilitates reconciliation between Morocco and Mauritania", Yabiladi.com, April 8, 2016.
59   There is a vast theoretical literature on this subject. See, for example: K.R. Dark (ed.), *Religion and International Relations*, (Basingstoke, Palgrave Macmillan, 2000); Vendulka

has led Morocco to reposition itself vis-à-vis religious identities and renew its approach to political Islam. A new definition of Islam, based on the 'principle of the golden mean',[60] thus emerged at the advent of the reign of Mohammed VI. As early as 2002, the launch of a vast project of reconstruction of the religious field on the institutional and normative levels made this ambition concrete. For the first time in the history of Morocco, Sufism became one of the three official components of state Islam, alongside the Malikite school and the Ascharite doctrine. Ahmed Toufiq, the new Minister of Habous and Islamic Affairs, appointed by the King in 2002, is a Sufi. He replaced a former minister considered too complacent with the Salafist movement. Represented in Morocco by numerous local and transnational brotherhoods, Sufism is practised by elites and the working classes. Presented as a bulwark against extremism (Wahhabi or Salafist) because of its mystical and spiritual dimension,[61] it allows the King, Commander of the Faithful, to revalorise the bonds of allegiance that have united transnational African religious communities to the sultans of Morocco at different times in Morocco's history, and to claim a singular role in the continent's security, which derives its legitimacy from the monarch's symbolic power. The institutionalisation of Sufism by the state came after a long period when Salafist doctrine dominated the field of religious thought among the ulemas. In the aftermath of independence, when the definition of national identity had rapidly become a partisan issue, Allal al-Fassi—ideologue of the Istiqlal Party and theorist of the 'Greater Morocco' project—displayed a public preference for reformist Salafism[62] (not to be confused with contemporary Salafism[63]). Allal al-Fassi was the son of a prominent ulema of Fez, rector of the Al Quaraouiyine Theological University, whose vision he had inherited. For him, Morocco had to return to its roots, to a more pious era, destroyed by the

---

Kubálková, "Towards an International Political Theology", *Millennium—Journal of International Studies* 29, no. 3 (January 2000): 675–704; Fabio Petito and Pavlos Hatzopoulos (eds.), *Religion in International Relations. The Return from Exile*, (Basingstoke, Palgrave Macmillan, 2003) Scott M. Thomas, *The Global Resurgence of Religion and the Transformation of International Relations*, (Basingstoke, Palgrave Macmillan, 2005).

60 "Speech by H.M. King Mohammed VI ON THE occasion of the first anniversary of the Sovereign's Inauguration", *Maroc.ma*, July 30, 2000.

61 "HM King Mohammed VI, Amir Al Mouminine, addresses a message to the participants in the first edition of the Sidi Chiker national meetings of Sufi followers", *Morocco. ma*, September 10, 2004.

62 Khalid Zekri, "Aux sources de la modernité marocaine", *Itinéraires. Littérature, textes, cultures*, n° 2009-3, (2009): 43–55.

63 Abdessamad Dialmy, "L'Islamisme marocain: entre révolution et intégration", *Archives de sciences sociales des religions*, no. 110, Éditions de l'École des hautes études en sciences sociales, (2000): 5–27.

westernisation introduced by France. To achieve this goal, the Arabic language and Islamic culture had to be disseminated through national education. In this scheme, the Amazigh vernacular languages also represented a threat to the unity of national identity: it was, therefore, necessary to arabise the Amazigh people from primary school onwards,[64] to erase their 'pagan' rituals as well as all forms of Islamic confraternity (Sufi) and maraboutic practices. Very quickly, a large part of the Moroccan bourgeois elite adhered to al-Fassi's ideal of the 'original' identity of the Moroccan nation, ignoring the fact that the concept of the nation-state had been imported from the European experience.

However, a new, more conservative and populist form of Salafism gradually emerged during the 1980s. Initially, this Salafism was introduced by the state to counteract revolutionary movements. However, radical and violent groups slowly developed around the Salafist ideology. It was particularly intending to counter this movement that Mohammed VI, once in power, wished to redefine the values of Moroccan Islam and reorganise religious institutions. The terrorist attacks of 16 May 2003 in Casablanca also contributed to accelerating the 'restructuring plan of the religious field', to use the expression used by its technocrats, the main components of which were the reorganisation of the Ministry of Habous and Islamic Affairs, the recomposition and enlargement of the Council of ulemas, and the rationalisation of Islamic education in public schools. This redefinition involved a set of reforms aimed at improving the state's control over the religious field and at combating Salafism by clarifying the principles of the new official Moroccan Islam. Among the areas of these reforms were the control of the origin of imams' fatwas (only state fatwas are now authorised), better supervision of Islamic teaching to verify its conformity with official Islam, the monitoring of the origin of mosque funding, better information on Salafist centres, and the diversification and professionalisation of religious representatives (in particular through the introduction of the function of 'mourchidates', preachers specialising in Islamic jurisprudence). These reforms have partly achieved the desired objectives, namely 'the rationalisation, modernisation and unification of Islamic education [...] which, instead of forming obtuse and sclerotic minds, will, on the contrary, favour openness to other cultures'.[65] However, the religious milieu, in particular that of the ulemas, remains very conservative and cannot accommodate the mentality changes desired by the King.

---

64 Karim K. Mezran, *Negotiation and Construction of National Identities*, (Boston, Martinus Nijhoff Publishers, 2007).
65 Ministry of Habous and Islamic Affairs, *Royal speech on the restructuring of the religious field in Morocco*, April 20, 2004.

The resignation of Asmaa Lamrabet, the only woman who had managed to—temporarily—join the Rabita Mohamadya of Ulemas thanks to this reform momentum, is a convincing illustration of the severe resistance to any form of modernisation in this field. Her webpage explains that her resignation was linked to 'differences in the approach to gender equality within the religious frame of reference'.[66] Thus, the plan to restructure the religious field has essentially focused on the security dimension, i.e. 'to protect Morocco from the vectors of extremism and terrorism, and to preserve its identity which bears the seal of moderation and tolerance',[67] with some success at this stage.

With this institutional and normative restructuring underway, Morocco also aims to disseminate its religious model to consolidate its cultural, spiritual and political influence in favour of a so-called moderate and tolerant approach. In this perspective, as a founding member of the OIC,[68] Morocco has presided over the organisation twice and competes fiercely with Turkey on the vision of the role it should play.[69] Addressing the leaders of Islamic countries, Mohammed VI promotes, in a context of rising jihadist extremism, the Moroccan vision of the golden mean and its potential to 'redress the shining image of Islam'.[70] In this optic, the diplomatic apparatus has been duly summoned to ensure the dissemination of this identity.[71]

---

66 Press release by Dr Asma Lamrabet explaining the reasons for her resignation from the Centre for Women's Studies in Islam within the Rabita alMohamadya of the Ulemas of Moroccoe, http://www.asma-lamrabet.com/articles/communique-de-presse-du-dr-asma-lamrabet-explicitant-les-raisons-de-sa-demission-du-centre-d-etudes-feminines-en-islam-au-sein-d/

67 *Discours royal relatif à la restructuration du champ religieux au Maroc.*

68 Organisation of the Islamic Conference, now the Organisation of Islamic Cooperation, established at the Rabat Summit, 1969.

69 Belhaj, *La dimension islamique dans la politique étrangère du Maroc*, 201–202.

70 'Based on our firm attachment to the ideals of our safe Islamic civilisation, which advocates a just middle ground and moderation, dialogue and tolerance, openness to and respect for the Other, we say the following to our partners in the international community: Come and agree together to refer to these sublime divine principles in our relations and the management of our differences: Come and agree together to refer, in our relations and the management of our disputes, to these sublime divine principles': "Speech by HM King Mohammed VI to the consultative meeting of the leaders of Islamic countries", *Maroc.ma*, February 26, 2003.

71 'We have developed an integrated and coherent diplomatic vision that affirms and enshrines Morocco's secular civilisational identity. (...) It is also the duty of Moroccan diplomacy to work, with the same ardour, to highlight the fundamental assets of the Kingdom and to make the most judicious use of them, through a coherent and effective positioning, in line with Morocco's values and higher interests, and with the fundamental develop-

To ensure this influence, the government created in 2004 a radio and television channel called Mohammed VI of the Holy Quran (Assadissa),[72] broadcast on the Hot Bird satellite (covering Europe and Asia Minor through the Mediterranean Basin) and Nile Sat (covering North Africa, the Near East and the Middle East). The channel broadcasts continuously in Arabic, Amazigh and French and participates in promoting Moroccan Islam as defined by the Ministry in 2002. More broadly, according to one leader, the objective of this channel is to contribute to 'counteracting extremists who damage the image of Islam'[73] with the same technological means. At the same time, the government encourages the publication of scientific and theological research through the organisation of the 'Mohammed VI Prize' for Islamic studies, promoting themes that align with the 'progressive' approach instituted by the organisers.[74]

The institutionalisation and control of the religious field by the monarchical apparatus thus served as a model for US officials in Algeria, who encouraged dialogue between the government and moderate Islamists.[75] Pierre Vermeren observes that from the 2000s onwards, 'the stability of the Moroccan regime, to whose side the French and Americans committed themselves, appears to be of capital interest amid a troubled Arab world'.[76] According to the Palace, there is no doubt that 'moderate and open Sunni Malikite Islam […] has always provided the receptacle and the crucible in which all the constituent components of the national identity, in its unity, richness and diversity of its various and multiple civilisational tributaries, have been happily blended'.[77] Although the moderation of the Maliki rite is not essential but relative, the proclamation of this historical individuality constitutes the irrefutable justification of the validity of a bridging role between African, Eastern and Western regions.

Strengthened by its stability and the recognition of this stability by the Western powers, and advantaged by its shared borders with three geo-civilisational

---

ments in international relations': "Message of the Sovereign to the 1st Conference of Ambassadors of HM the King".

72 Channel website: http://www.idaatmohammedassadiss.ma/.
73 Ministry of Habous and Islamic Affairs, *Launch of Mohammed VI Holy Qur'an Assadissa Channel*, June 16, 2004.
74 Website of the Ministry of Habous and Islamic Affairs: http://habous.gov.ma/fr/division-des-%C3%A9tudes-islamiques/377-Etudes-Islamiques/sce-organisation-prix-and-competition-aff-isl/24-presentation-of-the-mohammed-prize-vi-of-thought-and-study-islamiques-1433h-2012.html.
75 Yahia H. Zoubir, "Algeria and U.S. Interests: Containing Radical Islam and Promoting Democracy", *Middle East Policy* 9, no. 1 (2002): 64–81.
76 Vermeren, *Le Maroc de Mohammed VI*, 38.
77 "Speech of H.M. King Mohammed VI ON THE occasion of the Throne Day", *Maroc.ma*, 2015.

areas, the monarchy tends to legitimise its role in Africa by the 'mediation' that characterises the Kingdom's identity. It affirms that 'Moroccans have remained attached to the Malikite rite [...] thus demonstrating that moderation goes hand in hand with the very essence of Moroccan identity'.[78]

All of this discursive rhetoric contributes to the legitimisation of Moroccan action in West Africa, considering, in the words of the former prime minister, its secular 'spiritual leadership' in this region.[79] Thus, the Palace considers that diplomacy must henceforth redress Morocco's image by 'highlighting the assets of its spiritual influence, its historical heritage and its geo-strategic situation'.[80] The ability of the government to carry out this undertaking of symbolic legitimisation makes it a force for organisation and the embodiment of a collective identity, reinforced by the development of cultural and religious diplomacy on an African scale, the content of which I will analyse in the next chapter. At the top of this system, the monarch reinforces his symbolic power.

---

78 "Royal speech on the occasion of the 4th Throne Day anniversary".
79 Interview with Abdelilah Benkirane on Jordanian national television Quoted in: Amine Larbi, "Benkirane: L'africanité du Maroc, inébranlable par les manœuvres de ses ennemis", *Lemag.ma*, March 18, 2013.
80 "Speech by H.M. King Mohammed VI on the occasion of the 49th anniversary of the Revolution of the King and the People".

CHAPTER 6

Africa as a Field of Expression for an Indirect Strategy

1   Introduction

How can a country like Morocco use its internal development to serve an Africa policy? How can it exert its influence and consolidate its continental integration? How can it recover from its absence from the main pan-African cooperation structures? These are the challenges facing the Kingdom in the exercise of its Africa policy.

Morocco is a small power on the international scale and a medium power on the regional scale. Small and medium powers are generally recognised by their delayed socioeconomic growth, structural and administrative weaknesses, and lack of human resources with broad competencies. However, with the rise of multilateralism and the diversification of foreign policy levers, these states are no longer merely pivots used by great powers: they are recognised as sovereign, autonomous and influential actors. As Peter Katzenstein notes, they are able to defend their role in the international system 'not because they have found a solution to the problem of change but because they have found a way to live with change'.[1]

It can therefore be seen that the particularity of the Moroccan approach consists not in the specialisation of its diplomacy in one particular field,[2] but in the extensive use of the fields of diplomacy (humanitarian, economic, cultural, religious), its levels (bilateral, multilateral, trilateral, global) and its scales (informal, public, state, secret) in the service of a specialisation of its role identity. Diplomacy is thought of as a mechanism, or even a system, which, given Morocco's material resources, constitutes an ultra-reduced model of a great power's diplomatic apparatus. The objectives pursued and the expected results are therefore different. For example, the cultural diplomacy deployed by the

---

1   Peter J. Katzenstein, "Small States and Small States Revisited", *New Political Economy 8*, no. 1 (March 1, 2003): 9–30.
2   Several theorists defend the postulate of a systematic specialisation of diplomacy by small and medium powers. See in particular: Jordaan, "The concept of a middle power in international relations: distinguishing between emerging and traditional middle powers."

Kingdom is not part of a *soft power* strategy but part of a more modest form of diplomacy of influence, which I will define below.

Second, Morocco finds itself confronted, willingly or unwillingly, with the shadow of great external powers such as France. However, it is precisely the positioning of Morocco in relation to this shadow that determine the contours, physicality and density of its Africa policy. In this respect, the main challenge of distancing itself from projecting an area of cooperation is the Kingdom's ability to use and enhance the cultural and institutional legacy left by France in the region while affirming its specificity and difference. Unlike Brazil, for example, which has succeeded in asserting its presence in the Portuguese-speaking African region thanks to the withdrawal of Portugal[3] and a reversal of the balance of power between the two countries,[4] and which continues to extend its sphere of influence to other non-Lusophone countries,[5] Morocco is faced with power that is still firmly rooted in the French-speaking region but also in other regions of Africa. The challenge is not to compete with France or to try to dominate the multilateral Francophone institutions but to convert the French shadow into a light projected in the African space.

Third, since the early 2000s new African powers have emerged and developed on the one hand, and new instruments of pan-African cooperation on the other. The African Union, in particular, as well as the regional organisations with which it closely collaborates, have gradually become the main manifestations of an 'Africanisation of peace diplomacy', to use the expression of one senior UN official.[6] Although the AU still faces many structural difficulties and is the theatre of opposed conceptions of the role it should play, it is now present at all levels and in all areas of intra-African cooperation. Since it departed from the organisation in 1984, the Kingdom has been deprived of valuable cooperation frameworks. This failure has publicly raised the issue of the need for a strategy to be defined by all Moroccan leaders to circumvent this institutional obstacle.

---

3   Portugal has maintained close cultural and political ties with its former African colonies but has no real diplomatic influence. It has virtually no presence in the other major countries of the continent. João Gomes Cravinho and Mohammad-Saïd Darviche, "Les relations postcoloniales portugaises", *Pôle Sud*, no. 22 (2005): 89–100.
4   Francisco Santana Ferra, "Un 'espace phonique' lusophone à plusieurs voix? Enjeux et jeux de pouvoir au sein de la Communauté des Pays de Langue Portugaise (CPLP)", *International Journal of Comparative Politics 14*, no. 1 (2007): 95–129.
5   Carolina Milhorance de Castro, "La politique extérieure Sud-Sud du Brésil de l'après-Lula. Quelle place pour l'Afrique", *Afrique contemporaine*, no. 248 (2014): 45–59.
6   Stalon, "L'africanisation de la diplomatie de la paix".

As André Beaufre rightly reminds us, 'many people do strategy more or less unconsciously'.[7] This is very much Morocco's case: there is no official report or white paper on Morocco's Africa policy that sets out the objectives and broad doctrinal lines as defined by the Palace or the government, nor are there any strategists' guidelines to which the leaders refer. As demonstrated in the first chapter of this study, it is mainly the royal speeches that constitute, taken together, a body of doctrinal texts on foreign policy. In this context, it is obviously difficult to trace a clear strategic line. Nevertheless, this does not mean that the Kingdom conducts its Africa policy blindly and illogically. On the contrary, the study of this mechanism shows that the Kingdom does deploy a strategy, which I will describe as an indirect strategy.

In terms of defence, strategy is 'the art of using military forces to achieve the results set by policy'.[8] This definition, taken up by Beaufre, is faithful to the definitions proposed by Clausewitz, Liddel Hart and Raymond Aron. Similarly, it can be said that in foreign policy, strategy is the art of using diplomatic levers to achieve the results set by the policy, the lever being defined as an active force used as a means of action in the framework of diplomatic practice. More generally, in defence, as in foreign policy, strategy is 'the art of the dialectic of wills using force to resolve their conflict'.[9] The choice of means, therefore, depends closely on the definition of enemies and friends: who should be convinced? Similarly, the choice of the strategic model is closely linked to the means and objectives of the policy. If an actor has powerful means, if the threat is direct and its ambitions are high, it will generally employ a direct strategy. If, on the other hand, the means are weak, if the threat is comatose or dissuasive, and its ambitions are more modest, it will most often employ an indirect strategy.[10]

In the field of defence, the indirect strategy consists 'in not confronting the enemy in a direct showdown, but in approaching him only after having worried, surprised and unbalanced him by an unexpected approach, carried out by diverted directions': a manoeuvre which 'is imposed on the one of the two adversaries who is not sure of being strong enough to beat the enemy in a battle fought on the ground chosen by the adversary'.[11] In foreign policy, the definition of such a strategy is significantly different: the field of international politics,

---

7   Beaufre, *Introduction à la stratégie*.
8   Ibid., 33.
9   Ibid., 34.
10 There are other strategic models defined by Beaufre, such as the strategy of 'successive actions', the strategy of 'prolonged low-intensity total struggle' and the strategy of 'violent conflict aimed at military victory'. These are not relevant models for our case study. Therefore, I will not discuss them.
11 Beaufre, *Introduction à la stratégie*, 145–146.

unlike the battlefield, is not defined by the relationship with the enemy alone. Influence, recognition, stability, development and economic gains are all interests that guide and define the strategy's objectives. On the other hand, it must be recognised that in the case of Morocco, for example, Africa is a terrain chosen by the 'enemies of its territorial integrity' on which to wage a diplomatic battle. These two dimensions must therefore be taken into account simultaneously in defining the indirect strategy.

In foreign policy, I will therefore call indirect strategy the approach that consists of practising an extensive and offensive use of diplomacy in a field different from that of the adversary to avoid any direct confrontation and bypass the conflictual space. This manoeuvre is necessary for an actor who cannot confront opponents using the same means they have and who wishes to obtain additional gains unrelated to the confrontation with the opponent, such as recognition, influence or economic gains. If successful, the indirect strategy allows both the development of a new form of power and the paralysis of the adversary through the multiplication of means of diplomatic dissuasion, in the manner of the Lilliputians facing Gulliver.

2 Fifteen Years of Offensive Bilateralism in the Service of a Sectorisation of Cooperation

The history of Morocco's Africa policy reveals that the Kingdom has long lived with the legacy of its withdrawal from the AU and the policy of exclusion practised by its African adversaries. The conduct of an Africa policy during the Cold War highlighted seemingly intractable problems. After several diplomatic failures on the continent in the 1980s and 1990s, the arrival into power of Mohammed VI marked the beginning of a strategic reorientation: the end of the 'Hallstein doctrine', during which Morocco systematically broke off relations with African countries that supported the Polisario Front, through diplomatic recognition, and the revaluation of Morocco's image through an increased and multisectoral presence on the continent.

Long accused of defending its territorial interests to the detriment of a vision of solidarity with Africa, the Kingdom now intends to demonstrate that the defence of its interests is not incompatible with the expression of this solidarity. In this perspective, bilateral diplomacy appears to be the most favourable framework for a re-engagement that is both prudent and progressive. This approach is based on direct exchanges in a framework institutionalised by the two actors: a face-to-face meeting which allows the Kingdom to control the entire negotiation chain, limiting the risks.

This strategy of pragmatic influence replaces a policy that was struggling to overcome a sense of national betrayal. The royal pre-eminence over foreign policy plays a central role in this process, since the durability of cooperation agreements effectively rests on the symbolic endorsement provided by the monarch and on the maintenance of high-level links with African heads of state. More generally, bilateral diplomacy has the advantage of being able to sectorise cooperation according to the means and objectives of the government and to the degree of understanding shared with each state. In this context, bilateral diplomacy is tailor-made, free from globalised norms, veto rights and political quarrels; it is enhanced by the ability to give each relationship an exceptional character. The choice of bilateralism and the means mobilised have reinforced the postulate of an indirect strategy deployed by the Kingdom in this context.

Moroccan–African bilateral cooperation has been based, in the first instance, on official visits by the monarch to African states.[12] The first manifestation of this new Africa policy was Mohammed VI's visit to Mauritania in 2001, a significant event in that it was the first time that a Moroccan king had visited Mauritania. It should be recalled that Mauritania was the subject of territorial claims by Morocco after independence. The Kingdom finally recognised Mauritania's sovereignty in 1969, but relations between the two countries have continued to be marked by mutual distrust, fuelled by Algeria. The 2001 royal visit was therefore completely unprecedented. It led to the signing of some 30 cooperation agreements, the reopening of the Moroccan–Mauritanian borders in 2002 and the announcement by Mauritania of the construction of the last section of road linking Morocco to West Africa.[13] The construction of this new trans-Saharan road should eventually facilitate economic and human exchanges. It is also a symbolic illustration of the integration of the Maghreb with sub-Saharan Africa.

On the other hand, the royal visits directed the diplomatic apparatus towards countries considered strategic within the Africa policy. After several state visits to Mauritania, Senegal, Cameroon and South Africa between 2001 and 2004, the monarch began his first major 'African tour' by 2004, defining the geographical contours of the new privileged space of influence. Senegal, Niger, Cameroon, Benin and Gabon cordially welcomed the royal procession, com-

---

12 For an overview, see Appendix 1 and Appendix 1bis.
13 However, Mauritania refused the Moroccan proposal to finance 50% of the construction. Alain Antil and Armelle Choplin, "Le chaînon manquant. Notes sur la route Nouakchott-Nouadhibou, dernier tronçon de la transsaharienne Tanger-Dakar", *Afrique contemporaine*, no. 208 (2005):115–126,. See also Appendix 9.

posed of numerous public and private delegations at the King's bedside. Two years later, in 2006, a new African tour took Mohammed VI to Senegal, Gambia, Congo, DRC and Gabon. In 2009, he visited Equatorial Guinea. In 2013 he made his third African tour to Gabon, Côte d'Ivoire, Mali and Senegal. The following year he repeated his trips to Mali, Côte d'Ivoire, Gabon and Guinea (Conakry). In 2015, he completed his fourth African tour in Côte d'Ivoire, Gabon, Senegal and Guinea-Bissau. Let us stop with these few examples for now.

A study of the chronology of visits, agreements and conventions signed with Gabon,[14] Côte d'Ivoire[15] and Senegal attests to continuous cooperation effort with these three countries. The royal tours have further strengthened these exchanges by supervising and monitoring the preparation of dozens of new public–private and private–private partnerships, especially during the third and fourth tours in 2014 and 2015.[16] The 2014 visit to Gabon, for example, ended with the signing of 24 agreements in the fields of training, agriculture, energy and new technologies. This figure contrasts sharply with the average number of agreements concluded during the usual commissions or state visits by African presidents to Morocco (between four and six).

In countries with which exchanges have been poorly or irregularly maintained, the royal tours have raised the level of cooperation to a higher level. This is the case with Guinea, for example—a country that the monarch visited for the first time in 2014 accompanied by, among others, almost 600 businesspeople.[17] A year earlier, Mohammed VI had met President Alpha Condé on the fringes of the royal visit to Bamako in 2013. In 2012, the Palace supported the organisation of the 6th Joint Intergovernmental Commission after a long period of inaction. The new partnership with Guinea was thus clearly prepared in less than two years, nonetheless resulting in the conclusion of 21 cooperation agreements in various fields (hydraulics, fishing, mining, tourism , etc.), as well as the creation of a Moroccan–Guinean Business Council, during the royal visit. While in 2012 only 6% of Moroccan FDI was injected into the Guinean economy, Guinea became Morocco's fourth-largest African trade client after Senegal, Mauritania and Côte d'Ivoire just two years later.[18]

---

14   "Chronologie des conventions et accords de coopération signés entre le Maroc et le Gabon", MAP, March 5, 2014.
15   "Chronologie des accords et conventions liant le Maroc et la Côte d'Ivoire", Abidjan.net, March 19, 2013.
16   See Appendix 1 and Appendix 1bis.
17   Fouâd Harit, "Maroc-Guinée: les grandes décisions de Mohammed VI et Alpha Condé", Afrik.com, March 5, 2014.
18   "Relations Maroc-Afrique: l'ambition d'une 'nouvelle frontière'".

Finally, within the countries that recognised the Polisario Front as a state, the royal visits initiated a significant change in the orientation of bilateral cooperation. This is the case for Guinea-Bissau, for example—a Portuguese-speaking country in West Africa with which the Kingdom has engaged in numerous discussions on the Sahara. As a result of this effort, the government of Guinea-Bissau withdrew its recognition of the RASD in 2010 and opened a chancery in Rabat the following year, after 26 years of rupture. It is worth noting that during its royal visit in 2015, Morocco had sent 12,000 tons of medicine as well as a medical team to provide free consultations and surgeries to the citizens of Guinea-Bissau,[19] a sign of effective and not only discursive involvement in South–South cooperation. More than a state visit to launch sectoral cooperation, the monarch's trip to Guinea-Bissau illustrates the Kingdom's diplomatic progress: the progressive softening of the Polisario Front's protectors, the expansion of the Moroccan cooperation area to non-French-speaking countries and the beginning of regional integration by multilateral institutions.

Indeed, although Morocco has maintained sustained diplomatic relations with some of these African states since the 1960s, the legal frameworks of bilateral ties were developed mainly under the reign of Mohammed VI. With Senegal, for example, a country historically close to the Kingdom, this legal framework was only instituted in 2006.[20] This is also the case with the Joint Commissions: the first Joint Commission with the Congo was instituted in 2007.[21] The royal visits thus help to establish new frameworks for Moroccan–African cooperation before delegating their management to members of the government. These visits led each minister to prepare a convention or a partnership proposal with his African counterpart. Once signed, during a ceremony under the aegis of the two heads of state (in the case of royal visits) or an Intergovernmental Joint Commission, the private sector was immediately put to work in achieving the objective promoted by the agreement. The government is obliged to align itself with royal decisions. A promise of partnership that bears the King's seal cannot be neglected. All the ministries (transport, tourism, energy and education) involved in this undertaking therefore redoubled their efforts to establish a legal framework, norms and rules for cooperation that will facilitate the work of both the public and the private sectors. Following or in preparation for the royal visits, the travels of the Minister of Foreign Affairs ensure the smooth running of the negotiations. The former Minister of Foreign Affairs from 2002 to

---

19 "Mohamed VI on Wednesday in Guinea-Bissau, a first for a Moroccan king", *Telquel. ma*, May 25, 2015.
20 Portal of the Ministry of Foreign Affairs and Cooperation, 'Bilateral relations: Senegal',.
21 Portal of the Ministry of Foreign Affairs and Cooperation , 'Bilateral relations: Congo'.

2012, and current foreign affairs advisor to the King, Taieb Fassi Fihri, has played an essential role in this process, as have the directors of African affairs in the Ministry of Foreign Affairs, from Abdellatif Bendahane to Mohammed Sbihi.

The royal tours are finally intended to establish a climate of trust. In the eyes of African leaders, the monarch's visit is tangible proof of the Kingdom's commitment. The media coverage of these events also allows African heads of state to convince public opinion of the usefulness of such a cooperation.

For the Moroccan private sector too, it is a guarantee of opportunities. As one ambassador notes: 'Morocco's strategy is to make South–South cooperation a foreign policy priority. His Majesty has made about 20 visits to Africa and encourages companies to set up in these countries. When the King visits a country, it is a kind of guarantee for companies. It means that things will go well. Let's not forget that many Moroccans are still reluctant to invest in Africa'.[22] This is why private investment is also encouraged by the political negotiation of a legal framework aimed at securing the interests of Moroccan investments, as well as the negotiation of agreements to ease customs rules with African countries. Customs cooperation now includes the training of African customs officers in Morocco, agreements on the avoidance of double taxation to encourage trade, granting tariff preferences to African countries, abolishing visas and establishing common standards. In addition to the states concerned with the royal visits, many African countries have also concluded this type of agreement with Morocco. This is the case for Togo, for example, which sent a delegation to Rabat for this purpose.[23]

In addition, to ensure the smooth running of public and private bilateral negotiations, the Moroccan strategy has shown initiative in the political field, notably by getting involved in mediation. In this case, the monarch offered mediation in the Mano River conflicts in 2002. The Mano River conflicts refer to the fighting in Sierra Leone and Liberia since 1989, which ended with the voluntary exile of Liberian president Charles Taylor and a general peace agreement signed between the different rebel factions in 2003.[24] A year earlier, Mohammed VI had indeed brought together presidents Charles Taylor, Lansana Conté and Tejan Kabbag at a summit in Rabat, at the request of the Mano River Women's Peace Network.[25] This was an important event, as the various attempts to mediate by Muammar Gaddafi had never resulted in a direct meeting of the three presidents. Morocco deployed a diplomatic approach consist-

---

22 Interview with a serving ambassador to Africa no. 21, July 2013.
23 "Customs Cooperation with Morocco", *Togolese Republic*, March 18, 2016.
24 Paul Richards, "La terre ou le fusil?", *Afrique contemporaine*, no. 214 (2005): 35–57.
25 Mano River Women's Peace Network: http://www.marwopnet.org/resolutionconflits.htm.

ing of meetings between the representatives of these three countries on the one hand and Taieb Fassi Fihri (former Minister of Foreign Affairs and current King's advisor) on the other.

However, no Moroccan parliamentary report or study of the Mano River conflict mentions the role of Moroccan mediation in resolving the conflict. Although Morocco regularly claims to be involved in resolving the crisis as a guarantee of its 'goodwill' for the continent's development, it is difficult to know what the actual conditions were, as there are few sources on this subject.

In addition, Moroccan leaders find in the policy of donations made by the Kingdom in Africa a more visible way of reinforcing the implementation of bilateral cooperation agreements. Construction of field hospitals (Niger in 2005, Mali in 2012), donations of medicines, medical equipment or foodstuffs (34 tonnes to Mali, 12 tonnes to Liberia and Sierra Leone, 10 tonnes to Senegal, etc.): Morocco is massively reproducing a policy of solidarity that used to be mainly directed towards the Arab-speaking world, as well as a policy of royal donations traditionally practised within the Kingdom to mitigate the shortcomings of the welfare state. In Africa, these donations are as much part of real humanitarian diplomacy deployed by Morocco on a global scale (other countries such as Haiti and Paraguay have benefited from substantial donations) as they are part of a consolidating the legitimisation framework of a 'Morocco of solidarity' at the service of the success of bilateral continental cooperation. As an essential partner in this humanitarian diplomacy, the RAF are responsible for the construction of hospitals, the transport of humanitarian convoys, and the medical service, and represent, along with the Moroccan Agency for International Cooperation, the main actors of these projects. The use of the military in the service of this diplomacy is a skilful way of enhancing the image and role of the army on the continent.

The encouraging results of this policy are that in 15 years, between 2001 and 2016, more than 500 agreements have been signed with nearly 40 African countries.[26] This diplomacy has also been effectively sectoralised: health, education, industry, transport, agriculture and culture are all areas of Moroccan–African cooperation. Unlike other levels of cooperation, bilateral sectoral cooperation has the advantage of being less subject to political uncertainties since once institutionalised, it remains the responsibility of ministers and their African counterparts. This approach also has the advantage of selecting the countries with which cooperation is most likely to succeed. The division of cooperation into sectoral stakes generally facilitates the negotiation process.

---

26 "Les relations Maroc-Afrique: l'ambition d'une nouvelle frontière".

Sectoral cooperation introduces a new form of inter-ministerial competition that energises public policies in the context of modernising the administrative apparatus. In the long term, the public fragmentation of state diplomacy will signify the Kingdom's development and democratisation. Indeed, bilateral diplomacy under Mohammed VI already has the features of a public policy (i.e. publicised and governmentalised in the terms defined in the previous chapters), albeit highly dependent on the executive. It contrasts sharply with Cold War diplomacy, which relied mainly on a system of high-level, personalised and secret exchanges. Today, official and secret diplomacy are no longer opposed but appear to be two sides of the same process: while negotiations may be hidden, policy orientation is made public. Secret diplomacy takes the form of a complement or a mode of preparation rather than a substitute for official diplomacy. Negotiation, however, remains in the hands of a small number of special envoys.

3 The Acquisition of Material Resources through Trilateral Cooperation

While providing humanitarian aid to African countries, Morocco is itself a recipient of financial aid from major powers and international institutions. It is thus both a recipient and a donor of international aid. Its specialisation in triangular or trilateral cooperation has, however, provided a framework for developing its diplomatic action in Africa and enhancing its role as a bridge. As one report formulates it, triangular cooperation is a way for the government to 'channel international aid funds to finance infrastructure projects in Africa and to entrust their management to Moroccan companies' as well as to 'serve as a support point for greater intensification of Morocco's economic relations with the countries of the continent'.[27] Trilateral cooperation achieves a double objective: obtaining external funds for state actions in Africa and strengthening its identity as a golden mean.

The Agence Marocaine de Coopération Internationale (AMCI) is the main body responsible for implementing this form of cooperation.[28] Among its most important projects is TICAD, a partnership between Japan as a donor, Morocco as a pivotal country and French-speaking African countries as recipients. This five-year agreement began in 1998 and has grown considerably over the past

---

27 "Relations Maroc-Afrique : l'ambition d'une 'nouvelle frontière'".
28 See the AMCI website: https://www.amci.ma

decade. It includes Japan's support to Morocco in organising training for other French-speaking African nationals, mainly in water sanitation, seafood processing, and maternal and child healthcare. On the Japan International Cooperation Agency website, the organisation highlights Morocco's progress in terms of water (the rate of access to clean water rose to 97% in cities and 60% in rural areas in 2006) and development. This is how the Japanese agency justifies its choice for Morocco: 'Morocco has developed considerably over the last two decades, offering other African countries a familiar and adaptable model on the same continent [...] This is why South–South cooperation with Morocco is the focus of attention.'[29] In 2013, for example, nearly 300 African nationals from 27 countries received training in Morocco as part of this trilateral cooperation. In addition to this aid, Japan has made numerous donations to the Kingdom (a recent donation involved the construction of a shellfish research and technology centre): a way of ensuring that its interests are met, mainly concerning the exploitation of fisheries resources on the Moroccan coast.[30]

Another notable project, triangular cooperation with the Food and Agriculture Organisation (FAO), has given Morocco the means to play a significant role in the development of agriculture in Burkina Faso, Djibouti and Niger, as part of the support for South–South cooperation instituted by the organisation. According to the FAO website, it appears again that the Kingdom places itself as an actor rather than a beneficiary of South–South cooperation: 'Morocco has requested no South–South cooperation in its favour. On the other hand, the country is very active in this programme.'[31] Its support for the implementation of projects instituted by the FAO in these three countries has included a technical assistant and the sending of human resources to the field in countries such as Burkina Faso, Niger and Djibouti. Today, other programmes are at work, now including Moroccan banks such as Crédit Agricole, which has committed to financing tripartite food security projects.

At a less institutionalised level, Morocco regularly collaborates with European states in the framework of African development programmes. These include Belgium, with which the Kingdom signed a triangular cooperation

---

29 Japan International Cooperation Agency website: http://www.jica.go.jp/french/news/focus_on/ticad_v/articles/article22.html#anco1. (Accessed July 2016).
30 About the donation: 'This project is also expected to strengthen relations between Japan and Morocco, a country of particular diplomatic importance to Japan which imports many fish products such as octopus, squid and tuna': http://www.jica.go.jp/french/news/press/150617_01.html. (Accessed July 2016).
31 FAO website: http://www.fao.org/maroc/programmes-et-projets/nos-projets/programme-de-la-cooperation-sud-sud/en/.

agreement in 2007, targeting eight countries (DRC, Burundi, Rwanda, Benin, Niger, Senegal, Burkina Faso and Mali), mainly in the drinking water and agriculture sectors.[32] However, it is with France that this type of exchange appears to be the most constant, while paradoxically being the least formalised. According to one ambassador, for example, 'very often, instead of sending Gabonese people to train in France, Paris asks that Morocco send teachers here. If the French government sent these students to France, they would benefit from suitable structures but face other realities on their return. Also, it is less expensive with Morocco.'[33] In the field of training, as in other sectors, trilateral cooperation between France, Morocco and Africa is undoubtedly the most developed.

Finally, on an informal scale, the Kingdom has instituted its own trilateral strategy through the 'breakdown' of the FDI and grants it receives in Africa.[34] The 'sectoral breakdown', in financial jargon, consists of the distribution of these investments in the different sectors of the economy. It should be recalled that France is the leading investor in Morocco (36% of FDI received), followed by the United Arab Emirates (8.6% of FDI received) and Singapore (8.1%).[35] The scale of these investments contributes to consolidating the economic power of the Kingdom, the first recipient of FDI in North Africa and the second in Africa. Despite the uprisings observed during the Arab Spring, and for reasons mentioned in the first chapter of this book, the interest of international investors has continued to grow. Every year, FDI flows into the Kingdom increase: for example, France in particular, increased its share by 64% year-on-year between 2011 and 2013. In Morocco, the sectoral breakdown is mainly directed towards trade, tourism, banking, holding companies, energy, mining, real estate and industry.

However, it can be observed that another dynamic is taking place, which could be described as 'external breakdown' and consists of indirectly redirecting part of these investments outside the Kingdom, more specifically to Africa. Among the destinations of Moroccan FDI, Mali, Côte d'Ivoire, Senegal, Gabon and Cameroon are the most important.[36]

Finally, trilateral diplomacy appears to be a lever to adapt to the recommendations of international institutions on South–South cooperation while being

---

32   Portal of the Moroccan Ministry of Foreign Affairs and Cooperation, 'Cooperation between Morocco and European Union countries for the benefit of African countries',.
33   Interview with an incumbent ambassador no. 21, July 2014.
34   See Appendix 7.
35   "Les IDE au Maroc en 2013", *French Embassy in Morocco, Regional Economic Service*, June 2014.
36   See Appendix 10.

part of a golden-mean role identity, which extends its political use. Moreover, it also strengthens Morocco's bilateral ties with its African 'friends'. More than a complementary, or even secondary, diplomatic instrument, it is an integral part of this multifaceted diplomatic arsenal intended to ensure the recognition of the Moroccan role in Africa. Trilateral cooperation presents the pivotal states as countries with recognised expertise, linguistic and cultural links and diplomatic affinities with the beneficiary countries. In this sense, it gives the Kingdom the means not only to strengthen its means of action in African countries but also to demonstrate the stability of its institutions, economic climate and technical expertise. One can observe the application of such a strategy by Brazil, for example, which, despite the internal socioeconomic imbalances that characterise it, invests massively in human diplomacy and trilateral cooperation in Africa to consolidate its leadership. Abdenur demonstrates that in the case of Brazil, trilateral cooperation constitutes 'a specific tactic for national self-promotion within a broad foreign policy strategy'.[37]

4 Circumventing the Absence from the AU through Parallel Multilateral Diplomacy

While bilateral and trilateral policies between 2000 and 2016 produced positive results at the continental level, many African leaders felt that Morocco was depriving itself of a real political foothold as long as it did not play the AU's multilateral game. Morocco's strategy during this period was to try to represent Africa in global institutions with the aim of demonstrating its capacity to deploy a dynamic multilateral African diplomacy despite its absence from the AU. This strategy was illustrated first and foremost by its African initiatives within the UN. As one diplomat points out, 'Morocco has chaired the UN Counter-Terrorism Committee. It chaired the Security Council when the resolution on the intervention in Mali was adopted. It was also the first country to sound the alarm on the arms issue in Libya.'[38]

In the minds of Moroccan diplomats, the Kingdom's political integration within the continent could be achieved only if the country played a leading role in defending African interests within international institutions. This is why the Kingdom reintegrated the Geneva 'African Group' to the UN in 2004. Before that date, it had participated sporadically in this group from which it was

---

37 Adriana E. Abdenur, "The Strategic Triad: Form and Content in Brazil's Triangular Cooperation Practices", *International Affairs Working Paper New York University*, 1007/6, (2007).
38 Interview with a diplomat no. 6—Ministry of Foreign Affairs and Cooperation, May 2013.

informally excluded, although the UN did not notify it of this exclusion. From 2004 onwards, despite the Algerian attempt to reduce its presence in the form of 'African Union member states + Morocco' to replace the Africa Group, the Kingdom continued to practice offensive diplomacy by holding several responsibilities within the group. From 2006, it became coordinator of the African Human Rights Group, then vice-president of the UN Human Rights Council, representing African interests.[39] These developments are part and parcel of an Africa policy that is re-engaging in diplomatic areas that have long been ignored. However, the Kingdom's efforts are marred by the numerous altercations between Moroccan diplomats and nationals of countries that support the Polisario Front,[40] limiting the scope of this tactic. Its legitimacy as an African Group actor is thus threatened by the numerous Algerian and South African attempts to exclude the Kingdom from these bodies.

Confronted with the need to prove its Africanness after 25 years of mutual exclusion, Morocco has reoriented its strategy to divide the African opinion on the Polisario Front while demonstrating its commitment to the continent through federative actions, illustrating the application of an indirect strategy.

During the pre-colonial period (1830–1912), this strategy consisted of supporting European dissent to delay the occupation, which is why it was the last African state to be colonised.[41] At the beginning of independence, the Kingdom also created French–Spanish divisions by playing on the interests of both countries in favour of the defence of its interests in the Sahara and those relating to the evolution of French–Moroccan cooperation.[42] During the Cold War,

---

39 Portal of the Ministry of Foreign Affairs and Cooperation 'L'Afrique Priorité partagée du Royaume du Maroc et de l'ONU'.

40 "Vive altercation entre le Maroc et le Venezuela à l'ONU au sujet du Sahara", *Telquel.ma*, June 15, 2016, https://telquel.ma/2016/06/15/vive-altercation-entre-le-maroc-et-le-venezuela-a-lonu-au-sujet-du-sahara_1502056, accessed on September 04; 2016 editorial, La, 'Altercation between the Algerian and Moroccan ambassadors at the UN', *Algeria Focus*, 24 February 2013, http://www.algerie-focus.com/2013/02/altercation-entre-lambassadeur-algerian-and-moroccan-a-lonu/, accessed on September 42016.

41 Benjelloun, *Visages de la diplomatie marocaine depuis 1844*, 10 and 114. The author describes this tactic as the 'pendulum game'.

42 In February 1957, the Moroccan government authorised the Spanish government to reintroduce it in countries where the Kingdom did not yet have an embassy, which greatly annoyed French representatives, who did everything possible to upgrade the terms of their cooperation with independent Morocco. The Moroccan-Spanish negotiations also threatened French interests in the Sahara since Spain now envisaged territorial sacrifices in favour of independent Morocco in this region to obtain in return a strengthening of its position in the Presidencies and political advantages that would give Morocco, in terms of interdependence, a position as advantageous as that recognised to France : Note from the

the indirect strategy resided in the policy of neutrality or 'non-dependence' practised towards the two poles,[43] and was illustrated in reality by the discreet maintenance of its relations with the East despite the affirmation of its anti-communist orientation.[44] The political historiography of Morocco thus reveals a remarkable continuity of this foreign policy, which is sometimes permeated by its hesitations, sometimes firm in its neutrality, but systematically maintained as a de-ideologised pendulum axis.

Mohammed VI resumed this indirect strategy by integrating the Kingdom, as a permanent member or simple observer, into African regional and sub-regional organisations. This approach has enabled Morocco to build pro-Moroccan coalitions by bringing together states allied with its enemies while affirming its ability to act within a multilateral framework. Justifying such a choice, the King declared at the Élysée Summit on peace and security in Africa that

> these sub-regional organisations should be the pivot of any action plan emanating from our debates, the keystone of any strategy for stability and development in the Continent, the framework for any economic integration undertaking and the platform for coordination to meet the challenges of climate change and sustainable development.[45]

Ultimately, the integration of regional organisations offered diplomats a smaller and less antagonistic multilateral framework for action than that of

---

General Directorate of Moroccan and Tunisian Affairs. Mauritania affair. Spanish attitude. Paris, February 25, 1957. No. 542. See also documents no. 154 and 171. *Documents diplomatiques français Tome. I, 1 January–30 June* 1957.

[43] According to Abdeljabar Brahime 'Moroccan neutrality is not, however, intended to dissuade foreign powers to take an interest in Morocco, but rather to "bait" them, to make them compete for aid, to balance their presence and thus neutralise their influence.' Brahime Abdeljebbar, "Les facteurs d'élaboration de la politique étrangère au Maroc: étude de cas", (Thèse de 3e cycle, France: Université Paris Ouest Nanterre La Défense, 1984), 200.

[44] According to this former ambassador, 'there was no instruction for Ambassadors to take sides. Besides, the Moroccan embassy in Moscow was more important than the one in Algiers. Just as one could live with a large embassy in China'. Interview with a retired ambassador, Rabat, April 2013.

See also: Misk Hassane Milacic, Slobodan, "Les relations bilatérales entre le royaume chérifien et l'union soviétique 1956–1991 analyse combinatoire des jeux symboliques et enjeux matériels", (Thèse de Sciences Politiques, Bordeaux 1,1993), 412 f. p.

[45] Ministry of Foreign Affairs and Cooperation, *Message Royal au Sommet de l'Élysée sur la paix et la sécurité en Afrique*, January 6, 2013.

the AU and its UN corollary, the African Group. It has allowed Moroccans to exchange with their African counterparts in a restricted sphere that facilitates their ability to build coalitions in their favour. In this perspective, Morocco joined CEN–SAD (Sahel) as a permanent member in 2001, ECOWAS (West Africa) as an observer member in 2005[46] and ECCAS (Central Africa) as an observer member in 2014[47]—three regional organisations covering the cooperation space favoured by Morocco. The Kingdom's presence in CEN–SAD, first and foremost, contributes to its recognition as a geographical part of the Sahelian space in a context where Algeria regularly states that the Kingdom should not and cannot be considered a Sahelian country and more generally seeks to exclude Morocco from any form of African multilateral integration. This regional economic organisation, composed of 23 countries of the Sahel–Saharan strip, has also reinforced Morocco's place as a security actor in this region. The participation of diplomats in the various meetings is all the more facilitated since Algeria is the only country in the region not to be a member of the organisation due to its historical rivalry with Gaddafi, formerly the leading promoter of CEN–SAD. Taking advantage of this dual situation (the absence of Algeria and the lack of leadership since the fall of the Libyan regime), the Kingdom defends its South–South cooperation project, cooperation in the fight against terrorism and Moroccan sovereignty in the Sahara.[48]

Similarly, within ECOWAS the government has affirmed its willingness to 'support this organisation in its efforts to counter the security and socioeconomic challenges threatening the countries of the Sahel–Saharan region'.[49] In concrete terms, this support has taken the form of opening an institutional dialogue with ECOWAS members, granting humanitarian aid to Mali, Burkina Faso and Mauritania in a bilateral framework, and a financial contribution of US$5 million to the African-led international mission in Mali (MISMA). The institutionalisation of Morocco's participation in ECOWAS, in the form of observer status, has allowed the King to spread his messages to the organisation. These messages are intended to highlight Morocco's actions regarding development and security on the continent and to distinguish the Kingdom's policy from that of its neighbours. This was the case, for example, in this speech:

46 *Ministry of Foreign Affairs and Cooperation, Politique étrangère: Organisations sous-régionales*, n.d.
47 "Cooperation: The King of Morocco accredits his ambassador to the Céac | adiac-congo.com: all the news from the Congo Basin", http://adiac-congo.com/content/cooperation-le-Moroccan-king-accredits-his-ambassador-to-the-eac-8289, accessed on July 202016.
48 "Politique étrangère: Organisations sous-régionales".
49 "Ms Bouaida meets with the President of the CEDEaO", *MAP Maroc.ma*, April 22, 2014.

I would like to express my fervent wish that the Maghreb States will soon come before you, united and committed, to build fruitful and forward-looking interregional relations with the ECOWAS. If, despite the difficulties and obstacles, the five countries of the Maghreb Union have long been able to develop a dialogue with the five European countries of the Western Mediterranean and, beyond that, with the European Union, why do they still hesitate to establish it with their immediate southern neighbours with whom they share so much, in terms of challenges and threats, but also and above all, in terms of fraternity, potential and proximity of all kinds?[50]

It appears, therefore, that the Kingdom's contribution to African regional organisations is as much about strengthening the legitimacy of its diplomatic action as it is about an indirect strategy to persuade Africans of the prospect of absolute gains, to reduce blocking coalitions and to isolate its enemies.

Apart from African regional and sub-regional organisations, UN bodies, international forums, summits and multilateral conferences are a critical field of action for the government. To be at the heart of these projects, Morocco hosts some of their regional offices (e.g. the regional office of the Economic Commission for Africa, a UN body based in Rabat). Both private and public actors have been at the origin of the launch of several multilateral initiatives, such as the African Congress on the maintenance and safeguarding of heritage (created in 2016, based in Marrakech), the Mohammed VI Foundation of African Ulemas (created in 2016, based in Fez), the Forum of Press Agencies of Atlantic and West Africa (launched in 2014, based in Rabat), the Ministerial Conference of African Atlantic States (created in 2009, based in Rabat) and the African Conference on Human Development (created in 2007, based in Rabat). These are all structures or events that multiply the opportunities for meetings and cooperation between Moroccan and African leaders. Moreover, some of them are reduced or specialised duplicates of forums and conferences that already exist in Africa but have had little development. This is the case for the 2nd Regional Ministerial Conference on Border Security supported by Morocco, about which Algeria recalled the existence of a similar structure under the aegis of the AU. It is therefore clear that Morocco's creation of African forums and conferences is part of a simple indirect strategy that has enabled it to circumvent its absence from the AU through diplomacy of multilateral sectoral initiatives.

---

50 "Message of HM the King to the 42nd Ordinary Summit of the ECOWAS", *Maroc.ma*, April 14, 2013.

5 Morocco's Return to the AU: The End of the Indirect Strategy?

The 'Kigali Speech', transmitted by the King's emissaries at the African Union Summit in Kigali on 18 July 2016, is historic: it was the first time since its withdrawal from the OAU in 1984 that the Kingdom had clearly and officially formulated its readiness to reoccupy a seat in the organisation. Does this announcement sound the death knell of the indirect strategy? Is it a consecration of the diplomatic efforts deployed by Morocco in the framework of its indirect strategy, or a new stage in its implementation?

It was Morocco that applied for membership in the AU, but several African countries that had been inviting it for several years. The more the Kingdom developed its cooperation policy in Africa, the more the representatives of its African allies, including Gabon and Senegal, publicly called on the Kingdom to join the AU, assuring Morocco that the problem of the Polisario Front would be better resolved from within. This was the case, for example, with the former Senegalese Minister of Foreign Affairs, Cheikh Tidiane Gadio, who told Moroccan diplomats at a conference in Rabat:

> It is time to make a collective self-criticism. Africa has neglected its responsibilities by relegating the issue of the RASD. Morocco must return to take its seat in the AU. I know that Mohammed VI is very open on the issue. Let's go together to the AU: avoiding the problem is not the way to solve it.[51]

The Moroccan Minister of Foreign Affairs responded with a formula as categorical as it was illustrative of the Moroccan stance that has characterised the last 30 years: 'I am very surprised, positively, by this intervention. We would like to return to the AU, but the AU must first correct this severe mistake it has made.'[52]

Continuing its indirect strategy not to rejoin the AU unconditionally, Morocco has built up a special status with the organisation in recent years,[53] visible in its episodic participation in thematic meetings. At the beginning of his reign, Mohammed VI had already met with several African heads of state to discuss the conditions for his return: as early as 2001, the issue was raised at the AU's

---

51   Conference on the occasion of the 'Africa Day' at the Ministry of Foreign Affairs and Cooperation, which I attended, Rabat, May 23, 2013.
52   Response by Saad Eddine El Othmani, Ibid.
53   Terence McNamee *et alii*, *Morocco and the African Union. Prospects for Re-engagement and Progress on the Western Sahara*, (Johannesburg, 2013).

annual summit in Zambia.[54] In the following years, the Moroccan strategy consisted of a series of secret diplomatic negotiations on the margins of AU conferences, supported by Mohammed VI's meetings with African heads of state or their special envoys. Moroccan diplomacy has thus undergone both a quantitative and qualitative evolution since the multiplication of representation missions to the various African structures was coupled with real prospective negotiations. This approach offered Morocco the possibility of limiting its isolation from multilateral institutions without derogating from the principle of not returning without certain conditions being met. However, the reproduction of the scenarios of disputes between Moroccan and Algerian diplomats in multilateral arenas, sometimes preventing the regular running of thematic sessions, has weakened Moroccan efforts. Moreover, the strengthening of South African and Nigerian hostility after 2004[55] has also accentuated the existing divisions within the AU between pro- and anti-Polisario factions, demonstrating once again that the issue of Moroccan territorial integrity is, from beginning to end, a problem hijacked by several African countries.

Within the AU, Morocco's new allies, such as Guinea-Bissau, have nevertheless been particularly sensitive to the policy of Moroccan cooperation on the continent. Acting as the Kingdom's spokespersons in the wings of pan-African organisations, their representatives have warned the AU against the risks of division that could be accentuated in the long run by supporting a proto-republic not recognised by the UN to the detriment of a stable, secular, emerging Kingdom that is now integrated into the continent. The other argument mobilised by the latter evoked the possibilities of developing economic integration between Africa and Europe through Morocco, which is well positioned to play the role of relay.[56] The most tangible result of this indirect strategy deployed by Morocco is that between 2000 and 2015, ten African countries of the 26 that had usually supported the Algerian positions, officially withdrew their recognition of the RASD.[57] This was the case, for example, with Kenya and Chad in 2006, two sub-regional security powers whose foreign policy had long favoured the consensus established trilaterally by Algeria, South Africa and Nigeria. The arbitration by Kenya and Chad in favour of a UN solution reversed the pre-existing trend within the AU. The most recent pledges of withdrawal

---

54   "OAU considers Morocco readmission", BBC News, July 8, 2001.
55   See previous Title.
56   McNamee *et alii*, *Morocco and the African Union. Prospects for Re-engagement and Progress on the Western Sahara*.
57   See Appendix 5 and 5bis.

by Zambia[58] and Tanzania[59] have similarly strengthened Morocco's position with countries that, like the latter, formulated their orientation according to the regional powers they were influenced by. Despite the relative and provisional nature of these gains, they have helped to mature the problem of the neutrality of member states within the AU and to increase the chances of a decisive shift in the balance in Morocco's favour.

Assured of the likelihood of obtaining a majority coalition, the King therefore engaged in a dialogue with the President of Rwanda, the host country of the 25th African Union Summit held in July 2016. Paul Kagame's visit to Morocco in June 2016[60] was historic: first, because it was the first time that a head of state from Rwanda,[61] a country that supported the Polisario Front and, more generally, from the southern region of Africa (in which an overwhelming majority of countries also support it), had visited Morocco in a bilateral framework at the invitation of the King; second, because the visit focused on the Kingdom's desire to end its empty chair policy. Although the content of the negotiations during this meeting was not made public, the Moroccan request seemed to have found favour with Paul Kagame, since it led to the King sending several messengers to nearly 42 African countries before the date of the summit. Among the most significant of these were the lightning visits by the Minister of Foreign Affairs to seven African countries (Senegal, Côte d'Ivoire, Cameroon, Ethiopia, Sudan, Libya and Egypt) and the trip by the King's foreign affairs advisor to Kenya. The two leaders met with the heads of state of these countries and delivered a message from the King on his return to the AU. At the same time, the Minister Delegate for Foreign Affairs, Nasser Bourita, and the head of the Direction Générale des Études et de la Documentation (DGED), Yassine Mansouri, went to Algeria to meet President Bouteflika in order to warn

---

58 "Zambia withdraws recognition of pseudo 'rasd'", *Maghress*, http://www.maghress.com/en/eljadida24en/1305, accessed on January 10, 2016.
59 "Tanzania is moving towards the withdrawal of recognition of the chimeric 'RASD'", *le360.ma*, April 7, 2015.
60 The welcome given to the Rwandan President was a measure of the importance of this meeting. The government, the army, economic operators and social organisations took turns presenting the Kingdom's development progress and its commitment to South–South cooperation in Africa.
61 A year earlier, Paul Kagame was the only African head of state invited to attend the Medays in Tangiers, a multilateral conference organised by a Moroccan think tank run by the son of the Royal Advisor on Foreign Affairs, Taïeb Fassi Fehri, who awarded him the prize for the 'most inspiring leader in Africa'. This first Moroccan–Rwandan meeting thus constituted a framework for informal rapprochement between the two heads of state, favourable to preparing the official visit of Paul Kagame the following year. https://www.medays.org

their neighbour of this manoeuvre and to be able to engage in calm dialogue on the issue. At that time, the idea of Morocco's return to the AU had not been considered by the local press, which shows *a posteriori* that the negotiations had remained discreet until 18 July. At the end of their missions, the Minister of Foreign Affairs and the King's advisor on foreign affairs went to the AU Summit in Kigali, bringing the royal message to the audience's attention, creating a media surprise effect.

The content of the Kigali message[62] Is fully illustrative of the representations, intentions and discursive legitimisation framework of Morocco's diplomatic action in Africa. It combines all of the language elements mobilised in these different contexts and analysed in the previous chapters. In the first part of this speech, the King recalls that he is a 'King of an African country' and a personal connoisseur of Africa, stating: 'I know Africa and its cultures better than many others can claim. Through my many visits, I also know the reality on the ground, and I affirm this by measuring my words.' He then went on to champion a pan-Africanism that is not limited to black Africa: 'Some countries continue to claim that Morocco has no vocation to represent Africa because its population is not predominantly black. Africa cannot be reduced to one colour. To continue to insinuate this is to misunderstand our realities.' He continued by inscribing his action as a continuation of the policy led by Hassan II and Mohammed V while emphasising the novelty of this diplomacy as it was conceived. He concluded: 'More than three decades later, Africa has never been so central to Morocco's foreign policy and international action'. After summarising the main actions undertaken by the Kingdom on the continent over the past 15 years (South–South cooperation policy, integration into regional organisations, contribution to the PKOs, security policy and diplomatic mediation in the Mano River region, Libya and Mali), he defended the relevance of his approach by relating it to the postulate of Africa's emergence in international relations: 'The era when it was only an object in international relations is over. It is asserting itself, making progress and assuming its role on the international scene. It now presents itself as an active and respected interlocutor in the debate on global governance.'

In the second part of the speech, the monarch strongly criticised the AU's position towards the Kingdom. He returned to the illegal nature of the admission of the RASD and called for the AU's neutrality on this subject: 'Is the African Union not in obvious contradiction with international legality? [...] Would the AU remain out of step with the national position of its member states, since

---

62 Full text Appendix 10.

at least 34 countries do not recognise this entity?' He then announced that Morocco would soon return to the AU on the grounds that 'our friends have been asking us to return to them for a long time', and that 'after reflection, it became clear to us that when a body is sick, it is better to treat it from the inside than from the outside'. Finally, he highlighted the benefits that both Morocco and the AU could draw from this meeting:

> Acting from within, it will contribute to making it a stronger organisation, proud of its credibility and relieved of the trappings of an outdated period [...] Cooperation—already intense with many countries on a bilateral level—will be amplified and enriched. Morocco's expertise and know-how will then be able to be deployed in an even wider and better-organised field. This is particularly true of security issues and the fight against terrorism.

By not explicitly issuing any conditions for its return to the AU, the Kingdom broke with the policy it had adopted over the past 30 years, suggesting the end of the practice of indirect strategy in favour of a direct strategy. On the other hand, this break was prepared in the long term by means of various diplomatic levers, the content of which I will analyse below, and in the short term, through a series of painstaking negotiations with African heads of state. The Kigali speech, which was immediately made public, was a success. Within hours, 28 African states[63] tabled a motion to the current chairperson of the AU calling for the suspension of the Rasd from AU activities and organs. Addressed by Ali Bongo on behalf of the 28 states, this motion appeared as spontaneous as it was prepared, suggesting that the Kigali speech and its preparations were the expression of an indirect strategy. Among the motion's signatories was Ghana, which had previously supported the Polisario Front. Among the non-signatory states were Tunisia, Mali and Mauritania, states that the Kingdom thought it had definitively convinced but which were still under direct or indirect pressure from Algeria. It should be remembered that the Polisario Front issue is an African problem before it is international; if it is resolved within the continent, it will undoubtedly be resolved on a global scale. The Polisario Front does

---

63   Motion addressed to Ali Bongo Ondimba, President of the Gabonese Republic, on behalf of Benin, Burkina Faso, Burundi, Cape Verde, Comoros, Congo, Côte d'Ivoire, Djibouti, Eritrea, Gabon, Gambia, Ghana, Guinea, Guinea-Bissau, Central African Republic, Liberia, Libya, Democratic Republic of Congo, Sao Tome, Senegal, Seychelles, Sierra Leone, Somalia, Sudan, Swaziland, Togo, Zambia. See also the full text Appendix 11.

indeed have support in Latin America, but the Kingdom is already developing an active policy of cooperation with all the countries of the South American continent.[64]

---

[64] Yousra Abourabi, "Les relations internationales du Maroc", in *Le Maroc au Présent*, Baudouin Dupret (et all.), (Centre Jacques Berque, Éditions de la Fondation Ibn Saoud, Casablanca).

CHAPTER 7

Constructing Diplomatic Levers of Action to Promote a Role Identity

1   The Subordination of the Economic Tool to Political Imperatives

The economy has historically been omnipresent in international relations. Since the beginning of the last century, however, a new manifestation of the economic factor within these relations has emerged: economic diplomacy. Developed in the context of state capitalism and global trade liberalisation, economic diplomacy can contribute to intensifying or resolving new economic wars between groups of both private and public actors. The extent of economic wars is such that political scientists have now resorted to the jargon of military strategy to describe the phenomenon.[1] Since the end of the Cold War, many states have reformulated their diplomacy to adapt to the globalisation of trade and the postulate of a new international order characterised by the victory of liberalism. The Moroccan monarchy fully adheres to this normative framework and considers, for example, that the '"Least Developed Countries" are entitled to welcome the emergence of a new world order marked by interdependence and the universality of the values of political and economic liberalism'.[2] In this respect, the Kingdom's Africa policy is presented as a means of accompanying the economic emergence of Africa on the international scene, an emergence conceived in particular in terms of growth.[3]

Many international relations theorists tend to demonstrate a movement towards subordinating states' foreign policy to economic imperatives.[4] Morocco is not exempt from these changes. Some national companies, such as RAM, Maroc Telecom and Attijariwafa Banque, have acquired political power

---

1   Edward N. Luttwak, "Power relations in the new economy", *Survival 44*, no. 2 (June 1, 2002): 7–18.
2   "Message of H.M. King Mohammed VI to the Extraordinary Ministerial Conference of the MPC", *Maroc.ma*, March 25, 2013.
3   See on this subject Part I, Title Chapter 1, B.
4   Susan Strange, *States and Markets*, (New York, N.Y.: Blackwell Publishers, 1988); Robert Owen Keohane, *Power and Governance in a Partially Globalized World*, (London; New York: Routledge,; 2002); Joseph S. Nye, *Soft Power: The Means to Success in World Politics*, (New York: PublicAffairs, 2004); Guy Carron de La Carrière, *La diplomatie économique: le diplomate et le marché*, (1998).

within the Kingdom, to the point that their representatives are systematically part of the King's African tours, while Moroccan diplomats are obliged to make themselves available to these Moroccan companies that are setting up on the continent.[5]

In the space of 15 years, Mohammed VI's Morocco has gradually become the fifth African power on the continent, the second-largest African investor after South Africa and the largest investor in West Africa. Presented in this order, these figures give Morocco's Africa policy a significant economic dimension. For this reason, many journalists see the African orientation of Morocco's foreign policy as a way of meeting the interests of Moroccan companies, both public and private.[6] Several researchers believe that the Kingdom's economic diplomacy is based on a representation of West Africa 'as a possible substitute market, a countervailing space in which Morocco can weigh'.[7] Others are convinced that 'Morocco relies on its economic diplomacy to boost its economic growth and improve its trade balance'.[8] In an official report, the Ministry of Economy and Finance argues that the development of Moroccan–African relations has occurred because of 'the importance of the sub-Saharan African market in strategic, economic and commercial terms'.[9] Although based on different conceptions of the role of the economy, all of these assumptions tend to demonstrate that private economic interests guide the Kingdom's foreign policy. It appears, however, that this subordination movement is mainly carried out in the other direction: the inclusion of economic actors in the Kingdom's Africa policy indirectly serves eminent political ends.

Indeed, on the one hand, there is a significant gap between the enthusiasm expressed by economic actors about their benefits and the material extent of this economic diplomacy. On the other hand, it appears that this discursive optimism is rather an argument to lead Moroccan entrepreneurs to set up more operations in Africa. Compared with emerging middle powers such as Turkey, South Africa or Brazil, Morocco is not yet a sufficiently competitive country on the international scene.[10] The media success of this economic diplomacy

---

5   Interview with a diplomat N° 21.
6   Dafir, "La diplomatie economique marocaine en Afrique subsaharienne".
7   Alain Antil, "Le Maroc et sa 'nouvelle frontière': lecture critique du versant économique de la stratégie africaine du Maroc", *Institut français des relations internationales* (2010).
8   Dafir, "La diplomatie économique marocaine en Afrique subsaharienne".
9   Ministry of Economy and Finance, "Performance commerciale du Maroc sur le marché de l'Afrique subsaharienne", in *Annuaire marocain de la stratégie et des relations internationales*, ed. Abdelhak Azzouzi, (Centre marocain interdisciplinaire des études stratégiques et internationales, Rabat, L'Harmattan, 2013).
10 Morocco ranks 72nd among the most competitive countries in the world, behind Mauri-

lies much more in promoting Morocco's African identity and in legitimising its investments through the discursive framework of South–South cooperation than in real economic influence. Moreover, the Kingdom has very little power of coercion or economic pressure and, for the moment, has no interest in using it. It should be remembered that many Moroccan companies are still reluctant to invest in the African market, both for cultural reasons (linked to stereotypes) and strategic reasons (linked to the risks that such a deployment would generate), while the state does not occupy the strategic position of creditor of the continent. On the contrary, the example of the conditions of the withdrawal of RAM from Air Senegal shows that the interests of Moroccan companies can sometimes be sacrificed on the altar of good Moroccan–African[11] diplomatic relations.

The geographical area towards which investments and economic exchanges are directed initially coincided with the French-speaking countries then gradually, but timidly, expanded to other countries. The deployment of an economic diplomacy is one of the means of seduction mobilised and supported by the state, intended to strengthen its presence in these countries while differentiating itself from France. In the Kingdom's African embassies, there are now many 'economic advisors' responsible for promoting trade. In the long term, the national companies will be destined to take on the role of ambassador of the Kingdom. Many diplomats interviewed are convinced that Morocco's economic integration in Africa will solve its political problems. This ambition stems from a liberal vision, which considers free trade and economic interdependence as factors of peace and rapprochement. Not only does economic diplomacy appear in this context to be a regal activity, but it would seem that it is more of a geo-economy designed to compensate for the weak geopolitical role of states. Indeed, because the power of multinational firms dominates today's world and because the power of a state is judged by its economic health, geo-economics, which can be defined here as a state strategy based on the economics of rivalries in a territory or virtual space,[12] the Moroccan state cannot do without such a lever. As Yves Lacoste notes:

---

tius (46th), South Africa (49th), Rwanda (58th) and Botswana (71st). "Global Competitiveness Report 2015–2016".

11 Antil, "Le Maroc et sa 'nouvelle frontière': lecture critique du versant économique de la stratégie africaine du Maroc".

12 I will complete my definition with the more precise one of Pascal Lorot: 'Geoeconomics is the analysis of economic strategies—particularly commercial strategies—decided by States in the framework of policies aimed at protecting their national economy or certain well-identified parts of it, to help their "national companies" to acquire control of key technologies and/or to conquer certain segments of the world market relating to the production or marketing of a sensitive product or range of products, insofar as their pos-

geo-economics is a promising field. It is a relatively new and unfamiliar field for which all the work of exploration, mediation, explanation and bringing people into contact must be undertaken. We have power rivalries that can only be understood by a very small number of specialists, be they company directors, bankers, financial analysts or economists. With its tools, geo-economics must make them intelligible to the greatest number of people. Above all, it should raise awareness among those responsible for ensuring the nation's coherence in the eyes of the outside world and mobilising its capacity for influence.[13]

Unlike economic intelligence,[14] which is used more by companies to defend their economic interests and, to a lesser extent, by states to defend the economic interests of their companies, geo-economics integrates other factors of spatial rivalry into the analysis. Geo-economics serves political power, while economic intelligence serves economic power. The strategic watches resulting from these two approaches will lead to two forms of economic diplomacy.

This is where the difference lies between Morocco's economic diplomacy in Africa and that of Turkey, for example, which is mainly guided by a new generation of entrepreneurs attracted by the conquest of new markets. Ankara has indeed tripled the number of its embassies on the continent over the last 15 years, aiming to satisfy private actors,[15] while on the political level, it has not truly formulated an Africa policy. It is therefore more visible economically and culturally, than politically influential. Morocco is pursuing a different path.

---

session or control confers on the holder—State or "national" company—an element of power and international influence and helps to strengthen its economic and social potential. Geo-economics is concerned with the relationship between power and space, but a "virtual" or fluid space in the sense that its limits are constantly changing, i.e. a space free of the territorial and physical borders characteristic of geopolitics. As a corollary to this definition, a geo-economic system will group all the instruments available to a state, which it can use to satisfy all or part of the above-mentioned objectives it has set itself. Finally, geo-economic strategies are most often the work of developed states, but can, if necessary, be initiated by industrialised countries that are not members of the "Western club" in the classical sense. Pascal Lorot, "De la géopolitique à la géoéconomie", *Géoéconomie 3*, no. 50 (2009/3): 9–19.

13 Yves Lacoste, "Géopolitique, économie et nation", *Géoéconomie*, no. 50 (2009/3): 39–44.
14 For a definition of economic intelligence, see in particular Franck Bulinge and Nicolas Moinet, "L'intelligence économique: un concept, quatre courants", *Sécurité et stratégie 12*, (2013/1): 56–64.
15 For a comparison between Turkish and Moroccan economic diplomacy, see: Dafir, "La diplomatie économique marocaine en Afrique subsaharienne".

Therefore, it appears that Moroccan economic diplomacy is a lever, a tactical means subject to political imperatives, and not the opposite. This tendency could change as soon as the Kingdom reaches the status of an emerging middle power on an international scale, reinforcing its economic integration. In many cases, free trade agreements and the lack of visibility of companies' nationality have effectively reduced states' capacity to intervene in the economic field: the prevention of recourse to customs duties or currency exchange controls has eliminated the possibility of practising an adjustment policy. For the time being, unlike classical diplomacy, characterised by its tendency to remain discreet, economic diplomacy is characterised by its media value. The presence of 'expert' offices (think tanks, rating agencies, evaluation offices, etc.) has changed the game's rules: the objective is to know and make known. This new trend suits Moroccan diplomacy particularly well, as it offers it hyper-visibility. The economy, unlike war, is a commonplace of politics that is as strategic as it is dispassionate. To paraphrase Clausewitz,[16] it can be said that in the case of Morocco, economic diplomacy is simply the pursuit of power politics by other means.

2 Sectoral Investment Policies under the Banner of South–South Cooperation

Moroccan companies' presence in Africa results from a political will. It should therefore contribute to consolidating the legitimacy of Moroccan influence on the continent, supported by the Moroccan government's role identity of 'solidarity' and 'bridge between the North and the South'. As one report indicates: 'the economic strategy developed by Morocco towards the African continent aims to establish our country as a regional hub, at the service of co-development in the various key areas for our common future'.[17] The concept of co-development,[18] an element of language frequently used by the diplomatic apparatus, refers to the insertion of foreign economic policy in the framework of South–South cooperation advocated by the Kingdom and illustrated by the priority given to sectors that contribute to sustainable development rather than to the exploitation of resources. The King notably expressed this orientation

---

16   Carl von Clausewitz, *De la guerre*, (Paris: Éditions de Minuit, 1959).
17   "Relations Maroc-Afrique : l'ambition d'une 'nouvelle frontière'".
18   "Co-development', 'cornerstone' of His Majesty the King's diplomacy towards Africa (The National Interest)", *MAP Express*, April 30, 2014.

during his speech at the Abidjan Economic Forum,[19] taking care of his image as a travelling-salesman-King and defending the know-how of national companies.[20]

First, economic diplomacy consisted of the involvement of public or private companies—through public–private partnerships—in the implementation of national or local African projects relating to the development of infrastructure, agriculture, education and health by responding to public calls from the ministries in question. Among the most significant areas, we can list the following:

1. The construction of infrastructure: bridges, hospitals, roads, ports, railway networks and social housing. Examples include the urban redevelopment and ecological rehabilitation of Cocody Bay in Côte d'Ivoire, the construction of 15,000 units of social accommodation in Chad and the construction of the port of Malabo in Equatorial Guinea. These numerous projects have enabled leaders to demonstrate Morocco's commitment to modernising African infrastructure, a priority axis of the African Union Agenda 2063.

2. Water and electricity management: the ONEE (Office National de l'Électricité et de l'Eau potable) has carried out expert missions on urban sanitation (Dakar, Praia, Djibouti), electrification of the rural network (Mauritania, Cape Verde, Chad, Niger), and management by leasing of African water and electricity companies (Cameroon). These advances have enabled the Kingdom's leaders to demonstrate its capacities in the fight against exclusion in Africa, particularly in the context of the MDGs and then the SDGs (sustainable Development Goals).

3. Cooperation in agriculture: Morocco is the leading exporter of phosphates and has specialised in producing fertilisers and training agricultural engineers. Each year, the Meknes Agricultural Salon (SIAM) welcomes some 50 participating countries, including African heads of state such as Ali Bongo, a regular visitor to the show. These exchanges led to the signing of an agreement for the construction of two fertiliser factories in Morocco and Gabon, using Moroccan phosphate and Gabonese gas, and to the negotiation of other such projects. These prospects offered

---

19 'Credibility demands that the wealth of our continent should benefit, first and foremost, the African people. This implies that South/South cooperation should be at the heart of their economic partnerships': "Speech by HM the King at the Moroccan-Ivorian Economic Forum in Abidjan".

20 'Our own infrastructure projects are carried out entirely based on Moroccan expertise, from design to implementation and execution, whether it is, for example, highways, electrification, dams, ports or airports'. Ibid.

Moroccan leaders a way to confirm the development of a food security policy outside the framework of humanitarian donations instituted by the Palace.

In parallel to these public projects or public–private partnerships, the foreign economic policy is particularly dynamic in sectors that are not directly related to development cooperation. This strategy consists of investment in the form of the purchase of companies or shares in existing companies, a practice that is not exclusive to Moroccan private actors, since they are simply reproducing a method that already exists in Africa. In Malaysia, for example, 'South–South cooperation operations' are understood as 'operations to privatise African companies for their own benefit'.[21] The replication of this privatisation practice by the Moroccans can be observed mainly in the field of:

1. Finance (which represents 47% of Moroccan FDI): for example, in 2007 the Banque Marocaine du Commerce Extérieur (BMCE) acquired 35% of the shares of the Bank of Africa, which is present in about 15 countries. As one BMCE director points out, 'the sector that precisely justifies our role in Africa as a private group is obviously finance'.[22] This is also the orientation adopted by Attijarriwafa Bank, the largest Moroccan bank represented in Africa. The group now has a subsidiary in Senegal (CBaO), owns half of the Togolese bank BIA and Banque Internationale du Mali, and continues to expand in all the countries of West, Sahel and Central Africa.[23] Attijariwafa Bank has become the fourth-largest African bank, followed in fifth place by Groupe Banques Populaires, another Moroccan bank.[24] All of these Moroccan banks contribute to consolidating Morocco's Africa policy, as they invest in most of the infrastructure or agribusiness projects mentioned above.

2. Telecommunications (25% of FDI): for example, the company Maroc Telecom[25] acquired 54% of Mauritel (Mauritania) in February 2001, 51%

---

21 Jérôme Lauseig, "Quand la Malaysia Inc. Joue la carte Sud-Sud en Afrique subsaharienne", *Politique africaine*, no. 76 (2012): 63–75.

22 Brahim Benjelloun Touimi, "La présence de l'entreprise marocaine en Afrique: l'exemple de la BMCE Bank", in *Annuaire marocain de la stratégie et des relations internationales*, ed. Abdelhak Azzouzi, (Centre marocain interdisciplinaire des études stratégiques et internationales, Paris, l'Harmattan, 2013).

23 Ministère de l'Économie et des Finances, Direction des Études et des Prévisions Financières, *Point sur les relations du Maroc avec les pays de l'Afrique Subsaharienne*, (Rabat: May 2010).

24 "Attijariwafa Bank, 4th largest bank in Africa, according to The Economist", *Financial Afrik*, July 22, 2016.

25 The Moroccan state owns 30% of Maroc Telecom, and the UAE company Etisalat has

of Gabon Telecom in 2007, 51% of Onatel (Burkina Faso) in 2007[26] and 51% of Sotelma (Mali) in 2009. Since 2014, it has also owned the African operators Moov, present in Gabon, Togo, Benin, Côte d'Ivoire, Niger and the Central African Republic.

3. Holdings and industries (13% of FDI): Moroccan holding companies invest in diversified sectors, including industry (in particular, cement factories) but also tourism, renewable energies and mass distribution. The holding company Ynna (the group of the Chaâbi family) and SNI-ONA (the holding company of the royal family) are the most active in Africa. In the mining sector, the company Managem, a subsidiary of ONA, owns or operates several deposits in Guinea, Mali, Gabon, Burkina Faso and Niger.[27]

The government has generally encouraged all private companies, especially small and medium-sized enterprises (SMEs), by liberalising foreign investment through a circular dating from 2007.[28] In this perspective, a financial fund was created to encourage and support investments by Moroccan private operators in Africa. Similarly, the government has participated in the creation of bilateral economic forums with Côte d'Ivoire, Senegal, Mali, Guinea and Gabon, intended to encourage meetings, establish a climate of trust and help national companies to identify business opportunities. At the same time, a first 'Export Caravan' led by the government was initiated in 2009 in West Africa. This caravan has since been reorganised every year.

While Moroccan FDI in sub-Saharan Africa now represents more than half of total Moroccan direct investment abroad,[29] economic diplomacy is essentially envisaged in its bilateral dimension. Within the framework of its bilateral cooperation policy mentioned above, and intending to perfect the constitution of its area of influence, the Kingdom has institutionalised bilateral economic diplomacy by setting up a legal framework consisting of almost all 500 agree-

---

owned 51% since 2013. In 1999, Maroc Telecom was still 100% owned by the Moroccan state. The French company Vivendi gradually bought up shares in the company until it obtained 53% in 2007. Then the Emirati company Etisalat bought the French shares in 2013 in return for Etisalat's sale to Maroc Telecom of some of the operators it owned in Africa.

26   Maroc Telecom website: www.iam.ma. See also the 2014 activity report at: http://www.iam.ma/Lists/Publication/Attachments/63/RADD-MT2014.PDF.
27   Kamal Fahmi, "La stratégie de Managem pour son déploiement en Afrique", *Journée d'étude sur les relations maroco-africaines*, Rabat, Centre Jacques Berque, Centre of Saharan Studies, National Council for Human Rights, Kas Foundation, October 3 2014,. Coordination: Yousra Abourabi. https://www.youtube.com/watch?v=Gm_K4qV480Y.
28   Office des Changes, circular An 1720.increase in the amount transferable abroad was made in Circular 2010.1732.
29   See Appendix 10.

ments. The trade agreements proposed by the government are of three types, in line with international standards. Thus, there are agreements based on the Most Favoured Nation (MFN) clause, preferential-type agreements, and agreements relating to the Global System of Trade Preferences. Such a hierarchy of agreements can serve political purposes: the MFN, in particular, supports the existence of a special diplomatic relationship. Replicating a French economic strategy in Africa, the Kingdom had already signed 14 MFN-type trade agreements with West and Central African countries in the years 1970–1990.[30] This approach continues today. As an encouraging result of this policy, Morocco's trade balance with Africa, which was in deficit at the beginning of the 2000s (−7.2 million dirham/DH), has become a surplus (4.4 billion in 2018)—a good sign of the development of foreign trade. These exchanges have been increasing by 13% per year on average for ten years.

The government has therefore not embarked on this policy at a loss—far from it—but the economic gains are small compared with the means committed to achieving them. Moroccan exports represent only 0.4% of the sub-Saharan African market.[31] Similarly, the Kingdom's economic exchanges with Africa still represent only 6.4% of its foreign trade. It thus appears that the Kingdom's economic diplomacy is both unprecedented and relative, promising and fragile. There is a significant gap between how the Moroccan economic presence is mediatised and promoted, both in Morocco and in Africa, and the real anchoring of the Kingdom in the African economy, as the government struggles to mobilise the private sector (in particular SMEs) or to closely monitor the implementation of agreements due to a certain number of structural factors.[32] While the speed with which Morocco has imposed itself economically in Africa—thanks to large national and private companies encouraged by the King—appears remarkable, its weight in African trade is still largely negligible compared with medium-sized external powers such as Turkey. This gap reinforces the idea that economic diplomacy is a lever the political wishes to develop at its service and not the other way around.

The subordination of the economy to political imperatives in a country that claims to be liberal and that projects its power on the construction of a role identity raises a challenge: economic diplomacy, like other sectoral diploma-

---

30 "Morocco-Africa relations: the ambition of a 'new frontier'".
31 Ibid.
32 This is the case, for example, of Abdelkader Amara, Minister of Industry, Finance and New Technologies elected in (2011PJD), who is known to have been reluctant to open up the economy to Africa. See on this subject: Bachir Thiam, "Caravane de l'export: Ratés diplomatiques?", *L'Économiste*, June 5, 2012.

cies, must therefore necessarily bear an identity mark. To solve this equation, Morocco, once again, reproduces practices that are well known in neoliberal states that have adopted NPM as a practice of government bureaucracy. These include *nation branding*.

3 Promoting State Identity through Nation Branding and Intangible Capital

Given the structural weaknesses of the national economy and the long road ahead for Moroccan companies to become competitive in the African market, Morocco is trying to use its national identity to serve its economic diplomacy. In this perspective, the government resorts to the marketing strategy of labelling, namely *nation branding*. Nation branding is a way of promoting a country's identity using instruments inspired by business management. Simon Anholt (political advisor specialising in territorial marketing, vice-chair of the British Government Diplomacy Council) is the author of the concept. According to him, the 'national brand is the national identity made tangible, robust, communicative and above all useful'.[33] The government creates its brand, with one or more logos affixed to local products (crafts, edible goods, cultural and audio-visual production, etc.) whose authenticity it guarantees. Its implementation will enhance the country's image, strengthen its attractiveness to investors and tourists, and promote its culture. This policy should make it possible to strengthen cooperation between the Ministry of Tourism and the Ministry of Industry, for example, through consultation on the communication strategy and the choice of products to be promoted. To convince governments of the merits of this strategy, Simon Anholt defends the idea that 'the only type of government that can afford to ignore the impact of its national reputation is one that does not wish to participate in the global community, and that does not intend its economy, its culture or its citizens to benefit from the rich influences and opportunities offered by the rest of the world'.[34] Thus, in recent years, several states seduced by this new approach have become interested in nation branding at a rapid pace, leading to an instant domino effect.

---

[33] Cited in: Melissa Aronczyk, "Research in Brief How to Do Things with Brands: Uses of National Identity", *Canadian Journal of Communication Corporation 34*, (2009): 291–296. See also: Simon Anholt, *Competitive Identity. The New Brand Management for Nations, Cities and Regions*, (Basingstoke: Palgrave Macmillan, 2006).

[34] Anholt, *Competitive Identity. The New Brand Management for Nations, Cities and Regions*, 13.

Switzerland was one of the first nations to create a dedicated body called 'Swiss Presence' in 2001. In South Korea, in 2009, the Presidential Council of Nation Branding was also created in order to move up the ladder of the Anholt-GfK Ropers Nation Brands Index.[35] Similarly, the 'Marca España' was created in 2012,[36] the 'Marque France' in 2013,[37] as well as a series of other national brands. Within the Cherifian Kingdom, a 'Morocco Label' saw the day in 2013.

The idea seems simple: if the United States can export their 'American Dream', the Germans their 'Deutsche Qualität', and South Korea its 'Gangnam Style', Morocco can also offer its specificity. The important thing is to have an 'economic story' to tell. In this perspective, like the emergence plans mentioned in the first part of this study, many public and private actors are participating in the reflection on the values or goods specific to the Moroccan identity. The issue is decisive: the Royal Institute for Strategic Studies has made it a key area of research as part of its reflections on Morocco's 'global competitiveness'. According to the Alawite monarch, 'the promotion of the 'Morocco Label' is not a simple slogan, but rather a strategic objective whose realisation will make it possible to concretise all possible opportunities for cooperation in all fields'.[38] Like Canada,[39] which has made nation branding a focus of public diplomacy and a component of its soft power, Morocco has made the labelling of the country an essential component of its economic diplomacy.

On the other hand, Morocco is also trying to overcome its structural weaknesses and go beyond the principle of growth by developing its intangible resources. Since 2014, the state has been interested in identifying and developing its 'intangible capital'. Unsurprisingly, the term also originates from neo-institutional theories and is widely used within liberal normative structures. Borrowed from business jargon, intangible capital originally meant the appreciation of a company's intangible assets, such as the intelligence of its human resources, the quality of its software or its innovation potential. In business circles, it is believed that the more a company communicates about its intangible capital, the longer its stock exchange listing will be.[40] This capital, also called

---

35 Juliette Schwak, "South Korea Nation Branding: Global Recognition As The Final Step in A Successful Capitalist Development", *International Perspectives*, (2015).
36 See the dedicated website: http://marcaespana.es/.
37 "Launch of the 'France brand' mission", *The portal of the Ministry of the Economy and Finance*, January 30, 2013.
38 Ministry of Foreign Affairs and Cooperation, *Speech by His Majesty the King to the Ambassadors' Conference*, August 30, 2013.
39 Evan H. Potter, *Branding Canada: Projecting Canada's Soft Power through Public Diplomacy*, (Montreal: McGill-Queen's University Press, 2009).
40 Yosra Bejar, "La Valeur Informnelle du Capital Immatériel: Application aux Entreprises

structural or relational capital, has been introduced into economic theories in an attempt to propose an alternative to the financialised approach to growth while preserving a capitalist economy.

It was in 2006 that the term became a policy concept following the publication of a World Bank report entitled *Where is The Wealth Of Nations?* According to this report, 'intangible capital includes raw labour, human capital, social capital and other important factors such as the quality of institutions'[41] innovation and scientific research, artistic production, worker productivity, social trust and the quality of institutions can be defined as components of the intangible capital of states. In addition to natural and produced capital, intangible capital is one of the three components of the wealth of nations which must now be recognised and measured. By subtracting the value of natural and produced capital from the total monetary wealth of the country, we obtain the value of the percentage of intangible capital. The higher the rate, the greater the country's potential for sustainable development. Seduced by this theory, many countries have therefore set up institutions dedicated to identifying and valuing their intangible capital, such as France, which created a commission on the economy of intangible assets in 2006. In Morocco, the search for intangible capital is an idea introduced by a royal speech in 2014. According to the monarch, 'intangible capital is now asserting itself as one of the most recent parameters that have been retained at the international level to measure the overall value of states and companies'.[42] The interest in this concept demonstrates the importance that the state attaches to the valorisation of its identity. This supports the idea that economic diplomacy, although viewed from a liberal perspective, appears to be equally linked to the construction of an identity and the search for diplomatic recognition.

Technologiques Nouvellement IPO (1997–2004)", (PhD thesis, Université Paris Dauphine–Paris IX, 2006).

41 The World Bank, "Where is The Wealth Of Nations? Measuring Capital for the 21st Century", (Washington, D.C.: The World Bank, 2006) 17.

42 "Royal speech on the occasion of the 15th anniversary of the Throne Day", *Maroc.ma—Le portail officiel du Maroc*, July 30, 2014.

4 Accelerating Trade to Achieve Regional Integration: The Race to Maritime Transport

A priori, all of these efforts should have led to an increase in trade between Morocco and Africa over the last 20 years.[43] In reality, this statistical increase is mainly due to the growth of gas imports from Algeria, while in sub-Saharan Africa, trade has increased timidly. The products traded have not diversified much over the period studied,[44] even though all of the studies carried out on the subject tend to show that the potential of this trade is truly promising. Among the factors which slow down the development of regional trade, one can sometimes count the lack of interest of entrepreneurs, the inefficient use of the preferential trade regime set up by the state, the insufficient relay of success stories of Moroccan companies in Africa, the unsuitability of products intended for export to the African market, the lack of information on the opportunities and facilities offered by the continent (role of economic advisors),[45] the lack of competitive investment resources, but above all the absence of direct land or sea lines that could facilitate trade with many African countries, as well as public policies to secure investments.

While transport is the main vehicle for regional inter-state economic integration, Africa has a considerable lack of transport networks. Their development is also one of the main objectives of NEPAD-AUDA. A study of the geography of African networks helps to explain this shortcoming. On the land front, the continent is characterised by low road density: a single road, completed in 2002 after the construction of the missing section in Mauritania, links Morocco to West Africa, running along the maritime coast; no major trans-Saharan national road links the Kingdom to the Sahelian countries.[46] The same applies to the railways: Morocco appears to be totally isolated from its south.[47] Maritime transport, one of the most important means of transport in terms of trade in Africa (more than 90% of trade is exchanged by sea), is somewhat more developed (there are about 80 major ports in Africa). However, it suf-

---

43 See Appendix 12.
44 "Relations Maroc-Afrique : l'ambition d'une 'nouvelle frontière'".
45 It appears that the contacts between the economic advisors of the embassies and the entrepreneurs are still not very institutionalised, as mentioned in this official report:
    'This information deficit is not limited to the lack of dissemination of the opportunities and facilities offered by this framework to economic operators, in fact, the latter are virtually absent from the entire process of preparation and negotiation of agreements': "Point sur les relations du Maroc avec les pays de l'Afrique Subsaharienne".
46 See Appendix 13.
47 "Point sur les relations du Maroc avec les pays de l'Afrique Subsaharienne".

fers from a lack of equipment, insecurity and environmental problems due to sanitation. Despite the extent of this network, Morocco also suffers from the lack of direct links with African countries. There are generally few direct links between African countries: in many cases, ports serve extra-continental rather than regional traffic. Air transport is ultimately the most developed mode of transport in recent years, but it is used primarily for passenger transport. While the passenger rate in Africa is higher than in Latin America, the freight rate is well below the world average.

In line with the evolution of air traffic on the continent, RAM serves 26 countries in Africa,[48] whereas it was present in only half of that number a few years ago. In addition to directly serving Morocco's foreign policy by transporting government officials and businesspeople, RAM is helping to make the country known. It is gradually becoming the airline of choice for Africans travelling to and from Europe via Casablanca. Currently the fourth-largest African airline, RAM is an exemplary case of a company benefiting materially from opening up to Africa. In turn, it contributes to supporting the Kingdom's Africa policy. In this respect, the company's press releases are particularly evocative of the state's discursive legitimisation framework. One press release states, for example, that the development of RAM is based on a:

> strategy of strengthening its roots in its natural environment by developing its network in the continent and improving its offer and services for the benefit of customers in Africa [...] Royal Air Maroc has achieved this result thanks in particular to its genuine and responsible involvement in the continent's development per the policy of solidarity adopted by the Kingdom in Africa.[49]

At this stage, air transport is used much more for transporting passengers than for exchanging goods.

To develop its foreign trade and meet the continent's development objectives, notably the SDGs and Agenda 2063, Morocco is considering filling the land infrastructure gap through its participation in public works, some examples of which were given earlier, as well as turning to maritime trade. Until the early 2000s, Morocco had only one major commercial port, the port of

---

48 Algeria, Tunisia, Libya, Mauritania, Senegal, Burkina Faso, Mali, Côte d'Ivoire, Ghana, Cape Verde, Nigeria, Guinea-Bissau, Benin, Niger, Angola, Congo, Equatorial Guinea, Liberia, Sierra Leone, Cameroon, Central African Republic, Gambia, DRC, Togo, and Gabon.

49 Press release 'Marché Afrique', RAM, Casablanca on 30-12-2014 http://lecalame.info/?q=node/1547#:~:text=Royal%20Air%20Maroc%20a%20transporté,rapport%20à%20l%27exercice%20précédent.

Casablanca, linked mainly to Europe and the Mediterranean. In 2002, the construction of a larger port in Tangier, on the Strait of Gibraltar, the second-busiest seaway in the world, was entrusted to a public agency. Since its inauguration in 2007, the port of Tanger-Med has progressively established itself as one of the most important ports in Africa and presents itself as a future vehicle for Euro-African economic integration. Indeed, Tanger-Med breaks radically with the Moroccan port system. Its conception and organisation are inspired by the Asian model of Singapore, Malaysia and China: it includes numerous free trade and industrial zones, while its activities are oriented towards export trade.[50] As a result, many shipping lines have been established between European and African ports via Tanger-Med.[51] For the moment, these lines are operated mainly by foreign companies. In the long run, the government aims to encourage the creation of national shipping companies focused on African trade. In this perspective, the government has supported creating a Moroccan–Nigerian company (MNM African Shipping Line) which serves West African ports from Tangier and Casablanca. Morocco is still struggling, however, to establish direct transport lines. According to this specialist in Moroccan maritime policy: 'Any shipowner wanting to participate in Moroccan traffic (direct call) to the COA (West African coast) is obliged to combine with European or other ports to make his operation profitable. Therefore, any direct line created should be subsidised to support the additional costs.'[52] Faced with competition from foreign shipowners using the port of Tanger-Med, Moroccan entrepreneurs cannot impose themselves without the help of the state.

The race for maritime transport is therefore a geo-economic issue: the state's ability to negotiate the opening of direct maritime lines and to set up the representations of the Chamber of Commerce in African countries would encourage the development of a new generation of Moroccan businesspeople who would participate in the economic integration of Morocco within the continent. This is exactly what the government is looking for: the commercial representation of the Kingdom in the whole of Atlantic Africa. In the long term, the government's ambition is to achieve regional integration on all levels: financial and commercial but also monetary.[53] Intra-African trade represents only about

---

[50] Nora Mareï, "Le détroit de Gibraltar dans la mondialisation des transports maritimes", *EchoGéo*, February 10, 2012, no. 19.
[51] See Appendix 14.
[52] "Maroc-Afrique de l'Ouest: trop peu de lignes maritimes?", *Africa News Agency*, March 19, 2014, http://www.africanewsagency.fr/?p=1738, accessed on September 52016.
[53] "Relations Maroc-Afrique : l'ambition d'une 'nouvelle frontière'".

15% of the continent's total economic exchanges. The Kingdom therefore does not necessarily need to do much to mark its difference and be recognised, on the diplomatic scene, as a player in intra-African integration. Many Moroccans idealistically believed that it was possible that by the end of the 2010s, 'an Economic Union or even a Monetary Union would prevail: the African Economic Community'.[54] In this perspective, the government had already signed non-double taxation agreements with many countries and had joined or negotiated partnerships with Regional Economic Communities: the West African Economic and Monetary Union (UEMOA), the Common Market for Eastern and Southern Africa (COMESA) in the Sahel in 2001, and the Economic and Monetary Community of Central Africa (CEMAC). Although not well known internationally, all of these transformations still demonstrate a strong political will for regional integration.

5 Influence Diplomacy: The Role of Cultural and Religious Levers

Economic diplomacy and religious diplomacy are commonly accepted to be the two main levers of Joseph Nye's soft power, defined as 'the ability to get what you want through attraction rather than coercion or payment'[55] and, more specifically, as 'the ability to affect others with the cooptative goal of shaping the agenda, persuading and eliciting positive attraction in order to achieve one's preferred outcomes'.[56] Nye distinguishes the concept of soft power as a power of co-option and seduction from hard power as a power of coercion. For the author, soft power is not dependent on hard power and should not be confused with influence, in that it does not allow the achievement of a specific goal rather an impact on the achievement of a goal. According to the author, influence should be seen as a form of hard power and only works against less-powerful states. In contrast, co-option is the ability to shape what others want. Attraction must be based on shared values and the duty to contribute to those values. This is what Adam Smith called, in economics, the invisible hand that drives the market. As such, Nye has identified three main resources of soft power:

---

54 Benjelloun, "La présence de l'entreprise marocaine en Afrique: l'exemple de la BMCE Bank".
55 Joseph S. Nye, *Soft Power: The Means to Success in World Politics*, (New York: PublicAffairs, 2004), 11.
56 Joseph S. Nye, *The Future of Power*, (New York: PublicAffairs, 2011), 20–21.

- the attractiveness of culture, which includes not only the cultural elements of a country, the beliefs and the language but also the iconic commercial products (America's Coca-Cola, Japan's Pokémon);
- political values, which should help to spread a positive image of the country (cases of segregation, repression and other forms of violence practised by a state towards its population erode soft power);
- foreign policy, which must be seen as legitimate and having moral authority (the Gulf Wars made the US unpopular, for example).

Theorised in the 1990s to describe the resources of US hegemony, the concept is now very popular, as much criticised[57] as it is used in many empirical cases. On the one hand, it provides researchers with a simple theoretical concept that is broad enough to identify the full range of power resources other than military coercion or economic embargoes, to the point that its heuristic character is a veritable gold mine. On the other hand, it offers the leaders of small and large states the hope of exercising political power based simply on the popularity of their national brands and cultures. Embraced by Hillary Clinton, Barack Obama and many other leaders, soft power, hard power and the combination of the two known as smart power[58] have become standard expressions of political language. In Morocco, scholars and journalists often identify the cultural and religious resources mobilised by the state as diplomatic tools in the service of royal soft power.[59] Similarly, the government helps to legitimise this concept. In its speeches, the monarchy affirms that 'the wealth of a country is measured not only by economic indicators but also and above all by its soft power, its stability, its history, its cultural wealth and the density of its heritage',[60] and intends to

---

57 Todd Hall, "An Unclear Attraction: A Critical Examination of Soft Power as an Analytical Category", *The Chinese Journal of International Politics 3*, no. 2 (June 2010): 189–211; Janice Bially Mattern, "Why 'Soft Power' Isn't So Soft: Representational Force and the Sociolinguistic Construction of Attraction in World Politics", *Millennium—Journal of International Studies 33*, no. 3 (January 2005): 583–612; Colin S. Gray, *Hard Power and Soft Power: The Utility of Military Force as an Instrument of Policy in the 21st Century*, (Strategic Studies Institute, 2012).

58 It was Susan Noessel who first introduced the concept of smart power in an article in *Foreign Affairs* in 2004. The term was later used by Hillary Clinton in her speeches, and Joseph Nye commented on the concept in his work on hard and soft power. See: Susan Noessel, "Smart Power", *Foreign Affairs*, (March/April 2004).

59 "Le 'Soft Power', nouvelle arme de la diplomatie marocaine?", *L'opinion.ma*, October 8, 2014, "Les Marocains du monde, un soft power au service du Maroc", *Challenge*, February 20, 2015, Youssef Aït Akdim, "La Tidjaniyya, arme secrète du 'soft power' marocain en Afrique", *Le Monde.fr*, April 29 2016; Nazarena Lanza, "La Tijaniyya fait partie du soft power marocain", *Al Huffington Post Maghreb*, July 25, 2016.

60 "Full text of the Royal Message on the occasion of the first Mediterranean Concert", *Maroc.ma*, July 9, 2016.

use the dissemination of its cultural and identity model in the framework of its diplomacy. This shows that soft power appears to be an accurate and relevant concept to describe Moroccan power, for both the actors and the observers.

It should be stressed that soft power is not, as its name suggests, a form of power in itself, which leads to multiple confusions. A reading of the numerous empirical studies that use the concept shows that there is a significant gap between soft power as a resource and soft power as a type of power. If soft power is understood as a resource, it would be just as appropriate to refer directly to the cultural, economic, public and other diplomacies at work in the exercise of power. If soft power is a type of power, its hegemonic dimension, as conferred by Joseph Nye, is relevant in the case of the United States but effectively excludes Morocco from this category.

Indeed, among the measures that constitute Moroccan soft power as a type of power, we can first mention the creation of Moroccan cultural centres abroad. Like France with its French Cultural Centres or China with its Confucius Institutes (Hanban), the Kingdom inaugurated its first Maison du Maroc (Dar Al Maghrib) in Montreal in 2012. Since then, other centres have been opened or are under construction in European capitals with large Moroccan communities. These cultural centres are not so much intended to disseminate the Moroccan cultural model among other nationalities but more to offer Moroccans living abroad a place to preserve the 'Moroccan identity' of their children. In Africa, however, there are already 65 Chinese Confucius Institutes and 23 Confucius Classrooms,[61] about 50 French Cultural Centres,[62] 23 German Goethe Institutes[63] and some 15 Spanish Institutos Cervantes.[64] Similarly, Turkey has built seven Yunus Emre in Africa in recent years,[65] and Brazil already coordinates eight Centros Culturais Brasileiros on the continent. In contrast to these countries, the Kingdom has not planned to teach its dialects or make its arts and cultures known on a large scale in Africa due to the small presence of Moroccans living in these countries and the government's lack of interest in this type of leverage, which is precisely a soft power issue.

Morocco is not, at present, a normative, cultural, economic or religious model on an international or even regional scale, allowing it to exercise soft

---

61 Confucius Institute website: https://ci.cn/en/gywm/pp
62 See the list at: https://www.data.gouv.fr/fr/datasets/liste-des-instituts-francais-and-of-the ir-antennas/.
63 Goethe Institute website: https://www.goethe.de/en/wwt.html.
64 Cervantes Institute website: https://clic.cervantes.es/en/cursos/sobre-nosotros
65 Yunus Emre Institute website: http://www.yee.org.tr/en/.

power to satisfy its national interests. On the other hand, it does deploy a set of cultural, normative and religious policies that are part of a median 'diplomacy of influence'. Often associated with soft power, influence diplomacy is indeed commensurable with it but refers more precisely to the intensive use of diplomatic leverage (instead of military operations or sanction policies) through its sectoral diversification. The end of the Moroccan version of the Hallstein doctrine together with the announced end of the empty chair policy at the AU suggest that foreign policy is moving towards influence diplomacy. Influence diplomacy aims at influence through legitimisation and the search for recognition of an identity (of norms, values and beliefs). Soft power aims at hegemony by spreading this identity and trying to have it adopted. This is why diplomacy of influence seems more adapted to the ambitions and capacities of the Kingdom. Morocco's Africa policy must be interpreted in light of this latter concept. While it relies on means substantially similar to those described by Joseph Nye in relation to soft power, these means are insufficient or sometimes too recent to meet the political objectives defined by Morocco.

Moreover, while soft power depends essentially on non-state levers (associations, cultural institutions, universities, companies, individuals) and can be promoted only *a posteriori* by governments (for Nye, the success of soft power depends on the state's withdrawal from this field), influence diplomacy is, on the contrary, extremely centralised and is based on the state's choice to control all of the vectors likely to spread its power. This is also why soft power is better suited to the US case than small and medium-sized emerging powers. The US media and the US Agency for International Development (USAID) do not have the same relationship with their government as Al Jazeera has with the Qatari state, MBC with Saudi Arabia or Reliance with India.[66] The latter are much more closely linked to the government and are more a matter of public diplomacy or more broadly influence diplomacy than soft power. In Morocco, the development of the Medi1 group (radio, television and press) on the continent was directly the result of bilateral agreements signed under the presidency of the King and his African counterparts. The radio station has been broadcasting in Gabon since 2013 and in Côte d'Ivoire since 2015. The Medi1 television channel

---

66 'For largely bureaucratic reasons, much of what the U.S. government has undertaken in support of foreign media, education reform, and democratisation has not been considered 'public diplomacy' per se, and has been implemented primarily by agencies other than those dedicated explicitly to public diplomacy—in particular, the U.S. Information Agency (USIA), the *U.S.* Agency for International Development (USAID), and the U.S. *National Endowment for Democracy*.' Carnes Lord, "Public Diplomacy and Soft Power", *American Politics*, no. 3 (2012): 61–72.

also directly illustrates the new form that French–Moroccan cooperation takes in Africa. The channel was initially French-Moroccan, before becoming Moroccan and then private. It was created in 2006 jointly by the French (at the request of Jacques Chirac) and Moroccan governments, with the aim of promoting French-Maghrebi culture in the region. Since 2015, two versions of the channel exist: a French-speaking version intended for broadcasting in Africa (reinforcing the policy of Francophonie) and an Arabic-speaking version focused on the Maghreb. Although Medi1 has been the object of a progressive disengagement of the state, its presence in Africa is directly encouraged and supported by the diplomatic apparatus; a notable illustration of the centrality of the role of the state in the process of cultural diffusion, supporting the idea that this is a diplomacy of influence and not soft power. This influence diplomacy will mobilise other instruments such as expert missions, university training, particularly in French,[67] or the institutionalisation of relations and exchanges with trans-Saharan Sufi confraternity networks.

6   The Institutionalisation of Exchanges with trans-Saharan Sufi Confraternity Networks

The Sufi brotherhoods constitute a key player among the various resources mobilised in the framework of this diplomacy of influence. By being assigned a religious mission instituted by the Commander of the Faithful status, the sultans of Morocco have maintained allegiance links with certain transnational Sufi brotherhoods in West Africa since the nineteenth century. The Tijâniyya Brotherhood in particular has progressively imposed itself as a major transnational relay in Morocco's cultural and religious diplomacy in Africa. Established mainly in North Africa, West Africa and the Sahel (from Morocco to Tunisia, from Senegal to Sudan, from Sierra Leone to the Central African Republic), the Tijâniyya Brotherhood distinguishes itself from other Sufi brotherhoods by its apologetic discourse[68] as well as by the exceptional character of its propagation and success. The Tîjânes are also known to have played a decisive role in the conquest of power in the Sudanese-Sahelian world. Initially a Maghrebian brotherhood, it now takes on a more trans-Saharan identity, as it has been so successful in this region: its adaptation to the effects of modernity, and its social and spiritual anchoring, have been at the origin of its popularity in the

---

67   Yousra Abourabi, "Le Maroc francophone: identité et diplomatie africaine".
68   Jean-Louis Triaud and David Robinson, *La Tijâniyya: une confrérie musulmane à la conquête de l'Afrique*, (Karthala Éditions, 2000), 9–17.

newly decolonised states. This anchoring also stems from the support given by colonial France to the brotherhood and vice versa. For example, in 1916, at the request of Marshal Lyautey, the main representatives of the brotherhood sent dozens of letters to Moroccan leaders asking them to help France extend its political authority through the religious authority of the Tîjânes. Similarly, in 1925, during the Rif War, Sufi sheikhs deployed extensive propaganda among the Rifans to convince them to submit to France.[69] Many Tijân masters declared their loyalty to the Republic. This political compromise with the French further encouraged the development of the Tijâniyya in West Africa during this period.[70] This is one of the many reasons why the brotherhood now considers itself exclusive and asks its followers to abandon their other affiliations.

In Morocco, the Tijâniyya Brotherhood does not have a mass character but develops around a core of elites protected by the power. The city of Fez, the former capital of the Cherifian Empire and today the spiritual capital of the Kingdom, is a significant place of pilgrimage for all its followers, as it contains the tomb of its founder, Ahmed Al-Tijânî.[71] There are also other Tijân *zaouias* (spiritual centres) in different Moroccan cities, frequented by Moroccans as well as sub-Saharans, especially Senegalese. In Senegal, in fact, the Tijân represent more than half of the Muslims. Senegal also hosts three of the four main spiritual seats (Tivaouane, Kaolack and Madina-Gounass). For this reason, the Tijân have significant political power in the country, especially as they play a central role in preserving the 'Muslim identity' of society in the face of animism and Western values.[72] For many Senegalese Tîjânes, the possession of an *ijaza* (i.e. the right to initiate another into the practices of the brotherhood) from a Moroccan sheikh is a mark of legitimacy, as Moroccan Tijân sheikhs symbolically occupy a high position in the hierarchy of the brotherhood.[73] This spiritual recognition also reinforces the historical allegiance of the Tijân to the Alawite throne, which the independent Kingdom wished to institutionalise within the modern state. Thus, religious figures have been at the centre of political exchanges between Senegal and Morocco since independence. An example of this trend is the fact that Mohammed V was welcomed in Dakar by

---

69 Jean-Louis Triaud, "La tijâniyya, voie infaillible ou 'voie soufie réinventée'. Autour du pamphlet anti-tijânî d'Ibrâhîm Al-Qattân", in *La Tijâniyya: une confrérie musulmane à la conquête de l'Afrique*, eds. Jean-Louis Triaud and David Robinson, (Karthala, 2000), 198.
70 Triaud and Robinson, *La Tijâniyya*, 9–17.
71 Johara Berriane, "Intégration symbolique à Fès et ancrages sur l'ailleurs: Les Africains subsahariens et leur rapport à la zaouïa d'Ahmad al-Tijânî", *L'Année du Maghreb*, no. 11 (December 2014): 139–153.
72 Sambe, *Islam Et Diplomatie*, 75.
73 Ibid., 104–105.

Tijani personalities[74] on his return from exile in Madagascar. This was also the case for Hassan II, who always devoted time to meeting Sufi dignitaries as part of his diplomatic exchanges with Senegalese leaders.

Among these dignitaries, some are political leaders. Sheikh Ibrahim Mahmoud Diop, for example, had met Mohammed V and Hassan II and maintained close relations with Moroccan ulemas, ministers and scholars. During his theological lectures in Moroccan universities or at the Palace, he regularly pleaded for the development of diplomatic cooperation between Morocco and Senegal. He was at the origin of a gathering of international figures of the Tijâniyya in Fez, most of them coming from West Africa. During a famous 1987 conference he led entitled 'Where is Muslim Africa going?', the sheikh publicly submitted to the King a request for scholarships for West African theology students and won the case with Hassan II. The latter immediately ordered the ministries in question to 'hold a meeting to take steps to implement the Sheikh's proposals'.[75] Therefore, the Tijâniyya Brotherhood was the initiator of the development of a religious diplomacy by the Moroccan government, including a theology training policy for African students.

Ibrahim Mahmoud Diop was also behind the creation of the 'League of Moroccan and Senegalese ulemas for Friendship and Islamic Cooperation' inaugurated in 1985 under the patronage of King Hassan II and President Abou Diouf, and which he headed until his death in 2014. This league, funded in particular by the Moroccan Ministry of Islamic Affairs and Habous, has reinforced the weight of politico-religious exchanges and the scholarship policy for West African students in general and Senegalese students in particular. On the whole, it is clear that the connivance between Ibrahim Mahmoud Diop and Hassan II was at the origin of a new form of institutionalisation of religious exchanges by the state.

Today, the membership of a politician, whether Moroccan or Senegalese, in the Tîjâne network predisposes him to play a key role in developing bilateral or regional cultural diplomacy. As Bakary Sambe notes, 'the religious imaginary sometimes exceeds the real scope of Senegalese–Moroccan relations, which it roots in a symbolic or even sacred framework. Thus, policies orient their action according to this imaginary which, in the end, will become the basis of real bilateral cooperation.'[76] In the case of Senegal, it is impossible to talk about Moroccan–Senegalese relations without mentioning the Tijâniyya

---

74   Sambe, *Islam And Diplomacy*.
75   Quoted in: Cheikh Ibrahima Diop fils, "À propos des relations maroco-sénégalaises", Dakaractu.com, May 21, 2015.
76   Sambe, *Islam Et Diplomatie*, 76–77.

Brotherhood. The Moroccan–Senegalese couple constitutes a sort of 'French–German couple' on the scale of Islam in West Africa: although he is of Mouride obedience, Mohammed VI's new counterpart, Senegalese president Abdoulaye Wade (2000–2012), paid his respects with his delegation at the mausoleum of Ahmed Tijani in Fez during his first official visit to Morocco. This political gesture reinforced the consecration of religious links as the main lever of Moroccan–Senegalese diplomatic relations. It contributed to the institutionalisation of a bridge diplomacy (as previously defined) on the dissemination of Sufism and Malekism in Africa.

The city of Fez now hosts a large community of sub-Saharan migrants, particularly Senegalese, followers of the Tîjâniyya Brotherhood, who indirectly contribute to this political effort.

This historical legacy is today reconsidered and revalorised, on the discursive and institutional levels, within the framework of a religious diplomacy notably characterised by the development of a trans-Saharan politico-religious network. As soon as Mohammed VI was enthroned in 1999, the Minister of Islamic Affairs was charged with transmitting a royal message to the Tîjânes of Senegal (without going through classic diplomatic channels), reiterating the attachment of the Alawite throne to the brotherhood. For their part, the Senegalese Tîjânes reaffirmed 'the allegiance of the Brotherhood and its sheikhs to the Alaouite throne'.[77] Mohammed VI, for his part, reinforced the process of institutionalising relations between the brotherhood and the government by appointing an official representative of the Tarîqa Tijâniyya in Morocco. The restructuring of the religious field from 2002 onwards, the appointment of a new Minister of Habous and Islamic Affairs (Ahmed Toufiq) and the integration of Sufism among the components of the 'official Islam' of the Moroccan state are also part of this process.

The institutionalisation of exchanges between the brotherhoods and the state was carried out gradually. Initially, the Minister of Habous and Islamic Affairs, Ahmed Toufiq, was responsible for organising the first General Meeting of the Tarîqa Tijâniyya in Fez in 2007, which brought together many African Sufi masters, and for reading the royal message regarding the commitment of the Alawite dynasty to supporting the brotherhood. This policy continued with the organisation of the International Tijâniyya Conferences (in 2007, 2009 and 2014), and then the annual Conference of the Tijâniyya Brotherhood in Fez from 2012, in the aftermath of the crisis in Mali: a transnational religious

---

77 Statement by Sheikh Maodo Sy, quoted in: Bakary Sambe, "Tidjaniya: usages diplomatiques d'une confrérie soufie", *Politique étrangère Hiver*, no. 4 (Janvier 2011): 843–854.

event entirely supported by the Kingdom. At the same time, the government announced travel grants for pilgrims and a donation of Qur'ans for the 70 million followers of the brotherhood in Africa. In addition to the Ministry of Habous and Islamic Affairs, the Ministry of Tourism was also asked to contribute to this effort. According to the vice-president of the Regional Council of Tourism (CRT) of Fez, the objective promoted 'is to enrich the spiritual with a cultural dimension, by approaching it not only from the point of view of religious practice but also by associating it with the entire history of Fez'.[78] RAM was asked to offer plane tickets to the followers making a pilgrimage to Fez or to at least offer preferential tariffs, thus contributing to a reinvention of the trans-Saharan routes. It is mainly Malians who have benefited from this policy: for example, in 2015, between 6 and 7 million Malian Tîjânes benefited from preferential tariffs with RAM to travel to Fez.[79]

It should be noted that this religious diplomacy very quickly took on a tourist and commercial dimension. Together, the Regional Council of Tourism of Fez and RAM created an eight-day trip package called 'ziara tîjânia' to attract new pilgrims. Faced with this commercial strategy, other travel agencies began competing in Senegal and Morocco to sell travel packages to pilgrims, recovering in their favour the presentation of the Kingdom as the main spiritual centre of the Tijâniyya.[80] As of 2014, the number of religious tourists to Morocco had reached 41,267 people,[81] illustrating the close correlation between the Kingdom's economic diplomacy and its cultural and religious diplomacy.

On the political level, the annual meetings of the Tijâniyya in Fez are an opportunity to disseminate a royal message read to all pilgrims, which reinforces the visibility of the throne's support for the brotherhood, ensures the dissemination of the Moroccan religious model south of the Sahara, contributes to the promotion of Morocco as a host country for transnational Sufi networks, and consolidates the role of the brotherhoods as a political lever in the development of diplomatic cooperation with certain countries, such as Senegal and Mali. In this respect, the King has received representatives of other transnational Sufi brotherhoods, such as the Tarîqa Qadirya and the Tarîqa Mouridia,

---

78   "Fez promotes itself in Cameroon", *L'Économiste*, May 24, 2006.
79   "Royal Air Maroc signs a partnership agreement with the Federal Council of the Tîjânes of Mali in Bamako", *Le Matin*, February 23, 2014.
80   Nazarena Lanza, "Quelques enjeux du soufisme au Maroc: le tourisme religieux sénégalais et la construction d'un imaginaire sur l'amitié", in *Migrants au Maroc, cosmopolitisme, présence d'étrangers et transformations sociales*, eds. Nadia Khrouz and Nazarena Lanza, (Rabat, 2015), 65–72.
81   "Official visit of HM the King to Senegal", 2015.

and is exercising the same institutionalisation of links on a smaller scale. During the Islamic conferences led by Mohammed VI in Rabat, the most representative religious leaders of the African brotherhood landscape are now invited. The Tijâniyya Brotherhood, however, has a particular status in Moroccan diplomacy. More than a religious lever in the service of cultural diplomacy, the support given to the Tijâniyya is also part of a policy aimed at spreading the Islam of the golden mean advocated by the Kingdom.

7 The Spreading of a Golden-Mean Islam in Africa through Religious Training

For centuries, the Moroccan empires have contributed to disseminating the precepts and rites of the Maliki school in Africa. Even today, promoting Malikism south of the Sahara is a central concern for the Kingdom, as this link forms the basis of any discourse on Moroccan–African cultural ties. Under Hassan II, the republication of the classical texts of the Malekite rite, such as *Ibn 'Ashir's Matn*, reinforced their teaching in Senegalese madrasas.[82] In this respect, Hassan II declared that 'Morocco considers itself invested with the mission of preserving and disseminating the Muslim religion through universities, mosques, ulama and teachers'.[83] Similarly, the Makhzen of Mohammed VI claims that Morocco has 'the merit of having propagated Islamic values' in Africa.[84]

Nowadays, faced with the extent of movements associated with the Wahhabi rite (e.g. Salafists) operating in the region, Morocco has taken on the role of promoting the Malikite rite and Sufism as religious models capable of preserving the customs of local populations against any form of extremism. The war in Mali in 2012 was an opportunity for the Kingdom to initiate a new form of religious cooperation. Since Mali shares the Maliki rite and the Sufi practice with Morocco, and by virtue of a bilateral agreement between the two countries, Mohammed VI initiated the creation of a training centre for Malian imams in Moroccan Islam in 2013. This establishment was initially dedicated to the training of 500 Malian imams, but it now aims to train imams from various countries that have requested it (Nigeria, Tunisia, Côte d'Ivoire, Guinea, Senegal, etc.)

---

82 Sambe, *Islam Et Diplomatie*, 53.
83 Hassan II, Press Conference in Taif, February 9, 1980, in: *Speeches and Interventions of King Hassan II*, ((1982)1983)166.
84 "HM the King, Amir Al-Mouminine, presides in Casablanca over the ceremony announcing the creation of the Mohammed VI Foundation of African Ulemas", *Maroc.ma*, n.d.

This training centre's particularity lies in its providing not only theology courses but also history (the history of Moroccan–African relations, among others), geography, human rights, media analysis, health and astronomical calculations.[85] Built in less than a year, the centre resembles a modern and well-equipped university campus, attended by both Moroccans and foreigners. Women are also trained there as mourchidates (female religious preachers), to ensure the feminisation of the religious body. The government entirely pays for the years of study: the students are fed, lodged and taken care of and receive a small monthly grant of around 200 euros. Also, in order to enable African imams, in particular, to find a remunerative activity once they return to their country, the centre has integrated ad hoc professional training workshops (electricity, building jobs, culture, agriculture, IT, etc.).

Called the Mohammed VI Institute for the Training of Imams, this training centre aims to counter Wahhabi and Salafist tendencies and to advocate a more 'tolerant' Islam. It is a lever of the government's preventive security policy. At the same time, according to the government, the training of imams is part of the development of the 'historical capital of Morocco, a country of openness and tolerance, a place of coexistence and interaction between cultures and civilisations'.[86] Through this rhetorical legitimisation framework, the Kingdom constructs its role identity on the religious and cultural levels. In this perspective, Moroccan Islam is described as the Islam of the golden mean, as I announced at the beginning of this study, per the dialogical network established by the leaders.

The definition of a religious diplomacy through the paradigm of the golden mean takes place in a dialectical logic: 'The Kingdom of Morocco remains a model of attachment to Sunni Islam advocating the golden mean and tolerance and proscribing extremism, fanaticism and ostracism'.[87] More generally, it would seem that for the monarchy, beyond Morocco's religious values, its 'ancestral cultural values are also based on moderation and the golden mean'.[88] Within the government, the diplomatic dissemination of a golden-mean Islam is carried out primarily by the liberals. In an analysis of the Moroccan legislative campaigns, Mounia Bennani-Chraïbi identifies four approaches to religious policy:

---

85   "500 Malian imams soon to be trained in Morocco", *Jeune Afrique*, November 12, 2013.
86   Message of the King of Morocco to the first Ambassadors' Conference. August 30, 2013.
87   "Speech of HM the King to the Nation on the occasion of the 13th anniversary of the Throne Day", July 30, 2012.
88   "Speech by H.M. King Mohammed VI on the occasion of the 9th anniversary of the Throne Day", *Maroc.ma*, July 30, 2008.

A totalising vision of Islam, an Islam of the 'golden mean' combined with Moroccan 'common sense', a pole confining the religious to the private sphere, and an 'elitist' tendency inviting the production of authenticity by breaking away from the imitation of the past and the other, by reviving creativity and the critical thinking.[89]

The author identifies these four trends with four socio-professional groups, respectively: 'the educated and Islamised counter-elite, the Entrepreneurs, a left-wing group led to redefining its relationship with Islam, and a small intellectual and artistic elite'.[90] Beyond the liberals, more and more political groups support and appropriate this concept to define Moroccan Islam.

Presented as the Islam of the golden mean, the Moroccan religious model is constructed, tailored and adjusted for political purposes. Since its launch in 2012, the training of imams has undeniably contributed to the spreading and institutionalisation of the Malikite rite and Sufism, as well as Morocco's doctrinal and ritual choices. Indeed, the strength of the Moroccan proposal must be recognised: following the announcement of the training of Malian imams, the local and foreign press took up the subject with great enthusiasm. Several countries, such as Tunisia, Nigeria, Guinea, Côte d'Ivoire and Gabon, wanted to benefit from this training. Beyond the region, this approach has seduced other countries, such as Chechnya, the Maldives, and France, which sent some 50 imams to Rabat in 2015. Foreign organisations have also seized the opportunity to support Morocco financially in these projects.

Very quickly, in July 2015, the King created the Mohammed VI Foundation of African Ulemas, placed directly under his presidency and under the presidency-delegation of the Minister of Habous and Islamic Affairs. According to the latter, the creation of this institution is part of the continuity of the exercise of a religious influence illustrated by 'the construction of mosques in these countries, the regular presence of African ulemas at the Ramadan Hassanian talks, the creation of the League of ulemas of Morocco and Senegal, the establishment of the Institute of African Studies and the organisation of conferences on Sufi tarîqa'.[91] The objective promoted by this institution, which brings together the main Muslim religious representatives of West, Central and Sahelian Africa, is to promote the Islam of the golden mean in the region, to institutionalise and control religious exchanges, and to consolidate Moroccan–

---

89   Bennani-Chraïbi, *Scènes et coulisses de l'élection au Maroc*, 155.
90   Ibid.
91   "HM the King, Amir Al-Mouminine, presides in Casablanca over the ceremony announcing the creation of the Mohammed VI Foundation of African Ulemas".

African diplomatic relations.[92] In parallel with the construction of this network, the Kingdom has multiplied the donations offered to Islamic organisations in West Africa and the Sahel. In Côte d'Ivoire, for example, the Conseil supérieur islamique (COSIM), the Conseil national islamique (CNI) and the Ligue islamique des prédicateurs de Côte d'Ivoire (LIPCI) have already received Moroccan support.[93]

All of this dynamism, the repercussions of which cannot yet be measured, points to the need to experiment with innovative approaches to the rise of extremism. The partial effectiveness of the military approach and the difficulty of building a shared vision of regional security facilitates the enthusiasm for this type of initiative, even though it is difficult to predict the consequences. I will therefore attempt to outline this in the following chapter.

92 Ibid.
93 Mamadou Bamba, "Mobilité des Musulmans ivoiriens au Maroc: entre formation islamique et tourisme religieux", in *Migrants au Maroc, cosmopolitisme, présence d'étrangers et transformations sociales*, eds. Nadia Khrouz and Nazarena Lanza, (Rabat, 2015), 72–80.

CHAPTER 8

The Consequences of Morocco's Africa Policy: Between Relative Gains and Geopolitical Transformations

1   Introduction

One of the main debates in international relations is the definition of the ontological dynamics of the international order: does the structure determine the behaviour, interests and identity of the agents, or do the agents, as autonomous actors, determine the structure? In other words, which of the international system and its actors determines the other? After 30 years of debate between the different classical schools of international relations,[1] the most logical answer was given by the constructivists: the agents and the structure are co-constituted in a reflexive way. On the one hand, the global social structure influences the behaviour and nature of state and non-state actors; on the other hand, the state and non-state actors help to shape the international system.

On the one hand, certain international norms and certain geopolitical data inherited from the continent's history have shaped the Kingdom's identity, representations and interests. This is the case with the influence of liberalism on the national emergence strategy or the influence of the colonial heritage in the administrative culture. Other geopolitical transformations at work continue to influence Morocco's identity and behaviour as a state agent, such as the development of trans-Saharan migration and the emergence of the war against terrorism in the Sahel, or climate change. By broadening the analysis framework, we can also see that the new global power relations linked to the emergence of China and the Russian–US rivalry impact the way Morocco develops its Africa

---

1   For individualists, the agent determines the structure: the social relations the agent maintains may affect their behaviour but do not determine their identity or interests. For structuralists, the opposite is true. Structure has a constitutive effect on their identities and interests and helps to shape them. For Waltz, for example, 'structure operates as a cause' that structures the agent. On the agent–structure debate, see for example: Alexander E. Wendt, "The Agent-Structure Problem in International Relations Theory", *International Organization 41*, no. 3 (1987): 335–370; David Dessler, "What's at stake in the agent-structure debate?" (1989): 441–473; Shiping Tang, "International System, not International Structure: Against the Agent—Problematic Structure in IR", *The Chinese Journal of International Politics 7*, no. 4 (2014): 483–506.

policy. There is therefore no doubt about the influence of the structure, defined as an international social process, on the constitution of the identity of the Moroccan power. This last major section will tend to confirm this postulate.

On the other hand, Morocco has also distinguished itself from other state agents by the progressive construction of a singular role identity, constituted in particular by the style and the dual symbolic and executive authority of the monarch, the claim to a role as a geo-civilisational bridge, and the dissemination of a golden-mean Islam. The question that arises is therefore the following: does the Kingdom's foreign policy, and more specifically its Africa policy, contribute to shaping this new 'multiplex'[2] world order? This question leads directly to two other theoretical issues already raised in this book: what is the weight of small and medium-sized powers in the international system, and conversely, how do these types of powers adapt to the transformations of the environment? Ambitious, Morocco's foreign policy is forced to follow through on its intentions and assume its new responsibilities: developing security policies that preserve its identity and role on the continent. Limited in its means and support, this policy must also explore and anticipate future international developments in order to maximise its gains. These are the issues that will be examined in this section.

2   The Effects of Cultural and Religious Diplomacy in the Development of Migration to Morocco

Morocco's economic emergence, its political transition, and its religious and cultural diplomacy in Africa, as well as geopolitical developments in the region, have transformed the migration landscape within the Kingdom. Known historically as a land of emigration (15% of the population resides abroad[3]), Morocco has been since the mid-1990s a destination for migrants, mainly from sub-Saharan Africa.

The number of sub-Saharans staying for a short period (for hospital care, religious tourism, short-term professional training, military training) is gradually increasing, and the share of immigrants who settle in Morocco for a medium or long period has risen sharply in recent years, making Morocco a real migratory crossroads at the gateway to Europe.

---

2   Acharya, *Rethinking power, institutions and ideas in world politics*, See note no. 20.
3   United Nations Economic Commission for Africa Office for North Africa, *The Problem of Migration in Development Policies and Strategies in North Africa*, (Rabat: 2014), 97.

Indeed, while Morocco has one of the highest student expatriation rates in the world, it has become just as coveted by international and, more specifically, African students. As of 2012, there were nearly 15,577 foreigners from 134 countries, most of whom were sub-Saharan, in Morocco. If this figure still seems derisory, it should be noted that the rate of increase in the number of foreign students residing in Morocco between 2000 and 2009 was 732%.[4] This student mobility continues to grow, reaching 20,000 students per year. Therefore, it is conceivable that the number of sub-Saharan students and young graduates living in Morocco will become truly significant over the next decade. Already, almost 44% of these students claim not to have a second migration project planned after Morocco and intend to remain working after their studies for at least a few years.[5] Also, those who could not renew their scholarship at the time of their master's degree are already starting to integrate into the labour market by finding small jobs for students. According to a survey conducted among sub-Saharan students,[6] while their choice may have been Morocco due to a lack of opportunities in a Northern country (France in particular), half of the respondents claim to have a link with the Kingdom, most often via a family member who used to reside or still resides in the country. Therefore, the networks of students, religious people, politicians and sub-Saharan workers who have lived or stayed in Morocco are strongly intertwined. More generally, this stay is an opportunity for these students to experience a foreign country without going far, as the Moroccan culture is so different from the one they know, and is also a means to develop their professional careers. As one report notes: 'For African graduates from sub-Saharan Africa, such as doctors, artists, entrepreneurs, traders, Morocco offers new economic opportunities for social advancement that Europe no longer offers'.[7]

These different migratory networks are now asserting their presence in both their quantitative dimension and their social visibility. The presence of Christians, in particular, has led to the revitalisation of official churches (those recognised by the Moroccan authorities), particularly evangelical churches, with a Pentecostal dominance. In parallel to this, many informal places of worship

---

4   Souley Mahamadou Laouali and Jean-Baptiste Meyer, "Le Maroc, pays d'accueil d'étudiants étrangers", *Hommes et migrations. Revue française de référence sur les dynamiques migratoires*, no. 1300 (2012): 114–123.
5   Ibid.
6   Johara Berriane, "Les étudiants subsahariens au Maroc: des migrants parmi d'autres?" *Revue géographique des pays méditerranéens / Journal of Mediterranean geography*, no. 113 (2009): 147–150.
7   "La problématique de la migraton dans les politiques et stratégies de développement en Afrique du Nord", 16.

are emerging due to the restrictions on authorised worship in Morocco. No figures are available on attendance at these informal places of worship. Still, it is known that the official churches currently have nearly 3,000 members, 95% of whom are from sub-Saharan Africa: the main nationalities represented are Congo, DRC, Côte d'Ivoire, Cameroon and the Central African Republic,[8] all of which are Francophone countries. This possible correlation between the Kingdom's cultural diplomacy and the increase in migration is also raised by many observers. According to a survey on the attendance of Moroccan churches by sub-Saharans, 'the respective weight of nationalities varies according to the university cooperation agreements signed by Morocco'.[9]

Supporting this hypothesis, there is an increasingly significant presence of sub-Saharan pilgrims, directly linked to the institutionalisation of the Palace's links with the brotherhood networks, as well as to the residency facilities that result from the commercial policy that accompanies this diplomacy. According to a study on Ivorian migrants, 'Morocco has become a reference, even a model, in the eyes of Ivorian Muslims, and more particularly the Tîjâne community': 'in Côte d'Ivoire, these students sometimes present themselves as true scholars of the Islamic sciences and participate, in turn, in the propagation of Malikite Islam in the country'.[10] This is why more and more religious people are staying in Morocco for a medium or long period. The best-represented religious people are, unsurprisingly, the Senegalese, confirming the existence of a Moroccan–Senegalese 'inter-state couple'[11] working to spread Sufi Islam in the region. The immigration of the Senegalese to Morocco is the oldest: it began in the years 1960–1970.[12] The recent institutionalisation of links with the Tijâniyya Brotherhood and the migration networks established by the latter have nevertheless favoured the installation of new Senegalese people in Fez, some of whom have married Moroccan women. This flow has led to other flows:

---

8   Bernard Coyault, "L'africanisation de l'Église évangélique au Maroc: revitalisation d'une institution religieuse et dynamiques d'individualisation", *L'Année du Maghreb*, no. 11 (2014): 81–103.
9   Ibid.
10 Bamba, "Mobilité des Musulmans ivoiriens au Maroc: entre formation islamique et tourisme religieux".
11 The interstate couple is a metaphor that involves contemporary international actors 'engaged in security cooperation, more or less firmly attached, and involved in a process of international transformation' Brigitte Vassort-Rousset, *Building Sustainable Couples in International Relations*, (London: Palgrave Macmillan UK, 2014), 1.
12 Fatima Ait Ben Lmadani "La migration des Sénégalais au Maroc", *Study day on Moroccan-African relations*, Rabat, Centre Jacques Berque, Centre d'Études Sahariennes, Conseil National des Droits de l'Homme, Fondation kaS, 3 October 2014, Rabat. Coordination: Yousra Abourabi. Video URL: https://www.youtube.com/watch?v=YwCgHbAMKjA.

there are now Senegalese women domestic workers, sportspeople, and traders in Morocco.[13] Despite this close interweaving, religious people do not consider themselves ordinary migrants, as their status is highly political. According to one survey, they 'are generally part of the affluent middle class and are not confronted with the problem of migration. On the contrary, they are keen to maintain the distance between themselves and the "migrants" with whom they share only their nationality.'[14] Nevertheless, they sometimes mix with students who seek to join Sufi networks in search of their compatriots or workers who wish to strengthen their practice of Islam.

Morocco has supported this mobility of students, religious people and, to a lesser extent, workers, by relaxing the laws on entry and residence conditions for Africans. Some nationalities have benefited from these consular facilities for a long time. This is the case with the Senegalese, in the first place, who do not need a visa to travel to Morocco, and who also have the right to reside and work, according to a convention signed in 1964 that stipulates that 'without prejudice to conventions concluded or to be concluded between the two contracting parties, the nationals of each of the parties shall have access to public employment in the other State under the conditions determined by the legislation of that State'.[15] More recently, visa waiver agreements have been signed with Gabon, Côte d'Ivoire, Guinea-Conakry, Mali, Congo and Niger. On the diplomatic level, the discourse elaborated by the leaders tends to disseminate a welcoming image of the Kingdom towards its African 'brothers', even though, on a continental scale, Morocco is not one of the most open countries for Africans. According to the AfDB's 2016 African Visa Openness Index, Morocco ranked 41st among 54 African countries.[16]

In addition, apart from visa restrictions, some of the migrants residing in Morocco, except perhaps the religious ones, encounter difficulties in integrating, which encourages them to withdraw into the sub-Saharan communities within which solidarity links emerge. On the one hand, as one sociologist notes, Moroccans' stigmatisation of sub-Saharan students and the cultural gaps they are sometimes subjected to distance them from Moroccan students.[17] While religion could have been a factor of rapprochement among Muslims, it

---

13   Ibid.
14   Lanza, "Quelques enjeux du soufisme au Maroc: le tourisme religieux sénégalais et la construction d'un imaginaire sur l'amitié".
15   "Convention d'établissement entre le Gouvernement de la République du Sénégal et le Gouvernement du Royaume du Maroc", http://adala.justice.gov.ma/, December 22 1965.
16   "Africa Visa Openness Index", *African Development Bank*, n.d.
17   Berriane, "Les étudiants subsahariens au Maroc".

appears paradoxically that some Muslim sub-Saharan students consider themselves surprised by the 'lack of religiosity' of Moroccans[18]—so different are their approaches and practices—which pushes them to withdraw towards their compatriots and to claim their national or regional identity. This complex community under construction is therefore superimposed on another community resulting from an informal transnational migratory network that is developing massively in Morocco—the African migrants who are heading for Europe—making it even more difficult for the authorities to manage such a phenomenon. Fortunately, another part of the student and worker population is perfectly integrated, while those who suffer from exclusion phenomena are supported by a part of Moroccan civil society largely mobilised in associative networks for integration or in support of the Moroccan integration policy. In both cases, the growing presence of African migrants in Morocco is a consequence of its geographical position at the gateway to Europe, but also and increasingly of an economic policy geared towards emergence and the promotion of this position by an African diplomacy that defends openness and integration.

3 Towards a Mix of Foreign and Domestic Policies: The Example of Climate and Environmental Policy

The second consequence and perspective of Morocco's Africa policy lies in the increasingly deep interweaving of domestic and foreign policies, where each one relies on the other to serve the same objective, becoming more and more concerted and interdependent—whereas for a long time, let us remember, foreign policy remained a compartmentalised domain, which escaped publicisation and governmentality more than other public policies, although less than defence policy. With Jean-Noël Ferrié, I will call this phenomenon the domestic–foreign mix of public policies.[19] Morocco's environmental and climate policy offers a convincing example of this new trend at work. Over the past ten years, the institutionalisation of a global climate governance,[20] aimed at strengthening cooperation in the fight against global warming, has been accelerating. This has been supported by a range of studies that seek to link

---

18   Ibid.
19   Yousra Abourabi, Jean-Noël Ferrié, "Morocco's environmental diplomacy in Africa: an inside-out mix", *Telos*, June 7, 2018.
20   The concept of global climate governance was first formalised in the United Nations Framework Convention on Climate Change (UNFCCC) in 1992.

the environment to *high politics*: in addition to the well-documented scientific reports of the Intergovernmental Panel on Climate Change (IPCC), environmental concerns have moved up the agenda of decision-makers through the securitisation of this issue, supported by committed epistemic communities.[21] While in Africa, environmental concerns were long perceived as a 'Western luxury', a secondary interest that could only be considered once the continent's socioeconomic development and its integration into globalisation had been achieved, environmental protection and adaptation to climate change are now presented as the conditions for the continent's economic, food, health and, more generally, political security.

New political speeches reflect this shift in representation. Meles Zenawi, former prime minister of Ethiopia and the African Union's chief negotiator at the Copenhagen Climate Change Conference (COP 15), said that 'We all know that Africa has contributed almost nothing to global warming, but it is the first one to suffer from the heaviest consequences'.[22] Within this new vision advocated by the African Group of Negotiators, it is no longer a question of presenting Africa as the only victim demanding compensation, but one of mobilising local actors and making both political and financial efforts. Therefore, it is no coincidence that, a few years later, the 2016 COP 22 in Marrakech, tasked with encouraging the ratification of the Paris Agreement formulated at COP 21, was conceived and presented as an African COP. This was the wish of France, expressed by Ségolène Royale in her capacity as president of the COP 21, who put forward 'Africa as a victim of global warming, but also Africa as a solution';[23] and it was also the ambition of Morocco, which saw it as a diplomatic opportunity to provide further substance to its Africa policy. At this stage, it is less important to know the factors behind Africa's growing integration into the international climate regime[24] than to understand how it fits into it and, above all, how Morocco is trying to play a role.

---

21   See on this subject Daniel Compagnon, "Chapter 38. L'environnement dans les RI", in: *Traité de relations internationales*, eds. Balzacq Thierry, Ramel Frédéric, (Paris, Presses de Sciences Po (P.F.N.S.P.), 'Références', 2013), 1019–1052. URL: https://www.cairn.info/traite-de-relations-internationales-9782724613308-page-1019.htm.

22   *Speech to the Copenhagen Summit on December 16, 2010.*

23   Adrien Barbier, "For Ségolène Royal, the November COP in Marrakech must be African" *Le Monde Afrique*, August 7, 2016,: https://www.lemonde.fr/afrique/article/2016/08/07/pour-segolene-royal-la-cop-de-novembre-a-marrakech-doit-etre-africaine_4979478_3212.html#mfhIFxKi7JyEGwHB.99.

24   This has been the subject of an abundant literature. In French, see the synthesis by Yann Bérard and Daniel Compagnon, "Politiques du changement climatique: des controverses scientifiques à l'action publique", *Critique internationale*, no. 62 (2014/1): 9–19.

It should be recalled that African states are represented at the COP meetings through the African Group of Negotiators (AGN), a group of senior officials responsible for formulating and defending the common climate interests of the various AU member states. For a long time, the latter exclusively defended the 'polluter pays' principle, demanding external funding for African adaptation to climate change.[25] With the above-mentioned change in vision, some leaders are recognising and accepting the UN principle of 'common but differentiated responsibilities', which takes into account the historical responsibility of the polluting powers, global economic disparities and the need for global participation.

After creating a Climate Change and Desertification Unit, appointing a Heads of State and Government Committee on Climate Change (HOSCC) and giving birth to the African Climate Policy Centre in 2008,[26] the AU formulated its first African Climate Change Strategy in 2014.[27] The new objective advocated within this strategy is to 'forge a continent that works as a team and speaks with one voice to address the impacts of climate change'.[28] The strategy document recognises that the green economy is fundamental to ensuring food security and employment on the continent and proposes some 50 targets to be met and almost 200 actions to be taken by states for adaptation, mitigation and funding. A series of continental programmes have also been set up, such as the famous Climate Information Development Programme for Africa (Clim-Dev) in 2010 and the African Renewable Energy Initiative in 2015.

At this stage, and despite this promising momentum, African climate measures have not been clearly defined or are still marked by the conditionality of external aid. Many countries have not yet formulated a dedicated strategy or policy. Although encouraged within the COPs to formulate national adaptation and mitigation plans, the majority of African states are still struggling to define their needs and objectives, or where these have been the subject of specific policies, the implementation phase is constantly postponed. Good practices or success stories are still marginal, unambitious or poorly publicised, while immediate political, diplomatic and security imperatives take precedence over

---

25   *Climate Governance in Africa. A Handbook for Journalists*. Heinrich Böll Foundation and IPS Africa, (Johannesburg, 2012). URL: https://ng.boell.org/sites/default/files/climate_governance_handbook_english_version.pdf.
26   The Centre is responsible for assisting the Member States in formulating policy guidelines in this area.
27   African Union, *African Strategy on Climate Change*, (Addis Ababa, May 2014). https://stg-wedocs.unep.org/bitstream/handle/20.500.11822/20579/AMCEN_15_REF_11_Draft_African_Union_strategy_on_climate_change_English.pdf?sequence=1.
28   Ibid., 26.

long-term environmental strategies. There are many reasons for this: in addition to a lack of information, interest, skills, technologies and funding, intra-African governance in this field struggles to embrace the international climate regime. The latter's ability to impose binding agreements on states or even to mobilise on a large scale within a bottom-up approach is itself in question.[29]

Within the continent, Morocco stands out as a 'good student' internationally. According to the 2019 Climate Change Performance Index (CCPI) drawn up by the NGOs Germanwatch, NewClimate Institute and Climate Action Network International, unveiled during COP 24, Morocco is the second-best-performing country in this fight, after Sweden.[30] It had already been in fifth place for several years. This is mainly due to the energy transition initiated by the state and its ambitious commitments, motivated precisely by its Africa policy.

Indeed, at the moment of the deployment of its Africa policy, Morocco quickly established the objectives of a National Plan against Global Warming and a National Energy Strategy, one of the roles of which is to define the means of this energy transition. Thus, several public institutions were created between 2010 and 2011: the Moroccan Solar Energy Agency (MASEN), the Agency for the Development of Renewable Energy and Energy Efficiency (ADEREE), the Institute for Research in Solar Energy and New Energies (IRESEN) and the Energy Investment Company (SIE). The latter has mobilised an effective means of promoting large energy projects, namely sharing the risk with the promoters by participating in the company's capital and withdrawing once the project is completed. All of these contributions demonstrate that the energy transition project is indeed considered a national priority. This effort is determined by 'eco-eco' interests, i.e. economic-ecological,[31] giving way to the win-win logic. This includes the possibility of attracting external investment and developing the local industrial fabric in order to move away from energy dependence. It is also a question of consolidating economic growth while simultaneously adopting an ecological perspective that allows the mitigation of global warming.

Through this new financial strategy, Morocco's ambition is to increase the weight of renewable energies in the energy mix to 42% by 2020 and to 52% by 2030, exceeding the European objectives. These energies would mainly come

---

29 Steinar Andresen, "Do We Need More Global Sustainability Conferences?", in *Handbook of Global Environmental Politics* (2nd ed.), ed. Peter Dauvergne (Cheltenham, Edward Elgar, 2012), 87–96.
30 However, not all African countries have been assessed. Nevertheless, those that were are among the last. These are Egypt (24th), South Africa (39th) and Algeria (47th).
31 Several researchers defend this model based on a neoliberal vision. See in particular: Lester R. Brown, *Eco-Economy. Une autre croissance est possible, écologique et durable*, (Paris, Seuil, 2003).

from solar and wind sources. Since 2013, hydropower and wind energy have effectively represented more than 16% of electricity production. The Tarfaya wind farm, which has been operational since 2014, is already the largest wind farm in Africa.

The Noor solar power plant, inaugurated in 2016 in the Ouarzazate region, is projected to be the largest solar power plant in the world.

It is important to note that these renewable energy development programmes are partly funded and implemented by the Moroccan state. In addition, the leaders have been able to call on the help of several donors, such as the World Bank, the ADB, the UN Environment Programme (UNEP), GIZ and Agence Française de Développement. The Energy Development Fund also supports some programmes, mainly funded by Saudi Arabia and the United Arab Emirates. Several French (Quadran) and Spanish (Abengoa) investors also contribute to the direct financing of projects. The effort to involve this complex network of actors was such that the resulting governance is closely coordinated at the highest levels of the state.

The energy transition has quickly become a policy as sensible as it is required by the development of a continental climate diplomacy that consolidates Morocco's Africa policy. The organisation of COP 22 in 2016 marked the start of this policy with the launch, at the initiative of Mohammed VI, of the 'African Action Summit'. During this summit, which brought together some 50 states, Morocco endeavoured to present itself as a climate leader capable of defending African states' interests, particularly on funding issues. In his discursive strategy, the King declared that Africa 'pays a heavy price in the "climate" equation' and that the 'actors do not lack commitment or goodwill, but they sometimes lack the resources'.[32] It is no coincidence that the Noor solar power plant was also inaugurated on the sidelines of COP 22. It was a way for the Kingdom to show its ability to attract colossal financing (and not just aid) for equally ambitious projects while fulfilling its commitments. At the same time, Moroccan representatives offered African countries their services to help them obtain financing. In the same perspective, a large number of programmes, such as the African Agriculture Adaptation Initiative (AAA)[33] and the Climate Change Competence Centre (4C),[34] were inaugurated with the objective, as stated by a former environment minister, of 'pooling existing expertise in Morocco and

---

32 "Speech by King Mohammed VI at the 1st African Action Summit", Marrakech, November 16, 2016.
33 See the website at: http://aaainitiative.org/fr/initiative.
34 See the website at: https://www.4c.ma/fr.

deploying it to African countries, as part of Morocco's leadership role in combating the effects of climate change in Africa'.[35]

The ambition of Morocco's climate policy is undeniably a consequence of its Africa policy insofar as the implementation of an energy transition has been envisaged as a political opportunity. This opportunity is emerging in a continental context marked by both the AU's declared interest in the fight against climate change and structural difficulties in implementing the related policies within the states. Although this energy transition does not make the Kingdom an ecological country,[36] and although there are still some cautious positions within the leadership regarding environmental commitment, the prospects for Moroccan climate policy in Africa are numerous.

Morocco's climate policy illustrates a new mechanism of public action at work, the 'domestic–foreign mix',[37] through which public policies (in this case, energy policy) can be developed in a way that is consistent with a foreign policy orientation so that the state makes new international commitments that in turn become binding domestically.

4 Enshrining the End of a MENA/sub-Saharan Africa Divide: A Socially Constructed Regionalist Project

In the space of a decade, Morocco has become the leading African investor in West Africa and rejoined the African Union after 33 years of absence. Strengthened by its new position, the Kingdom now intends to integrate into ECOWAS. On 24 February 2017, the Ministry of Foreign Affairs and International Cooperation formulated a request for membership in ECOWAS[38] in a communiqué sent to Ellen Johnson Sirleaf, president of the organisation. This decision was unusual because it was the first time that Morocco had applied to join an

---

35 Hakima El Haite quoted in "Mohammed Nbou appointed Director of the Climate Change Competence Centre", Energy & Strategy, no. 46, Q1 2017, p. 16. URL: http://www.fedenerg.ma/wp-content/uploads/2017/04/ES_46.pdf.

36 The protection of the ecosystem, the separation of waste and the use of polluting products are not the subjects of ambitious policies.

37 Jean-Noël Ferrié and Yousra Abourabi "La diplomatie environnementale du Maroc en Afrique: un mix intérieur-extérieur".

38 Established in 1975, the Economic Community of West African States (ECOWAS) promotes economic integration and political cooperation among its 15 member states. This regional community is bound by a multilateral treaty, the latest version of which was revised in 1993. ECOWAS has shown many developments in the field of free movement, harmonisation of policies, and standards and security cooperation.

African Regional Economic Community (REC) as a full member, the first time that ECOWAS had faced such a request[39] and the first time that the AU had seen a member state seeking membership of a new REC. Morocco is part of the AMU in the division accepted by the AU, and no other country has ever requested to change or combine its membership of two regions.

Initially, ECOWAS gave its 'agreement in principle' in June 2017, surprising the entire political class. Six months later, the agreement was questioned at the Summit of Heads of State and Government in Abuja. There were many questions about the relevance of such integration: is Morocco not an economic competitor? Does it not have hegemonic intentions? Does its population consider itself African? More fundamental questions, touching on the very identity of ECOWAS, were also exchanged: if we wanted to, how could we admit a new member? Is the state identity advocated by Morocco compatible or soluble with the West African identity? The issues raised in the discussions revealed reticence, which halted the process—so much so that in Morocco, while the decision to apply for membership of ECOWAS had not been the subject of consultation, it did become a subject of public debate, revealing domestic reticence about opening borders to the West African grouping, about adhering to the principle of the secular nature of the state and even, in the longer term, about the possibility of exchanging the Moroccan dirham for a common currency.

On the part of ECOWAS, in order to show that the request was taken seriously, not to contradict the agreement in principle and not to offend the Moroccan partner, a group of five states (Nigeria, Côte d'Ivoire, Ghana, Guinea, Togo) was entrusted with the task of carrying out an in-depth impact study. In parallel to this study—whose deliverables have not been determined—and to show goodwill, the ECOWAS Commission was tasked with defining the 'preconditions and pre-requisites' for the accession of any new member and for drawing up a Draft Community Act 'which will define the decision-making process'.

This process has thus made it possible to reveal the groups of West African actors most reluctant about regional integration as desired by Morocco. These are, first and foremost, the employers' associations of the various countries (particularly in Nigeria and Senegal) and political groups supporting the Algerian and South African positions on the Polisario Front. In response to these geopolitical representations, Nigeria is particularly the subject of sustained

---

39 The possibility of enlargement of the Community was never envisaged in the founding text. See Community of West African States, *ECOWAS Revised Treaty*, Economic Abuja, 1993 https://ecowas.int/wp-content/uploads/2022/08/Revised-treaty-1.pdf

bilateral diplomacy.[40] Indeed, around the Nigerian state, it is the employers, in particular the Manufacturers Association of Nigeria (MAN), whose power of influence is important, which seems to perceive Moroccan ambitions as a threat to its own economic interests. The competition that the arrival of large Moroccan companies (and Moroccan products) could provoke is perceived as inevitable and harmful by the latter. The launch of the AfCFTA (the African Continental Free Trade Area) may partly render this debate moot, but other issues (e.g. the question of regulatory convergence) remain problematic. The Moroccan argument has been that the potential collaboration of Moroccan and West African companies could actually generate more benefits. Employers are not the only reluctant stakeholder group. Also in Nigeria, a group of ex-ambassadors has clearly spoken out against the Moroccan Sahara and the relevance of such membership. Other groups of actors (diplomats, politicians, researchers, farmers' groups and officials within ECOWAS) in the various countries of the region are reluctant for other reasons: Morocco's request for membership is perceived as a diplomatic offensive that would only serve hegemonic Moroccan interests, in a context where West Africa is struggling to achieve the objectives it has set for itself. These actors are struggling to see what Morocco could bring to the table in terms of strengthening governance, security or development, for reasons linked to historical perceptions, mentioned at the beginning of the book.

In response to this reticence, the official message transmitted by the Moroccan state, through the president of the Amadeus Institute, is that 'Morocco is not in a hurry'. Through this discursive legitimisation framework, Morocco reinforces the idea that it is indeed planning a regionalist rather than a regionalisation strategy. As Daniel Bach aptly points out, 'the notion of regionalism takes into account ideas or ideologies, programmes, policies and objectives that aim to transform and identify social space into a regional project'.[41] More specifically, regionalism 'postulates the explicit construction of an identity, as opposed to its formation. It refers to the implementation of an agenda or even the definition of a strategy. It can be institutional construction within the framework of an IGO, but also the conclusion of bilateral political-legal arrangements.'[42] Regionalisation differs from regionalism in that it 'refers to processes. These processes can be the result of the realisation of regionalist

---

40   Yousra Abourabi: "Morocco-Nigeria: towards the reconstruction of regional geopolitics", *Middle East Eye*, June 23, 2018, https://www.middleeasteye.net/fr/opinions/maroc-nig-ria-towards-a-reconstruction-of-west-african-policy-211542393.
41   Bach, "Regionalismes, regionalisation and globalisation", 346.
42   Ibid.

projects. Regionalisation can also result from aggregating individual strategies, independent of any identified regionalist aspiration or strategy'.[43] This strategy is effectively based on two axes: on the one hand, the state is striving to mobilise non-state actors more through developing public diplomacy (economic, cultural, etc.). On the other hand, it places its desire for integration within the framework of formal requests submitted to regional institutional actors, without any extensive desire to capture the sovereignty of these multilateral organisations and without wanting to use club diplomacy to 'force' membership.

At the same time, it is a question of regionalism 'from above', constructed by the Moroccan leaders in such a way as to support a more global Africa policy. It should be noted that a few months after this request, the King publicly stated the failure of the AMU and the need for Morocco to rethink its continental integration circles. For the King, 'it is clear that the flame of the AMU has been extinguished because faith in a common interest has disappeared' (Addis Ababa speech, 2017), and that consequently 'alas, the AMU no longer exists' (Abidjan speech, 2017). More generally, he will seek to valorise ECOWAS at the expense of the AMU, declaring that 'the AMU is the least integrated region on the African continent, if not on the planet', and presenting ECOWAS as 'a reliable space for the free movement of people, goods and capital' (Addis Ababa speech, 2017).

Morocco's application is a regionalist project and not a regionalisation project because this application is formulated *a priori*, and not *a posteriori*, of effective integration, be it transnational or institutional, as well as based on the will to recognise a shared identity or a community of values (which is not necessarily the case in regionalisation). Nevertheless, this regionalist project under construction aims to achieve regionalisation in the form of a 'holistic' integration,[44] i.e. a form of political integration that is part of a process of re-founding pan-Africanism, in which the gap between regionalism and regionalisation is the narrowest. This regionalist vocation calls into question the relevance of a Maghrebian space separated from a West African space, and more generally, that of a North African space or the 'MENA' region distinct from the sub-Saharan space. On the contrary, Morocco's Africa policy opens the way to new research perspectives that will have to redraw new regional areas from the point of view of the actors in order to better understand them as observers.

---

43   Ibid., 347.
44   Ibid.

CONCLUSION

Morocco: A Median Power

In the space of 20 years, Mohammed VI's Morocco has made significant progress: poverty has been reduced, the middle class has grown, public infrastructure has been developed, and the health, education and administration systems have been modernised. On the economic front, the steady increase in the growth rate (from 1.8% in 1999 to 4.4% in 2015[1]) due to manufacturing and services, the opening up of trade, as well as the boom in foreign investment have enabled the Kingdom to claim the status of an emerging country and the fifth-largest economy on the continent.[2] Currently, other projects are underway, continuing this dynamic. For example, the Noor solar park, inaugurated in 2016, was at that point the largest solar power plant on the continent. The Cherifian Kingdom already aims to be recognised as an actor at the forefront of the African energy transition. The COP 22, organised in Marrakech in November 2016, symbolically marked the starting point for deploying this new climate diplomacy.[3]

This general observation obscures the phenomenon of growing socioeconomic disparities, the consequences of this development for the environment and the ecological balance of the Kingdom, and the delays in improvement in the areas of education, social development, gender equity and other human rights. But despite these limitations, and as is often the case on the international scene, it is primarily macroeconomic data, growth statistics and major national projects (infrastructure, institutional reforms, social programmes) that, when well publicised and promoted, count in the first place in the appreciation of the value of a state by its peers. As a result, the Kingdom's ambition is precisely to be recognised as an emerging power by 2030.

Morocco also illustrates a more general trend, where participation in the global economy and the assimilation of certain liberal norms is also an instrumental choice to support the regime. This instrumental capacity can be used as a lever in the defence of national interests at the international scale, as well as in the current regime's recognition as an essential and credible interlocutor. Morocco has thus made the hosting of regional offices of international insti-

1 World Bank data: https://data.worldbank.org/indicator/NY.GDP.MKTP.KD.ZG?locations=MA
2 See in particular Title 2.
3 See the Moroccan website on the Conference: http://www.cop22.ma/.

tutions, political NGOs and multilateral conferences an important element of the recognition of its role identity.

At the heart of this enterprise, the monarchy is the primary decision-maker in the Kingdom's domestic and foreign policy. After initiating a political transition and undertaking important democratic reforms, under the combined effect of social demands and international pressure, and certainly of his own will, the King has transformed the Moroccan sociopolitical landscape. With the strength of his lineage (the Alawite dynasty has reigned in Morocco since the sixteenth century), his symbolic authority (as Commander of the Faithful) and his political status (at the top of the decision-making system), Mohammed VI has taken over the political and institutional legacy of Hassan II, while distancing himself from the late monarch and developing his own style. The reforms initiated by the King have thus strengthened his legitimacy as much as his popularity. In this regard, I recall the observation by Jean-Noël Ferrié and Baudouin Dupret, quoted at the beginning of this study: 'Morocco is the only country in North Africa and the Middle East to have succeeded in undertaking reforms in such a profound manner that one can no longer—except in a polemical manner—simply say that it is authoritarian.'[4] Illustrating this trend, unlike Hassan II, Mohammed VI has never been the object of a coup attempt, and his legitimacy was not questioned during the Arab Spring.

Monarchical authority thus took a less absolute and more executive form with the advent of the reign of Mohammed VI. The latter's style change is also linked to an evolution in the definition of royal interests. These interests lie not in the preservation of the legitimacy of power, as this is well consolidated, but more generally in the defence of the old and new roles of the monarch: Commander of the Faithful, king of the poor, entrepreneurial king, guarantor of the nation's traditions and defender of territorial integrity—so many roles that result from a slow construction of the public identity of the monarchy. Mohammed VI represents the embodiment of these roles on a domestic and external scale, gradually giving Moroccan diplomacy a singular character.

The diplomatic apparatus has developed thanks to the gradual emergence of the country, on the one hand, and the encouragement of the monarch, on the other. The administration imperfectly but stubbornly tries to reproduce Western institutional frameworks designed according to the principles of NPM and promoted by its international donors, actors of a powerful neoliberal epistemic community. At the same time, the socio-academic profile of diplo-

---

4   Dupret and Ferrié, 'B. Dupret and J.N. Ferrié. The Moroccan 'exception''.

mats has diversified, while the training of young recruits has become more professional. In addition, embassies are now numerous, especially in Africa. As modern diplomacy covers new areas (cultural, public, economic diplomacy, etc.), there is a greater assumption of responsibility by the government for foreign policy issues that are not in the vital or supreme interests of the nation. The various waves of replacements of consuls and ambassadors that have taken place in recent years on the King's orders are part of this trend aimed at giving the diplomatic apparatus the means to assume its prerogatives.

However, the Ministry of Foreign Affairs remains a 'ministry of sovereignty'. In other words, although diplomats have more significant means and responsibilities in carrying out their duties, foreign policy is, more than any other public policy, conceived and directed primarily by the monarchy. Within the Royal Cabinet, the foreign affairs advisor and his team assist the monarch in this decision-making process and work with the minister on issues deemed strategic. More generally, the main foreign policy orientations are communicated by the monarchy through its official speeches, which diplomats must strive to implement, under the supervision and assiduous control of the Palace. All of these implementation efforts are part of a power policy, defined intrinsically as the pursuit of economic and political emergence, relationally as the projection of influence in sectoral fields, and intersubjectively as the construction and search for recognition of a unique role identity. These three dimensions of power are closely intertwined.

We can therefore observe that a dialogical network around the notion of the golden mean has gradually emerged within the political, academic and media spheres. Understood as a moderate practice of Islam but also as a geo-cultural identity, the golden mean is not a political doctrine formulated *a priori* but an element of language that can characterise the norms, values and roles that the Moroccan state disseminates or exercises, through which it wishes to be recognised as a power

In other words, the golden mean allows for the defining of Morocco's 'role identity' on the international scene. The use of this concept developed by Wendt[5] should not be seen as an attempt to strictly apply the author's theory to the Moroccan empirical case but rather as a conceptual borrowing of a definition that suits my purpose well. Indeed, the Kingdom intends to use its geographical location at the crossroads of different geo-cultural areas, its national identity redefined in the sense of a better consideration of cultural

---

5 Wendt, *Social Theory of International Politics*, 224.

diversity, the new style of the monarchy, both rooted and popular, and the politico-religious values that advocate moderation and tolerance to serve its power policy.

Guided by these new ambitions, the Kingdom of Mohammed VI has progressively made the African continent, particularly sub-Saharan Africa, the privileged terrain of its foreign policy. One could easily have imagined that the Arab-Muslim world would be the Kingdom's primary concern. However, it appears that Africa is at the top of the Moroccan diplomatic agenda due to several historical and geopolitical determinants, to the point where Morocco calls itself African and not just Arab or Muslim any more.

First, the status of the Sahara has been a contentious issue between the Polisario Front, a pro-independence movement supported by Algeria, and the Moroccan state since the decolonisation of the territory by Spain in 1975. More generally, Moroccan territorial claims in what is now Mauritania and Algeria, formulated in the aftermath of independence through the 'Greater Morocco' project based on pre-colonial systems of allegiance, have aroused the enmity of many African leaders. Accentuated by the ideological divide of the Cold War, this dissension led to the OAU's recognition of the Polisario Front as an independent republic called the RASD, and the Kingdom's departure from this organisation in 1984 in protest, denouncing the violation of its territorial integrity. In the following 15 years, Morocco's version of the 'Hallstein doctrine' accentuated its exclusion from the main spheres of pan-African influence. The Sahara conflict was thus seen as an African problem, an issue in relation to which it now lies within the Kingdom's ability to regain the confidence of former Eastern Bloc states and assert its presence on the continent more generally. In the Moroccan geopolitical representation, the Sahara is its 'link' with sub-Saharan Africa, without which it would remain geographically and politically cut off from the rest of the continent.

Second, France's Africa policy during the Cold War partly determined the Kingdom's representations and behaviour in Africa. As an ally of a powerful France, Hassan II's Morocco carried out numerous African operations to support liberation movements and counter the advance of communism. The Francophile community of interest supported by the Republic also enabled the late King to forge close ties with the leaders of France's main allied states, particularly Senegal, Côte d'Ivoire and Gabon. On the strength of its experience, the Kingdom relied on this network to engage militarily, this time officially, in one of the most important armed conflicts on the continent at the time, in the Congo. Little by little, the government developed its own cooperation policy with these states, under France's sometimes benevolent and sometimes malevolent gaze.

At the beginning of Mohammed VI's reign, these historical conditions determined the Moroccan ruling class's geopolitical representations. On the one hand, Algeria and its African allies, particularly Nigeria and South Africa, but also Angola, Mozambique and Ethiopia, formed a 'hostile axis' in relation to Moroccan claims and were long represented as 'enemies of territorial integrity' and therefore *hostis* in the Schmittian sense. On the other hand, the countries of West, Central and Sahelian Africa, which are also mainly French-speaking countries, are designated as 'brotherly countries' with which the Kingdom envisaged developing its cooperation in the first place and strengthening its diplomatic and political ties. From these representations, two main foreign policy axes are derived.

Concerning this first group of actors, the Moroccan leadership sometimes adopted a restricted policy, in the sense that for many years little effort was made to exchange, negotiate or cooperate. When this was the case, efforts were strongly limited or weakened by the hostility of these countries towards the Kingdom. This is the case with South Africa, whose potential for cooperation was severely undermined by its support for the Polisario Front. In other instances, Morocco has been able to gloss over the feeling of enmity in favour of a policy of reaching out, marking a break with its version of the Hallstein doctrine.

Thus, the Kingdom's objective is to strengthen its alliances and broaden them to countries hostile to its territorial claims, in a logic of deconstruction of ideological postures and highlighting of Morocco's assets. This is a policy that bears the seal of Mohammed VI, since, as head of the executive, he contributes to giving it a singular tone, reflecting the role identity defended by the Kingdom. Nicknamed 'Mohammed VI the African' by the local and international press, he has resolutely launched this Africa policy through his numerous official visits to the continent,[6] which have helped to spread the image of a supportive and entrepreneurial King.

Mohammed VI's Africa policy is thus defined by his own style, the historical determinants that have shaped the representations of African states, and the means available to the Kingdom in the era of neoliberal globalisation. It is conditioned by ambitions of power, which are formulated not only in structural and economic terms through plans for emergence but also in relational and geopolitical terms through the exercise of diplomatic influence in a territorial space. In order to affirm this new status, a framework of legitimisation was deployed. This is based on different discursive repertoires formulated induc-

---

6 See Appendix 1 and 1bis.

tively, i.e. by finding *a posteriori* links between commonly accepted normative frameworks and Moroccan diplomatic action. Thus, Morocco presents itself as an African state by demonstrating the age-old ties between the former empires and the Saharan countries, to the point where its African identity was included as an essential character of its national identity in the last constitution of 2011. It also presents itself as a state of solidarity by appropriating the normative framework of South–South cooperation and global security and placing its cooperation policy within this framework. Finally, it presents itself as a moderate and open state by promoting its identity as one of playing a golden-mean role on the diplomatic level. These different discursive legitimisation frameworks have reinforced the interest of many African countries in the Kingdom, an interest that is visible in the emotional diplomacy displayed by their leaders.

Despite these new prospects, Morocco was still confronted with the difficulty of exercising its Africa policy due to its exclusion from the institutional mechanisms of the AU and the hostility of the most important continental powers. This double limitation led it to develop an 'indirect strategy', which I have defined in diplomatic terms as the offensive and extensive practice of diplomacy by a state in fields and areas different from those of its adversaries to avoid direct confrontation, bypass the conflict area and obtain additional gains unrelated to the conflict with the latter.

Indeed, the Kingdom initially favoured selective bilateral diplomacy in Africa, which has the advantage of being able to sectorise cooperation, to develop relations according to the degree of understanding and the means of the government, and to have the capacity to give each relationship its own originality. Thus, the policy deployed within the French-speaking countries initially consisted of the multiplication of bilateral cooperation agreements rather than a regional approach conducted through a multilateral mechanism. On the other hand, the government was interested in trilateral (also called triangular or tripartite) cooperation, which generally brings together a donor actor (Northern countries), a pivotal state (Morocco) and one or more recipient states (in Africa). This type of cooperation generally allows the pivotal state to raise funds on the one hand and to play an expert role on the other. Finally, in order to circumvent its absence from the AU while demonstrating its ability to play the game of multilateralism, Morocco was at the origin of the creation of new African multilateral organisations and forums, not attached to the AU, as well as having integrated, as an observer member, into the main regional organisations of West, Sahel and Central Africa. These different approaches confirm that the conduct of the Kingdom's diplomacy is situated within its own strategic framework, based on the multiplication of means of action rather than on specialisation in niche diplomacy.

More concretely, this diplomacy covers various fields, in line with the increase in international diplomatic activity and the multiplication of the stakes and actors of this diplomacy. In this sense, it can be said that Morocco is adapting well to modernity. Thanks to its economic diplomacy, it has established itself as the second-largest African investor on the continent (after South Africa) and the largest in West Africa: the construction of infrastructure, real estate projects, the purchase of banks and telephone operators, and agricultural investments are all projects that have been carried out under the banner of South–South cooperation. Thanks to the deployment of cultural diplomacy, Morocco is gradually becoming a university hub for African students. Finally, the deployment of religious diplomacy reinforces the symbolic authority of the monarch beyond the national borders and participates in disseminating a Moroccan religious model known as the Islam of the golden mean. These different areas of diplomacy have mobilised the Palace, the government, and non-state actors such as entrepreneurs, the media, civil society and transnational religious brotherhoods to illustrate a real modernisation of the diplomatic apparatus. Overall, this policy has not yet had a decisive effect on the economy of African countries. Still, it has strengthened the presence and weight of the Kingdom in Africa, just as it has raised its ambition to make this space its strategic depth. Morocco's return to the AU in 2017 is the most relevant illustration of this.

As with any foreign policy, it is necessary to consider the consequences of Morocco's Africa policy for its geopolitical environment as well as for the evolution of the state's recognition as a power. These consequences are of three kinds. First, Morocco has become a migratory crossroads. Indeed, it is no longer just a transit point but an actual stopover for migrants who settle for up to 12 years,[7] thanks to the Kingdom's socioeconomic development and the dissemination of a welcoming image within the continent, reinforced by religious and cultural diplomacy, as well as the abolition of visas for several West African countries, which has also favoured the migration phenomenon. A new form of migration, both academic and religious, is manifesting itself in the Moroccan social landscape. The increase in economic migration has led to the securitisation of this issue, illustrated by a certain amount of violence observed against undocumented migrants and by the unabashed expression of anti-black racism within social networks, altering the image of an African and supportive Kingdom. This phenomenon has nevertheless accelerated the

---

7 Association Marocaine d'Études et de Recherche en Migrations (AMERM), "Enquête sur la migration subsaharienne au Maroc 2007", June 2008, 43.

formulation of a migration policy aimed at the regularisation and integration of migrants. Despite European pressure to make Morocco a buffer zone, the country has taken into account the recommendations of the National Council for Human Rights to develop a new migration policy adapted to Moroccan interests in Africa and has submitted a project to the UN for the creation of a pan-African cooperation mechanism on the migration issue. Despite the limits and difficulties encountered in implementing this migration policy, it should be noted that the particularity of this mechanism under construction lies in the approach to the phenomenon. Migration is presented not as a security problem but rather as a development factor. Undoubtedly, these developments will contribute to favouring African migration to Morocco in the future.

Second, in the context of the development of global climate governance and a paradigm shift in the AU's interest in combating climate change, Morocco has used its energy transition as a lever to gain recognition for its leadership role in this field. Morocco's ability to attract external funding for ambitious industrial projects in the field of renewable energy has been promoted on the diplomatic front in such a way as to open up promising prospects for many African countries wishing to participate more in this global ecological effort. The 'African Action Summit' launch and many Moroccan-led continental programmes (such as the African Agriculture Adaptation Initiative) are examples of this ongoing phenomenon.

Third, Morocco now aims to draw a new geopolitical arc, grouping the West African countries together. In this perspective, an official request for membership was submitted to ECOWAS. This regionalist policy is the result of diplomatic efforts undertaken in these countries, reinforcing on the Moroccan side the representation of the Kingdom as a stakeholder in a West African space to the detriment of the Maghreb or Arab space. Comforted in this choice by the increase in transnational security threats (terrorism, organised crime, etc.) as well as the insertion of the Kingdom in a West African regional security complex, the leaders have also developed a new discursive framework of legitimisation around the need to develop regional cooperation in security matters.

Finally, on the strength of its political and institutional reforms, its economic and social development, and the deployment of its diplomacy in Africa, Morocco constitutes a remarkable case study in the analysis of small-country foreign policy. Guided by power interests (understood as the quest for emergence, the exercise of diplomatic influence within a territorialised space and the projection of a role identity), the Kingdom has experienced a considerable rise on the African scene in less than 20 years. This growth can be measured in the welcome given to the King during his African tours, in the emotional diplomacy exchanged by African heads of state and in the use of official Moroccan elements of language by the African media. Similarly, more and more African presidents are visiting Morocco. More generally, the areas of cooperation have expanded, particularly within the countries of West Africa. Finally, the Kingdom is playing an increasingly important role in Sahelian security.

The first relative gain[8] of this policy is that many states have withdrawn their recognition of the RASD. Of the 88 countries that had recognised the Polisario Front as an independent state (mainly during the Cold War), 43 have suspended their relations with this actor (mostly under the reign of Mohammed VI). In Africa, of the 36 countries that recognised the Polisario Front as an independent state, 22 have withdrawn this recognition or frozen their relations.[9]

The second gain related to this policy is the evolution of Morocco's relations with France. These relations are still as close as during the Cold War, but their nature seems to have changed. It is no longer a loyal alliance in the service of France's African and Arab policies but rather a compromise alliance, defined as a political pact that brings two states together in an asymmetrical relationship, but one that is sufficiently interdependent to allow the weaker state to participate in, or create for itself, another alliance system or sub-system. While during the Cold War, Moroccan–African relations were globally dependent on French strategic, political, institutional and normative arrangements, contemporary Africa policy is exercised through mechanisms that are common or similar to those of France while at the same time detaching itself in its foundations and interests from the Africa policy of the former colonial power. Moreover, Morocco now affirms its intention to diversify its international alliances in favour of Russia and China, without this sacrificing, threatening or altering the smooth running of its cooperation with France.

There are also absolute gains in this policy. These lie in the effects of the development cooperation deployed by the Kingdom on the continent. It is clear that the construction projects carried out, the aid granted to the Least Developed Countries, the humanitarian donations made and the professional training provided, although very insignificant compared with the amount of Chinese or French aid, all contribute to the development of the continent. The fact that they come from an African state in the process of achieving its own development makes them all the more remarkable, especially since Morocco does not demand immediate political compensation and does not project itself as a hegemonic power. Unlike China's attitude towards the recognition of Taiwan, the recognition of the Moroccanness of Western Sahara by

---

8   On the difference between absolute and relative gains, see Powell, "Absolute and Relative Gains in International Relations Theory".
9   Appendixes 5 and 5bis.

states is no longer a condition for the development of diplomatic relations. The case of Mali, a country that has long maintained relations with the Polisario Front but with which the Kingdom has engaged in close cooperation for several years, is particularly illustrative in this respect. Instead, it appears that Morocco's gains lie in its affirmation and recognition as an African power on the continent through the image it disseminates, confirming the constructivist paradigm according to which the search for recognition of a role identity can be conceived as a national interest as important as security or economic gain.

Internationally, Morocco is not a competitive economic power, an offensive military power or an influential normative power. Economically, its weight in African trade remains small compared with the weight of medium-sized powers outside Africa (Turkey, Brazil). In terms of innovation and industrial transformation, the government is still underperforming. Nevertheless, trade with Africa continues to grow by an average of 12% per year, which is considerable. Similarly, the trade balance has been in large surplus in Morocco's favour since 2008. While the Kingdom is still heavily dependent on external aid and investment, its ability to maintain or create links with external economic partners is remarkable.

On the military level, its army is seasoned and modern and constitutes the seventh-strongest army on the continent. However, although Morocco is present in many African conflict theatres through its participation in the PKOs, it does not plan to play a decisive role in terms of continental military security on a bilateral scale. The training provided to African officers allows it to build a network at the service of an influence diplomacy but does not aim to transform the African military landscape. Morocco does not wish to take the risk of intervening in offensive missions where its legitimacy is not recognised; similarly, its external deployment capacities are limited by the massive mobilisation of the army in securing the borders, while the costs of such deployments remain prohibitive. More generally, its strategic doctrine is defensive. The intelligence system seems to have been definitively modernised and, above all, seems to be working better in concert with the diplomatic system. However, on a continent marked by crises and wars and whose desire is to be able to resolve its own conflicts without the help of a foreign power, an African power will therefore be recognised according to its capacity to play a prominent role in this area, which constitutes a major challenge for the Kingdom.

On the normative level, although it strives to have its own normative framework of thought, particularly through the religious dimension, Morocco remains a real normative sounding board for external epistemic communities. As an international 'good student', it is pursuing with particular interest the upgrading of its institutions in the image of French institutions, measuring its progress against the criteria promoted by the IMF, the UN, the World Bank, the European Union and the various American expert offices. The content of the numerous reports published by the Ministry of Economy and Finance illustrates this trend. Although disseminating a model for the management of the religious field, based on the Moroccan Islam of the golden mean, constitutes an innovative normative vector, this experience is recent, still under construction, and it depends on the security context marked by the rise of transnational terrorism. At the African level, idealistic and regionalist projects such as the 'African Renaissance', the '*Pax Africana*' and Pan-Africanism have, at different times in history, constituted discursive frameworks that inscribe countries in the history of continental construction. Morocco discursively inscribes its action within the framework of South–South cooperation and 'the trust in Africa' and is not lacking in continental initiatives. However, it still faces the challenge of translating this discursive framework into a normative framework of its own that allows it to make a fundamental difference in its approach. This takes time.

Consequently, Morocco can be defined as a median power. This qualification makes it possible to escape the classic vertical hierarchical approach to power, which tends to rank powers from the greatest to the smallest. This vision, inherited from the Treaty of Chaumont (1814), was all the more considered during the Cold War to support the idea of a balance of power. 'Great power' refers to the realistic hegemon. The median power, whether 'traditional' or 'emerging', deploys a foreign policy that tends to favour multilateralism and cooperation.[10] The small power, unable to ensure its security by its own means, must rely on its alliances with great powers.[11] The qualification of median power also escapes the classical horizontal hierarchical approach to power, which tends to classify powers according to their projection field. The latter aims to account for the scope of power projection: regional, multilateral or global. The vertical and horizontal hierarchical approaches are relevant but imprecise in identifying the particularities of the Moroccan power. Moreover, notwithstanding this apparent scientificity, in both cases, there is no consensus on the definition of the attributes of a median power or a regional power, for example. These hierarchical views make it almost impossible for a researcher to understand the particular form of influence of a small state in the system. Is Morocco an emerging middle power like Turkey, a regional power like Nigeria or a small

---

10 Jordaan, "The concept of a middle power in international relations".
11 Robert L. Rothstein, *Alliances and small powers*, (New York: Columbia University Press, 1968).

sub-regional power like Senegal? Under which heading should this country be classified? The hierarchical approach to power appears all the more limited, as it suggests the existence of a permanent struggle between states to reach the highest status in the hierarchy. This normative masculinist postulate immediately obscures the specificities inherent in the interests of each power. The adjective 'median' thus has a double meaning here: relational on the one hand and relative to identity on the other.

On the relational level, the particularity of the Kingdom is to manage, despite its weak material resources, to place itself at a median level of sovereign and diplomatic autonomy. The idea of medianity should be considered not as a normative or subjective judgement but as a measuring instrument inscribed in a reflexive scale. In contrast to the middle, which is usually defined in terms of a normative scale, median power is identified in terms of the constant capabilities, resources and relationships of other states and the degree to which others recognise this sovereign and diplomatic autonomy.

Sovereign autonomy means, first of all, the intra-state order, i.e. the stability of the regime, the durability of institutions, the capacity of the power to resist internal contestation and integrate reforms, and the recognition of the legitimacy of this power. More generally, it is a question of the state's capacity to make its political choices freely and to legitimise its action while minimising its submission to the trials of other nations and its sensitivity to endogenous destabilisation attempts. The link between sovereignty and power has been emphasised by many authors, following the example of Raymond Aron, demonstrating in passing that the affirmation of sovereignty is not incompatible with the idea of democracy, since even within democratic regimes there remains the need to have 'a person or a group of persons who assume sole responsibility for the exercise of political authority', to take up a formula of Hans Morgenthau.[12] Sovereignty cannot be absolute or indivisible into several political units. Still, it is nevertheless a fundamental element of power. Conversely, power is manifested by, among other things, the ability to make the other accept at least a partial surrender of its sovereign autonomy. The idea of recognition is also essential in the definition of sovereign autonomy. While sovereignty alone can be legally accepted (in this sense, all decolonised states are now sovereign), sovereign autonomy refers to a degree of freedom in the elaboration of policy as well as to a degree of recognition of its legitimacy. At a time when many states are sacrificing part of this sovereign autonomy on the altar of globalisation, the ability of the government to maintain a popular and

---

12   Aron, *Paix et guerre entre les nations*, 725.

legitimate image is the *sine qua non for* mobilising all possible resources in the fulfilment of its foreign policy ambitions.

In the case of Morocco, order is subject to a single, supreme and recognised legitimate authority. I will not stop repeating this. The most recent example that illustrates this historical configuration is that of the waves of contestation in 2011: the monarchy emerged strengthened from the Arab Spring. The government has embodied the reformer's role and shown remarkable resilience in the face of destabilisation attempts. In fact, the new constitution, while contributing to the liberalisation and democratisation of the regime, strengthened the executive power of the monarch, as well as his legitimacy, as the King was very much a part of the change process. This trend has strengthened the Moroccan regime's legitimacy at the international level. It is illustrated first in the state's ability to not completely surrender to attempts to import external models while not being perceived as a protest state. The nature of the link between sovereign autonomy and power was also manifested in the ability of the sovereign to mobilise and federate new actors, in addition to the government, in the conduct of the Africa policy, such as the private sector and brotherhood networks, just as this policy attracted the support of the public opinion. This sovereign autonomy is also, at the international level, a guarantee of policy implementation. It reinforces the idea that a declared ambition will indeed be pursued, even if it takes time.

On the other hand, diplomatic autonomy means the capacity of the state to resist the influence of foreign powers in the choice of its diplomatic orientations in order to be able to satisfy all or part of its interests. Diplomatic autonomy is similar to strategic autonomy as defined in the field of defence, i.e. the autonomy of military means with a training capacity. It therefore refers to the autonomy of diplomatic means with the same training capacity applied to foreign policy, i.e. the adhesion and support of several actors to the proposals formulated by the state on the international scene. Finally, it refers to non-dependence on an alliance system or on protecting partners to satisfy interests considered vital.

Morocco has reached a median degree of diplomatic autonomy, visible first in the evolution of the French–Moroccan relationship, which, as recalled above, has evolved towards a compromise alliance.

The degree of dependence was thus minimised by the increase in the interdependence between the two countries. The assertion of autonomy in diplomatic orientations was manifested through the conditions of elaboration and conduct of this Africa policy and, more recently, through the Asian orientation of foreign policy. Finally, the leadership capacity was illustrated by the adherence of a certain number of countries to the golden-mean Islam advocated by

Morocco and the latter's participation in the religious training courses organised within the Kingdom.

Finally, in terms of identity, medianity refers to the role identity as constructed and projected by Morocco on the international scene. Its quest for legitimacy and recognition has progressively pushed it to define and assert its role identity, notably around the 'golden mean' notion. In addition to officially serving as a definition of religious identity, the golden mean can also characterise a diplomatic positioning. The search for a compromise between the lack of material or relational resources on the one hand, and the projection of new ambitions based on the assurance of autonomy on the other, implies, for a median power such as Morocco, seeking the role of bridge, mediator or moderator. This posture is visible in the strong interest in tripartite cooperation, the affirmation of the moderate character of political values and the affirmation of the Kingdom's geo-cultural identity. The specificity of this posture is that Morocco has the characteristics of a 'small state'[13] while having the foreign policy ambitions of a 'middle power.'[14] An opening suggested by this work is that a comparative analysis is necessary to complete the study and demonstrate the relevance of the concept of median power, both in its specificities and in its application to the Moroccan case.

In conclusion, Morocco's Africa policy, in addition to being a manifestation of its new ambitions, has effectively reinforced its status as a power. To say that Morocco is an African power is therefore no longer a figure of speech or a political slogan but an acknowledgement of a real trend that can be observed in the continent's international relations. Both at the level of its identity and in its political relations with other African states, the Kingdom has been able to seize the *kairos*, that decisive moment which, like the strategic decision in battle, represents the opportunity for favourable action. In an Africa on the move, on the verge of a historic turning point in its international relations, Morocco's foreign policy has opportunely placed the country at the heart of this new destiny.

---

13   Jeanne A.K Hey, *Small States in World Politics: Explaining Foreign Policy Behavior*, (Boulder: Lynne Rienner Pub, 2003).
14   Jordaan, "The concept of a middle power in international relations".

APPENDIX 1

State Visits of Mohammed VI Abroad, 2000–2016

Date of visit	Country
2016 (May)	China
2016 (April)	Saudi Arabia and UAE
2016 (March)	Russia
2015 (December)	UAE
2015 (November)	France
2015 (February)	France
2015 (May–June)	Côte d'Ivoire
2015 (May–June)	Gabon
2015 (May–June)	Guinea-Bissau
2015 (May–June)	Senegal
2015 (May)	Saudi Arabia
2014 (May)	Tunisia
2014 (March)	Gabon
2014 (March)	Guinea-Conakry
2014 (February)	Côte d'Ivoire
2014 (February)	Mali
2013 (November)	United States
2013 (September)	Mali
2013 (September)	Senegal
2013 (September)	Côte d'Ivoire
2013 (September)	Gabon
2012 (November)	Hawaii
2012 (May)	France
2009 (April)	Equatorial Guinea
2006 (November)	Senegal
2006 (February–March)	Democratic Republic of Congo
2006 (February–March)	Republic of Congo
2006 (February–March)	The Gambia
2005	Japan
2005 (July)	Niger
2005 (April)	Singapore

(*cont.*)

Date of visit	Country
2005 (February–March)	Burkina Faso
2005 (February–March)	Mauritania
2005 (February–March)	Senegal
2005 (February–March)	Gabon
2004 (November–December)	Argentina
2004 (November–December)	Peru
2004 (November–December)	Brazil
2004 (November–December)	Chile
2004 (November–December)	Dominican Republic
2004 (November–December)	Mexico
2004	Egypt
2004 (June)	Senegal
2004 (June)	Niger
2004 (June)	Benin
2004 (June)	Cameroon
2004 (January)	UAE
2003	Malaysia
2003 (June)	Mauritania
2003	Egypt
2002 (September)	South Africa
2002	Jordan
2002	Russia
2002 (September)	Gabon
2002	Kuwait
2002	Syria
2002	Lebanon (Arab Summit)
2002 (June)	Qatar
2002	Thailand
2002 (February)	China
2002 (January)	Saudi Arabia
2001 (January)	Cameroon
2001	Senegal
2001 (September)	Mauritania
2001 (February)	India
2000	Egypt

(cont.)

Date of visit	Country
2000	Italy
2000 **(March)**	France

SOURCE: PREPARED BY THE AUTHOR BASED ON MAP PRESS RELEASES.

APPENDIX 1

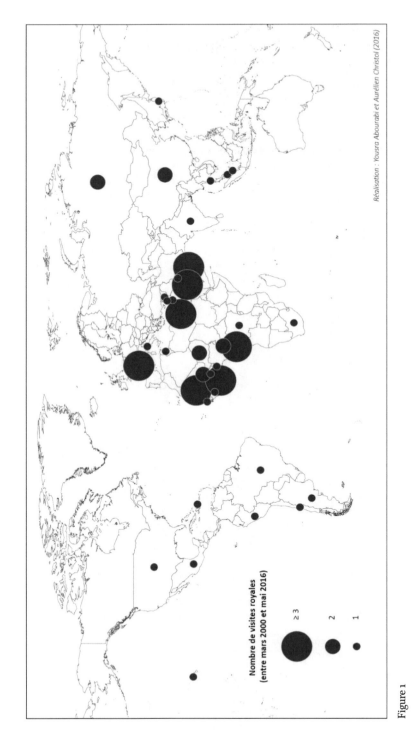

Figure 1
SOURCE: DRAWN BY THE AUTHOR

APPENDIX 2

The King's Speeches, 1999–2015: Statistics

Year	Number of messages and speeches
2015	11
2014	20
2013	52
2012	16
2011	11
2010	17
2009	17
2008	25
2007	16
2006	11
2005	25
2004	26
2003	26
2002	21
2001	31
2000	57
1999	25

SOURCE: PREPARED BY THE AUTHOR BASED ON THE MAP WEBSITE AND THE OFFICIAL PORTAL OF THE KINGDOM (MAROC.MA).

APPENDIX 3

FDI to Morocco (1) and (2)

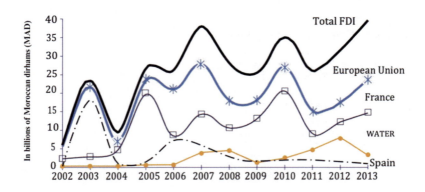

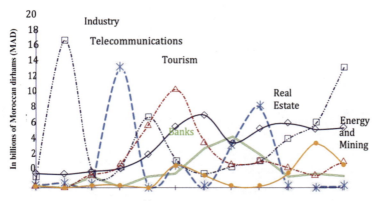

FIGURE 2 FDI to Morocco (1)
SOURCE: OFFICE DES CHANGES; FDI IN MOROCCO BY COUNTRY AND SECTOR. *BUDGET BILL FOR THE FINANCIAL YEAR 2015*, REPORT, RABAT, MINISTRY OF ECONOMY AND FINANCE, DIRECTORATE OF FINANCIAL STUDIES AND FORECASTING, 2015

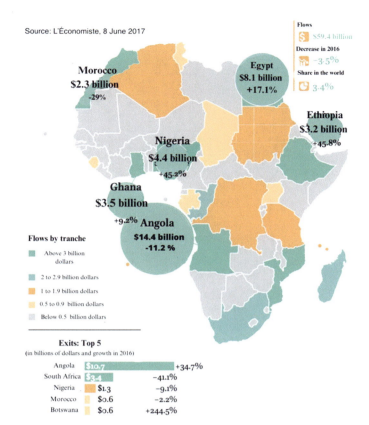

FIGURE 3   FDI to Morocco (2)

APPENDIX 4

Map of 'Greater Morocco'

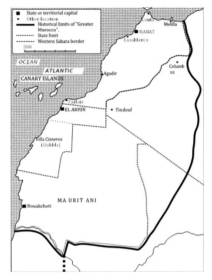

FIGURE 4
SOURCE: BUGWARABI, NICODEME, LA POLITIQUE SUDSAHARIENNE DU MAROC DE À 1956–1984, THÈSE DE DOCTORAT, PARIS, FRANCE: UNIVERSITÉ PANTHÉON-SORBONNE, P. 1997, 467

APPENDIX 5

Countries that Have Withdrawn Their Recognition of the RASD

Country	Date of withdrawal of recognition
Jamaica	14 September 2016
Suriname	9 March 2016
Paraguay	3 January 2014
Panama	20 November 2013 (resumed in 2016)
Haiti	11 October 2013
Saint Vincent and the Grenadines	13 February 2013
Barbados	12 February 2013
Zambia	3 March 2011
Papua New Guinea	3 April 2011
Burundi	25 October 2010
Saint Christopher and Nevis	16 August 2010
Antigua and Barbuda	12 August 2010
Grenada	11 August 2010
Commonwealth of Dominica	22 June 2010
Guinea-Bissau	30 March 2010
Malawi	16 September 2008
Seychelles	18 March 2008
Cape Verde	27 July 2007
Cambodia	14 August 2006
Chad	17 March 206
Madagascar	6 April 2005
Albania	10 November 2004
Serbia and Montenegro	October 2004
Ecuador	June 2004
Sierra Leone	2003
Dominican Republic	2002
Honduras	2002
Colombia	2000
Costa Rica	2000
Vanuatu	7 September 2000

(cont.)

Country	Date of withdrawal of recognition
Kiribati	3 September 2000
Tuvalu	3 September 2000
Nauru	3 September 2000
Liberia	1997
Swaziland	1997
Peru	1996
Burkina Faso	1996
Saint Lucia	1989

SOURCE: PREPARED BY THE AUTHOR FROM MULTIPLE SOURCES.

APPENDIX 6

Map of Diplomatic Postures regarding the Status of Moroccan Western Sahara

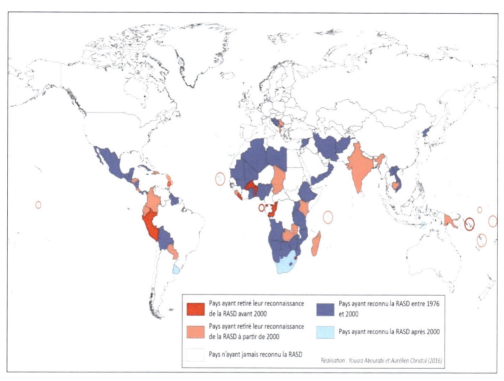

FIGURE 5   SOURCE: PREPARED BY THE AUTHOR

APPENDIX 7

Export of French War Material to Morocco (2008–2014)

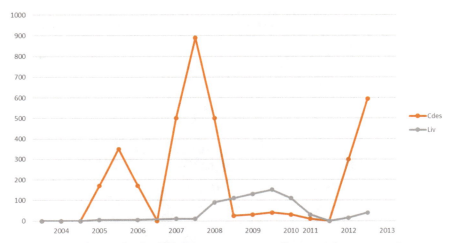

FIGURE 6 Evolution of orders/deliveries 2004–2013 in million euros (current euros)
SOURCE: RAPPORT AU PARLEMENT SUR 2014 LES EXPORTATIONS D'ARMAMENT DE LA FRANCE, PARIS, MINISTERE DE LA DEFENSE, 2014.

APPENDIX 8

Moroccan FDI in Africa (1)

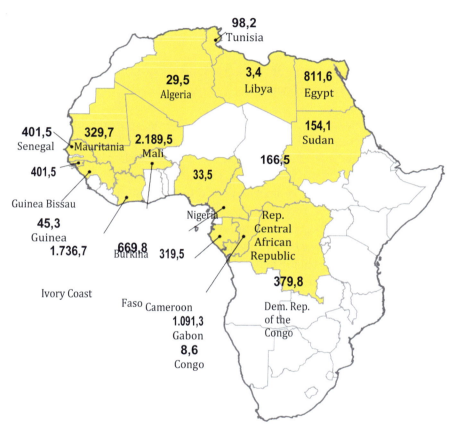

FIGURE 7   *Note*: 75% of the flows (in millions of DH) are concentrated in six countries.
SOURCE: 'MOROCCAN FDI IN AFRICA 41 BILLION DH INVESTED IN FIVE YEARS', THE ECONOMIST, 27 MARCH 2014.

APPENDIX 9

Legitimisation Framework for the Africa Policy: Example of a Document on South–South Cooperation

Source: 'Morocco, a country of solidarity: South–South cooperation', Ministry of Foreign Affairs and Cooperation

Morocco has always had close and deep ties with the countries of the South, especially those of sub-Saharan Africa.

As it has opened up to the world, Morocco has established cooperative relations with the countries of the Continent in various sectors. In this case the key sectors which constitute the backbone of this cooperation are those such as trade, fishing, transport, agriculture, training and health.

Morocco's African preoccupations were translated into action in the early years of its independence by the organisation, in 1960, of the Casablanca Conference under the aegis of the late S.M. Mohammed V, which brought together the main African leaders. These steps were crowned with great success and led to the creation, in 1962 in Addis Ababa, of the former Organisation of African Unity (OAU).

Morocco has therefore made it its duty to integrate the defence of African causes into its foreign policy. It is also committed to meeting the legitimate expectations of the continent's peoples for development that meets their expectations and aspirations.

Historically, the age-old links between Morocco and African countries reflect its roots in the continent, hence Morocco's duty of solidarity towards its brothers in the South in the development effort, as evidenced by the holding in Morocco of several conferences on African development.

Since 1983, Morocco has strengthened its position on the continent, maintaining exemplary political relations with most countries and conducting supportive and active South–South cooperation.

Morocco's commitment to South–South cooperation has been expressed at the highest level of the state. It is reflected in the actions of His Majesty King Mohammed VI, since his inauguration, to advocate active solidarity with sub-Saharan Africa.

His Majesty King Mohammed VI has thus increased his visits to several African countries, introducing a new aspect to Morocco's cooperation with

African countries, that of cooperation in the field of human development, in addition to sectoral cooperation in several areas.

Morocco has taken a series of concrete measures in terms of financial assistance. Thus, His Majesty King Mohammed VI decided, at the Africa–Europe Summit in 2000, to cancel all debts owed to Morocco's debts by the Least Developed African Countries (LDCs) and to offer duty-free and quota-free access to most of the export products from these countries. This measure has resulted in an increase in exports from these countries to Morocco.

Convinced of its strategic interest, Morocco has made South–South cooperation the main thrust of its foreign policy and is working, through various means, to strengthen this cooperation at the regional and interregional levels.

It is in this spirit that Morocco joined the Community of Sahel–Saharan States (CEN–SAD) in 2001. Morocco, which is also mobilised to promote the development of Africa by advocating a renewed partnership, has shown its support for the New Partnership for Africa's Development (NEPAD-AUDA) in all international forums, as well as for the promotion of trade within the framework of the West African Economic and Monetary Union (WAEMU).

At the international level, Morocco has never ceased to advocate and support the issue of development in the countries of the South. Thus, during its presidency of the Group of 77 and China in 2003, Morocco reaffirmed its commitment to South–South cooperation, particularly in the direction of sub-Saharan Africa.

In this sense, Morocco organised in 2007, in Rabat, in partnership with the UNDP, the first African Conference on Human Development. This conference aimed to respond to Morocco's ambition to promote balanced and harmonious global human development, through the strengthening of South–South cooperation and the implementation of commitments made in various international forums, in particular those related to the MDGs.

In a speech addressed to the participants of this conference, His Majesty King Mohammed VI reaffirmed Morocco's position of placing the development of South–South cooperation at the top of its foreign policy priorities, particularly in Africa.

The Rabat Declaration, adopted at the end of the conference, stated the commitment of African leaders to promoting cooperation in the field of human development through their strategies and action plans at regional and sub-regional levels.

Morocco's efforts to give South–South cooperation a human face and solidarity are reflected in its constant commitment to the noble causes of peace and development, as well as in the solidarity it has always shown with the concerns of the countries of the South and their aspirations for progress and well-being.

APPENDIX 10

The Road Linking Morocco to West Africa

The opening of the Moroccan–Mauritanian borders in 2002, and construction of the missing section (Nouadhibou–Nouakchott) in 2005.

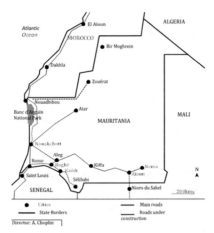

FIGURE 8
The road network in Mauritania
SOURCE: ALAIN ANTIL AND ARMELLE CHOPLIN, 'LE CHAÎNON MANQUANT. NOTES SUR LA ROUTE NOUAKCHOTT-NOUADHIBOU, DERNIER TRONÇON DE LA TRANSSAHARIENNE TANGER-DAKAR', *AFRIQUE CONTEMPORAINE*, OCTOBRE 1 NO. 2005, PP. 208, 115–126

APPENDIX 11

Moroccan FDI in Africa (2)

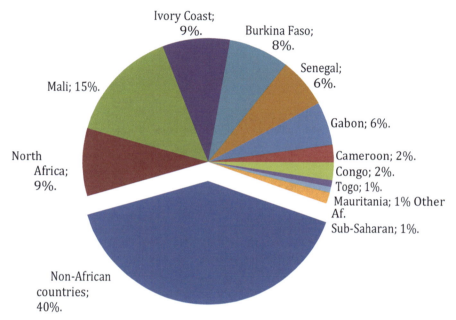

FIGURE 9   Geographical structure of Moroccan FDI flows abroad, 2003–2013 (preliminary figures)

Country	2003	2004	2005	2006	2007	2008	2009	2010	2011	2012	2013[a]
Mali	0	0	0	0	0	671	1647	1577	189	207	458
Ivory Coast	2	0	0	0	0	0	644	884	0	900	426
Togo	0	0	0	0	0	0	0	0	0	0	308
Maurice	0	0	0	0	0	0	0	0	0	0	123
Guinea	0	0	0	0	1	0	0	0	6	83	90
Cameroon	0	0	0	3	0	59	17	26	435	134	70
Central African Republic	0	0	0	0	0	0	0	0	39	31	53
Gabon	0	0	0	0	295	0	184	1271	19	62	24
Mauritania	0	0	0	0	0	2	1	79	98	32	24
Burkina Faso	0	0	0	2459	0	0	0	0	0	57	19

a   Preliminary figures

(*cont.*)

Country	2003	2004	2005	2006	2007	2008	2009	2010	2011	2012	2013
Congo	0	0	0	5	18	18	0	575	0	82	15
Ghana	0	0	0	0	0	0	5	0	0	0	10
Guinea-Bissau	0	0	0	0	0	0	0	0	0	0	7
Senegal	0	36	10	5	283	1431	297	12	2	21	
Guinea-Bissau	0	0	0	0	0	0	0	0	0	0	3
Ethiopia	0	0	0	0	0	0	0	0	0	0	2
Equatorial Guinea	0	0	0	9	16	0	0	0	1	1	0
Gambia	0	0	0	0	0	0	0	1	0	0	0
Nigeria	0	16	0	0	0	0	0	0	0	0	0
Total FDI in sub-Saharan Africa	2	52	10	2481	613	2181	2795	4424	788	1610	1637
Total FDI abroad	189	189	1511	4123	5082	4236	3839	5016	1710	3532	3015
Share of sub-Saharan Africa in % of total	1,3%	27,3%	0,6%	60,2%	12,1%	51,5%	72,8%	88,2%	46,1%	45,6%	54,3%

SOURCE: *MOROCCO–AFRICA RELATIONS: THE AMBITION OF A 'NEW FRONTIER'*, REPORT, RABAT, MINISTRY OF ECONOMY AND FINANCE, DIRECTORATE OF FINANCIAL STUDIES AND FORECASTING, 2014

APPENDIX 12

AU Motion of 28 States for the Suspension of the RASD

Source: 'Motion on behalf of twenty-eight countries for the upcoming suspension of the ghostly RASD from the activities of the African Union', *Le Matin.ma*, July 182016.

'Full text of the motion addressed by His Excellency, Ali Bongo Ondimba, President of the Gabonese Republic, on behalf of Benin, Burkina Faso, Burundi, Cape Verde, Comoros, Congo, Côte d'Ivoire, Djibouti, Eritrea, Gabon, Gambia, Ghana, Guinea, Guinea-Bissau, Equatorial Guinea, Liberia, Libya, Central African Republic, Democratic Republic of Congo, Sao Tome and Principe, Senegal and Togo, Guinea, Guinea-Bissau, Central African Republic, Democratic Republic of Congo, Liberia, Libya, Sao Tome, Senegal, Seychelles, Sierra Leone, Somalia, Sudan, Swaziland, Togo, Zambia.

'Mr President, twenty-eight Heads of State,
A. Bearing in mind the genuine ideals of African construction;
B. Faithful to the principles and objectives of the African Union, notably the achievement of greater unity and solidarity among African States, the defence of their sovereignty and territorial integrity, the promotion of peace, security and stability on the Continent, the promotion of international cooperation, with due regard to the Charter of the United Nations, and the creation of appropriate conditions to enable the Continent to play its proper role in the world economy;
C. Regretting the absence of the Kingdom of Morocco from the bodies of the African Union, and aware of the particular circumstances in which the 'Sahrawi Arab Democratic Republic' was admitted to the OAU

'Welcoming the contents of the historic Message addressed by His Majesty King Mohammed VI, King of Morocco, to the current Chairman of the 27th AU Summit for distribution to the participating Heads of State and Government.

1. Welcome the decision of the Kingdom of Morocco, a founding member of the OAU and whose active contribution to the stability and development of the Continent is widely known, to join the African Union and intend to work for this legitimate return to take place as soon as possible;
2. Decide to act towards the suspension, in the near future, of the 'Sahrawi Arab Democratic Republic' from the activities of the African Union and

all its organs, in order to allow the AU to play a constructive role and to contribute positively to the efforts of the United Nations for a final settlement of the regional dispute over the Sahara.

'On behalf of these twenty-eight countries, I would ask you to include this motion in the documents of this Summit and to have it distributed to the Member States.

Please accept, Mr. President, the assurance of my highest consideration.'

APPENDIX 13

Trade with Africa

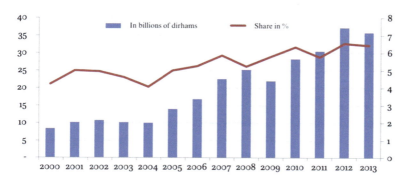

FIGURE 10 Morocco's trade with Africa (in billions of dirhams) source: office des changes, elaborations DEPF
SOURCE: *RELATIONS MAROC-AFRIQUE: L'AMBITION D'UNE 'NOUVELLE FRONTIÈRE'*, RAPPORT, RABAT, MINISTÈRE DE L'ÉCONOMIE ET DES FINANCES, DIRECTION DES ÉTUDES ET DES PRÉVISIONS FINANCIÈRES, 2014.

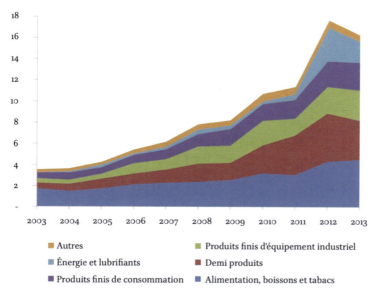

FIGURE 11 Moroccan exports to Africa (in billions of dirhams)
SOURCE: FOREIGN EXCHANGE OFFICES, DEPF ELABORATIONS

© KONINKLIJKE BRILL BV, LEIDEN, 2024 | DOI:10.1163/9789004546622_024

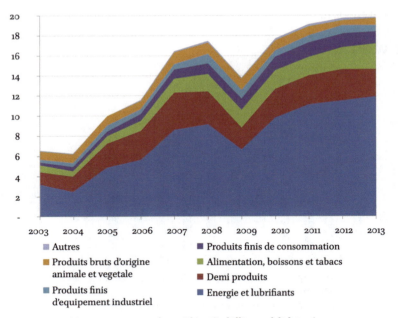

FIGURE 12   Moroccan imports from Africa (in billions of dirhams)
SOURCE: FOREIGN EXCHANGE OFFICES ELABORATIONS DEPF

APPENDIX 14

Transport Networks in Africa

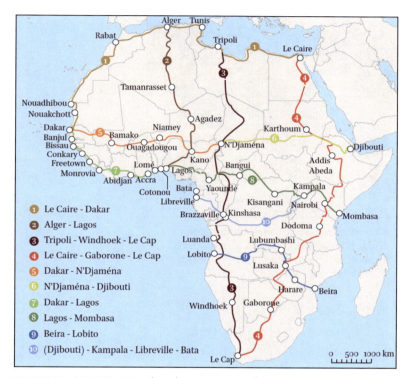

FIGURE 13   SOURCE: OCDE (2019), ACCESSIBILITÉ ET INFRASTRUCTURES DES VILLES FRONTALIÈRES, NOTES OUEST-AFRICAINES, N. 23, ÉDITIONS OCDE, PARIS, HTTPS://DOI.ORG/10.1787/256FCAA4-F

APPENDIX 15

Shipping Lines, Morocco–Africa

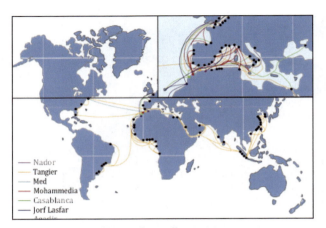

FIGURE 14   Main shipping lines affecting Moroccan ports
SOURCE: 'PORT STRATEGY ON THE HORIZON'
2030, FLAP: MINISTRY OF EQUIPMENT AND
TRANSPORT, 2011, P. 62

Bibliography

1 General Academic Sources

1.1 *Books and Theses*

Acharya, Amitav. *Rethinking Power, Institutions and Ideas in World Politics: Whose IR?* New York: Routledge, 2014.

Altoraifi, Adel. *Understanding the Role of State Identity in Foreign Policy Decision-Making: The Rise and Demise of Saudi-Iranian Rapprochement (1997–2009)*. London: The London School of Economics and Political Science, 2012.

Anholt, Simon. *Competitive Identity: The New Brand Management for Nations, Cities and Regions*. Basingstoke: Palgrave Macmillan, 2006.

Aron, Raymond. *Paix et guerre entre les nations*. Paris: Calmann-Lévy, 1962.

Aron, Raymond. *De Giscard à Mitterrand: 1977–1983*. Fallois, 2005.

Badie, Bertrand. *Un Monde Sans Souveraineté: Les États Entre Ruse et Responsabilité*. Fayard, 1999.

Balzacq, Thierry, and Frédéric Ramel, eds. *Traité de Relations Internationales*. Paris: Les Presses de Sciences Po.

Battistella, Dario, Franck Petiteville, Marie-Claude Smouts, and Pascal Vennesson. *Dictionnaire des Relations Internationales, 3rd edition*. Paris: Dalloz, 2012.

Beaufre, André. *Introduction à la Stratégie*. Paris: Armand Colin, Pluriel, 1963.

Bejar, Yosra. *La Valeur Informelle du Capital Immatériel: Application aux Entreprises Technologiques Nouvellement Introduites En Bourse (1997–2004)*. Thesis, Université Paris Dauphine–Paris IX, 2006.

Bevir, Mark, Oliver J. Daddow, and Ian Hall. *Interpreting Global Security*. London, New York: Routledge, 2014.

Bitterling, David. *L'invention du Pré Carré: Construction de l'Espace Français Sous l'Ancien Régime*. Paris: Albin Michel, 2009.

Booth, Ken, and Nicholas J. Wheeler. *The Security Dilemma: Fear, Cooperation and Trust in World Politics*. New York: Palgrave Macmillan, 2008.

Bourdieu, Pierre. *Interventions, 1961–2001: Science Sociale & Action Politique*. Marseille: Agone, 2002.

Braud, Philippe. *L'Émotion en Politique: Problèmes d'Analyse*. Presses de la Fondation Nationale des Sciences Politiques, 1996.

Bravo, Alain, Paul Friedel, and Alain Appriou. *La Sécurité Globale: Réalité, Enjeux et Perspectives*. Paris: CNRS Éditions, 2009.

Buzan, Barry, Ole Waever, and Jaap de Wilde. *Security: A New Framework for Analysis*. Boulder: Lynne Rienner Publisher, 1998.

Campbell, David. *Writing Security: United States Foreign Policy and the Politics of Identity, Revised edition*. Minneapolis: Univ Of Minnesota Press, 1998

Cardon, Dominique. *La Démocratie Internet: Promesses et Limites*. Paris: Seuil, 2010.

Carron de La Carrière, Guy. *La Diplomatie Économique: Le Diplomate et Le Marché*. Paris: Economica, 1998.

Clausewitz, Carl Von. *On War*. Paris: Éditions de Minuit, 1959.

Commission on Human Security, ed. *Human Security Now: Report of the Commission on Human Security*. Paris: Presses de Sciences Po, 2003.

Cooper, Andrew F., ed. *Niche Diplomacy: Middle Powers After the Cold War*. New York: Palgrave Macmillan, 1997.

Coutau-Bégarie, Hervé, and Martin Motte. *Approches de la Géopolitique: De l'Antiquité au XXIe Siècle*. Paris: Economica Institut de Stratégie Comparée, 2013.

Dark, K.R., ed. *Religion and International Relations*. New York, Basingstoke: Palgrave Macmillan, 2000.

Devin, Guillaume. *Sociologie des Relations Internationales*. Paris: La Découverte, 2013.

Dunn, Kevin C., and Timothy M. Shaw, eds. *Africa's Challenge to International Relations Theory*. Palgrave Macmillan, 2013.

Eckert, Denis, and Vladimir Kolossov. *La Russie: Un Exposé pour Comprendre, un Essai pour Réfléchir*. Flammarion, 1999.

Finnemore, Martha. *National Interests in International Society*. New York: Cornell University Press, 1996.

Foucault, Michel. *Les Mots et Les Choses: Une Archéologie des Sciences Humaines*. Paris: Gallimard, 1990.

Freund, Julien. *The Essence of Politics*. Paris: Dalloz, 2003.

Hall, Todd H. *Emotional Diplomacy: Official Emotion on the International Stage*. Ithaca: Cornell University Press, 2015.

Hey, Jeanne A.K., ed. *Small States in World Politics: Explaining Foreign Policy Behavior*. Boulder: Lynne Rienner Pub, 2003.

Hurrelmann, A., S. Schneider, and J. Steffek, eds. *Legitimacy In An Age Of Global Politics*. Basingstoke: Palgrave Macmillan, 2007.

Jaffrelot, Christophe, Jean-Jacques Gabas, Bruno Losch, and Jérôme Sgard. *L'Enjeu Mondial: Les Pays Émergents*. Paris: Les Presses de Sciences Po, 2008.

Jervis, Robert. *The Logic of Images in International Relations*. Princeton, N.J., USA: Princeton University Press, 1970.

Jervis, Robert. *Perception and Misperception in International Politics*. Princeton, N.J.: Princeton University Press, 1976.

Keohane, Robert Owen. *Power and governance in a partially globalized world*. London; New York: Routledge, 2002

Keohane, Robert Owen. *After hegemony: cooperation and discord in the world political economy*. Princeton, Princeton University Press, 2005.

Kessler, Marie-Christine. *Les ambassadeurs*. Paris: Les Presses de Sciences Po, 2012.

Kherad, Rahim (ed.). *Sécurité humaine: théorie et pratique(s)*. In honour of Dean Dominique Breillat, international colloquium [5 and 6 February 2009, Faculty of Law and Social Sciences of Poitiers]. Paris: A. Pedone, 2010.

Koschut, Simon and Oelsner, Andrea (eds.). *Friendship and international relations*. Basingstoke: Palgrave Macmillan, 2014.

Kupchan, Charles A. *How Enemies Become Friends: The Sources of Stable Peace*. Princeton, Princeton University Press, 2012.

Lacoste, Yves. *Geopolitics: The Long History of Today*. New Edition. Paris: Larousse, 2009.

Macleod, Alex and O'Meara, Dan. *Theories Of International Relations: Contestations And Resistances*. Athena Publishing (CAN), 2010.

Merle, Marcel. *Sociologie des relations internationales*. Paris: Dalloz, 1982.

Mezran, Karim K. *Negotiation and Construction of National Identities*. Boston, Martinus Nijhoff Publishers, 2007.

Nye, Joseph S. *Soft Power: The Means to Success in World Politics*. New York, PublicAffairs, 2004.

Nye, Joseph S. *The Future of Power*. New York, PublicAffairs, 2011.

Petito, Fabio and Hatzopoulos, Pavlos (eds.). *Religion in International Relations. The Return from Exile*. Basingstoke: Palgrave Macmillan, 2003.

Potter, Evan H. *Branding Canada: Projecting Canada's Soft Power through Public Diplomacy*. Montreal, McGill-Queen's University Press, 2009.

Rothstein, Robert L. *Alliances and small powers*. Institute of war and peace studies, New York, Columbia University Press, 1968.

Schmitt, Carl. *La notion de politique*. Paris: Flammarion, 1992.

Sindjoun, Luc. *Sociologie des relations internationales africaines*. Paris: Karthala, 2002.

Strange, Susan. *States and Markets*. New York, Blackwell Publishers, 1988.

Telhami, Shibley and Barnett, Michael N. *Identity and Foreign Policy in the Middle East*. Cornell University Press, 2002.

Thomas, Scott M. *The Global Resurgence of Religion and the Transformation of International Relations*. Basingstoke: Palgrave Macmillan, 2005.

Vassort-Rousset, Brigitte (ed.). *Building Sustainable Couples in International Relations*. London: Palgrave Macmillan, 2014.

Voss, James F. and Sylvan, Donald A. *Problem representation in foreign policy decision making*. Cambridge, Cambridge University Press, 1998.

Wendt, Alexander. *Social Theory of International Politics*. Cambridge, UK; New York: Cambridge University Press, 1999.

1.2   *Journal Articles and Book Chapters*

Acharya, Amitav. "Globalisation and Sovereignty: A Reassessment of their Relationship." *International Journal of Comparative Politics* 8 (2001): 383–394.

Albert, Mathias, and Barry Buzan. "Securitization, Sectors and Functional Differentiation." *Security Dialogue* 42, no. 4–5 (2011): 413–425.

Allison, Graham T., and Philip D. Zelikow. "The Essence of Decision Making: The Rational Actors Model." *Cultures & Conflicts* (March 2000): 36.

Aronczyk, Melissa. "Research in Brief: How to Do Things with Brands: Uses of National Identity." *Canadian Journal of Communication Corporation* 34 (2009): 291–296.

Bach, Daniel C. "Regionalisms, Regionalisation and Globalisation." In *Le Politique en Afrique—État des débats et pistes de recherche*, 343–361. Paris: Karthala, 2009.

Balzacq, Thierry. "La Sécurité: Définitions, Secteurs et Niveaux d'Analyse." *Fédéralisme Regionalism* (2003/2004): 4. Accessed online.

Balzacq, Thierry. "The Three Faces of Securitization: Political Agency, Audience and Context." *European Journal of International Relations* 11, no. 2 (January 6, 2005): 171–201.

Balzacq, Thierry, and Frédéric Ramel, eds. "La France." In *Traité de Relations Internationales*, 157–180. Paris: Les Presses de Sciences Po, 2013.

Boulding, K.E. "National Images and International Systems." *The Journal of Conflict Resolution* 3 (1959): 120–131.

Bourdieu, Pierre. "Sur le Pouvoir Symbolique." *Annales. Histoire, Sciences Sociales* 32 (1977): 405–411.

Braspenning, Thierry. "Constructivism and Reflexivism in the Theory of International Relations." *Annuaire Français des Relations Internationales* III (2002): 314–329.

Braudel, Fernand. "Histoire et Sciences Sociales: La Longue Durée." *Annales. Histoire, Sciences Sociales* 13 (1958): 725–753.

Criekemans, David. "Rehabilitation and Renovation in Geopolitical Thought." *Political Space. Online Journal of Political Geography and Geopolitics* (February 2011): 12.

Darviche, Mohammad-Saïd. "Exiting the Nation-State: Juan Linz with and beyond Max Weber." *International Journal of Comparative Politics* 13, no. 13 (September 1, 2006): 115–127.

David, Charles-Philippe, and Jean-François Rioux. "Le concept de sécurité humaine." In *La sécurité humaine : une nouvelle conception des relations internationales*, edited by Jean-François Rioux. Paris: l'Harmattan, Collection Raoul-Dandurand, 2002.

Dessler, David. "What's at stake in the agent-structure debate?" *International Organization* 43, no. 3 (June 1989): 441–473.

Dupret, Baudouin, Enrique Klaus, and Jean-Noël Ferrié. "Derrière le voile. Analyse d'un réseau dialogique égyptien." *Droit et Société* 68 (2008): 153–179.

Dussouy, Gérard. "Vers une géopolitique systémique." *Revue internationale et stratégique* 47, no. 3 (2002): 53–66.

Edobé, Joseph-Vincent, and Frank Ebogo. "Le Cameroun." In *Traité de relations internationales*, Paris: Les Presses de Sciences Po, 2013, 89–112.

Grosser, Pierre. "De l'usage de l'Histoire dans les politiques étrangères." In *Politique étrangère : nouveaux regards*, edited by Frédéric Charillon. Paris: Presses de Sciences Po, 2002, 361–388.

Hall, Todd. "An Unclear Attraction: A Critical Examination of Soft Power as an Analytical Category." *The Chinese Journal of International Politics* 3, no. 2 (June 2010): 189–211.

Hey, Jeanne. "Introducing Small State Foreign Policy." In *Small States in World Politics*, edited by Jeanne Hey. Lynne Rienner, Boulder, 2003, 1–11.

Honneth, Axel. "La reconnaissance entre États." *Cultures & Conflits* 87 (December 2012): 27–36.

Hopf, Ted. "The Promise of Constructivism in International Relations Theory." *International Security* 23, no. 1 (July 1998): 171–200.

Hopf, Ted. "The logic of habit in International Relations." *European Journal of International Relations* 16, no. 4 (January 2010): 539–561.

Jordaan, Eduard. "The concept of a middle power in international relations: distinguishing between emerging and traditional middle powers." *Politikon* 30, no. 1 (2003): 165–181.

Katzenstein, Peter J. "Small States and Small States Revisited." *New Political Economy* 8, no. 1 (March 2003): 9–30.

Kempf, Olivier. "Le Maréchal de Vauban, premier géopoliticien français?" *Stratégique* 99 (January 2010): 35–50.

Kessler, Marie-Christine. "La politique étrangère comme politique publique." In *Politique étrangère : nouveaux regards*, edited by Frédéric Charillon. Paris: Presses de Sciences Po, 2002, 167–192.

Kubálková, Vendulka. "Towards an International Political Theology." *Millennium— Journal of International Studies* 29, no. 3 (January 2000): 675–704.

Laïdi, Zaki. "Négociations internationales: la fin du multilatéralisme." *Esprit* 11 (November 2013): 108–117.

Lambert, Alain and Migaud, Didier. "La loi organique relative aux lois de finances (LOLF): levier de la réforme de l'État." *Revue française d'administration publique* 117, no. 1 (March 1, 2006): 11–14.

Lord, Carnes. "Diplomatie publique et soft power." *Politique américaine* 3, no. 3 (November 15, 2012): 61–72.

Löwenheim, Oded and Heimann, Gadi. "Revenge in International Politics." *Security Studies* 17, no. 4 (December 9, 2008): 685–724.

Luttwak, Edward N. "Power relations in the new economy." *Survival* 44, no. 2 (June 1, 2002): 7–18.

Macleod, Alex, Masson, Isabelle et Morin, David. "Identité nationale, sécurité et la théorie des relations internationales." *Études internationales* 35, no. 1 (2004): 7–24.

McEwan, Cheryl and Mawdsley Emma. "Trilateral Development Cooperation: Power and Politics in Emerging Aid Relationships." *Development and Change* 43, no. 6 (November 1, 2012): 1185–1209.

Öniş, Ziya and Kutlay, Mustafa. "The dynamics of emerging middle-power influence in regional and global governance: the paradoxical case of Turkey." *Australian Journal of International Affairs*, June 21, 2016. Accessed [online].

Petiteville, Franck. "De la politique étrangère comme catégorie d'analyse des relations internationales." *Critique internationale* 20, no. 3 (2003): 59–63.

Powell, Robert. "Absolute and Relative Gains in International Relations Theory." *The American Political Science Review* 85, no. 4 (1991): 1303–1320.

Putnam, Robert D. "Diplomacy and Domestic Politics: The Logic of Two-Level Games." *International Organization* 42, no. 3 (July 1, 1988): 427–460.

Ramel, Frédéric. "Représentations, images et politique étrangère: anciens débats, nouveaux outils." *Revue française de science politique* 50, no. 3 (2000): 531–538.

Ripley, Brian. "Psychology, Foreign Policy, and International Relations Theory." *Political Psychology* 14, no. 3 (1993): 403–416.

Simplicio, Francisco. "South-South Development Cooperation: A Contemporary Perspective." In *South-South Cooperation*, edited by Renu Modi, Palgrave Macmillan UK, International Political Economy Series, 2011, 19–41.

Smith, Karen. "International Relations in South Africa: A Case of 'Add Africa and Stir'?" *Politikon* 40, no. 3 (December 1, 2013): 533–544.

Snidal, Duncan. "Rational Choice and International Relations." In *Handbook of International Relations*, London, SAGE Publications, 2002, 73–94.

Tang, Shiping. "International System, not International Structure: Against the Agent—Structure Problématique in IR." *The Chinese Journal of International Politics* 7, no. 4 (January 12, 2014): 483–506.

Vernant, Jacques. "La recherche en politique étrangère." *Politique étrangère* 33, no. 1 (1968): 9–17.

Wendt, Alexander. "The Agent-Structure Problem in International Relations Theory." International Organization 41, no. 3 (July 1, 1987): 335–370.

Wendt, Alexander. "Anarchy is what States Make of it: The Social Construction of Power Politics." International Organization 46, no. 2 (April 1, 1992): 391–425.

1.3 *Studies*

Abdenur, Adriana E. *The Strategic Triad: Form and Content in Brazil's Triangular Cooperation Practices*. International Affairs Working Paper, New York University, 2007.

Charillon, Frédéric. "La Francophonie comme profondeur stratégique?" In *Francophonie et profondeur stratégique*, edited by Bagayoko Niagalé and Ramel Frédéric. Institut de Recherche Stratégique de l'École Militaire, coll. Études, no. 26, 2013, 5–9.

Gray, Colin S. *Hard Power and Soft Power: The Utility of Military Force as an Instrument of Policy in the 21st Century*. Carlisle: Strategic Studies Institute, US Army War College, 2012.

Holtom, Paul, Bromley, Mark, Wezeman, Pieter D., and Wezeman, Siemon T. *Trends in International Arms Transfers*. SIPRI Fact Sheet, SIPRI, March 2013.

Ramel, Frédéric. *Recherche ennemi désespérément. Origines, essor et apport des approches perceptuelles en relations internationales.* Chaire Raoul-Dandurand en études stratégiques et diplomatiques UQAM, Quebec, Cahiers Raoul Dandurand, no. 4, 2001.

2 Academic Sources on Morocco and Africa

2.1 *Books and Theses*

Abitol, Michel. *Histoire du Maroc.* Paris: Perrin, 2009.

Abourabi, Yousra. *Maroc.* Bruxelles: De Boeck, 2019.

Abusitta, Abdelgadir. "La dimension africaine dans la politique étrangère libyenne 1969–2002." Thèse, Université d'Auvergne–Clermont-Ferrand I, 2012.

Adebajo, Adekeye and Mazrui, Ali A. *The Curse of Berlin: Africa After the Cold War.* Oxford University Press, 2014.

Arrigoni, Michael. "La dimension militaire du conflit au Sahara occidental: enjeux et stratégies." Thèse, Université de Reims, 1997.

Ayache, Germain. *Études d'histoire marocaine.* Rabat, Maroc: SMER, 1979.

Bat, Jean-Pierre. *Le syndrome Foccart: La politique française en Afrique, de 1959 à nos jours.* Paris: Folio, 2012.

Belhaj, Abedessamad. *La dimension islamique dans la politique étrangère du Maroc.* Louvain: Presses univ. de Louvain, 2009.

Ben' Achir, Bou'Azza et Schérer, René. *Esclavage, diaspora africaine et communautés noires du Maroc.* Paris: L'Harmattan, 2005.

Benjelloun, Thérèse. *Visages de la diplomatie marocaine depuis 1844.* Casablanca: Eddif, 1991.

Bennani-Chraïbi, Mounia. *Scènes et coulisses de l'élection au Maroc : les législatives 2002.* Paris: Karthala, 2005.

Bensaâd, Ali (dir.). *Le Maghreb à l'épreuve des migrations subsahariennes : immigration sur émigration.* Paris: Karthala, 2009.

Berramdane, Abdelkhaleq. *Le Maroc et l'Occident : 1800–1974.* Paris: Karthala, 1987.

Berramdane, Abdelkhaleq. *Le Sahara occidental, enjeu maghrébin.* Paris: Karthala, 1992.

Boubkraoui, Lhouceine. "Essai de formalisation du fonctionnement de l'économie marocaine", PhD diss., Université Paris I Panthéon-Sorbonne, 1983.

Brahime, Abdeljebbar. "Les facteurs d'élaboration de la politique étrangère au Maroc : étude de cas", PhD diss., Université Nanterre La Défense, 1984.

Bugwarabi, Nicodeme. "La politique sudsaharienne du Maroc de 1956 à 1984", PhD diss., Université Panthéon-Sorbonne, 1997.

Centre D'études Internationales (dir.). *Une décennie de réformes au Maroc : 1999–2009.* Paris, France: Karthala, 2009.

Del Sarto, Raffaella A. *Contested state identities and regional security in the Euro-Mediterranean area*. New York: Palgrave Macmillan, 2006.

El Hamel, Chouki. *Black Morocco a history of slavery, race, and Islam*. Cambridge: Cambridge University Press, African studies, 2013.

El Houdaïgui, Rachid. *La politique étrangère sous le règne de Hassan II : acteurs, enjeux et processus décisionnels*. Paris: L'Harmattan, 2003.

Faligot, Roger, Guisnel Jean et Kauffer Rémi. *Histoire politique des services secrets français : de la Seconde Guerre mondiale à nos jours*. Paris: La Découverte, 2013.

Fernández-Molina, Irene. *La política exterior de Marruecos en el reinado Mohamed VI (1999–2008): actores, discursos y proyecciones internas*. Madrid: Universidad Complutense de Madrid, 2013.

Fernandez-Molina, Irene. *Moroccan Foreign Policy under Mohammed VI, 1999–2014*. Routledge, 2015.

Foucher, Michel. *Frontières d'Afrique : Pour en finir avec un mythe*. Paris: CNRS, 2014.

Jouve, Marie-Hélène. "Effet et usage de l'opinion publique dans les relations franco-marocaines : la crise des années 1990–1991", Paris: Mémoire de D.E.A., Université de Paris I Panthéon-Sorbonne, 1991.

Kontchou Kouomegni, Augustin. *Le Système diplomatique africain : bilan et tendances de la première décennie*. Paris: A. Pedone, 1977.

Laroui, Abdallah. *Les Origines sociales et culturelles du nationalisme marocain : 1830–191*. Paris: La Découverte, 1977.

Lugan, Bernard. *Histoire du Maroc : des origines à nos jours*. Paris: Ellipses, 2011.

Marfaing, Laurence and Wippel, Stephen. *Les relations transsahariennes à l'époque contemporaine : un espace en constante mutation*. Paris: Karthala, 2004.

Misk Hassane Milacic, Slobodan. "Les relations bilatérales entre le Royaume chérifien et l'union soviétique 1956–1991 analyse combinatoire des jeux symboliques et enjeux matériels" PhD diss., Université Bordeaux 1, 1993.

Modi, Renu (dir.). *South-South Cooperation: Africa on the Centre Stage*. Berlin: Springer, 2011.

Moha, Édouard. *Histoire des relations franco-marocaines ou Les aléas d'une amitié*. Paris: Picollec, 1995.

Mokhefi, Mansouria and Antil, Alain. *Le Maghreb et son Sud : vers des liens renouvelés*. Paris: CNRS, 2012.

Mouline, Mohammed Nabil. *Le califat imaginaire d'Ahmad al-Mansûr légitimité, pouvoir et diplomatie au Maroc*. Paris: Presses Universitaires de France, Proche Orient, 2008.

Otayek, René. *La politique africaine de la Libye : 1969–1985*. Paris: Karthala, 1986.

Regragui, Ismaïl. *La diplomatie publique marocaine une stratégie de marque religieuse?* Paris: L'Harmattan, Histoire et perspectives méditerranéennes, 2013.

Rivet, Daniel. *Lyautey et l'institution du protectorat français au Maroc : 1912–1925 Tome II*. Paris: L'Harmattan, 1996.

Rivet, Daniel. *Histoire du Maroc*. Paris: Fayard, 2012.

Riziki, Mohamed Abdelaziz. *Sociologie de la diplomatie marocaine*. Paris: L'Harmattan, 2014.

Saaf, Abdallah (dir.). *Le Maroc et l'Afrique après l'indépendance*. Rabat: Université Mohammed v, Institut des Études Africaines, Actes de colloque, 1996.

Sambe, Bakary. *Islam Et Diplomatie : La Politique Africaine Du Maroc*. Gaithersburg: Phoenix Press International, 2011.

Steffen, Marfaing Laurence Wippel. *Les relations transsahariennes à l'époque contemporaine*. Paris: Karthala, 2003.

Tozy, Mohamed. *Monarchie et islam politique au Maroc*. Paris: Presses de Sciences Po, 1999.

Triaud, Jean-Louis and Robinson David. *La Tijâniyya : une confrérie musulmane à la conquête de l'Afrique*. Paris: Karthala, 2000.

Vermeren, Pierre. *Le Maroc de Mohammed vi: la transition inachevée*. Paris, France: La Découverte, 2011.

Villers, Gauthier de. *De Mobutu à Mobutu : trente ans de relations Belgique-Zaïre*. Bruxelles: De Boeck Supérieur, 1995.

Waterbury, John. *The Commander of the Faithful: The Moroccan Monarchy and its Elite*. Presses Universitaires de France, 1975.

Wu, Shiwei. "Les échanges commerciaux et la coopération économique entre la Chine et les pays méditerranéens occidentaux: Le modèle d'intégration transrégionales". Thesis, Université Pascal Paoli, 2015.

Zartman, Ira William. *International relations in the new Africa*. New York: Prentice-Hall, 1966.

2.2 *Academic Articles and Book Chapters*

Abourabi, Yousra. "La découverte de pétrole au large des Iles Canaries : un facteur de conflit entre le Maroc et l'Espagne?" Paris: Centre Interarmées de Concepts de Doctrines et d'Expérimentations, 2014.

Abourabi, Yousra. "Le Maghreb face au sahel : des tentatives de coopération sécuritaire à l'avènement de diplomaties religieuses." In Monde arabe ; entre transition et implosion, edited by Abidi Hasni, 330 pages. Paris: éditions Erick Bonnier, collection Encre d'Orient, 2015.

Abourabi, Yousra. "Les relations internationales du Maroc." In Le Maroc au Présent, edited by Dupret B. et al., 1017 pages. Centre Jacques Berque, Éditions de la Fondation Ibn Saoud, Casablanca, 2015.

Abourabi, Yousra. "Penser les relations internationales africaines à travers l'étude des régionalismes." Revue Française de Science Politique 67, no. 5 (2017): 931–945.

Alaoui, Hicham Ben Abdallah El. "L'autre Maroc." Pouvoirs, no. 145, no. 2 (April 1, 2013): 59–69.

Alioua, Mehdi. "Le Maroc, un carrefour migratoire pour les circulations euro-africaines?" Hommes et Migrations, no. 1303 (2013): 139–145.

Antil, Alain, and Choplin Armelle. "Le chaînon manquant. Notes sur la route Nouakchott-Nouadhibou, dernier tronçon de la transsaharienne Tanger-Dakar." Afrique contemporaine 208 (October 1, 2005): 115–126.

Augé, Benjamin. "Les nouveaux enjeux pétroliers de la zone saharienne." Hérodote 142 (September 23, 2011): 183–205.

Ayache, Germain. "Le sentiment national dans le Maroc du XIXe siècle." Revue Historique 130 (October 1968): 393–410.

Bach, Daniel C. "Nigeria's 'Manifest Destiny' in West Africa: Dominance without Power." Africa Spectrum 42, no. 2 (2007): 301–321.

Baghdzouz, Aomar. "Le Maghreb, le Sahara occidental et les nouveaux défis de sécurité." L'Année du Maghreb III (November 1, 2007): 523–546.

Bamba, Mamadou. "Mobilité des Musulmans ivoiriens au Maroc : entre formation islamique et tourisme religieux." In Migrants au Maroc, cosmopolitisme, présence d'étrangers et transformations sociales, edited by Nadia Khrouz et Nazarena Lanza, 72–80. Konrad Adenauer Stiftung, Centre Jacques Berque, Rabat, 2015.

Barre, Abdelaziz. "La politique marocaine de coopération en Afrique." In Le Maroc et l'Afrique après l'indépendance, edited by Abadallah Saaf, 57–68. Rabat: Université Mohammed V, Institut des Études Africaines, 1996.

Belhaj, Abdessamad. "L'usage politique de l'islam : l'universel au service d'un État. Le cas du Maroc." Recherches sociologiques et anthropologiques 37, no. 2 (April 15, 2007): 121–139.

Belkaïd, Akram. "La diplomatie algérienne à la recherche de son âge d'or." Politique étrangère 2 (Été, 2009): 337–344.

Benchemsi, Ahmed. "Mohammed VI, despote malgré lui." Pouvoirs 145, no. 2 (April 1, 2013): 19–29.

Bendourou, Omar. "La consécration de la Monarchie gouvernante." L'Année du Maghreb VIII (October 12, 2012): 391–404.

Benhima, Yassir. "Le Maroc à l'heure du monde (XVe – XVIIe siècle). Bilan clinique d'une historiographie (dé)connectée." L'Année du Maghreb 10 (July 1, 2014): 255–266.

Benjelloun Touimi, Brahim. "La présence de l'entreprise marocaine en Afrique : l'exemple de la BMCE Bank." In Annuaire marocain de la stratégie et des relations internationales, edited by Abdelhak Azzouzi, 145–160. Paris: L'Harmattan CMIESI, 2012.

Benkhalloul, Mohamed. "Le traité d'union maroco-libyen d'Oujda (13 août 1984) dans la presse marocaine de langue arabe." Annuaire de l'Afrique du Nord (CRESM) 23 (1986): 693–704.

Benkhattab, Abdelhamid. "Le rôle de la politique saharienne franquiste dans l'internationalisation de l'affaire du Sahara occidental." In Le différend saharien devant l'Organisation des Nations Unies, edited by Centre d'Études Internationales, 27–45. Paris: Karthala, 2011.

Berriane, Johara. "Les étudiants subsahariens au Maroc : des migrants parmi d'autres?" *Méditerranée. Revue géographique des pays méditerranéens / Journal of Mediterranean geography* 113 (December 31, 2009): 147–150.

Berriane, Johara. "La formation des élites subsahariennes au Maroc." In *Le Maghreb et son Sud : vers des liens renouvelés*, edited by Mansouria Mokhefi and Alain Antil, 213–231. Paris: CNRS éditions, 2012.

Berriane, Johara. "Intégration symbolique à Fès et ancrages sur l'ailleurs : Les Africains subsahariens et leur rapport à la zaouïa d'Ahmad al-Tijânî." *L'Année du Maghreb* 11 (December 23, 2014): 139–153.

Boilley, Pierre. "Géopolitique africaine et rébellions touarègues. Approches locales, approches globales (1960–2011)." *L'Année du Maghreb* VII (December 20, 2011): 151–162.

Bouhout, El Mellouki Riffi. "La politique marocaine de coopération avec l'Afrique Subsaharienne." In *Le Maroc et l'Afrique après l'indépendance*, edited by Abdallah Saaf, 57–86. Rabat, Morocco: Université Mohammed V, Publications de l'Institut des Études Africaines, 1996.

Bouzidi, Mohammed. "Le Maroc et l'Afrique sub-saharienne." *Annuaire de l'Afrique du Nord* 17 (1979): 87–111.

Brière, Sophie, and Andrea Martinez. "Changements et résistances en matière d'institutionnalisation de l'égalité entre les sexes : le cas du Maroc." *Recherches féministes* 24, no. 2 (2011): 153.

Catusse, Myriam. "Le 'social': une affaire d'État dans le Maroc de Mohammed VI." *Confluences Méditerranée* 78, no. 3 (September 1, 2011): 63–76.

Catusse, Myriam. "Au-delà de 'l'opposition à sa Majesté': mobilisations, contestations et conflits politiques au Maroc." *Pouvoirs* 145, no. 2 (April 1, 2013): 31–46.

Chaponnière, Jean-Raphaël. "Le basculement de l'Afrique vers l'Asie." *Afrique contemporaine* 234 (September 22, 2010): 25–40.

Chena, Salim. "L'Algérie : de la puissance idéologique à l'hégémonie sécuritaire." In *Le Maghreb et son Sud : vers des liens renouvelés*, edited by Mansouria Mokhefi and Alain Antil, 19–40. Paris: CNRS éditions, 2012.

Chena, Salim. "Le Maghreb après les indépendances : (re)définition, (re)composition, (re)construction." *L'Espace Politique* 18 (November 22, 2012): 2–15.

Chéneau-Loquay, Annie. "L'Afrique au seuil de la révolution des télécommunications." *Afrique contemporaine* 234 (September 22, 2010): 93–112.

Chikh, Slimane. "La politique africaine de l'Algérie." *Annuaire de l'Afrique du Nord* 17 (1979): 1–54.

Coyault, Bernard. "L'africanisation de l'Église évangélique au Maroc : revitalisation d'une institution religieuse et dynamiques d'individualisation." *L'Année du Maghreb* 11 (December 23, 2014): 81–103.

Coyault, Bernard. "Les églises de maison congolaises de Rabat : la participation du secteur informel à la pluralisation religieuse au Maroc." In *Migrants au Maroc, cosmopolitisme, présence d'étrangers et transformations sociales*, edited by Nadia Khrouz and Nazarena Lanza, 55–64. Rabat: Konrad Adenauer Stiftung, Centre Jacques Berque, 2015.

Cravinho, João Gomes, and Mohammad-Saïd Darviche. "Les relations post-coloniales portugaises." *Pôle Sud* 22 (2005): 89–100.

Crouzel, Ivan. "La 'renaissance africaine': un discours sud-africain?" *Politique africaine* 77 (November 15, 2012): 171–182.

Dafir, Amine. "La diplomatie économique marocaine en Afrique subsaharienne : réalités et enjeux." *Géoéconomie* 63, no. 4 (February 1, 2013): 73–83.

Daguzan, Jean-François. "La politique étrangère de l'Algérie : le temps de l'aventure?" *Politique étrangère* 3 (September 2, 2015): 31–42.

Dalle, Ignace. "Pierre Vermeren. Le Maroc de Mohammed VI. La transition inachevée." *Afrique contemporaine* 239, no. 3 (January 25, 2012): 154–156.

Darracq, Vincent. "Jeux de puissance en Afrique : le Nigeria et l'Afrique du Sud face à la crise ivoirienne." *Politique étrangère* 2 (June 29, 2011): 361–374.

Delafosse, Maurice. "Les débuts des troupes noires du Maroc." *Hespéris—Institut des Hautes Études Marocaines*, 1923: 1–12.

Desrues, Thierry, and Kirhlani, Said. "Dix ans de monarchie exécutive et citoyenne : élections, partis politiques et défiance démocratique." *L'Année du Maghreb* VI (December 17, 2010): 319–354.

Dris-Aït Hamadouche, Louisa. "L'Algérie et la sécurité au Sahel : lecture critique d'une approche paradoxale." *Confluences Méditerranée* 90, no. 3 (2014): 105.

Durand, Hubert. "La France a-t-elle une politique marocaine?" *Confluences Méditerranée* 23 (Autumn 1997): 171–177.

Elhamadi, Mohsine. "Modernisation du champs religieux au Maroc 1999–2009." In *Une décennie de réformes au Maroc (1999–2009)*, 117–142. Karthala, 2009.

Ellis, Stephen. "Africa after the Cold War: new patterns of government and politics." *Development and change* 27, no. 1 (1996): 1–28.

Fernández-Arias, Carlos. "Sahara Occidental : Un año después de Baker." *Política Exterior* 19, no. 107 (2005): 73–82.

Ferra, Francisco Santana. "Un 'espace phonique' lusophone à plusieurs voix ? Enjeux et jeux de pouvoir au sein de la Communauté des Pays de Langue portugaise (CPLP)." *Revue internationale de politique comparée* 14, no. 1 (2007): 95–129.

Ferrié, Jean-Noël. "Les limites d'une démocratisation par la société civile en Afrique du Nord." *Études et Documents du CEDEJ* 7 (2004).

Ferrié, Jean-Noël, and Dupret Baudouin. "La nouvelle architecture constitutionnelle et les trois désamorçages de la vie politique marocaine." *Confluences Méditerranée* 78, no. 3 (2011): 25.

Ferrié, Jean-Noël. "Dispositifs autoritaires et changements politiques. Les cas de l'Égypte et du Maroc." *Revue internationale de politique comparée* 19, no. 4 (April 29, 2013): 93–110.

Ferrié, Jean-Noël. "Démocratisation de l'Afrique du Nord et du Moyen-Orient : l'impossible accélération de l'histoire." In *Monde arabe, entre transition et implosion : les dynamiques internes et les influences externes*, 2015. Paris: E. Bonnier, impr.

García, Raquel Ojeda, and Collado, Ángela Suarez. "El Sáhara Occidental en el marco del nuevo proyecto de regionalización avanzada marroquí." *RIPS : Revista de Investigaciones Políticas y Sociológicas* 12, no. 2 (December 5, 2013): 89–108.

Gèze, François. "Armée et nation en Algérie : l'irrémédiable divorce?" *Hérodote* 116, no. 1 (2005): 175–203.

Goldsmith, Benjamin. "Imitation in International Relations: Analogies, Vicarious Learning, and Foreign Policy." *International Interactions* 29, no. 3 (July 2003): 237–267.

Grimaud, Nicole. "L'introuvable équilibre maghrébin." In *La Politique extérieure de Valéry Giscard d'Estaing*, edited by Samy Cohen and Marie-Claude Smouts, 323–347. Presses de la Fondation Nat. des Sciences Politiques, 1985.

Hamadouche, Louisa Dris-Aït. "L'Algérie face au 'printemps arabe': l'équilibre par la neutralisation des contestations." *Confluences Méditerranée* 81 (July 17, 2012): 55–67.

Hassani-Idrissi, Mostafa. "Manuels d'histoire et identité nationale au Maroc." *Revue internationale d'éducation de Sèvres* 69 (September 1, 2015): 53–64.

Hibou, Béatrice. "La "décharge", nouvel interventionnisme." *Politique africaine* 1 (March 1999): 6–15.

Hillali, Mimoun. "Du tourisme et de la géopolitique au Maghreb : le cas du Maroc." *Hérodote* 127, no. 4 (November 27, 2007): 47–63.

Hugon, Philippe. "Les nouveaux acteurs de la coopération en Afrique." *International Development Policy | Revue internationale de politique de développement* 1 (March 1, 2010): 99–118.

Hugon, Philippe. "La crise va-t-elle conduire à un nouveau paradigme du développement?" *Mondes en développement* 150, no. 2 (July 12, 2010): 53–67.

Jacquemot, Pierre. "L'émergence de classes moyennes en Afrique." *Afrique contemporaine* 244 (February 18, 2013): 124–125.

Kaké, Ibrahima Baba. "L'aventure des Bukhara (prétoriens noirs) au Maroc au XVIIIe siècle." *Présence Africaine* 70 (June 1, 1969): 67–74.

Lamouri, Mohamed. "L'affaire du Sahara : de l'Organisation de l'Unité Africaine à l'Organisation des Nations Unies." In *Le différend saharien devant l'Organisation des Nations Unies*, edited by Centre d'études internationales, 65–79. Karthala, 2011.

Lanza, Nazarena. "Quelques enjeux du soufisme au Maroc : le tourisme religieux sénégalais et la construction d'un imaginaire sur l'amitié." In *Migrants au Maroc, cosmopolitisme, présence d'étrangers et transformations sociales*, edited by Nadia

Khrouz and Nazarena Lanza, 65–72. Konrad Adenauer Stiftung, Centre Jacques Berque., Rabat, 2015.

Lauseig, Jérôme. "Quand la Malaysia Inc. joue la carte Sud-Sud en Afrique subsaharienne." *Politique africaine* 76 (November 15, 2012): 63–75.

Lecoutre, Delphine. "Vers un gouvernement de l'Union africaine ? Gradualisme et statu quo v. immédiatisme." *Politique étrangère* 3 (October 20, 2008): 629–639.

Lewin, André. "Les Africains à l'ONU." *Relations internationales* (April 2006): 55–78.

Mahamadou, Laouali, Souley, and Meyer, Jean-Baptiste. "Le Maroc, pays d'accueil d'étudiants étrangers." *Hommes et migrations. Revue française de référence sur les dynamiques migratoires* (November 1, 2012): 114–123.

Mareï, Nora. "Le détroit de Gibraltar dans la mondialisation des transports maritimes." *EchoGéo*, no. 19 (February 10, 2012).

Maslouhi, Abderrahim El. "La gauche marocaine, défenseure du trône. Sur les métamorphoses d'une opposition institutionnelle." *L'Année du Maghreb* 5 (November 1, 2009): 37–58.

Méric, Édouard. "Le conflit algéro-marocain." *Revue française de science politique* 15, no. 4 (1965): 743–752.

Milhorance de Castro, Carolina. "La politique extérieure Sud-Sud du Brésil de l'après-Lula. Quelle place pour l'Afrique?" *Afrique contemporaine* 248 (June 25, 2014): 45–59.

Mohsen-Finan, Khadija, and Zeghal, Malika. "Opposition islamiste et pouvoir monarchique au Maroc." *Revue française de science politique* 56, no. 1 (March 1, 2006): 79–119.

Nigoul, Claude. "De Gaulle et Hassan II." In *De Gaulle et le Maroc*, edited by Mustapha Sehimi, 179–192. Publisud / Sochepress., Paris, Les Témoins de l'Histoire, 1990.

Noessel, Susan. "Smart Power." *Foreign Affairs*, March/April 2004.

Otayek, René. "Libye et Afrique : Assistance financière et stratégie de puissance." *Politique africaine* (May 1981) 1 (2): 77–98.

Rakotonirina, Haingo Mireille. "Le dialogue interrégional UE-Afrique depuis Cotonou : le cas de la facilité de soutien à la paix en Afrique." *Politique européenne* 22: 125–147.

Richards, Paul. "La terre ou le fusil?" *Afrique contemporaine* 214 (September 1, 2005): 37–57.

Saaf, Abdallah. "L'expérience marocaine de transition politique." *IEMed Institut Européen de la Méditerranée*, 2009.

Saaf, Abdallah. "Le partenariat euro-maghrébin." In *Le Maghreb dans les relations internationales*, edited by Khadija Mohsen-Finan, 189–211. Paris, CNRS Éditions, 2011.

Saidy, Brahim. "La politique de défense Marocaine : articulation de l'interne et de l'externe." *Maghreb–Machrek* 202 (December 1, 2009): 115–131.

Saidy, Brahim. "Relations civilo-militaires au Maroc : le facteur international revisité." *Politique étrangère* (December 1, 2007) Autumn, no. 3: 589–603.

Sakpane-Gbati, Biléou. "La démocratie à l'africaine." *Éthique publique. Revue internationale d'éthique sociétale et gouvernementale* 13, no. 2 (December 31, 2011).

Sambe, Bakary. "Tidjaniya : usages diplomatiques d'une confrérie soufie." *Politique étrangère*, January 14, 2011, Winter, no. 4: 843–854.

Sehimi, Mustapha. "L'influence gaullienne sur la constitution marocaine." In *De Gaulle et le Maroc*, edited by Mustapha Sehimi, 104–122. Publisud / Sochepress., Paris, Les Témoins de l'Histoire, 1990.

Serre, Françoise De La. "Les revendications marocaines sur la Mauritanie." *Revue française de science politique* 16, no. 2 (1966): 320–331.

Slyomovics, Susan. "Témoignages, écrits et silences : l'Instance Équité et Réconciliation (IER) marocaine et la réparation." *L'Année du Maghreb* IV (2008): 123–148.

Stalon, Jean-Luc. "L'africanisation de la diplomatie de la paix." *Revue internationale et stratégique* 66, no. 2 (June 1, 2007): 47–58.

Sylla, Ndongo Samba. "From a marginalised to an emerging Africa? A critical analysis." *Review of African Political Economy* 41, sup. 1 (October 3, 2014): 7–25.

Taylor, Ian, and Marchal Roland. "La politique sud-africaine et le Nepad." *Politique africaine* 91 (November 15, 2012): 120–138.

Triaud, Jean-Louis. "La tijâniyya, voie infaillible ou 'voie soufie réinventée'. Autour du pamphlet anti-tijânî d'Ibrâhîm Al-Qattân." In *La Tijâniyya : une confrérie musulmane à la conquête de l'Afrique*, edited by Jean-Louis Triaud and David Robinson, 165–199. Karthala, 2000.

Vircoulon, Alain. "L'Afrique du Sud et le Maghreb." In *Le Maghreb et son Sud : vers des liens renouvelés*, edited by Mansouria Mokhefi and Alain Antil, 59–72. Paris, CNRS éditions, 2012.

Vloeberghs, Ward. "Quand le Royaume rayonne : La géopolitique marocaine au prisme du commerce extérieur." *Confluences Méditerranée* 78, no. 3 (2011): 157.

Wyk, Jo-Ansie van. "Nuclear diplomacy as niche diplomacy: South Africa's post-apartheid relations with the International Atomic Energy Agency." *South African Journal of International Affairs* 19, no. 2 (August 1, 2012): 179–200.

Zekri, Khalid. "Aux sources de la modernité marocaine." *Itinéraires. Littérature, textes, cultures* (November 1, 2009): 43–55.

Zoubir, Yahia H. "Algeria and U.S. Interests: Containing Radical Islam and Promoting Democracy." *Middle East Policy* 9, no. 1 (March 1, 2002): 64–81.

Zoubir, Yahia H. "Les États-Unis et le Maghreb : primauté de la sécurité et marginalité de la démocratie." *L'Année du Maghreb* II (March 1, 2007): 563–584.

Zoubir, Yahia H. "Stalemate in Western Sahara: Ending International Legality." *Middle East Policy* 14, no. 4 (December 1, 2007): 158–177.

Zoubir, Yahia H. "Les États-Unis et L'Algérie : antagonisme, pragmatisme et coopération." *Maghreb–Machrek* 200, no. 2 (June 1, 2009): 71–90.

2.3 Studies and Seminars
2.3.1 Studies

Abourabi, Yousra, and Durand de Sanctis Julien. *The Emergence of African Security Powers: A Comparative Study*. Paris: Institut de Recherche Stratégique de l'École Militaire, 2016.

Antil, Alain. *Le Royaume du Maroc et sa politique envers l'Afrique sub-saharienne*. Paris: Institut français des relations internationales, November 2003.

Antil, Alain. *Le Maroc et sa 'nouvelle frontière': lecture critique du versant économique de la stratégie africaine du Maroc*. Paris: Institut français des relations internationales, June 2010.

Boulanger Martel, Simon Pierre. "Transfert d'armes vers l'Afrique du Nord. Entre intérêts économiques et impératifs sécuritaires." Note d'Analyse, GRIP, 24 mars 2014, 19 pages.

Cherkaoui, Mustapha. *Quel potentiel de développement des relations de coopération Maroc-Nigeria*. Rabat: Institut Royal des Études Stratégiques, 10 mai 2012.

Cordesman, Anthony H., and Nerguizian Aram. *The North African Military Balance. Force Developments & Regional Challenges*. Washington: Center For Strategic and International Studies—Burke Chair in Strategy, 2010, 124 p.

Enquête sur la migration subsaharienne au Maroc 2007. Association Marocaine d'Études et de Recherche en Migrations (AMERM), 2008, 125 p.

Intégrer la sécurité humaine dans les politiques de sécurité nationale dans le nord-ouest de l'Afrique. Centre pour le contrôle démocratique des forces armées—Genève (DCAF), 2010, 64 p.

Jaïdi, Larabi, and Abouyoub, Hassan. *Le Maroc entre le statut avancé et l'Union pour la Méditerranée*. Rabat: Friedrich Ebert Stiftung et Fondation Abderrahim Bouabid., Les cahiers bleus, no. 12, 2008, 56 p.

Kandel, Maria. "La stratégie américaine en Afrique : les risques et les contradictions du "light footprint"." In *La stratégie américaine en Afrique*, edited by Maria Kandel, Paris: Études, Institut de Recherche Stratégique de l'École Militaire., no. 36, 2014, pp. 13–32.

Lutz, Fanny. "Une décennie de frénésie militaire Dépenses militaires au Moyen-Orient et en Afrique du Nord." Note d'Analyse, GRIP, 26 février 2013, pp. 14–15.

McNamee, Terence, Mills, Greg, and Pham, Peter J. *Morocco and the African Union. Prospects for Re-engagement and Progress on the Western Sahara*. Discussion Paper, Johannesburg: The Brenthurst Foundation, 2013, 27 p.

Rhoufrani, Talal. *Les relations Maroc–Afrique du Sud : réalité et perspectives*. Rabat: Institut Royal des Études Stratégiques, 31 mai 2012.

Sahara occidental : le coût du conflit. International Crisis Group, Rapport Moyen-Orient/ Afrique du Nord no. 65, 11 juin 2007, 32 p.

Zouitni, Hammad. *La diplomatie marocaine à travers les organisations régionales (1958–1984)*. Casablanca: Fondation Konrad Adenauer, 1998, 252 p.

2.3.2 Oral Presentations at Seminars and Other Scientific Events

Ait Ben Lmadani, Fatima. "La migration des Sénégalais au Maroc", *Study Day on Moroccan–African Relations*, Rabat, Centre Jacques Berque, Centre d'Études Sahariennes, Conseil National des Droits de l'Homme, Fondation KAS, October 3, 2014, Rabat. Coordination: Yousra Abourabi. URL of the video: https:// www.youtube.com/ watch?v=YwCgHbAMKjA.

Anich, Rudolph, "Contexte et enjeux de la migration au Maroc," Journée d'étude sur les relations maroco-africaines, Rabat, Centre Jacques Berque, Centre d'Études Sahariennes, Conseil National des Droits de l'Homme, Fondation KAS, 3 October 2014. Coordination: Yousra Abourabi. URL of the video: https://www.youtube.com/watch?v=n1SNVKkWOvg.

Cherkaoui, Mustapha, former Ambassador of Morocco to Nigeria, "Le Maroc et la lutte contre l'extrémisme religieux: le cas de Boko Haram au Nigéria," Study Day on Morocco-African Relations, Rabat, Centre Jacques Berque, Centre d'Études Sahariennes, Conseil National des Droits de l'Homme, Fondation KAS, October 3, 2014. Coordination: Yousra Abourabi. URL of the video: https://www.youtube.com/watch?v=MsSEGV2NRAc.

Conference on the occasion of the 'Africa Day' at the Ministry of Foreign Affairs and Cooperation, which I attended, Rabat, May 23, 2013.

Fahmi, Kamal, "Managem's strategy for its deployment in Africa," Study day on Moroccan–African relations, Rabat, Centre Jacques Berque, Centre d'Études Sahariennes, Conseil National des Droits de l'Homme, Fondation KAS, October 3, 2014. Coordination: Yousra Abourabi. URL of the video: https://www.youtube.com/watch?v=Gm_K4qV48oY.

Gaïd Salah, Ahmed, "L'Armée de Libération Nationale, arme de l'information et de la diplomatie," Colloquium organised by the Direction de la Communication, de l'Information et de l'Orientation de l'État-Major de l'Armée Nationale Populaire, Algiers, October 22, 2014. URL: http://www.mdn.dz/site_principal/index.php?L=fr #undefined.

"Intervention by Nabil Adghoghi at the IRES seminar on the Morocco–GCC partnership," ires.ma, April 30, 2013.

3 Non-academic Sources

3.1 *Essays and Journalistic Works*

Alaoui, Moulay Hicham el. *Journal d'un prince banni : Demain, le Maroc*. Paris: Grasset, 2014. 368 p.

Bonnier, Henry. *Une passion marocaine*. Paris: Artège, 2015. 204 p.

Bruyère-Ostells, Walter. *Dans l'ombre de Bob Denard : Les mercenaires français de 1960 à 1989*. Paris: Nouveau Monde éditions, 2014. 391 p.

Hughes, Stephen O. *Le Maroc de Hassan II*. Rabat: Bouregreg, 2003. 473 p.

Péan, Pierre. *Affaires africaines*. Paris: Fayard, 1983. 213 p.

Péan, Pierre. *Nouvelles affaires africaines : Mensonges et pillages au Gabon*. Paris: Fayard, 2014. 96 p.

Saint-Prot, Charles. *Mohammed V ou la Monarchie populaire*, Monaco : Éditions du Rocher, 2012. 245 p.

3.2 *Press and Magazine Articles*

Abourabi, Yousra. "Morocco Nigeria: Towards a Reconstruction of West African Geopolitics." *Middle East Eye*, June 23, 2018. URL: https://www.middleeasteye.net/en/opinion-en/morocco-nigeria-a-reconstruction-of-geopolitics-west-african-countries.

Abourabi, Yousra, and Jean-Noël Ferrié. "La diplomatie environnementale du Maroc en Afrique: un mix intérieur-extérieur." *Revue Telos*, June 7, 2018. URL: https://www.telos-eu.com/fr/politique-francaise-et-internationale/la-diplomatie-environnementale-du-maroc-en-afrique.html.

Airault, Pascal. "La nouvelle diplomatie de M6." *Jeune Afrique*, January 26, 2009. URL: http://www.jeuneafrique.com/205594/politique/la-nouvelle-diplomatie-de-m6/.

Aït Akdim, Youssef. "Interview with Mohammed Bachir Rachdi: 'Morocco must ensure consistency in its strategies'." JeuneAfrique.com, June 10, 2014. URL: http://www.jeuneafrique.com/9339/economie/mohammed-bachir-rachdi-le-maroc-doit-watch-the-coh-rence-of-his-strat-gies/.

Aït Akdim, Youssef. "La Tidjaniyya, arme secrète du 'soft power' marocain en Afrique." *Le Monde.fr*, April 29, 2016. URL: http://www.lemonde.fr/international/article/2016/04/29/la-tidjaniyya-arme-secrete-du-soft-power-marocain-en-afrique_4911069_3210.html.

Akalay, Aïcha. "What is this Moroccan identity that we are envied according to Mohammed VI?" *Telquel.ma*, July 30, 2015. URL: http://telquel.ma/2015/07/30/what-moroccan-identity-that-we-envy-according-to-mohammed-vi_1457920.

Al Fassi, Allal. "Les revendications marocaines sur les territoires sahariens: le point de vue de M. Allal el-Fassi." *Le Monde diplomatique*, January 1, 1960. URL: http://www.monde-diplomatique.fr/1960/01/ALLAL_EL_FASSI/23406.

Alaoui, Hicham Ben Abdallah El. "Le 'printemps arabe' n'a pas dit son dernier mot." *Le Monde diplomatique*, February 1, 2014, no. 719, no. 2. URL: https://www.monde-diplomatique.fr/2014/02/EL_ALAOUI/50074.

Anouzia, Ali. "Ambassadorial appointments, what has changed?" *Lakome*, March 12, 2013. URL: http://www.maghress.com/fr/lakomefr/1502.

Aourid. "Thinking Our Diplomacy." *Zamane*, January 12, 2015. URL: http://zamane.ma/en/penser-notre-diplomatie/.

Belhaj, Soufiane. "Rajeunissement du corps diplomatique." *Aujourd'hui le Maroc*, November 10, 2008. URL: http://www.maghress.com/fr/aujourdhui/64998.

Belkaïd, Akram. "L'obsession des complots dans le monde arabe." *Le Monde diplomatique*, June 1, 2015. URL: https://www.monde-diplomatique.fr/2015/06/BELKAID/53074.

Benattallah, Halim. "Par-delà la participation du Maroc au Sommet des pays du CCG, quels messages en direction de l'Algérie?" *Le Quotidien d'Oran*, April 25, 2016. URL: http://www.lequotidien-oran.com/index.php?news=5228160&archive_date=2016-04-14.

Bennani, Driss, Benkhalloul, Mohamed. "La fin des ministères de souveraineté?" *La vie eco*, November 28, 2011. URL: http://www.lavieeco.com/news/politique/la-fin-des-ministeres-de-souverainete-20784.html.

Bennani, Driss. "Enquête. Voyage au cœur de la diplomatie marocaine." *Telquel*, March 28, 2012. URL: http://telquel.ma/2012/03/28/Enquete-Voyage-au-coeur-de-la-diplomati
e-marocaine_413_1702.

Berrada, Mohammed. "Moroccan-French relations for a renewed partnership." *National Defence*, October 1999.

Bin-Nun, Yigal. "Morocco and the Mossad, Israeli-Moroccan Secret Relations." *Le Journal Hebdomadaire*, July 3, 2004. URL: https://www.academia.edu/8566046/Le_Morocco_and_the_Mossad_The_Isra%C3%A8tes_Moroccan_Relations.

Bin-Nun, Yigal. "Nos contacts avec le Maroc datent de la guerre des Sables." *Le Courrier d'Algérie*, September 14, 2009. URL: https://www.academia.edu/8569160/Our_contacts_with_Morocco_date_from_the_Sand_War.

Blum, Elena, and Lamlili, Nadia. "Lobbying: What African countries spend in the US." JeuneAfrique.com, May 16, 2014. URL: http://www.jeuneafrique.com/163760/politics/lobbying-what-people-think-of-African-countries-in-the-US/.

Boucek, Christopher. "Saudi Extremism to Sahel and Back." *Carnegie Endowment for International Peace*, March 26, 2009. URL: http://carnegieendowment.org/2009/03/26/saudi-extremism-to-sahel-and-back-pub-22891.

Braeckmann, Colette. "Belgians and Zairians sign reconciliation agreement in Rabat." Lesoir.be, July 25, 1989. URL: https://www.lesoir.be/art/%252Fbelges-et-zairois-signent-a-rabat-l-accord-de-reconciliation_t-19890725-Z01V9W.html.

Brousky, Omar. "Le Maroc enterre trente ans d'arabisation pour retourner au français." *Le Monde.fr*, February 19, 2016. URL: http://www.lemonde.fr/afrique/article/2016/02/19/maroc-le-roi-mohamed-vi-enterre-trente-ans-d-arabisation-pour-retourner-au-francais_4868524_3212.html.

Cabirol, M. "Défense: la France a exporté pour 6,3 milliards d'euros d'armes en 2013." *La Tribune*, January 29, 2014.

Cheikh Ibrahima Diop fils. "À propos des relations maroco-sénégalaises." Dakaractu.com, May 21, 2015. URL: http://www.dakaractu.com/A-PROPOS-DES-RELATIONS-SENEGALO-MAROCAINES_a90207.html.

C.J. "Les trois grands mérites de l'intervention française." *Le Monde diplomatique*, May 1, 1977. URL: https://www.monde-diplomatique.fr/1977/05/C_J_/34239.

Dabo, Mamadou. "Au Mali de l'hospitalité et de l'africanité: Adieu-les-visees-azawadiennes-le-roi-marocain-sinstalle." *Mali Actu*, February 21, 2014. URL: http://maliactu.net/au-mali-de-lhospitalite-et-de-lafricanite-adieu-les-visees-azawadiennes-le-roi-marocain-sinstalle/.

Decraene, Philippe. "L'évolution politique: les résolutions adoptées à Casablanca suscitent les inquiétudes de certains Etats." *Le Monde diplomatique*, February 1961. URL: http://www.monde-diplomatique.fr/1961/02/DECRAENE/24053.

Delort, Nicolas. "Advanced status: moving from the symbolic to the practical." *Amadeus Institute*. 2010. URL: http://www.amadeusonline.org/publications/analyses/251-statut-avance-from-symbolism-to-practice.html.

Demetz, Jean-Michel and Lagarde, Dominique. "Moulay Hicham: 'La solution au Maroc: une monarchie réformée'." *L'Express*, May 15, 2011. URL: http://www.lexpress.fr/actualite/monde/moulay-hicham-la-solution-au-maroc-une-monarchie-reformee_992647.html.

Didi, Abdeljalil. "African anchorage enriches Morocco's local and national identity." Almaouja.com, November 19, 2014. URL: http://www.almaouja.com/ouarzazate-terre-d-afrique/815-ancrage-africain-enriches-local-and-national-identity-of-morocco.

Drugeon, Anthony. "In Africa, Moroccan diplomacy has listed its hostile countries." *Telquel.ma*, January 7, 2015. URL: http://telquel.ma/2015/01/07/en-afrique-diplomatie-marocaine-liste-ses-pays-hostiles_1429111.

Dupret, Baudouin and Ferrié Jean-Noël. "L' 'exception' marocaine: stabilité et dialectique de la réforme." *Middle East*, June 2012, no. 14. URL: http://www.cjb.ma/268-les-archives/164-archives-publications-des-chercheurs/376-archives-publications-des-chercheurs-2012/b-dupret-and-j-n-ferrie-l-exception-marocaine-stabilite-et-dialectique-de-la-reforme-1843.html.

El Affas, Aziza. "Mouvement dans le réseau diplomatique." www.leconomiste.com, March 12, 2013. URL: http://www.leconomiste.com/article/904385-movement-in-the-network-diplomatic. (Accessed May 2016)

Fauvet, Jacques. "La Mauritanie a toujours fait partie du Maroc." *Le Monde*, April 10, 1956. URL: http://www.lemonde.fr/archives/article/1956/04/10/bull-la-mauritania-has-always-been-part-of-morocco-which-it-gave-me-its-bull-name-it-is-not-logical-that-algeria-continues-to-live-under-a-regime-colonial-nous-sommes-p_3113854_1819218.html.

Gelfand, L. "Spend to Thrive, Country Briefing: Algeria." *IHS Janes Defense Weekly*, January 28, 2009.

Gravier, Louis. "Morocco defends its national interests away from antagonisms des Grands." *Le Monde diplomatique*, September 1, 1969. URL: http://www.monde-diplomatique.fr/1969/09/GRAVIER/29191.

Grosrichard, Ruth. "Le juif en nous. Au cœur de l'identité marocaine." *Telquel*, November 22, 2008. URL: http://juifdumaroc.over-blog.com/article-le-juif-en-nous-au-coeur-de-l-identite-marocaine-40476094.html.

Guerraoui, Driss. "La Semaine de Sa Majesté le Roi Mohammed VI à Hawaii en livre." *Quid.ma*, July 28, 2015. URL: http://www.quid.ma/politique/la-semaine-de-his-majesty-king-mohammed-vi-a-hawaii-in-book/. (Accessed June 2016)

Harit, Fouâd. "Maroc-Guinée: les grandes décisions de Mohammed VI et Alpha Condé." *Afrik.com*, March 5, 2014. URL: https://www.afrik.com/maroc-guinee-les-grandes-decisions-de-mohammed-vi-et-alpha-conde

Innocent, Marc. "La quête de 'l'émergence' en Afrique, ou la fin de l'afro-pessimisme." *Abidjan.net*, March 19, 2015. URL: http://news.abidjan.net/h/529149.html.

Iraqi, Fahd. "Omar Kabbaj: le conseiller Afrique de Mohammed VI." *Jeune Afrique*, June 21, 2016. URL: http://www.jeuneafrique.com/mag/334014/politique/omar-kabbaj-African-expertise/.

Jaïdi, L. "Trois vérités sur l'accord Maroc-USA." *La Vie Économique*, April 12, 2004. URL: http://lavieeco.com/news/debat-chroniques/trois-verites-sur-laccord-maroc-usa-4511.html.

Johnson, Matt. "The $20 Million Case for Morocco." *Foreign Policy*, February 26, 2014. URL: https://foreignpolicy.com/2014/02/25/the-20-million-case-for-morocco/.

Lacouture, Jean. "Les revendications sahariennes du Maroc s'affirment et s'étendent." *Le Monde diplomatique*, May 1958. URL: https://www.monde-diplomatique.fr/1958/05/LACOUTURE/22584.

Lacouture, Jean. "À chacun son neutralisme: il n'y a pas de non-alignement, il y a des pays non alignés." *Le Monde diplomatique*, October 1, 1961. URL: http://www.monde-diplomatique.fr/1961/10/LACOUTURE/24432.

Lacouture, Jean. "Le Maroc voit se prolonger son isolement diplomatique." *Le Monde diplomatique*, September 1, 1963. URL: https://www.monde-diplomatique.fr/1963/09/LACOUTURE/25544.

Lakmahri, Samir. "Morocco–South Africa: the underside of a mess." *Zamane*, December 6, 2013. URL: http://zamane.ma/fr/maroc-afrique-du-sud-les-dessous-dun-gachis-2/.

Lanza, Nazarena. "'Tijâniyya is part of Moroccan soft power'." *Al Huffington Post Maghreb*, July 25, 2016. URL: http://www.huffpostmaghreb.com/2016/07/25/softpower-maroc-lanza-naz_n_11179050.html. (Accessed August 2016)

Larbi, Amine. "Benkirane: L'africanité du Maroc, inébranlable par les manœuvres de ses ennemis." *Lemag.ma*, March 18, 2013. URL: http://www.lemonde.fr/economie/article/2015/02/08/swissleaks-sa-majeste-mohammed-vi-client-numero-5090190103-chez-hsbc_4572324_3234.html.

Lefèvre, Jean. "À propos de la crise congolaise. Le Maroc confirme la vocation africaine de sa politique étrangère." *Le Monde diplomatique*, September 1, 1960. URL: https://www.monde-diplomatique.fr/1960/09/LEFEVRE/23819.

Lhomme, Fabrice, Davet, Gérard, and Benchemsi, Ahmed. "'SwissLeaks': His Majesty Mohammed VI, client number one at 5090190103HSBC." *Le Monde*, February 8, 2015.

Majdi, Yassine. "Les secrets du lobbying marocain aux États-Unis dévoilés." *Telquel.ma*, February 27, 2014. URL: http://telquel.ma/2014/02/27/les-secrets-du-lobbying-Moroccan-in-the-United-States-devoiles_11425.

Marchat, Henri. "Les revendications marocaines sur les territoires sahariens: la réponse de M. Henri Marchat." *Le Monde diplomatique*, January 1, 1960. URL: http://www.monde-diplomatique.fr/1960/01/MARCHAT/23440.

Mathieu, O. "Course aux armes et leadership algérien." JeuneAfrique.com, May 5, 2012.

Mbaye, Amadou L. "Le Roi du Maroc en Afrique Subsaharienne: Mohammed VI, l'Africain." SeneNews.com, May 24, 2015. URL: http://www.senenews.com/2015/05/24/le-roi-du-maroc-en-afrique-subsaharienne-mohammed-vi-lafricain-2_128254.html.

Merchet, Jean-Dominique. "En 2020, le Maroc entend être une puissance industrielle émergente." *L'Opinion.fr*, April 7, 2014. URL: http://www.lopinion.fr/7-avril-2014/en-2020-maroc-entend-etre-puissance-industrielle-emergente-11078.

Monjib, Maâti. "Kadhafi et Hassan II, des ennemis de trente ans." *Zamane.ma*, March 24, 2014. URL: http://zamane.ma/fr/kadhafi-et-hassan-ii-des-ennemis-de-thirty-years-old-2/.

Mouhsine, Réda. "El Mostafa Sahel. Adieu conciglieri!" *Telquel.ma*, October 17, 2012. URL: http://telquel.ma/2012/10/17/El-Mostafa-Sahel-Adieu-conciglieri_540_4587.

Mounombou, Stevie. "Mohammed VI in Libreville." *Gabonreview*, June 3, 2015. URL: http://gabonreview.com/blog/mohammed-vi-a-libreville-le-4-juin/.

Nicet-Chenaf, Dalila. "Les pays émergents: performance ou développement?" *La Vie des Idées*, March 4, 2014. URL: [http://www.laviedesidees.fr/Les-pays-emergents-performance-ou.html] (http://www.laviedesidees.fr/Les-pays-emergents-performance-ou.html).

Rfaif, Najib. "L'arabattitude dans tous ses États." *La Vie Éco*, April 16, 2004. URL: http://lavieeco.com/news/debat-chroniques/larabattitude-dans-tous-ses-etats-4531.html.

Ribouis, Olivier. "Terrorisme en Tunisie: Alger accuse le Maroc." *La Nouvelle Tribune*, December 16, 2013. URL: http://www.lanouvelletribune.info/international/17306-terrorism-in-tunisia-algeria-accuses-morocco. (Accessed June 2016)

Schwak, Juliette. "South Korea Nation Branding: Global Recognition As The Final Step in A Successful Capitalist Development." *International Perspectives*, January 4, 2015.

Sehimi, Mustapha. "La réforme silencieuse." *Maroc Hebdo*, September 3, 2004, no. 630. URL: http://www.maghress.com/fr/marochebdo/118056.

Sfali, Adam. "Bernard Lugan: L'Africanité du Maroc, d'historique à agissante." *Lemag.ma*, March 3, 2014. URL: http://www.lemag.ma/Bernard-Lugan-L-Africanite-du-Morocco-d-history-acting_a81187.html. (Accessed June 2016)

Sfali, Adam. "Après le discours du Roi à Riyad, la Chine propose un accord de libre-échange au Maroc." *Lemag.ma*, April 23, 2016. URL: http://www.lemag.ma/-After-the-speech-of-the-King-a-Riyad-the-China-proposes-a-free-trade-agreement-au-Maroc_a98709.html. (Accessed June 2016)

Silmani, Leïla. "Un ambassadeur pas comme les autres." *Jeune Afrique*, May 3, 2010. URL: http://www.jeuneafrique.com/197123/politique/un-ambassadeur-pas-comme-the-others/.

Sudan, François. "Mohammed VI, African King." *Jeune Afrique*, June 15, 2015. URL: http://www.jeuneafrique.com/mag/235744/politique/mohamed-vi-african-king/.

Thiam, Adam. "Mohammed VI's African tour: Majesty, the people are waiting for you." *maliweb*, May 22, 2015. URL: http://www.maliweb.net/economie/cooperation/toure-africaine-de-mohammed-vi-majeste-ce-peuple-vous-attend-979012.html.

Thiam, Bachir. "Caravane de l'export: Ratés diplomatiques?" 2012. URL: https://www.leconomiste.com/article/895148-caravane-de-l-export-rat-s-diplomatiquesde-notre-envoy-sp-cial-libreville-bachir-thia

Thiam, El Hadji Abdoulaye. "Mohammed Chraibi, Consul Honoraire du Sénégal au Maroc: Le Sénégal a la chance d'avoir un homme de dossiers." *Lesoleil.sn*, April 20, 2012. URL: https://fr.allafrica.com/stories/201204021047.html

"Malian 500 imams soon to be trained in Morocco." *Jeune Afrique*, November 12, 2013. URL: http://www.jeuneafrique.com/Article/ARTJAWEB20131112102010/.

"75 000 femmes ont collaboré pour écrire un Coran offert à Mohammed VI », *Telquel*, June 19, 2015. URL : https://telquel.ma/2015/06/19/linattendu-cadeau-femmes-mohammed-vi_1452816

"Popular reception for King Mohammed VI in Abidjan." *Connectionivoirienne*, May 31, 2015. URL: https://connectionivoirienne.net/2015/05/31/cote-divoire-accueil-populaire-pour-le-roi-mohammed-vi-a-abidjan/

"Adoption of the Tannock report: The relentless entryism of opponents defeated." *MAP Maroc.ma*, October 23, 2013. URL: http://www.maroc.ma/fr/actualites/adoption-from-the-report-tannock-lentrism-achieved-adversaries-in-failure.

"Affair Georges Ouégnin humiliated: Mohamed VI honoured former chief instead du Protocole d'État." *Abidjan.net*, March 22, 2013. URL: http://news.abidjan.net/h/454889.html.

"Hezbollah Affair: Towards a standoff between Algeria and the Gulf monarchies at the Arab League." *Al Huffington Post*, July 4, 2016. URL: https://algeria-watch.org/?p=35373

"Affaire Karim Wade: Mohamed VI, négociateur de l'ombre?" Dakaractu.com, March 15, 2013. URL: https://www.dakaractu.com/Affaire-Karim-Wade-Mohamed-VI-negociateur-de-l-ombre_a40682.html

"Altercation between Algerian and Moroccan ambassador at UN" (*sic*.). *Algeria Focus*, February 24, 2013. URL: http://www.algerie-focus.com/2013/02/altercation-entre-algerian-and-moroccan-ambassador-a-lonu/.

"Amrani talks to Ivorian industry minister." *Maroc.ma*, May 22, 2013. URL: http://www.maroc.ma/fr/actualites/amrani-sentretient-avec-le-ministre-ivoirien-de-lindustrie.

"Attijariwafa Bank, 4th largest bank in Africa, according to The Economist." *Financial Afrik*, July 22, 2016. URL: https://www.financialafrik.com/2016/07/22/attijariwafa-bank-4e-banque-en-afrique-selon-the-economist/#:~:text=Le%20classement%20des%20banques%20africaines,à%203%2C156%20milliards%20de%20dollars.

"In the eyes of the Americans, Algeria is more important than it thinks—Francis Ghiles on Radio M (audio)." *Maghreb Émergent*, April 1, 2014. URL: https://maghrebemergent.net/aux-yeux-des-americains-l-algerie-est-plus-importante-qu-elle-ne-le-pense-francis-ghiles-sur-radio-m-audio/

"What the wave of ambassadorial appointments means for Moroccan diplomacy." *Al Huffington Post*, February 7, 2016. URL: http://www.huffpostmaghreb.com/2016/02/07/nomination-ambassadors-m_n_9180500.html.

"Chronologie des accords et conventions liant le Maroc et la Côte d'Ivoire." *Abidjan.net*, March 19, 2013. URL: http://news.abidjan.net/h/454618.html.

"How Mossad helped Morocco kill Ben Barka." *Courrier international*, March 26, 2015. URL: https://www.courrierinternational.com/article/renseignement-comment-le-mossad-aide-le-maroc-tuer-ben-barka#:~:text=L%27enquête%20révèle%20que%20le,ministre%20de%20l%27Intérieur%20marocain.

"Cooperation: The King of Morocco accredits his ambassador to ECCAS." *Adiac Congo*, February 17, 2014. URL: http://adiac-congo.com/content/cooperation-le-Moroccan-king-accredits-his-ambassador-to-the-eac-8289.

"Dakhla 2016: a la Coopération Sud-Sud au cœur du débat." *Guinée Matin—Les Nouvelles de la Guinée profonde*, February 17, 2016. URL: http://guineematin.com/actualites/dakhla-2016-lafrique-and-south-south-cooperation-au-coeur-du-debat/.

"Damen delivers a second Moroccan SIGMA frigate." MerEtMarine.com, February 13, 2012.

"In the Way of Development and Progress." *Le Monde diplomatique*, March 1, 1970. URL: http://www.monde-diplomatique.fr/1970/03/A/29529.

"Diplomacy: African Parliament wages war on Morocco." *le360.ma*, October 19, 2015. URL: https://fr.le360.ma/politique/diplomatie-le-parlement-africain-mene-une-guerre-contre-le-maroc-54739/

"Dossier. Mohammed VI, the African." *LE360.MA*. URL: https://fr.le360.ma/dossier/mohammed-vi-lafricain-40651/

"En Guinée-Bissau, un jour chômé pour la visite de Mohammed VI." *Telquel.ma*, May 28, 2015. URL: http://telquel.ma/2015/05/28/jeudi-28-mai-chome-en-guinee-bissau-en-raison-visite-mohammed-vi_1449245.

"Fez promotes itself in Cameroon." *L'Économiste*, May 24, 2006. URL: http://www.leconomiste.com/article/fes-fait-sa-promotion-au-cameroun.

"Morocco–France Partnership Forum in Paris." *MAP–Maroc.ma*, May 20, 2015. URL: http://www.maroc.ma/fr/actualites/forum-de-partenariat-maroc-france-paris.

"Hommage au Maroc pour la liberation de l'Angola." La Nouvelle Tribune, September 10, 2012.

"Moroccan FDI in Africa 41 billion DH invested in five years." *L'Économiste*, March 27, 2014. URL: https://www.leconomiste.com/article/927811-ide-marocains-en-afrique4 1-milliards-de-dh-investis-en-cinq-ans

"AfDB and Algeria redefine the basis for a strengthened partnership." *African Development Bank Group*, April 21, 2016. URL: http://www.afdb.org/fr/news-and-events/article/afdb-and-algeria-redefine-the-foundations-for-strengthened-partnership-1 5621/.

"L'africanitéduMarocnesj'estjamentie." *Afrique7*, September 19, 2013. URL: http://www.afrique7.com/politique/7815-lafricanite-du-maroc-ne-sest-jamais-dementie.html.

"Algeria uses the weapon of psychotropic drugs to harm Morocco."*LeMatin.ma*, August 2014. URL: [http://lematin.ma/express/2014/contrebande_l-algerie-se-sert-de-l-arm e-psychotropics-for-damage-in-Morocco/207415.html]

"Saudi Arabia facilitates reconciliation between Morocco and Mauritania." Yabiladi.com, April 8, 2016. URL: [http://www.actu-maroc.com/larabie-saoudite-facilite-la -reconciliation-between-morocco-and-mauritania/

"Russia welcomes Morocco's efforts to settle the Sahara conflict." *CORCAS*, March 2, 2007. URL: [http://www.corcas.com/Sahara-Occidental/La-Russie-salue-les-efforts-du-Maroc-pour-le-reglement-du-conflit-du-Sahara-738-1483-958.aspx (Accessed June 2016)

"Tanzania moves towards withdrawal of recognition of the chimeric 'SADR'." *le360.ma*, April 7, 2015. URL: https://fr.le360.ma/politique/la-tanzanie-se-dirige-vers-le-retrait -de-reconnaissance-de-la-chimerique-rasd-36715/

"Zambia withdraws recognition of pseudo 'rasd'." *Maghress*, April 4, 2011. URL: http://www.maghress.com/fr/eljadida24fr/1305.

"Le climat des affaires favourise les IDE au Maroc." *L'Économiste*, June 25, 2015. URL: https://www.leconomiste.com/article/973365-le-climat-des-affaires-favorise-les-id e-au-maroc

"'Co-development' as a 'cornerstone' of His Majesty the King's diplomacy towards Africa (The National Interest)." *MAP Express*, April 30, 2014. URL: [http://www.mapex press.ma/actualite/opinions-et-debats/le-co-developpement-stone-angles-of-the-diplomacy-of-his-majesty-king-versus-africa-national-interest/

"Congress reiterates US support for Moroccan Autonomy Plan for the Sahara." *Autonomy Plan*. URL: http://plan-autonomie.com/5265-le-congres-reitere-lappui-des-usa -at-moroccan-autonomy-plan-for-the-sahara.html.

"Bouteflika's provocative speech triggers tension in Moroccan-Algerian relations."*MAP Maroc.ma*, October 31, 2013. URL: http://www.maroc.ma/en/news/the-provocateur -speech-of-bouteflika-triggered-tension-in-Moroccan-relations.

"Le fait religieux, un incontournable de la diplomatie française." SaphirNews.com, November 8, 2013. URL: http://www.saphirnews.com/Le-fait-religieux-un-incontournable-de-la-diplomatie-francaise_a17874.html.

"Le Maroc aura son agence d'expertise." *L'Économiste*, June 15, 2015. URL: http://www.leconomiste.com/article/972830-le-maroc-aura-son-agence-d-expertise.

"Le Maroc consacre 175 millions de dirhams pour les loyers des ambassades et consulats." *Bladi.net*, November 7, 2015. URL: http://www.bladi.net/maroc-loyers-ambassades-consulats,43475.html.

"Morocco Decides to Recall His Majesty the King's Ambassador to Algiers for Consultation." MAP *Maroc.ma*, October 30, 2013. URL: http://www.maroc.ma/fr/news/morocco-decides-recall-in-consultation-of-his-majesty's-ambassador-majeste-le-roi-alger.

"Morocco welcomes Mali back into the Francophone family." *Maroc.ma*, November 8, 2013. URL: http://www.maroc.ma/fr/actualites/le-maroc-se-felicite-du-return-from-malaria-within-the-francophone-family.

"King Mohammed VI expected in Côte d'Ivoire on Sunday." *Connectionivoirienne*, February 22, 2014. URL: https://connectionivoirienne.net/2014/02/22/le-roi-mohammed-vi-attendu-dimanche-en-cote-divoire/

"Les Marocains du monde, un soft power au service du Maroc." *Challenge*, February 20, 2015. URL: http://www.ccme.org.ma/fr/medias-et-migration/41285.

"Les ministres de souveraineté." *Aujourdhui le Maroc*, August 20, 2002. URL: http://www.aujourdhui.ma/une/focus/les-ministres-de-souverainete-21610#.VnAvNcroGRt.

"Le 'Soft Power', nouvelle arme de la diplomatie marocaine?" *L'opinion.ma*, October 8, 2014. URL: http://www.lopinion.ma/def.asp?codelangue=23&id_info=41235.

"The first images of Chinese corvettes destined for Algeria." Médias24.com, August 25, 2014.

"Morocco-West Africa: Too few shipping lines?" *Africa News Agency*, March 19, 2015. URL: http://www.africanewsagency.fr/?p=1738.

"Moroccans of the World: Mohammed VI wants 'exemplary consulates'." *Bladi.net*, August 16, 2015. URL: http://www.bladi.net/marocains-monde-mohammed-6,42786.html.

"Morocco-Cameroon: Hand in Hand." *Journal Du Cameroun*, August 8, 2013. URL: https://fr.journalducameroun.com/maroc-cameroun-main-dans-la-main/

"Morocco: Fassi Fihri, the return." JeuneAfrique.com, May 3, 2013. URL: http://www.jeuneafrique.com/137551/politics/maroc-fassi-fihri-le-retour/.

"Morocco–France: Ces interventions militaires communes." *L'Économiste*, No. 46211, September 18, 2015. URL: https://www.leconomiste.com/article/977383-maroc-france-ces-interventions-militaires-communes

"Morocco: New consuls appointed." *Bladi.net*, October 19, 2015. URL: http://www.bladi.net/maroc-nouveaux-consuls,43345.html.

"Morocco/Nigeria: La normalisation des relations pas prête d'avoir lieu." Yabiladi.com, June 1, 2015. URL: http://www.yabiladi.com/articles/details/36246/maroc-nigeria-normalisation-relationships-prete.html.

"Morocco/Senegal: A perfect identity of views and a common will to promote a bilateral cooperation as fruitful as diversified." *MAP Express*, July 31, 2013. URL: http://www.mapexpress.ma/actualite/opinions-et-debats/marocsenegal-a-perfect-identity-views-and-a-common-volume-to-move-a-bilateral-cooperation-as-fruitful-as-diverse/.

"Mbarka Bouaida, ministre déléguée auprès du ministre des Affaires étrangères et de la Coopération." *Jeune Afrique*, April 5, 2015. URL: http://www.jeuneafrique.com/228943/politics/mbarka-bouaida-ministre-d-l-gu-e-aupr-s-du-ministre-des-transaffairs-and-coop-ration/.

"Mise en garde contre la collusion polisario-Aqmi-Mujao." *lematin.ma*, May 13, 2014. URL: https://lematin.ma/express/2014/tamek-a-washington_mise-en-garde-contre-la-collusion-polisario-aqmi-mujao/202122.html

"Mitterrand et l'Afrique: une relation marquée par le discours de La Baule." *RFI Afrique*, January 8, 2016. URL: https://www.rfi.fr/fr/afrique/20160108-mitterrand-afrique-discours-baule-democratie

"Mme Bouaida meets with ECOWAS president." *MAP Maroc.ma*, April 22, 2014. URL: http://www.maroc.ma/fr/actualites/mme-bouaida-sentretient-with-the-president-of-the-cedeao.

"Mohamed VI on Wednesday in Guinea-Bissau, a first for a Moroccan king." *Telquel.ma*, May 25, 2015. URL: http://telquel.ma/2015/05/25/mohamed-vi-mercredi-in-guinea-bissau-first-king-morocco_1448562.

"Mohammed VI plays the Putin card." *The Desk*, March 14, 2016. URL: https://ledesk.ma/grandangle/mohammed-vi-play-the-Putin-card/.

"Mohammed VI l'Africain." *Aujourd'hui le Maroc*, September 23, 2013. URL: https://aujourdhui.ma/focus/mohammed-vi-l-africain-105111

"Nelson Mandela and Morocco: A Long History of Friendship and Loyalty." *Medias24*, December 6, 2013. URL: https://medias24.com/2013/12/06/nelson-mandela-et-le-maroc-une-longue-histoire-damitie-et-de-fidelite/

"OAU considers Morocco readmission." *BBC News*, July 8, 2001. URL: http://news.bbc.co.uk/2/hi/africa/1428796.stm.

"Opening in Madrid of the 1st seminar on the Moroccan–Spanish Initiative for Mediation in the Mediterranean." *Atlasinfo.fr*, February 11, 2013. URL: http://www.atlasinfo.fr/ Opening in Madrid of the 1st seminar on the Moroccan–Spanish Initiative for Mediation in the Mediterranean.

"Global Competitiveness Report 2015–2016: African Countries Ranked." *Agence Ecofin*, September 3, 2014. URL: https://www.agenceecofin.com/gestion-publique/3009-32742-rapport-mondial-sur-la-competitivite-2015-2016-le-classement-des-pays-africains

4 Primary Sources

4.1 *Reports and Official Documents*

Berthélemy, Jean-Claude, Jean-Michel Salmon, Ludvig Söderling, and Henri-Bernard Solignac Lecomte. *Emerging Africa*. Paris: OECD, 2002, 232 pp.

Chaturvedi, Sachin. "The Growing Dynamism of South–South Cooperation." In *Development Cooperation 2014: Mobilising Resources for Sustainable Development*, OECD Publishing, Paris, 2015.

Huntginger, J. "Les Relations Économiques entre la France et le Maroc." Paris: Avis et Rapports du Conseil Économique et Social, May 21, no. 1987, pp. 10–25.

Lalumière, Catherine. *L'évolution de la Situation au Sahara Occidental*. Brussels: European Parliament—Ad Hoc Delegation to Western Sahara, 2002.

Lambert, Alain. *Rapport du Sénat sur la Proposition de Loi Organique Relative aux Lois de Finances*. Paris: Sénat, 2000.

Larbi, George A. *The New Public Management and Crisis States*. Geneva: United Nations Research Institute for Social Development, 1999, 65 p.

Lorgeoux, Jeanny, and Jean-Marie Bockel. *L'Afrique Est Notre Avenir*. Paris: Sénat—Commission des Affaires étrangères, de la Défense et des Forces Armées, 2013, 501 p.

Rhee, H. "South–South Cooperation." Seoul: KOICA (Korean International Cooperation Agency)—Working Paper, 2010.

Oxfam. "Un Maroc Inégalitaire, une Taxation Juste." Rapport, 2019.

Roatta, Jean. *Rapport sur le Projet de Loi (no. 3276) Autorisant l'Approbation de l'Accord entre le Gouvernement de la République Française et le Gouvernement du Royaume du Maroc Relatif au Statut de Leurs Forces*. Paris: Assemblée Nationale, 2007.

Tenzer, Nicolas. *L'Expertise Internationale au Cœur de la Diplomatie et de la Coopération du XXIe Siècle. Instruments pour une Stratégie Française de Puissance et d'Influence*. Report. Paris: Ministry of Foreign and European Affairs, 2008, 430 p.

Vergne, Clémence. "Le Modèle de Croissance Marocain: Opportunités et Vulnérabilités." Agence Française de Développement, June 2014, no. 14, *Macroéconomie & Développement*.

Zeleza, Paul Tiyambe. *Manufacturing African Studies and Crises*. Dakar: Codesria, 1997, 632 p.

Background Study for the Development Cooperation Forum. *Trends in South–South and Triangular Development Cooperation*. New York: ECOSOC, United Nations, 2008, 63 p.

Charte des Valeurs du Diplomate Marocain. Rabat: Ministère des Affaires étrangères et de la Coopération, 2011, 20 p.

Cinquentenaire de l'Indépendance du Royaume du Maroc—50 ans de Développement

Humain—Perspectives 2025. Document de synthèse du rapport général. Ambassade du Maroc en France, January 2006, 46 p.
Review of the Reports of the Administrator of the United Nations Development Programme. New York: United Nations High-level Committee on South–South Cooperation, 2012, 17 p.
Guide du Diplomate Marocain. Rabat: Ministère des Affaires étrangères et de la Coopération, May 2009, 202 p.
"The Definition of Human Security Continues to Divide Member States in the General Assembly." UN General Assembly, Informal Paper for the Information Media, Sixty-fourth session, 89th plenary—morning, 2010.
L'Afrique Priorité Partagée du Royaume du Maroc et de l'ONU. Document d'Analyse. Ministère des Affaires étrangères et de la Coopération, Date non précisée, 69 p.
Migration Issues in Development Policies and Strategies in North Africa [Report]. Rabat: United Nations Economic Commission for Africa Office for North Africa (UNECA), 2014, 97 p.
Human Security in West Africa: Challenges, Synergies and Actions for a Regional Agenda. Lomé, Togo: Sahel and West Africa Club/OECD, 2006, 56 p.
Human Security in Theory and Practice. Application of the Human Security Concept and the United Nations Trust Fund for Human Security. UN Office for the Coordination of Humanitarian Affairs, 2009, 86 p.
Loi des Finances 2015. Rapport. Rabat: Ministère de l'Économie et des Finances, Direction des Études et des Prévisions Financières, 2015, 187 p.
Open Government in Morocco. OECD Public Governance Reviews, OECD Publishing, 2015, 269 p.
Framework for Operational Guidelines on United Nations Support for South–South and Triangular Cooperation. New York: United Nations—High-level Committee on South–South Cooperation, 2012, 33 p.
Point sur les Relations du Maroc avec les Pays de l'Afrique Subsaharienne. Report. Rabat: Ministry of Economy and Finance, Directorate of Studies and Financial Forecasts, 2008, 15 p.
Projet de Loi de Finances pour l'Année Budgétaire 2015. Rapport. Rabat: Ministère de l'Économie et des Finances, Direction des Études et des Prévisions Financières, 2015, 141 p.
Rapport Annuel. Report. Rabat: Conseil Économique Social et Environnemental, 2013, 121 p.
Rapport au Parlement sur les Exportations d'Armement de la France 2014. Paris: Ministère de la Défense, 2014, 107 p.
Report of the High-level Committee on South–South Cooperation. Summary. United Nations General Assembly, 2007, 4 p.
Rapport sur le Budget Genre. Rapport. Rabat: Ministère de l'Économie et des Finances, 2014, 199 p.

Relations Maroc-Afrique: l'Ambition d'une 'Nouvelle Frontière'. Rapport. Rabat: Ministère de l'Économie et des Finances, Direction des Études et des Prévisions Financières, 2014, 29 p.

Where is The Wealth Of Nations? Measuring Capital for the 21st Century. Report. Washington, D.C.: World Bank, 2006, 208 p.

4.1.1   Working Documents, Minutes of Meetings, Resolutions, Decrees

"Order of June 27 Relating to the List of War Material and Assimilated Material Subject to Prior Authorization for Export and Defence-related Products Subject to Prior Authorization for Transfer." Legifrance. May 2014. Accessed at www.legifrance.gouv.fr.

"Chronologie des Conventions et Accords de Coopération Signés entre le Maroc et le Gabon." Ministry of Foreign Affairs and Cooperation, MAP. March 5, 2014.

"Press Release on the Occasion of the Announcement of the Constitutive Act of the Mohammed VI Foundation of African Ulemas." Ministry of Habous and Islamic Affairs. July 13, 2015.

"Consecration of the Ministry of Foreign Affairs and Cooperation during the Seminar on the Appropriation of the New LOF." Paris: Ministry of Foreign Affairs and Cooperation. October 21, 2015.

"Constitution of the Kingdom of Morocco." Kingdom of Morocco. 2011.

"Convention d'Établissement entre le Gouvernement de la République du Sénégal et le Gouvernement du Royaume du Maroc." Portal of the Moroccan Ministry of Justice. December 22, 1965.

"Customs Cooperation with Morocco." Portail de la République Togolaise. March 18, 2016.

"Cooperation between Morocco and European Union countries for the Benefit of African Countries." Portal of the Moroccan Ministry of Foreign Affairs and Cooperation.

"Tripartite Cooperation." Deutsche Gesellschaft für Internationale Zusammenarbeit (GIZ) GmbH. December 2013. Available at: https://www.giz.de/en/downloads/giz2014_fr_cooperation_tripartite_Maroc.pdf.

"Marrakech Declaration on the Occasion of the Media Forum on the African Continent." Morocco.ma. December 17, 2015.

"Marrakech Declaration on South–South Cooperation." Group of Seventy-Seven at the United Nations, General Assembly. January 2004, 14 p.

"Paris Declaration on Aid Effectiveness and the Accra Agenda for Action." OECD. 2005/2008, p. 26.

"Decree on the Attributions of the Minister of Foreign Affairs and Cooperation and the Organisation of the Ministry of Foreign Affairs and Cooperation." Ministry of Public Service and Modernisation of Administration. Decree no. 2-13-253 of Shaaban (11,434,20 June 2013).

"Press Kit—Seminar for Ambassadors of His Majesty the King Accredited in Africa." Rabat: Ministry of Foreign Affairs and Cooperation, Directorate of Public Diplomacy and Non-State Actors. August 2012.

"Press Kit: Seminar of Moroccan Ambassadors in Africa. Moroccan Diplomacy in Africa: A Renewed Approach in the Service of a Strategic Priority." Rabat: Ministry of Foreign Affairs and Cooperation, 2012.

"Presentation on the Draft Sectoral Budget of the Ministry of Foreign Affairs and International Trade de la Coopération." Paris: Ministry of Foreign Affairs and Cooperation. November 5, 2015.

"Africa Visa Openness Index." African Development Bank. http://www.afdb.org/fr/topics-and-sectors/initiatives-partnerships/africa-visa-openness-index/.

"International Women's Day: La Femme Diplomate à l'Honneur." Ministry of Foreign Affairs and Cooperation. March 8, 2012.

"Launch of the 'France Brand' Mission." Portal of the French Ministry of Economy and Finance. January 30, 2013.

"Morocco and South–South Cooperation / Least Developed Countries (LDCs)." Rabat: Ministry of Foreign Affairs and Cooperation.

"Morocco and Tripartite Cooperation." Portal of the Moroccan Ministry of Foreign Affairs and Cooperation.

"Les IDE au Maroc en 2013." French Embassy in Morocco, Regional Economic Service. June 2014.

Law No. 40/1975. Boletin Oficial, No. Madrid 278. November 20, 1975.

"Morocco, a Country of Solidarity: South–South Cooperation." Portal of the Moroccan Ministry of Foreign Affairs and Cooperation. Available at: https://www.diplomatie.ma/Portals/12/-%20-%20Cooperation%20Sud.pdf. (Accessed June 2016)

"Motion on Behalf of Twenty-Eight Countries to Suspend the Ghostly SADR from the Activities of the African Union." Full text of the motion published by Le Matin.ma. July 18, 2016.

"Note to the Minister of Foreign Affairs and Cooperation." American Affairs Division, DFAIT. October 2, 2014.

"Performance Commerciale du Maroc sur le Marché de l'Afrique Subsaharienne." In Abdelhak Azzouzi (ed.), *Annuaire Marocain de la Stratégie et des Relations Internationales*, Centre Marocain Interdisciplinaire des Études Stratégiques et Internationales, Rabat: L'Harmattan, 2012.

"Foreign Policy: Sub-regional Organisations." Portal of the Ministry of Foreign Affairs and Cooperation.

"Reflection on Morocco's Strategy Towards Africa." Rabat: Moroccan Ministry of Foreign Affairs. Diplomatic Document circulated by Chris Coleman. April 22, 2013. Available at: http://www.arso.org/Coleman/renouveau_de_la_pol_afr_du_Maroc.pdf.

"Bilateral Relations: Congo." Portal of the Ministry of Foreign Affairs and Cooperation.

"Bilateral Relations: Senegal." Portal of the Ministry of Foreign Affairs and Cooperation.

"Resolution adopted by the General Assembly 58/220: Economic and Technical Cooperation among Developing Countries." United Nations General Assembly, 2004.

"H.M. the King, Amir Al-Mouminine, Presides in Casablanca over the Ceremony Announcing the Creation of the Mohammed VI Foundation of African Ulemas." Maroc.ma. July 13, 2015.

"Visit of King Mohammed VI to Côte d'Ivoire." Portal of the Ministry of Foreign Affairs and Cooperation. 2014, 21 p.

"Official Visit of H.M. the King to Guinea-Conakry." Portal of the Ministry of Foreign Affairs and Cooperation. 2014, 49 p.

"Official Visit of H.M. the King to Senegal." Maroc.ma. 2015.

4.2 *Speeches and Books by Officials*

4.2.1 Publications by Officials

Alaoui, Mohammed Ben El Hassan. *La Coopération entre l'Union Européenne et les Pays du Maghreb* (based on Mohammed VI's thesis). Paris: Nathan, 1994, 237 p.

Basri, Driss. *Le Maroc des Potentialités: Génie d'un Roi et d'un Peuple*. Royaume du Maroc, Ministry of Information, 1989, 318 p.

Hassan II. *Le Défi*. Paris, France: A. Michel, 1976, 284 p.

Hassan II. "Assumer Son Destin." *Le Monde Diplomatique*, March 1, 1970.

Hassan II and Laurent Éric. *La Mémoire d'un Roi: Entretiens avec Eric Laurent*. Paris, France: Plon, 1993, 304 p.

Robert, Maurice, and Renault André. *Maurice Robert 'Minister' of Africa. Entretiens avec André Renault*. Paris: Seuil, 2004, 410 p.

4.2.2 Published Speeches, Statements and Interviews

Ouattara, Alassane. "Statement by President Alassane Ouattara on His Return from Morocco" [Video]. RtI Channel, 2015. URL: https://www.youtube.com/watch?v=AuV8ShQOjkw.

Mitterrand, François. "Speech at La Baule, June 1990."

Chirac, Jacques. "Speech by the President of the Republic Jacques Chirac on the Occasion of the State Dinner Offered in Honor of His Majesty Hassan II, King of Morocco." May 7, 1996.

King Hassan II. *Speeches and Interviews of H.M. King Hassan II Volume VI, [1978–1980]*. Rabat: Ministry of Information, 1990, 574 p.

Condé, Alpha. "Interview with Alpha Condé, President of the Republic of Guinea." Le Matin.ma, May 3, 2014.

Fabius, Laurent. "Interview of Mr. Laurent Fabius, Minister of Foreign Affairs and Inter-

BIBLIOGRAPHY

national Development, with the Moroccan Radio Station 'Medi1'." Diplomatie.gouv.fr, March 10, 2015.

Bouteflika, Abdelaziz. "Intervention by President Bouteflika at the NEPAD-AUDA Stakeholders' Dinner-Debate, El Mouradia—Presidency of the Republic." October 22, 2004.

"Intervention of the President of the Republic in front of the French Community at the Lycée Lyautey in Casablanca." Portal of the Presidency of the French Republic, April 5, 2013.

"Mezouar Announces a Large Movement in the Consular Corps Concerning About 70% of the Consulates" [Video]. Medi1TV, August 6, 2015.

N.B.: Mohammed VI's speeches below are listed by date.

"Speech on the Occasion of the Youth Day." *Maroc Hebdo*, July 11, 1998.

"1st Speech from the Throne by His Majesty King Mohammed VI." *Maroc.ma*, July 30, 1999.

"L'Allocution de S.M. le Roi Mohammed VI lors du Dîner Officiel Offert en l'Honneur du Président Jacques Chirac." *Maroc.ma*, March 20, 2000.

"Speech on the Occasion of the First Anniversary of the Sovereign's Induction." *Maroc.ma*, July 30, 2000.

"Royal Message to the Participants in the Colloquium Organised in Rabat on the Occasion of the Celebration of the National Day of Moroccan Diplomacy." *Maroc.ma*, April 28, 2000.

"Speech at the 21st Summit of Heads of State and Government of Africa and France." *Maroc.ma*, January 17, 2001.

"Interview given by His Majesty King Mohammed VI to the French daily 'Le Figaro'", *Maroc.ma*, September 4, 2001.

"Message of H.M. the King, Amir Al Mouminine, to the participants of the inter-faith meeting in Brussels on 'God's peace in the world'", *Maroc.ma*, December 18, 2001.

"Speech by H.M. King Mohammed VI on the occasion of the 49th anniversary of the Revolution of the King and the People", *Maroc.ma*, August 20, 2002.

"Speech by H.M. King Mohammed VI at the Consultative Meeting of Leaders of Islamic Countries", *Maroc.ma*, February 26, 2003.

"Royal speech on the occasion of the 4th Throne Day anniversary", *Maroc.ma*, July 30, 2003.

"Speech by H.M. King Mohammed VI at the Arab Summit in Tunis", *Maroc.ma*, March 29, 2004.

"Royal speech on the restructuring of the religious field in Morocco", *Ministry of Habous and Islamic Affairs*, April 20, 2004.

"Speech of H.M. the King on the occasion of the Throne Day", *Maroc.ma*, July 30, 2004.

"H.M. King Mohammed VI, Amir Al Mouminine, addresses a message to the participants of the first edition of the Sidi Chiker national meetings of the followers of Sufism", *Maroc.ma*, September 10, 2004.

"Speech by H.M. King Mohammed VI on the occasion of the 5th anniversary of the Trône", *Maroc.ma*, July 30, 2005.

"Speech by H.M. the King to the participants of the UN General Assembly meeting", *Maroc.ma*, September 14, 2005.

"Message from His Majesty King Mohammed VI to the UN Millennium Summit", *Maroc.ma*, July 2, 2006.

"Message of H.M. the King to the XIth Summit of Heads of State and Government of the Francophonie", *Maroc.ma*, August 2006.

"H.M. King Mohammed VI addresses a message to the participants of the first African conference on human development", *Maroc.ma*, April 6, 2007.

"Speech by H.M. King Mohammed VI on the occasion of the 9th anniversary of the Throne Day", *Maroc.ma*, July 30, 2008.

"Speech by H.M. the King to the Nation on the occasion of the 34th anniversary of the Green March", *MAP*, November 6, 2009.

"Speech of H.M. the King to the Nation on the occasion of the 11th anniversary of the Throne Day", *Maroc.ma*, July 30, 2010.

"Speech of H.M. the King to the Nation on the occasion of the 13th anniversary of the Throne Day", *Maroc.ma*, July 30, 2012.

"Royal Message to the Élysée Summit on Peace and Security in Africa", *Morocco.ma*, January 6, 2013.

"H.M. the King addresses a message to the 42nd ordinary summit of ECOWAS", *Maroc.ma*, February 27, 2013.

"Message of H.M. King Mohammed VI to the Extraordinary Ministerial Conference of LDCs", *Maroc.ma*, March 25, 2013.

"H.M. the King sends a message of thanks to President Ali Bongo at the end of His official visit to Gabon", *Maroc.ma*, April 13, 2013.

"Message of H.M. King Mohammed VI to the Africa–France Summit", *Maroc.ma*, May 31, 2010.

"Message of the Sovereign to H.M. the King's First Ambassadors' Conference", *Morocco.ma*, September 1, 2013.

"Speech by H.M. the King on the occasion of the 38th anniversary of the Green March", *Morocco.ma*, November 6, 2013.

"H.M. the King sends a message of thanks to the Malian president at the end of His official visit to Mali", *Maroc.ma*, February 23, 2014.

"Speech by H.M. the King at the Moroccan-Ivorian Economic Forum in Abidjan", *Maroc.ma*, February 24, 2014.

"Speech of H.M. the King to the participants of the 4th Africa-European Union Summit in Brussels", *Maroc.ma*, April 3, 2014.

"Royal speech on the occasion of the 15th Throne Day anniversary", *Maroc.ma*, July 30, 2014.

"Speech by H.M. the King on the occasion of the 61th anniversary of the revolution of the King and the people", *Maroc.ma*, August 20, 2014.

"Speech by H.M. the King to the nation on the occasion of the 39th anniversary of the Green March", *Maroc.ma*, November 5, 2014.

"Royal speech on the occasion of the 16th Throne Day anniversary", *Maroc.ma*, July 30, 2015.

"Full text of the speech delivered by H.M. the King at the 3rd India-Africa Forum Summit", *Maroc.ma*, October 29, 2015.

"Royal speech on the occasion of the 40th anniversary of the Green March", *Maroc.ma*, November 6, 2015.

"Message of H.M. the King to the participants of the Crans Montana Forum in Dakhla", *Maroc.ma*, March 18, 2016.

"Full text of the Royal Message on the occasion of the first Mediterranean Concert", *Maroc.ma*, July 9, 2016.

"Speech by H.M. the King to the nation on the occasion of the 63th anniversary of the Revolution of the King and the People", *Maroc.ma*, August 20, 2016.

4.3 Archives

Documents diplomatiques français: Vol. 1956. *II*, Paris, Ministère des Affaires étrangères, Commission de publication des documents diplomatiques français, 1989, 697

French Diplomatic Documents 1957. Tome I, 1 January–30 June, Paris, Ministry of Foreign Affairs, Commission de publication des documents diplomatiques français, 1990,1008

Documents diplomatiques français 1962, Tome I, 1 January–30 June, Paris, Ministry of Foreign Affairs, Commission de publication des documents diplomatiques français, 1998,717

4.4 Interviews

The interviews with the diplomats remain anonymous and are not mentioned in this list. Therefore, to preserve the confidentiality of the interviews, no names are mentioned in the study.

5 Sitography

Japan International Cooperation Agency: www.jica.go.jp.
Moroccan Agency for International Cooperation: www.amci.ma.
World Bank: www.banquemondiale.org or www.worldbank.org.

Mohammed VI Radio and Television Channel: www.idaatmohammedassadiss.ma.
House of Representatives in Morocco: www.chambredesrepresentants.ma.
CIA, The World Factbook: https://www.cia.gov/the-world-factbook/
European Conference of Support and Solidarity with the Sahrawi People: www.eucoco
 madrid.org.
Advisory Council for Saharan Affairs: www.corcas.com.
Global Fire Power: www.globalfirepower.com.
Group of 77 at the United Nations (UN) www.G77.org.
Instance Centrale de Prévention de la Corruption (Morocco): www.icpc.ma.
Arab World Institute: www.imarabe.org.
Algerian Ministry of National Defence: www.mdn.dz.
Minister Delegate for Foreign Affairs, Youssef Amrani: www.youssef-amrani.ma.
Moroccan Ministry of the Civil Service and Modernisation of the Administration: www
 .mmsp.gov.ma.
Moroccan Ministry of Foreign Affairs and Cooperation: www.diplomatie.ma.
Moroccan Mission in Geneva (UNO): www.mission-maroc.ch.
Moroccan Mission to Hawaii: www.morocco-in-hawaii.com.
Open Government Partnership: www.opengovpartnership.org.
United Nations: www.un.org.
Food and Agriculture Organization of the United Nations: www.fao.org.
Moroccan Autonomy Plan for Western Sahara: plan-autonomie.com.
Official portal of Morocco: www.maroc.ma.
Presidency of the Algerian Republic: www.el-mouradia.dz.
Presidency of the French Republic: www.elysee.fr.
Mano River Women's Peace Network: www.marwopnet.org.

Index

Acharya, Amitav 18n, 38,
Advanced Status (EU-Morocco Relations) 41, 42
African
  identity 177, 178, 218, 255, 263
  integration 89, 172, 231
  multilateralism 64, 73, 154
  regionalism (regional system) 27, 36, 207, 209, 265
  unity 64, 66, 67, 136
  security 37, 67
African Union
  Peace and Secrity Council 37
Al Fassi, Allal 58, 59, 60, 62, 64, 69, 160, 161, 188
Al Quds Committee 43, 109, 127
Aron, Raymond 11, 14, 19, 79, 117n, 138, 160n, 269

Bach, Daniel 36, 37, 153n, 163n, 175, 256
Bat, Jean-Pierre 73n, 79, 80n, 82n, 164
bridge 44, 52, 66, 74, 202, 220, 245, 271
  diplomacy 127, 128, 129, 130, 238
  geo-strategic 45

Casablanca
  Conference 67, 76
  Group 66, 67, 68
cooperation
  military 42, 83, 87, 88, 151
  south-south 38, 53, 109, 115, 129, 154, 172, 175, 176, 180–184, 187, 199, 203, 204, 208, 213, 218, 220–222, 263, 264, 268, 286, 287
  triangular 88n, 129, 130, 166, 167, 183, 184, 202, 202, 263, 302, 324, 325

diplomacy (Diplomatic)
  cultural 193, 237, 240, 245, 247, 264
  economic 109, 110, 144, 154, 216–219, 220, 221, 223–227, 231, 264
  mediation 130
  religious 48, 65, 176, 192, 231, 235, 237, 238, 239, 241, 245, 264
  sectoral 55, 201, 224

emergence 3, 5, 30, 31, 32, 33, 40, 45, 57, 115, 116, 244, 259, 262
  economic 29, 38, 216, 245
  model 29, 30
epistemic community 10, 33, 54, 267, 259

Gaddafi, Muammar 73, 74, 76, 82, 85, 95, 200, 208
geopolitical 4, 16, 27, 51, 53, 59, 134, 141, 146, 175, 244, 264
  approach 20, 23, 25
  order 57, 58
  space 6
  system 6
golden mean 4, 46–49, 50–54, 66, 126, 130, 169, 188, 190, 202, 240–242, 242, 260, 264
globalisation 1, 36n, 51, 54, 117, 216, 250, 256, 262, 269
grandism 58, 59
greater 43, 59
  'Greater Morocco' project 58, 59, 61, 68, 76, 160

Hallstein, Walter 72
  Hallstein Doctrine 72, 85, 89, 135, 196, 234, 261
Hassan II 46, 50, 52, 68, 70–79, 80–88, 92, 101–103, 110–112, 147, 162, 170, 174, 177, 180, 213, 237, 240, 259, 261, 304

identity 4, 15, 48, 127, 139, 234, 244, 245, 256, 271
  collective 6, 16, 17, 133
  construction 13
  national 25, 52, 176, 260
  religious 27, 271
  state 23, 27, 45, 127
international relations 1, 4, 8, 12, 13, 16, 17, 19, 23, 41, 127, 138, 181, 187, 216
  African 7, 213, 271
  constructivist approach 5, 8, 9, 10–13, 100, 169, 244, 267
  debates 244
  multiplex world order 18, 34, 245

post-hegemonic multilateralism   38, 39
theories   25

legitimisation
    framework   1, 28, 58, 132, 175–179, 180, 187, 201, 213, 229, 241, 256, 262
    strategy   28, 53, 176

Malikite   191, 247
    school   188
    rite   48, 56, 192, 240, 242
Mohammed VI, King   5, 30, 41, 44, 45, 49, 92, 103, 109, 110, 122, 162, 166, 170, 189, 238, 240, 258
    foreign policy   148, 155, 163, 171, 197, 198, 200, 202, 273, 286, 287
    personality   18, 101, 102, 105
    reign   1, 2, 31, 43, 99, 100, 112, 115, 117, 167, 180, 188, 196, 199, 259, 266
    speech   47, 52, 128, 161, 185, 186, 192
    style   107, 108, 114, 165, 174, 262
Monrovia Group   67
multilateralism   85, 131, 134, 135, 152, 193, 263, 268

N'Krumah, Kwamé   67
National Liberation Army   61, 62
neoliberalism   38, 54, 55, 119, 225, 259, 262
    norms   29, 30, 40, 52
neutrality   25, 94, 134n, 207, 212, 213
    active   51
    formal   69, 79
new frontier   53, 54, 55, 142, 160, 224n
norms, values and beliefs   13, 15, 16, 45, 234, 260

Perrault, Gilles   86
political
    realism   68
    system   3, 76, 80
    transition   2, 3, 41, 245

Pompidou, Georges   78, 169
post-bipolar Africa   34, 35, 116, 117
projection   4, 40, 45, 143, 153, 271
    power   55, 268
    space   3
power
    median   258, 268, 271
    medium   40, 193
    middle   40, 268, 269, 271
    policy   4, 73, 260, 261

regionalism (regional)   36, 39, 175, 256, 257
    cooperation   265
    integration
representation   15, 19, 20, 24, 40, 53, 59, 103, 130–134, 136, 148, 149, 151, 154, 160–164, 175
    framework   28, 55, 131, 133
    geocultural   127
    geopolitical   43, 58, 89, 135, 261
    neoliberal   54, 55
role
    diplomacy   40, 41,
    identity   4, 15, 16, 28, 45, 46, 53, 56, 66, 69, 126, 130, 169, 176, 205, 224, 241, 245, 259, 260, 262 265, 267, 271
    projection   15, 175, 265

Sahrawi Front (Polisario)   70, 71, 90, 91, 92, 95, 97, 138, 147, 148
small powers   39, 40, 168, 268, 299
structural   31, 168, 227
    adjustment   29, 33, 84
    development   28, 34, 41, 116

territorial integrity   58, 68, 72, 74, 76, 79, 91, 93, 95, 96, 101, 103, 109, 115, 134, 135, 136, 143, 146, 177, 196, 211, 259, 262
Treaty of Oujda   74, 75, 82

Printed in the United States
by Baker & Taylor Publisher Services